Lecture Notes in Computer Science　　　7588

Commenced Publication in 1973
Founding and Former Series Editors:
Gerhard Goos, Juris Hartmanis, and Jan van Leeuwen

T0218391

Fei Wang   Dinggang Shen
Pingkun Yan   Kenji Suzuki (Eds.)

Machine Learning in Medical Imaging

Third International Workshop, MLMI 2012
Held in Conjunction with MICCAI 2012
Nice, France, October 1, 2012
Revised Selected Papers

Springer

Volume Editors

Fei Wang
IBM Research Almaden
650 Harry Road, San Jose, CA 95120, USA
E-mail: wangfe@us.ibm.com

Dinggang Shen
University of North Carolina, School of Medicine
Department of Radiology and Biomedical Research Imaging Center
130 Mason Farm Road, Chapel Hill, NC 27599, USA
E-mail: dgshen@med.unc.edu

Pingkun Yan
Chinese Academy of Sciences, Xi'an Institute of Optics and Precision Mechanics
17 Xinxi Road, New Industrial Park, Xi'an, Shaanxi 710119, China
E-mail: pingkun.yan@opt.ac.cn

Kenji Suzuki
The University of Chicago, Department of Radiology
5841 South Maryland Avenue, Chicago, IL 60637, USA
E-mail: suzuki@uchicago.edu

ISSN 0302-9743   e-ISSN 1611-3349
ISBN 978-3-642-35427-4   e-ISBN 978-3-642-35428-1
DOI 10.1007/978-3-642-35428-1
Springer Heidelberg Dordrecht London New York

Library of Congress Control Number: 2012953042

CR Subject Classification (1998): I.4.3, I.4.6, I.4.0-1, I.4.7-10, I.5.2, J.3, I.2.1, I.2.6, I.2.10, H.2.8, I.3.3

LNCS Sublibrary: SL 6 – Image Processing, Computer Vision, Pattern Recognition, and Graphics

Typesetting: Camera-ready by author, data conversion by Scientific Publishing Services, Chennai, India

Printed on acid-free paper

Springer is part of Springer Science+Business Media (www.springer.com)

Preface

The Third International Workshop on Machine Learning in Medical Imaging (MLMI) 2012 was held at the Acropolis Convention Center, Nice, France on October 1, 2012, in conjunction with the 15th International Conference on Medical Image Computing and Computer-Assisted Intervention (MICCAI).

Machine learning plays an essential role in the medical imaging field, including computer-aided diagnosis, image segmentation, image registration, image fusion, image-guided therapy, image annotation, and image database retrieval. With advances in medical imaging, new imaging modalities and methodologies such as cone-beam/multi-slice CT, 3D ultrasound imaging, tomosynthesis, diffusion-weighted MRI, positron-emission tomography (PET)/CT, electrical impedance tomography and diffuse optical tomography, and new machine-learning algorithms/applications are demanded in the medical imaging field. Single-sample evidence provided by the patient's imaging data is often not sufficient for satisfactory performance. Because of large variations and complexity, it is generally difficult to derive analytic solutions or simple equations to represent objects such as lesions and anatomy in medical images. Therefore, tasks in medical imaging require learning from examples for accurate representation of data and prior knowledge.

MLMI 2012 was the second in a series of workshops on this topic. The main aim of this workshop is to help advance scientific research within the broad field of machine learning in medical imaging. This workshop focuses on major trends and challenges in this area, and it presents work aiming to identify new cutting-edge techniques and their use in medical imaging. We hope the series of workshops becomes a new platform for translating research from bench to bedside.

The range and level of submissions for this year's meeting were of very high quality. Authors were asked to submit full-length papers for review. A total of 67 papers were submitted to the workshop in response to the call for papers. Each of the papers underwent a rigorous double-blinded peer-review process, with each paper being reviewed by at least two (typically three) reviewers in the Program Committee composed of 51 known experts in the field. Based on the reviewing scores and critics, a total of the 33 best papers (49%) were accepted for presentation at the workshop and chosen to be included in this Springer LNCS volume. The large variety of machine learning techniques necessary for and applied to medical imaging was well represented at the workshop.

We would like to thank our invited keynote speaker, Anand Rangarajan, Department of Computer and Information Science and Engineering, University of Florida, whose keynote address was a highlight of the workshop. We are grateful to the Program Committee for reviewing submitted papers and giving constructive comments and critiques, to the authors for submitting high-quality papers, to the presenters for excellent presentations, and to all those who supported MLMI 2012 by attending the meeting.

August 2012

Fei Wang
Dinggang Shen
Pingkun Yan
Kenji Suzuki

Organization

Program Committee

Akinobu Shimizu	Tokyo University of Agriculture and Technology, Japan
Anant Madabhushi	Rutgers - State University of New Jersey, USA
Axel Wismueller	University of Rochester, USA
Bram van Ginneken	Radboud University Nijmegen Medical Centre, The Netherlands
Clarisa Sanchez	Radboud University Nijmegen Medical Center, The Netherlands
Daniel Rueckert	Imperial College London, UK
Daoqiang Zhang	Nanjing University of Aeronautics and Astronautics, China
Edward H. Herskovits	University of Pennsylvania, USA
Emanuele Olivetti	Fondazione Bruno Kessler, Italy
Ghassan Hamarneh	Simon Fraser University, USA
Guangzhi Cao	GE Healthcare, USA
Guorong Wu	University of North Carolina, Chapel Hill, USA
Guoyan Zheng	University of Bern, Switzerland
Heang-Ping Chan	University of Michigan Medical Center, USA
Hidetaka Arimura	Kyusyu University, Japan
Hongtu Zhu	University of North Carolina, Chapel Hill, USA
Hotaka Takizawa	University of Tsukuba, Japan
Ipek Oguz	University of North Carolina, Chapel Hill, USA
Jianming Liang	Arizona State University, USA
Jianwu Xu	University of Chicago, USA
Joachim Hornegger	Friedrich Alexander University, Germany
Kazunori Okada	San Francisco State University, USA
Kevin Zhou	Siemens Corporate Research, USA
Kilian Pohl	University of Pennsylvania, USA
Li Shen	Indiana University School of Medicine, USA
Luping Zhou	CSIRO, Australia
Marc Niethammer	University of North Carolina, Chapel Hill, USA
Marius Linguraru	National Institutes of Health, USA
Marleen de Bruijne	University of Copenhagen, Denmark
Min C. Shin	UNC Charlotte, USA
Minjeong Kim	UNC Chapel Hill, USA
Nico Karssemeijer	Radboud University Nijmegen Medical Centre, The Netherlands

Table of Contents

Transductive Prostate Segmentation
for CT Image Guided Radiotherapy

Yinghuan Shi[1,2], Shu Liao[2], Yaozong Gao[2], Daoqiang Zhang[2,3],
Yang Gao[1], and Dinggang Shen[2]

[1] State Key Laboratory for Novel Software Technology, Nanjing University, China
[2] Department of Radiology and BRIC, UNC Chapel Hill, U.S.
[3] Department of Computer Science and Engineering,
Nanjing University of Aeronautics and Astronautics, China

Abstract. Accurate 3-D prostate segmentation is a significant and challenging issue for CT image guided radiotherapy. In this paper, a novel transductive method for 3-D prostate segmentation is proposed, which incorporates the physician's interactive labeling information, to aid accurate segmentation, especially when large irregular prostate motion occurs. More specifically, for the current treatment image, the physician is first asked to manually assign the labels for a small subset of prostate and non-prostate (background) voxels, especially in the first and last slices of the prostate regions. Then, transductive Lasso (tLasso) is proposed to select the most discriminative features slice-by-slice. With the selected features, our proposed weighted Laplacian regularized least squares (wLapRLS) is adopted to predict the prostate-likelihood for each remaining unlabeled voxel in the current treatment image. The final segmentation result is obtained by aligning the manually segmented prostate regions of the planning and previous treatment images, onto the estimated prostate-likelihood map of the current treatment image for majority voting. The proposed method has been evaluated on a real prostate CT dataset including 11 patients with more than 160 images, and compared with several state-of-the-art methods. Experimental results indicate that the promising results can be achieved by our proposed method.

1 Introduction

In clinical application, the prostate region in CT images usually requires time consuming manual segmentation in a slice-by-slice manner by the physician for image guided radiation therapy. Recently, many computer-aided prostate segmentation methods [3–5, 8] have been developed and achieved much success in CT image guided radiotherapy. Unfortunately, when large irregular motion occurs within prostate region, it is difficult for previous methods to achieve good segmentation results. In this case, the domain specific prior knowledge, which is usually given by the experienced physician, is extremely useful for segmentation. The specific prior knowledge includes the first and the last slices within prostate regions that can help deal with large irregular prostate motion, and confusing voxels which lie on boundary of prostate and background since in some case prostate and background voxels are quite similar. In this paper, a novel

F. Wang et al. (Eds.): MLMI 2012, LNCS 7588, pp. 1–9, 2012.

transductive method for 3-D prostate segmentation is proposed, which aims to improve the segmentation results by using additional physician's interactive labeling information.

When a new treatment image comes, the physician is allowed to give some prior information on (i) the first and last slices in prostate regions and (ii) voxels which lie on boundary of prostate and background if they are difficult to distinguish according to physician's consideration (Several typical examples are shown in Fig.1). Meanwhile, the planning image and treatment images obtained in the

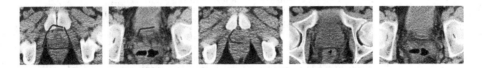

Fig. 1. The typical examples of physician's labeling. Blue curves denote the labeled background voxels, and red curves denote the labeled prostate voxels.

previous treatment days from the same patient can also be used to guide accurate segmentation, with their manual segmented results often available. Therefore, our goal is to incorporate physician's current labeled information as well as information obtained from the planning and previous treatment images for accurate segmentation. In this paper, physician's labeled voxels in the current treatment image are called '**labeled voxels**'; voxels in the planning and previous treatment images are called '**auxiliary voxels**' and the remaining voxels in the current treatment image are called '**unlabeled voxels**'. Our aim is to predict the labels (prostate or background) for the unlabeled voxels.

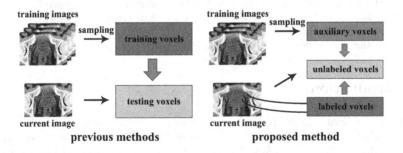

Fig. 2. The difference between previous methods and the proposed method. Our proposed method uses the information from both the physician's knowledge as well as the planning and previous treatment images. Red and blue lines in the current slice of the proposed method mean prostate and background voxels labeled by the physician, respectively.

The proposed transductive prostate segmentation method is mainly based on (i) transductive Lasso (tLasso) for discriminative feature selection, which is an extension of traditional supervised Lasso [13] to the transductive manner;

and (ii) weighted Laplacian regularized least squares (wLapRLS) for prostate-likelihood prediction, which imposes the prior label constraint [14] for the unlabeled voxels. Main steps of the proposed method can be summarized as: **firstly**, all previous and current treatment images are rigidly aligned to the planning image of the same patient based on their pelvic bone structures by following the same method in [8]. **Secondly**, the physician is allowed to label several voxels, as mentioned before. For each 2-D slice in the current treatment image, combining with voxels sampled from the planning and previous treatment images, 2-D low-level features are extracted, tLasso is then applied to select the most discriminative features, and wLapRLS is further adopted to predict the 2-D prostate-likelihood map for unlabeled voxels in the current slice. **Thirdly**, the predicted 2-D prostate-likelihood map in each slice will be merged into a 3-D map. The final 3-D prostate-likelihood map is obtained by fusing the 3-D maps along y-axis and z-axis. **Finally**, to make full use of prostate shape information, manual segmented prostate regions in the planning and previous treatment images will be rigidly aligned to the prostate-likelihood map. We adopt majority voting on the multiple aligned results to get the final segmentation result.

2   Proposed Method

2.1   Preprocessing and Notations

For each patient, we have one planning image, several previous treatment images, and one current treatment image; all of them are manually segmented by physician except the current treatment image. We first extract the pelvic bone structure from each image using threshold-based segmentation, and then each treatment image will be rigidly aligned to the planning image based on their pelvic bone structures [8]. For feature representation of each voxel, we extract three different kinds of features from its neighborhood in 2-D slice which include histogram of oriented gradient (HoG) [2], local binary pattern (LBP) [11] and multi-resolution Haar wavelet [9].

When asking physician to label the current treatment image, we will not ask him/her to label several voxels in each slice, which is too time-consuming. Instead, after ROI extraction, we only ask physician to label several prostate and background voxels in the first and last slices within the prostate region, as well as one slice in every 3-5 slices within the central part of prostate region. Normally, the physician only needs to label at most 8 slices for an image during segmentation process according to our observation.

In this paper, the matrices (2-D and 3-D) are denoted by bold upper case letters, the vectors are denoted by bold lower case ones, and the scalars are denoted by lower case ones. For each patient, the planning image and its corresponding manual segmented result are denoted as $\mathbf{I}^{\mathbf{P}}$ and $\mathbf{G}^{\mathbf{P}}$, respectively. We also denote the nth treatment image $\mathbf{I}_n$ as the current treatment image. The previous treatment images and their corresponding manual segmented results are denoted as $\mathbf{I}_1, ..., \mathbf{I}_{n-1}$ and $\mathbf{G}_1, ..., \mathbf{G}_{n-1}$, respectively. Also, the final 3-D prostate-likelihood map and its segmentation result by applying our method to the current treatment image $\mathbf{I}_n$ are denoted as $\mathbf{P}'_n$ and $\mathbf{G}'_n$, respectively. For the sth slice in $\mathbf{I}_n$, we denote the labeled, auxiliary, and unlabeled voxels as $(\mathbf{x}^L_{i,s}, y^L_{i,s})_{i=1,...,n_l}$,

$(\mathbf{x}_{i,s}^A, y_{i,s}^A)_{i=1,...,n_a}$ and $(\mathbf{x}_{i,s}^U, y_{i,s}^U)_{i=1,...,n_u}$, respectively. For each pair $(\mathbf{x}_{i,s}^L, y_{i,s}^L)$, $\mathbf{x}_{i,s}^L$ and $y_{i,s}^L$ denote the feature vector and corresponding label for the ith labeled voxels in the sth slice, respectively, which are the same for the auxiliary and unlabeled voxels. n_l, n_a, n_u are the numbers of the labeled, auxiliary and unlabeled voxels, respectively. For simplicity, we denote $n_t = n_l + n_a + n_u$. It is worth noting that, to predict the prostate-likelihood for the sth slice in $\mathbf{I}_n$, the auxiliary voxels are sampled within slices $[s - \bigtriangledown s, s + \bigtriangledown s]$ in the planning and previous treatment images. $\bigtriangledown s$ is the slice-offset, which is set to 1 in this paper. The reason for introducing $\bigtriangledown s$ is that auxiliary voxels in adjacent slices have similar distribution in feature space, which guarantees enough auxiliary voxels are sampled, especially on the top and bottom part of prostate.

2.2 Feature Selection by tLasso

For feature selection, we consider using tLasso, an extension of traditional supervised Lasso [13] to the transductive manner. In tLasso, our aim is not only to minimize the empirical loss on the labeled and auxiliary voxels by using different selected features, but also to preserve the local structure for the labeled, auxiliary, and unlabeled voxels. The key point of tLasso is that Laplacian regularized term is imposed. The objective function of tLasso is as follows:

$$\min_{\beta} \left\{ \|\mathbf{J}(\mathbf{y} - \mathbf{F}\beta)\|_2^2 + \frac{\gamma_G}{n_t^2}\beta^\top \mathbf{F}^\top \mathbf{L}\mathbf{F}\beta + \gamma_S\|\beta\|_1 \right\}, \tag{1}$$

where $\beta \in \mathbb{R}^d$ is the parameter to be optimized, and d is the dimension of feature space. $\gamma_G \in \mathbb{R}$ and $\gamma_S \in \mathbb{R}$ are the two parameters to control the weights for the last two terms; we will report the method for automatically selecting γ_G and γ_S in the experiments. $\mathbf{F} \in \mathbb{R}^{n_t \times d}$ and $\mathbf{y} \in \mathbb{R}^{n_t}$ are the feature matrix and labels, respectively, in which the first n_l rows are the labeled voxels, the middle n_a rows are the auxiliary voxels, and the last n_u rows are the unlabeled voxels (for the unlabeled voxels in tLasso, the initial labels in $\mathbf{y}$ are set to 0). n_l, n_a, n_u and N are defined in the notations. $\mathbf{L} \in \mathbb{R}^{n_t \times n_t}$ is graph Laplacian, which is with similar definition as that in [1][12]. Since labels of unlabeled data are unknown, $\mathbf{J} \in \mathbb{R}^{n_t \times n_t}$ is used to indicate voxels which are unlabeled. $\mathbf{J}$ is a diagonal matrix and defined as $\mathbf{J} = \text{diag}\left[\overbrace{\alpha_l/n_l, ..., \alpha_l/n_l}^{n_l}, \overbrace{\alpha_a/n_a, ..., \alpha_a/n_a}^{n_a}, \overbrace{0, ..., 0}^{n_u}\right]$, where α_l and α_a $(0 \le \alpha_l, \alpha_a \le 1)$ are the two weights to balance the influences of the labeled and auxiliary voxels, respectively. Larger α_l (α_a) leads to more emphasis on the labeled (auxiliary) voxels. In Eq.1, the first term is to measure the empirical loss on the labeled and auxiliary voxels by selecting features according to β, the second term is to preserve the similarity information for all the voxels [1], and the last term is L_1 norm to guarantee the sparsity of β. Eq.1 can be efficiently solved by Nesterov's method [10] or gradient descent method [15]. In this paper, we solve Eq.1 using CVX toolbox [6]. By obtained β, we can select the corresponding d' $(d' < d)$ features with non-zero entries in β. Also, we can generate a new feature matrix $\mathbf{F}' \in \mathbb{R}^{n_t \times d'}$ by using the selected d' features to replace $\mathbf{F}$.

2.3 Prostate-Likelihood Prediction by wLapRLS

To make full use of the information obtained from the planning and previous treatment images, we propose wLapRLS to extend LapRLS [1] by imposing the prior label constraint for unlabeled voxels, which has been demonstrated useful in domain adaptation problem [14] since the feature distributions in current treatment image and previous images are not always similar. The objective function of wLapRLS is defined as follows:

$$\min_{\boldsymbol{\omega}} \left\{ \|\mathbf{J}'(\mathbf{y}' - \mathbf{K}\boldsymbol{\omega})\|_2^2 + \gamma_C \boldsymbol{\omega}^\top \mathbf{K} \boldsymbol{\omega} + \frac{\gamma_G}{n_t^2} \boldsymbol{\omega}^\top \mathbf{K} \mathbf{L}' \mathbf{K} \boldsymbol{\omega} \right\}, \qquad (2)$$

where $\boldsymbol{\omega} \in \mathbb{R}^{n_t}$ is the parameter to be optimized. $\gamma_C \in \mathbb{R}$ and $\gamma_G \in \mathbb{R}$ are the two parameters to control the weights for the last two terms, we will report the method for automatically selecting γ_C and γ_G in the experiments. $\mathbf{K} \in \mathbb{R}^{n_t \times n_t}$ and $\mathbf{L}' \in \mathbb{R}^{n_t \times n_t}$ are Gram matrix and graph Laplacian generated from feature vectors $\mathbf{F}'$ with selected feature in tLasso. $\mathbf{K}$ and $\mathbf{L}'$ are with the same definition as that in literature [1][12]. $\mathbf{y}' \in \mathbb{R}^{n_t}$ is the initial label, which is slightly different from $\mathbf{y}$ in Eq.1. For $\mathbf{y}$, unlabeled voxels' initial labels are set to 0; while in $\mathbf{y}'$, we assign the initial labels for unlabeled voxels as prediction by a classifier, which is trained on auxiliary voxels. Therefore, $\mathbf{y}'$ can be defined as $\mathbf{y}' = \left[y_{1,s}^L, ..., y_{n_l,s}^L, y_{1,s}^A, ..., y_{n_a,s}^A, P_A(\mathbf{x}_{1,s}^U), ..., P_A(\mathbf{x}_{n_u,s}^U) \right]^\top$, where $P_A(\mathbf{x}_{i,s}^U)$ means the classification result for $\mathbf{x}_{i,s}^U$ by using the auxiliary classifier P_A trained on the auxiliary voxels. In this paper, we use support vector machine (SVM) to train P_A with selected features by tLasso. The advantage of using P_A is that the results can be benefited from auxiliary voxels [14]. To balance the influences of the labeled, auxiliary and unlabeled voxels, $\mathbf{J}' \in \mathbb{R}^{n_t \times n_t}$ is introduced, which is defined as $\mathbf{J}' = \text{diag}\left[\overbrace{\alpha_l'/n_l, ..., \alpha_l'/n_l}^{n_l}, \overbrace{\alpha_a'/n_a, ..., \alpha_a'/n_a}^{n_a}, \overbrace{\alpha_u'/n_u, ..., \alpha_u'/n_u}^{n_u} \right]$, where α_l', α_a' and α_u' are the non-negative weights for labeled, auxiliary and unlabeled voxels, respectively, which satisfies $\alpha_l' + \alpha_a' + \alpha_u' = 1$. In Eq.2, the first term is the empirical loss term, the second term is the smoothness term, and the last term takes all the voxels' structural information into account [1]. The $\boldsymbol{\omega}$ can be computed as a close-form solution as follows:

$$\boldsymbol{\omega} = \left[\mathbf{J}'\mathbf{J}'\mathbf{K} + \gamma_C \mathbf{I} + \frac{\gamma_G}{n_t^2} \mathbf{L}'\mathbf{K} \right]^{-1} \mathbf{J}'\mathbf{J}'\mathbf{y}', \qquad (3)$$

where $\mathbf{I}$ is the identity matrix. Finally, by using the Representer Theorem, the prostate-likelihood of an unlabeled voxel $\mathbf{x}_{j,s}^U$ in the current treatment image can be calculated as $f(\mathbf{x}_{j,s}^U) = \sum_{i=1}^{n_t} \mathbf{K}(\mathbf{x}_{i,s}, \mathbf{x}_{j,s}^U)\boldsymbol{\omega}_i$. With calculated prostate-likelihood of the unlabeled voxels, 2-D prostate-likelihood map for each slice in the current treatment image can be generated.

For all slices in the current treatment image, the obtained 2-D predicted likelihood maps will be merged together to generate the 3-D prostate-likelihood map according to the order of original slices. In [8], the authors found that the combination of segmentation results along two directions (z-axis and y-axis) is helpful to improve the performance. Therefore, we generate 3-D predicted prostate-likelihood map $\mathbf{P}_n'$ by averaging $\mathbf{P}_{\mathbf{z},n}'$ and $\mathbf{P}_{\mathbf{y},n}'$, where $\mathbf{P}_{\mathbf{z},n}'$ and $\mathbf{P}_{\mathbf{y},n}'$ are the 3-D prostate-likelihood maps generated along z-axis and y-axis, respectively. Without loss of generality, the details of generating $\mathbf{P}'_{\mathbf{z},n}$ are summarized in Alg.1. Since $\mathbf{P}'_{\mathbf{z},n}$ is obtained from the slices cut from z-axis, similarly $\mathbf{P}'_{\mathbf{y},n}$ can also be obtained from Alg.1 by cutting the slices along y-axis.

Algorithm 1. Generating 3-D prostate-likelihood map $\mathbf{P}'_{\mathbf{z},n}$

Input: previous images $\mathbf{I}^{\mathbf{P}}, \mathbf{I}_1, ..., \mathbf{I}_{n-1}$ and their manual segmentations $\mathbf{G}^{\mathbf{P}}, \mathbf{G}_1, ..., \mathbf{G}_{n-1}$, current treatment image $\mathbf{I}_n$ (size $S_x \times S_y \times S_z$), and slice-offset $\triangledown s$

Output: 3-D prostate-likelihood map $\mathbf{P}'_{\mathbf{z},n}$

1: **for** $s \leftarrow 1, ..., S_z$ **do**
2:     $(\mathbf{x}^A_{i,s}, y^A_{i,s})_{i=1,...,n_a} \leftarrow$ sampling from slices $[s - \triangledown s, s + \triangledown s]$ in $\mathbf{I}^{\mathbf{P}}, \mathbf{I}_1, ..., \mathbf{I}_{n-1}$
3:     **if** s^{th} slice in $\mathbf{I}_n$ is labeled by physician **then**
4:         $(\mathbf{x}^L_{i,s}, y^L_{i,s})_{i=1,...,n_l} \leftarrow$ physician's labeling
5:     **else**
6:         $(\mathbf{x}^L_{i,s}, y^L_{i,s})_{i=1,...,n_l} \leftarrow$ labeled voxels in the nearest slice from s^{th} slice
7:     **end if**
8:     $\beta \leftarrow$ solution returned by tLasso in Eq.1
9:     $\omega \leftarrow$ solution returned by wLapRLS in Eq.2
10:    **for** $j \leftarrow 1, ..., n_u$ **do**
11:       $f_{\mathbf{z}}(\mathbf{x}^U_{j,s}) \leftarrow \sum_{i=1}^{n_t} \mathbf{K}(\mathbf{x}_{i,s}, \mathbf{x}^U_{j,s}) \omega_i$
12:    **end for**
13:    assign $f_{\mathbf{z}}(\mathbf{x}^U_{j,s})_{j=1,...,n_u}$ as prostate-likelihood for the sth slice in $\mathbf{P}'_{\mathbf{z},n}$
14: **end for**

2.4 Rigid Alignment-Based Majority Voting

To generate segmentation result $\mathbf{G}'_n$ by using obtained prostate-likelihood map $\mathbf{P}'_n$, we consider using shape information from the planning and previous treatment images to guide the segmentation. Firstly, $\mathbf{G}_1, ..., \mathbf{G}_{n-1}$ and $\mathbf{G}^{\mathbf{P}}$ will be rigidly aligned to $\mathbf{P}'_n$; Then, the final prostate segmentation result can be achieved by majority voting on all the aligned manual segmentations.

3 Experimental Results

The proposed method was evaluated on a prostate 3-D CT-image dataset consisting of 11 patients. The original resolution of each image is $512 \times 512 \times 61$, with in-plane voxel size as 0.98×0.98 mm^2 and the inter-slice voxel size as 3 mm. All the images are manually segmented by experienced physician. We used the first 3 images (i.e., the planning image and the first two treatment images) as training images, from which auxiliary voxels are sampled and the segmentation ground truths are available. In our experiments, we use two common evaluation metrics: Dice ratio, and centroid distance (CD).

For parameter setting in tLasso, two important regularization parameters γ_G and γ_S are chosen by leave-one-out cross validation. Specifically, for each patient, to segment the current treatment image $\mathbf{I}_n$, we will use brute-force-search strategy to estimate γ_G from 10^{-i} ($i = 1, ..., 10$), as well as γ_S from 10^{-j} ($j = 1, ..., 10$), using leave-one-out cross validation on the 3 training images. The

γ_G and γ_S, which obtain the best result in cross validation, will be chosen as the final parameters. In the experiment, $\gamma_G = 10^{-6}$ and $\gamma_S = 10^{-8}$ are found to be the best. For α_l and α_a, we empirically set them as 0.5 and 0.5, respectively, which means that the labeled and auxiliary voxels are equally important. We use the same parameter choosing method for wLapRLS, and $\gamma_C = 10^{-6}$ and $\gamma_G = 10^{-5}$ in wLapRLS are found to be the best. For α_l', α_a' and α_u', we empirically set them as 1/3, 1/3 and 1/3, respectively.

The comparisons among different methods are listed in Table. 1. The results of [3] and [5] are listed for reference since different datasets are used. From Table.1, it is obvious that our proposed method outperforms [8] in terms of higher Dice ratio. Moreover, our centroid distances in 3 directions, i.e., lateral (x-axis), anterior-posterior (y-axis) and superior-inferior (z-axis), are significantly lower than [8] (except the CD in y-axis, where our -0.04 is slightly higher than -0.02 in [8]). We can infer that physician's interactive labeling information is quite useful for predicting the possible central location of prostate. In Fig.3, we illustrate the centroid distances for all 11 patients in 3 directions, respectively. Since we use the same data set as the one used in [8], it is known that the patients 2, 3 and 8 are with larger prostate motion. For patient 2, the median Dice ratio is 0.905 (around 0.87 in [8]); for patient 3, the median Dice ratio is 0.888 (around 0.89 in [8]); for patient 8, the median Dice ratio is 0.906 (around 0.86 in [8]). It is demonstrated that our proposed method is useful when large irregular motion occurs within prostate regions. We also illustrate some typical segmented examples in Fig.4, indicating that our results are very close to the manual segmentations.

Table 1. Comparison of mean Dice and CD among different methods, with the best results marked by bold font

methods	Feng *et al.*[5]	Davis *et al.*[3]	Li *et al.* [8]	our method
Patients	24	3	11	11
Images	306	40	161	161
Mean Dice	0.893	0.820	0.908	**0.917**
Mean CD(x/y/z)(mm)	N/A	$-0.26/0.35/0.22$	$0.18/-0.02/0.57$	$-0.10/-0.04/-0.09$

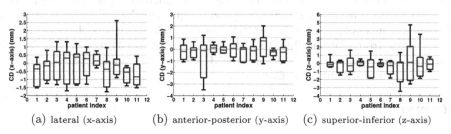

(a) lateral (x-axis)   (b) anterior-posterior (y-axis)   (c) superior-inferior (z-axis)

Fig. 3. Centroid distances along the lateral (x-axis), anterior-posterior (y-axis), and superior-inferior (z-axis) directions, respectively. Five horizontal lines (ascending order in values) means the min, 25% percentile, median, 75% percentile, and the max value, respectively.

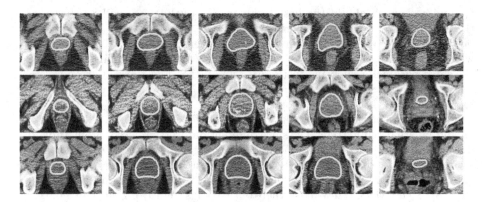

Fig. 4. The typical examples of segmentation results. Yellow curves denote the results using the proposed method, and red curves denote the manual delineation results.

4   Conclusion

In this paper, we propose a novel transductive 3-D prostate segmentation method for CT image guided radiotherapy. Our proposed method can incorporate the physician's interactive labeled information as well as the patient-specific information obtained from the planning image and previous segmented treatment images. Two novel methods: tLasso for transductive feature selection, and wLapRLS for transductive prostate-likelihood prediction, are also proposed. We test our proposed method on a real CT-prostate dataset. Based on the experimental results, our proposed method can obtain promising results, especially for the cases with large irregular prostate motion. It has demonstrated that physician's interactive information is quite useful for guiding accurate segmentation.

Acknowledgments. The work was supported by the grant from the National Science Foundation of China (Grant Nos. 61035003, 61175042, 61021062), the National 973 Program of China (Grant No. 2009CB320702), the 973 Program of Jiangsu, China (Grant No. BK2011005) and Program for New Century Excellent Talents in University (Grant No. NCET-10-0476). The work was also supported by the grant from National Institute of Health (Grant No. 1R01 CA140413). Y. Shi was a one-year visiting student at UNC Chapel Hill under the scholarship from the Chinese Scholarship Council.

References

1. Belkin, M., Niyogi, P., Sindhwani, V.: Manifold regularization: a geometric framework for learning from labeled and unlabeled examples. Journal of Machine Learning Research 7, 2399–2434 (2006)
2. Dalal, N., Triggs, B.: Histograms of oriented gradients for human detection. In: CVPR, pp. 886–893 (2005)

3. Davis, B.C., Foskey, M., Rosenman, J., Goyal, L., Chang, S., Joshi, S.: Automatic Segmentation of Intra-treatment CT Images for Adaptive Radiation Therapy of the Prostate. In: Duncan, J.S., Gerig, G. (eds.) MICCAI 2005. LNCS, vol. 3749, pp. 442–450. Springer, Heidelberg (2005)
4. Freedman, D., Radke, R.J., Zhang, T., Jeong, Y., Lovelock, D.M., Chen, G.T.: Modelbased segmentation of medical imagery by matching distributions. IEEE Trans. Med. Imag. 24, 281–292 (2005)
5. Feng, Q., Foskey, M., Chen, W., Shen, D.: Segmenting CT prostate images using population and patient-specific statistics for radiotherapy. Medical Physics 37, 4121–4132 (2010)
6. Grant, M., Boyd, S.: CVX: Matlab Software for Disciplined Convex Programming, version 1.21 (April 2011), http://cvxr.com/cvx
7. Jenkinson, M., Bannister, P., Brady, M., Smith, S.: Improve optimization for the robust and accurate linear registration and motion correction of brain images. NeuroImage 17, 825–841 (2002)
8. Li, W., Liao, S., Feng, Q., Chen, W., Shen, D.: Learning Image Context for Segmentation of Prostate in CT-Guided Radiotherapy. In: Fichtinger, G., Martel, A., Peters, T. (eds.) MICCAI 2011, Part III. LNCS, vol. 6893, pp. 570–578. Springer, Heidelberg (2011)
9. Mallat, G.: A theory for multiresolution signal decomposition: the wavelet representation. IEEE Trans. on Pattern Analysis and Machine Intelligence 11, 674–693 (1989)
10. Nesterov, Y.: Introductory lectures on convex optimization: a basic course. Kluwer Academic Publishers (2004)
11. Ojala, T., Pietikainen, M., Maenpaa, T.: Multiresolution gray-scale and rotation invariant texture classification with local binary patterns. IEEE Trans. on Pattern Analysis and Machine Intelligence 24, 971–987 (2002)
12. Shi, Y., Gao, Y., Wang, R., Zhang, Y., Wang, D.: Transductive cost-sensitive lung cancer image classification. Applied Intelligence (2012), doi:10.1007/s10489-012-0354-z
13. Tibshirani, R.: Regression shrinkage and selection via the lasso. Journal of the Royal Statistical Society: Series B 58, 267–288 (1996)
14. Yang, J., Yan, R., Hauptmann, A.G.: Cross-domain video concept detection using adaptive svms. In: ACM Multimedia Conference, pp. 188–197 (2007)
15. Zhang, D., Liu, J., Shen, D.: Temporally-Constrained Group Sparse Learning for Longitudinal Data Analysis. In: Ayache, N., Delingette, H., Golland, P., Mori, K. (eds.) MICCAI 2012, Part III. LNCS, vol. 7512, pp. 264–271. Springer, Heidelberg (2012)

Model-Driven Centerline Extraction
for Severely Occluded Major Coronary Arteries

Yefeng Zheng, Jianhua Shen, Huseyin Tek, and Gareth Funka-Lea

Imaging and Computer Vision, Siemens Corporate Research, Princeton, NJ, USA
yefeng.zheng@siemens.com

Abstract. Almost all previous approaches on coronary artery centerline extraction are data-driven, which try to trace a centerline from an
automatically detected or manually specified coronary ostium. No or little high level prior information is used; therefore, the centerline tracing
procedure may terminate early at a severe occlusion or an anatomically
inconsistent centerline course may be generated. In this work, we propose a model-driven approach to extracting the three major coronary
arteries. The relative position of the major coronary arteries with respect to the heart chambers is stable, therefore the automatically segmented chambers can be used to predict the initial position of these
coronary centerlines. The initial centerline is further refined using a machine learning based vesselness measurement. The proposed approach
can handle variations in the length and topology of an artery, and it is
more robust under severe occlusions than a data-driven approach. The
extracted centerlines are already labeled, therefore no additional vessel
labeling procedure is needed. Quantitative comparison on 54 cardiac CT
datasets demonstrates the robustness of the proposed method over a
state-of-the-art data-driven approach.

1   Introduction

Cardiac computed tomography (CT) is the primary non-invasive imaging modality to diagnose coronary stenosis thanks to its superior image resolution. To
facilitate the diagnosis, coronary centerlines are often extracted before the detection and quantification of the stenosis. However, automatic centerline extraction is challenging due to the presence of severe occlusions, imaging artifacts,
and insufficient contrast agent, etc. Furthermore, large anatomical variations of
the coronary tree are another major challenge. For example, depending on the
dominance pattern, the posterior descending artery (PDA) and posterolateral
branch (PLB) artery can be fed by either the right coronary artery (RCA) or
the left circumflex artery (LCX). Various coronary centerline extraction methods have been proposed in the literature [1,2]. Almost all previous approaches
are data-driven, which try to trace a centerline from an automatically detected
or manually specified coronary ostium. The prominent advantage of these approaches is the potential to handle anatomical variations. However, since no or
little high level prior information is used, the centerline tracing procedure may

F. Wang et al. (Eds.): MLMI 2012, LNCS 7588, pp. 10–18, 2012.

terminate early at a severe occlusion or an anatomically inconsistent centerline course may be generated. In clinical practice, reporting is made more efficient if the correct label (*i.e.*, the branch name) is assigned to each branch in the extracted coronary tree. Previously, the coronary tree is extracted first, followed by a post-processing for branch labeling [3]. Labeling is not an easy task if the coronary tree is not extracted completely or there is wrong tracing of some branches into non-coronary structures. Such a two-step sequential approach is not optimal. Each step is made un-necessarily difficult due to the limited usage of the high level prior information. Recently, Kitamura *et al.* [4] proposed a method to build the coronary shape model composed with 30 discrete nodes sampled from three major coronary arteries and two coronary veins. The coronary shape model is then fitted to the detected coronary candidates via an optimization procedure. However, one global shape model may have difficulty to handle anatomical variations of coronary arteries.

Though the connectivity of coronary arteries exhibits large variations, the position of major coronary arteries relative to the heart chambers is quite stable [5]. Such prior constraints can significantly improve the centerline extraction robustness, especially for patients with severe occlusions. In this work, we propose a model-driven approach to extracting the proximal and middle segments of the coronary arteries, which are normally consistently present at a predictable position. To be specific, the relative positions of the heart chambers and the proximal/middle segments of the major coronary arteries are learned from a set of training data and embedded in a mean shape model. During testing we first segment all four heart chambers. The deformation field from the mean shape to the input volume is calculated using the chamber meshes, and then used to warp the coronary mean shape toward the input volume. After a chamber-based prediction, we get a rough estimate of the course of the coronary arteries, which is further refined using a dynamic programming based shortest path computation with a machine learning based vesselness measurement as the path cost. A classifier is trained to distinguish a centerline point from the others and the classification score is taken as the vesselness. Our learning based vesselness is more accurate than the previous handcrafted vesselness measurements [6,7]. At last, the extracted centerlines are verified and extended to the distal end.

The proposed approach has a few advantages compared to the previous data-driven approaches: 1) It is much more robust under severe occlusions. Clinically relevant occlusions mostly occur at the proximal or middle segment of a major artery and this part is extracted using a more robust model-driven approach; 2) By combining model-driven and data-driven approaches, it can handle variations in the length and topology of an artery; and 3) We combine the centerline extraction and vessel labeling into the same procedure. Consequently, the extracted centerlines are already labeled once detected.

2 Building Coronary Model

Due to the anatomical variations, it is impossible to have a single model for the major coronary arteries, not to mention the whole coronary tree. Compared to

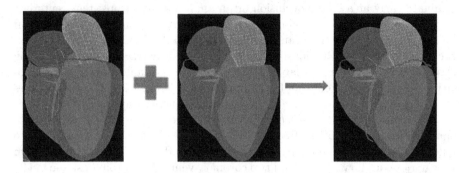

Fig. 1. Heart chamber based prediction of major coronary arteries. **Left**: Mean shape of the heart chambers and coronary arteries built from a training set. **Middle**: Segmented heart chambers on an input dataset. **Right**: Predicted coronary arteries.

the RCA and LCX, the left anterior descending (LAD) artery is simpler since its distal extent is not affected by the variations of the dominance pattern. But, its visible length inside a volume varies either due to anatomical variation or insufficient contrast agent inside the vessel. To handle the length variation, we truncate the LADs from all patients to the same relative length. Here, we measure the relative length against the distance between the left coronary ostium and the left ventricular apex. The truncation threshold is set to the lower 5th percentile over the given training set to ignore a few outliers with very short LADs. The truncation threshold can be tuned to adjust how much of the centerline we want to extract from the model-driven approach and how much we want to leave for a data-driven procedure. On average, we model 80% of the full length. After truncation, the LADs are evenly resampled to 64 points.

The distal segment of the LCX and RCA varies a lot in topology. Depending on the coronary dominance, they may bifurcate into the PDA or PLB. Therefore, we cannot model their full length. Since both the proximal and middle segments of the LCX and RCA run inside the atrioventricular groove, we only model this part. They are truncated with a similar approach to the LAD and then evenly resampled to 64 points. About 60% of the full lenght of the LCX and 75% of the RCA are preserved and therefore modeled.

After extracting the consistent part of all major coronary arteries, we add them into the four-chamber heart model. The left sub-image of Fig. 1 shows the mean shape model with both the heart chambers and coronary arteries. The relative position of the coronary arteries with respect to the chambers is embedded in this mean shape model, which will later be used to predict the initial position of coronary arteries on an unseen volume.

3   Model-Driven Coronary Centerline Extraction

Given an input volume, the heart chambers are segmented using the method presented in [8], and they are then used to predict the initial position of the

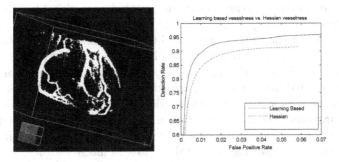

Fig. 2. Learning based vesselness. **Left**: Detected coronary artery voxels for one volume. The voxel classification score is thresholded for visualization purpose. **Right**: Detection rate vs. false positive rate of the learning based vesselness and Hessian vesselness.

coronary arteries. Since the heart chambers are available in both the mean shape and the input volume, we use them to estimate a deformation field. Here, the well-known thin-plate spline (TPS) model [9] is used to estimate the deformation field. In addition, the left and right coronary ostia are also automatically detected using the method proposed in [10] and they are added as anchor points for TPS deformation.

A dynamic programming based optimization is then applied to refine the initial centerline path. The initial centerline is represented as a set of evenly sampled points P_i, for $i = 0, 1, \ldots, n-1$. For each point P_i, we uniformly sample 41×41 candidate positions P_i^j on a plane perpendicular to the centerline path at this point. The candidates P_i^j are sampled on a regular grid of 20×20 mm^2 with grid spacing of 0.5 mm. Now, the problem is how to select the best position for each point P_i. It can be formulated as a shortest path computation problem,

$$\bar{P}_0^{J(0)}, \bar{P}_1^{J(1)}, \ldots, \bar{P}_{n-1}^{J(n-1)} = \arg\min_{P_i^{J(i)}} \sum_{i=0}^{n-1} C(P_i^{J(i)}) + w \sum_{i=0}^{n-2} \|P_i^{J(i)} - P_{i+1}^{J(i+1)}\|. \quad (1)$$

The first term is the cost for a single node, measuring how likely this point is at the center of the vessel. Here, a machine learning based vesselness (more details in the next paragraph) is used as the node cost. The second term in Eq. (1) is the total length of the path by summing the Euclidean distance between two neighboring points on the path. Free parameter w, which is used to balance the two terms, is heuristically tuned on a few datasets and then fixed throughout the experiments. The optimal path can be calculated efficiently using dynamic programming.

Various vesselness measurements have been proposed in the literature, $e.g.$, the Hessian vesselness [6], medialness [7,11], and cylinder model based vesselness [12]. Based on a simple geometric assumption of the artery shape, these handcrafted vesselness measurements have difficulty to detect the coronary bifurcations. In this work, we exploit machine learning techniques to train a classifier, which can tell us whether a voxel is at the center of a coronary artery or not. The annotated centerline points are treated as positive training samples. The voxels with a large distance to the centerlines are treated as negative samples. Here, we set the distance threshold to 5 mm (which is about the maximum diameter of a coronary artery) to avoid collecting negative samples inside a coronary lumen. The steerable features [8], which are efficient and capable of capturing complicated image patterns, are extracted for classification. Around a given position, we sample $5 \times 5 \times 5$ points using the regular sampling pattern of the steerable features. The distance between neighboring sampling point is set to 3 mm. We extract 24 local features at each sampling point based on the image intensity and gradient, resulting in a total of 125×24 image features. The probabilistic boosting tree (PBT) [8] is used to train a classifier. The PBT outputs a real-valued classification score within [0, 1], which is treated as a vesselness measurement as used in Eq. (1). Fig. 2a shows the detected coronary voxels in a typical volume. The coronary tree structure is clearly visible with only a few false positive detections. As shown in Fig. 2b, our learning based vesselness achieves consistently a higher detection rate under any false positive rate, compared to the well-known Hessian vesselness [6]. It preserves the vessel junctions quite well and is very efficient to compute.

4   Centerline Verification and Extension

The model-driven approach is robust under severe occlusions. However, it only models the consistent proximal and middle segments of a coronary artery. It needs to be combined with a data-driven approach to handle the anatomical variations. The data-driven procedure has two major goals: centerline verification and centerline extension.

The centerline generated by the model-driven step may be too long for a few datasets (*e.g.*, for the 5% shortest LADs excluded from the model training). On such cases the distal end of the centerline is traced into a non-coronary structure. We shrink the centerline from the end point, one by one, if the vesselness score is less than a threshold. After shrinking we extend the centerline from the current end point to the distal using shortest-path computation. Again, the learning-based vesselness is used as a cost for each node on the path. Starting from the current end point, we search all paths with a certain length (*e.g.*, 10 mm). We then pick the best path among them and append it to the current centerline. If a good path is found (with a path cost smaller than a threshold), we keep tracing. Otherwise, the tracing procedure stops. The LAD is traced quite well since there are no further bifurcations beyond the segment extracted by the model-driven procedure. However, for the LCX and RCA, there may still be a couple of long branches. For some confusing cases, it is hard to achieve a unanimous agreement even among physicians in determining which is the main trunk and which is a side branch. Our algorithm picks one branch among these candidates with some randomness.

5 Experiments

There is an open competition on coronary centerline extraction within the Rotterdam Coronary Artery Algorithm Evaluation Framework, which is a continuation of a MICCAI challenge in 2008 [2]. We did not participate in the competition because, besides the three major coronary arteries, it also evaluates a randomly picked side branch, which is missing in this work. Instead, we evaluate our algorithm on a more challenging dataset with severe occlusions and low image quality, and the evaluation is restricted to the three major coronary arteries. The whole dataset with 108 volumes is split into two equal sets with one set for training and the other for testing.

We use the same error measurements proposed in [2], including overlap (OV), overlap until first error (OF), overlap with the clinically relevant part of the vessel (OT), and average inside (AI). All measurements are based on point-to-point correspondence between the detected centerline and the ground truth. A centerline point is claimed to be detected correctly if its distance to the corresponding ground truth point is no more than a threshold (which is set to the radius at that point in [2]). Annotating the radius or lumen at each centerline point is quite time consuming and we do not have this information in our annotation. Instead, we set the threshold to 2.5 mm, which is roughly the radius of the proximal segment of a coronary artery. We found the error measurements are not sensitive to this threshold since when a centerline is traced to a wrong position, the distance to the ground truth centerline is normally much larger than 2.5 mm. In real applications, a small coronary segment close to the distal end is not clinically relevant. To calculate the overlap for the clinically relevant part (OT), the distal segment with a radius less than 0.75 mm is excluded in [2]. Again, since we have no radius annotation, we have to truncate the centerline differently. Here, we treat the segment that we use to build the mean shape model (Section 3) as the clinically relevant part, which corresponds to the proximal 80% of the LAD, and the segment inside the atrioventricular groove for the LCX and RCA.

We compare our method with a state-of-the-art data-driven approach [7], which won the second place on the MICCAI challenge in the category of automatic methods in 2008, and significant further improvements in robustness have been achieved recently [13]. Since the data-driven approach generates an unlabeled coronary tree, the ground truth centerline is used to pick the correct branch for evaluation. As shown in Table 1, our approach consistently outperforms the data-driven approach on all measurements for all three major coronary arteries. The improvement of overlap (OV) is significant for the LAD, and moderate for the LCX and RCA since our algorithm may pick up a distal branch inconsistent to the ground truth. The improvements in OF (72% vs. 56%) and OT (92% vs. 85%) are more significant since these measurements are dominated by the centerline quality of the proximal segment, which is extracted using a far more robust model-driven procedure in our approach.

Fig. 3 shows the curved multi-planar reformation view of the centerline extraction results on three example cases. All have mild to severe occlusions in the major coronary arteries. The first dataset has a short occlusion in the LCX.

Table 1. Quantitative comparison of the proposed method and a data-driven approach [7] on 54 cardiac CT datasets. OV, OF, and OT measure the overlap ratio between detected and ground truth centerlines, while AI is a distance measurement in millimeters [2].

	LAD				LCX				RCA				Over All			
	OV	OF	OT	AI	OV	OF	OT	AI	OV	OF	OT	AI	OV	OF	OT	AI
Data-Driven Method	76%	47%	84%	1.03	69%	57%	81%	0.99	79%	65%	89%	0.89	75%	56%	85%	0.97
Proposed Method	87%	76%	92%	0.61	71%	65%	89%	0.49	82%	74%	94%	0.56	80%	72%	92%	0.55

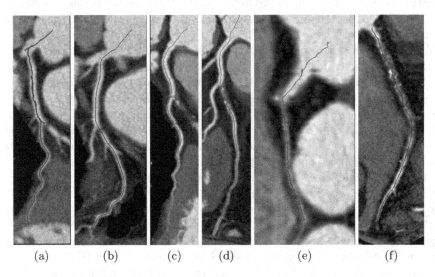

(a)   (b)   (c)   (d)   (e)   (f)

Fig. 3. Coronary centerline extraction results on three datasets. (a), (c), and (e) are the results of a data-driven approach [7], while (b), (d), and (f) are the results of the proposed method. Though the major coronary arteries have mild or severe occlusions, the proposed method works well. The data-driven approach fails to pick the correct main trunks, instead tracing into side branches.

The data-driven approach outputs a branch terminated at the occlusion and it also outputs a long side branch. Therefore, the following vessel labeling algorithm is very likely to pick the long side branch as the main trunk. For the other two examples, the data-driven approach fails to trace the main trunks too. The proposed method is very robust under occlusions and it works well even on long severe occlusions (the last example in Fig. 3).

The proposed method is computationally efficient, compared to other algorithms in the literature. The whole process takes about 7.5 s on a computer with quad-core 2.33 GHz CPU and 3 GB memory, including 4.0 s for chamber segmentation and 3.5 s for centerline extraction. However, chamber segmentation is already part of our cardiac CT analysis workflow. Therefore, centerline extraction only incurs 3.5 s additional computation time. For comparison, the data-driven approach [7,13] takes about 15 s to process a volume on the same computer, which is already the fastest among all automatic algorithms that participated in the MICCAI challenge [2]. Please note, this is not a head-to-head comparison in speed since the data-driven approach generates the whole coronary tree without branch labels. Our algorithm outputs only three major coronary arteries, but they are properly labeled.

6 Conclusion

In this work, we proposed a model-driven centerline extraction method, which leverages the prior information embedded in a combined shape model with both heart chambers and coronary arteries. The proposed method is robust under severe occlusions inside a vessel. Another advantage is that the extracted centerlines are already labeled properly, therefore no vessel labeling post-processing is needed. In the future we plan to extend our work to extract the whole coronary tree. For example, we can detect the bifurcations on the major coronary arteries and, at each bifurcation, data-driven branch tracing can be initiated. In this way all side branches can be extracted and labeled, and the dominance pattern of the coronary tree can also be identified automatically.

References

1. Lesage, D., Angelini, E.D., Bloch, I., Funka-Lea, G.: A review of 3D vessel lumen segmentation techniques: Models, features and extraction schemes. Medical Image Analysis 13(6), 819–845 (2009)
2. Schaap, M., Metz, C.T., van Walsum, T., et al.: Standardized evaluation methodology and reference database for evaluating coronary artery centerline extraction algorithms. Medical Image Analysis 13, 701–714 (2009)
3. Lu, L., Bi, J., Yu, S., Peng, Z., Krishnan, A., Zhou, X.S.: A hierarchical learning approach for 3D tubular structure parsing in medical imaging. In: Proc. Int'l Conf. Computer Vision, pp. 1–8 (2009)
4. Kitamura, Y., Li, Y., Ito, W.: Automatic coronary extraction by supervised detection and shape matching. In: ISBI, pp. 234–237 (2012)
5. Lorenz, C., von Berg, J.: A comprehensive shape model of the heart. Medical Image Analysis 10(4), 657–670 (2006)
6. Frangi, A.F., Niessen, W.J., Vincken, K.L., Viergever, M.A.: Multiscale Vessel Enhancement Filtering. In: Wells, W.M., Colchester, A.C.F., Delp, S.L. (eds.) MICCAI 1998. LNCS, vol. 1496, pp. 130–137. Springer, Heidelberg (1998)
7. Tek, H., Gulsun, M.A., Laguitton, S., Grady, L., Lesage, D., Funka-Lea, G.: Automatic coronary tree modeling. The Insight Journal (2008)
8. Zheng, Y., Barbu, A., Georgescu, B., Scheuering, M., Comaniciu, D.: Four-chamber heart modeling and automatic segmentation for 3D cardiac CT volumes using marginal space learning and steerable features. IEEE Trans. Medical Imaging 27(11), 1668–1681 (2008)
9. Bookstein, F.: Principal warps: Thin-plate splines and the decomposition of deformations. IEEE Trans. Pattern Anal. Machine Intell. 11(6), 567–585 (1989)

10. Zheng, Y., Tek, H., Funka-Lea, G., Zhou, S.K., Vega-Higuera, F., Comaniciu, D.: Efficient Detection of Native and Bypass Coronary Ostia in Cardiac CT Volumes: Anatomical vs. Pathological Structures. In: Fichtinger, G., Martel, A., Peters, T. (eds.) MICCAI 2011, Part III. LNCS, vol. 6893, pp. 403–410. Springer, Heidelberg (2011)
11. Krissian, K., Malandain, G., Ayache, N., Vaillant, R., Trousset, Y.: Model based detection of tubular structures in 3D images. Computer Vision and Image Understanding 80(2), 130–171 (2000)
12. Friman, O., Kühnel, C., Peitgen, H.: Coronary artery centerline extraction using multiple hypothesis tracking and minimal paths. The Insight Journal (2008)
13. Tek, H., Zheng, Y., Gulsun, M.A., Funka-Lea, G.: An automatic system for segmenting coronary arteries from CTA. In: Proc. MICCAI Workshop on Computing and Visualization for Intravascular Imaging (2011)

MRI Confirmed Prostate Tissue Classification with Laplacian Eigenmaps of Ultrasound RF Spectra

Mehdi Moradi[1,2], Christian Wachinger[3], Andriy Fedorov[2],
William M. Wells[2,3], Tina Kapur[2],
Luciant D. Wolfsberger[2], Paul Nguyen[2], and Clare M. Tempany[2]

[1] Department of Electrical and Computer Engineering,
University of British Columbia, Vancouver, Canada
moradi@ece.ubc.ca
[2] Brigham and Women's Hospital, Harvard Medical School, Boston, MA
[3] Massachusetts Institute of Technology, Cambridge, MA

Abstract. The delivery of therapeutic prostate interventions can be improved by intraprocedural visualization of the tumor during ultrasound-guided procedures. To this end, ultrasound-based tissue classification and registration of the clinical target volume from preoperative multiparametric MR images to intraoperative ultrasound are suggested as two potential solutions. In this paper we report techniques to implement both of these solutions. In ultrasound-based tissue typing, we employ Laplacian eigenmaps for reducing the dimensionality of the spectral feature space formed by ultrasound RF power spectra. This is followed by support vector machine classification for separating cancer from normal prostate tissue. A classification accuracy of 78.3±4.8% is reported. We also present a deformable MR-US registration method which relies on transforming the binary label maps acquired by delineating the prostate gland in both MRI and ultrasound. This method is developed to transfer the diagnostic references from MRI to US for training and validation of the proposed ultrasound-based prostate tissue classification technique. It yields a target registration error of 3.5±2.1 mm. We also report its use for MR-based dose boosting during ultrasound-guided brachytherapy.

1 Introduction

Prostate tumors can not be visualized in the ultrasound B-mode images used for interventional guidance. As a result, the current methodology of transrectal ultrasound (TRUS) guided biopsy is a systematic sampling approach, which can potentially miss or under sample cancerous tissue or may incorrectly stage the disease. Similarly, for therapeutic interventions such as brachytherapy and surgery, the lack of reliable radiologic characterization of the tissue forces the choice of radical treatment as opposed to focal therapy. In order to enable image-based targeting, 3T MRI-guided prostate intervention is currently performed in a small number of institutions including Brigham and Women's Hospital. The motivation for MRI guidance is the proven performance of multiparametric

F. Wang et al. (Eds.): MLMI 2012, LNCS 7588, pp. 19–26, 2012.

MRI, which includes diffusion weighted imaging (DWI) and dynamic contrast enhanced (DCE) imaging, in detection and characterization of prostate cancer [1]. However, MR-guided procedures are costly due to the high cost of the scanner and the required MR compatible tools. Therefore, the search for an ultrasound-based solution for intraoperative tumor visualization is vital. Ultrasound can play an important role both in tissue typing for cancer detection and as an intraoperative modality to enable registration of the preoperative diagnostic maps or targets to the interventional field of view. In this paper, we report advances in both ultrasound-based tissue classification and in registration to MRI.

Ultrasound B-mode and RF signals have been used for tissue typing in prostate [2]. The use of RF signals enables the access to the echoes before going through the nonlinear process of envelope detection and filtering that results in the B-mode image. It also enables normalization to remove the effects of the employed transducer from the RF signals to acquire a system-independent tissue response. The tissue typing features are extracted from the normalized power spectrum of short segments of RF signals. The commonly used features are the slope and the intercept of a line fitted to the RF power spectrum [3]. This parametrization process does not take advantage of all the information in the reflected signals. A dimensionality reduction approach that uses the entire length of the spectrum can potentially result in a more informative set of features. We propose the use of Laplacian eigenmap on the feature space formed by the average RF power spectra for dimensionality reduction in ultrasound-based tissue classification. This method builds a adjacency graph that incorporates the neighborhood information of the data points in the spectral space and calculates the eigenvalues of the graph Laplacian. This neighborhood dependent quality results in robustness to noise compared to principal component analysis (PCA). The original application of this geometrically inspired dimensionality reduction method is in embedding manifolds in lower dimensions [4]. In the context of ultrasound imaging, the method was previously used for breathing gating in 4D ultrasound imaging [5]. In our work, the reduced feature space is used with a support vector machine (SVM) classifier for separating cancer from normal tissue regions.

The diagnostic label of the data used in SVM training of this work is determined by a radiologist on multiparametric MRI data and further confirmed with biopsy results. In order to map the diagnosis to the ultrasound image space, we report a contour-driven deformable registration approach for aligning ultrasound to MRI. The reported registration method is innovative and practical within the context of prostate brachytherapy where gland contouring is routinely performed for dose planning. We also report the clinical use of this registration scheme to enable MR-assisted TRUS guided prostate brachytherapy.

2   Methods

2.1   Clinical Data

The patient population consisted of those who had biopsy evidence of low to intermediate grade prostate cancer, and were candidates for low dose brachytherapy.

From Dec. 2011 to Feb. 2012, six patients were imaged for brachytherapy volume study at Brigham and Women's Hospital in Boston, MA and the images were used in complaince with HIPPA and the approval of the institutional review board. All patients underwent mpMRI exams in a GE 3T MR scanner using an endorectal coil. T1w, T2w, DWI and DCE sequences were included. Slice spacing was 3 mm. An expert radiologist (CMT) contoured areas of the prostate suspicious of cancer on T2w (low SI), raw DCE (rapid enhancement and wash out after gadolinium agent administration) and Average Diffusion Coefficient ADC (low SI) sequences. These findings were compared to biopsy outcomes and tumors with positive radiology finding on MRI confirmed by a positive biopsy finding from the same anatomic area were used as regions with a cancer label in our machine learning algorithm. The normal tissue was from the peripheral zone of the prostate gland of the same patients where the opposite criteria applied (no MRI or biopsy evidence of cancer).

The TRUS data was acquired during ultrasound volume studies performed days prior to the brachytherapy procedure. The data was acquired using a Pro Focus UltraView 800 (BK Medical Systems, Herlev, Denmark) with the transverse array of the BK 8848 transducer. For all cases the focal zone was set to 2 cm and all TGC settings were set to the middle value. To acquire the RF data, we equipped a personal computer with a frame grabber (X64-CL Express, Dalsa, Montreal, Canada) and used a camera link connection to the BK UA2227 research interface. We also established a TCP/IP connection between the ultrasound machine and the PC for transferring the imaging parameters. The imaging protocol was to use a standard brachytherapy stepper unit and capture axial RF and B-mode frames from base to apex, starting with the axial image at the bases and retracting with 5 mm steps to cover the entire length of the gland. The 5 mm slice spacing was chosen based on the locking step size of the stepper unit. Between 8 and 12 slices covered the entire length of the gland.

The contouring and processing of the prostate images was performed in the open-source 3D Slicer 3.6.3 software package [6]. The attending radiation oncologist (PN) contoured the prostate gland on both the axial T2w MRI and B-mode images of the prostate. The Model Maker module in 3D Slicer software was used to create the 3D surface meshes (smoothing iterations = 10).

2.2   MR to TRUS Registration

Due to the effect of the endorectal coil used during MR imaging and also the different patient positions between MR and TRUS image acquisitions, deformable registration is required to map the diagnostic MRI labels onto the US images. Intensity-based deformable registration of ultrasound to MRI is a challenging open problem due to the poor signal to noise ratio and lack of well defined features in ultrasound images. Several works have used deformable surface-based registration to tackle this problem [7,8]. Surface-based registration techniques commonly use a biomechanical finite element model of the surface mesh and are computationally expensive. We use a simple contour-driven deformable registration method. Unlike the surface-based methods, it uses a B-spline transform to elastically align the binary 3D label maps resulting from manual contouring. The key point is to use a coarse B-spline grid to ensure that warping does not unrealistically deform the detailed features within the prostate gland. It should be noted that the poor visibility of the prostate contour, particularly in the apex area, negatively affects the registration accuracy of both our method and the surface-based techniques. The registration approach was fully implemented in 3D Slicer and consisted of the following steps (the notation: USS: ultrasound surface model, MRS: MRI surface model, UL: binary label map volume acquired by contouring the gland in ultrasound, ML: binary label map from MRI, MR: grayscale T2w MRI volume, US: grayscale US volume, MRD: binary diagnostic label map marked on MRI):

- Use the iterative closest point (ICP) registration method [9] to obtain a rigid transformation ($T^r_{MRS \to USS}$).
- Apply the ICP transform to MR labels as the initial transform: $\widehat{ML} = T^r_{MRS \to USS} \bullet ML$.
- Define a coarse B-spline grid, with cell size of around half the length of the gland, on $\widehat{ML}$. We used the cell size of 30 mm.
- Use mutual information maximization [10] to obtain the following B-spline transform on binary label maps: $T^B_{\widehat{ML} \to UL}$.
- Obtain the transformed grayscale MR image, re-sampled with US image as the reference image: $\widehat{MR} = T^B_{\widehat{ML} \to UL} \bullet MR$.
- Re-sample the MR diagnostic map with the US image as the reference image: $\widehat{MRD} = T^B_{\widehat{ML} \to UL} \bullet MRD$.

The resulting $\widehat{MRD}$ was in the ultrasound image raster and was used as the diagnostic label to define cancerous and normal areas in ultrasound. $\widehat{MR}$ was used for evaluating the registration.

2.3   Dimensionality Reduction on RF Power Spectra

The proposed tissue typing features were extracted from regions of interest (ROIs) of approximate physical size 1×1 mm, equivalent to windows of length 64 samples in the axial direction and 4 lines in the lateral direction of the RF frames. The ROIs were overlapping by 25% in both lateral and axial directions. Using the FFT algorithm, the frequency spectra of the four line segments in each ROI were calculated and averaged. Since the RF signal is real, the power spectrum of the ROI was fully represented with half the length of the RF line segments, *i.e.* $k=32$. Given m regions of interest equivalent to points in the form of $\mathbf{S}_1, ..., \mathbf{S}_m$ in the spectral feature space, the adjacency graph was formed by considering an edge between points $\mathbf{S}_i$ and $\mathbf{S}_j$ if point $\mathbf{S}_i$ was among the n nearest neighbors of $\mathbf{S}_j$. We set the weight for the graph connections to $W_{ij}=1$ if

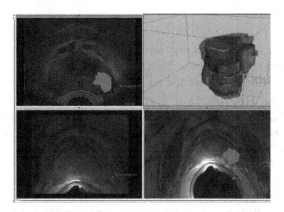

Fig. 1. The MR-TRUS registration: Top-right shows the moving MRI surface model (red) and the fixed TRUS surface model built from manual contouring of the gland in the two modalities, registered with ICP, Bottom-right: original MRI image with the outlined clinical target volume, Bottom-left: the warped MR image, Top-left: the resampled clinical target volume shown on the B-mode image

the vertices i and j were connected and 0 otherwise. Following [4], the eigenvectors $\mathbf{f}_i$, corresponding to the smallest l non-zero eigenvalues ($\lambda_i, i = \{1, ..., l\}$), computed by solving the generalized eigenvalue problem:

$$\mathbf{L}\mathbf{f} = \lambda D\mathbf{f} \tag{1}$$

were used for the embedding of the data in the l dimensional space, where $l < k$. In Eq. 1, D is a diagonal matrix formed as $D_{ii} = \sum_j W_{ij}$ and L = D-W is the Laplacian. We set the neighborhood size to $n=100$. The reduced dimension of the feature space was set to $l=2$ based on the observation that adding more eigenvalues to the feature vectors did not improve the classification result. Since the registered diagnostic label maps were on the B-mode images, the resulting RF feature maps were scan converted and resampled to the B-mode raster.

2.4 Classification

Support vector machine classification was used to examine the performance of the proposed features in separating cancer from normal ROIs [11]. The SVM implementation called LIBSVM and reported in [12] was used for this purpose. The radial basis function (RBF) kernel was employed and the parameter values of the RBF exponent and the slack variable weight coefficient were set with a grid search as described in [12]. For cross validation, a leave-10%-out approach was used, and repeated 100 times, each time with a random permutation of data points prior to partitioning to ten bins. We report the average and standard deviation of the 1000 tests.

3   Results

From the six patients, two did not have tumors with positive radiologic and biopsy finding from the same area. Since the reference diagnostic labels were not available for these case, the reported results are from the other four cases.

Evaluation of the Registration: Figure 1 shows the results of the proposed registration method on a clinical case. To evaluate the registration accuracy, an expert radiologist who routinely reads prostate MRI images, contoured structures such as the verumontanum, calcifications, and cysts that were visible on both modalities. The tip of verumontanum and the geometric center of the matched calcifications/cysts were used as fiducial points. In all four cases, we also used the leftmost point on the prostate contours in the axial plane as an additional fiducial point. In total, 11 landmarks were identified from the four cases (at least two in each). We applied the transformation $T^B_{\widehat{ML} \to UL}$ to the fiducial points. The distance from the transformed MR fiducial points to the matching ultrasound fiducial points was measured as the target registration error (TRE). The average TRE was 3.5 mm with a standard deviation of 2.1 mm. It should be noted that the identification of matching landmarks that were visible on both TRUS and T2w MR images was challenging, particularly due to the different slice spacing in the two modalities. We noted that the worst measured registration error (5.3 mm) was in a case in which the original ultrasound fiducial point and the transformed MRI fiducial point were in different axial slices in the ultrasound space. The radiation oncologist qualitatively evaluated the warped MR images to ensure the internal deformations were reasonable.

In the most recent case, the MR-TRUS registration was used during the patient's prostate brachytherapy procedure to enable dose boosting. The clinical target volume, marked on T2w MRI by a radiologist, was registered onto the axial ultrasound images and visualized in OR using 3D Slicer (Figure 2). The dose in the clinical target volume was set to at least 150% of the prescribed 145 Gy dose, boosted from at least 100% (biopsy Gleason grade: 3+4, age: 73).

Tissue Classification Accuracy in Ultrasound Data. The average B-mode intensity in the eight bit gray scale images was 18.1±11.2 in the areas marked as cancer and 21.8±9.9 in the areas marked as non-cancer. Figure 3 shows an example of the marking of the cancerous and normal areas and the distribution of the first two Laplacian eigenvalues extracted from the RF power spectra of the ROIs within these areas. SVM classification results are reported in Table 1 for both Laplacian eigenvalue features and the two largest PCA eigenvectors for comparison. With an average accuracy of 78.3±4.8%, the Laplacian eigenvalues provide a more accurate classification of the ROIs compared to PCA.

Table 1. SVM classification outcomes, PCA and Laplacian eigenvalues

Dimensionality reduction method	accuracy %	sensitivity %	specificity %
Laplacian eigenvalues	78.3±4.8	72.4 ±9.6	82.5±2.5
PCA	73.2±4.6	61.4 ± 10.4	80.8 ±5.9

Fig. 2. The proposed MR-TRUS registration was used during the prostate brachyther-apy surgery to boost the dose to the clinical target volume

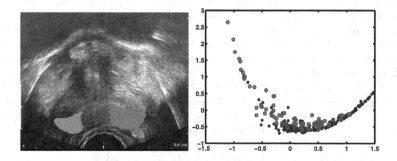

Fig. 3. Left: The cancer label map (green) registered from MRI to US and the non-cancer region (red) on the peripheral zone of the prostate gland. Right: The distribution of the first (horizontal axis) and the second (vertical axis) eigenvalues computed from the RF power spectra in the normal (blue stars) and cancer regions (red circles).

4   Conclusions

In this work we reported a machine learning framework for prostate tissue clas-sification from ultrasound data. The regions of interest in the tissue were rep-resented by the average power spectrum of the RF line segments within each ROI. We used the geometrically inspired eigenvalue decomposition of the graph Laplacian to reduce the size of the feature space from 32 to 2. The proposed method is a significant improvement compared to PCA-based RF features. Our goal is to further improve this cancer detection performance with combining the MRI features, in paticular ADC, with the ultrasound features for tissue typing. This was not feasible within the context of the present dataset due to the fact that the reference diagnostic labels were derived based on ADC among other MR sequences. It should also be noted that due to the small number of cases, we did not perform leave-one-subject-out cross validation. Therefore, clinical significance of the cancer detection rate can not be established at this stage.

To enable mapping of the reference diagnostic maps from MRI to ultrasound, we also reported the contour-driven registration of the two modalities. Our reported registration accuracy is close to slice spacing limit and comparable to those reported for surface-based methods [8].

Acknowledgement. The National Center for Research Resources and the National Institute of Biomedical Imaging and Bioengineering of the National Institutes of Health through Grant Numbers P41EB015898 and P41RR019703, and R01CA111288. The contents are solely the responsibility of the authors and do not necessarily represent the official views of the NIH. M. Moradi received partial support from US DoD PCRP Award W81XWH-10-1-0201.

References

1. Moradi, M., Salcudean, S.E., Chang, S.D., Jones, E.C., Buchan, N., Casey, R.G., Goldenberg, S.L., Kozlowski, P.: Multiparametric MRI maps for detection and grading of dominant prostate tumors. J. Magn. Reson. Imaging 35(6), 1403–1413 (2012)
2. Scheipers, U., Ermert, H., Sommerfeld, H.J., Garcia-Schurmann, M., Senge, T., Philippou, S.: Ultrasonic multifeature tissue characterization for prostate diagnosis. Ultrasound in Medicine and Biology 20(8), 1137–1149 (2003)
3. Feleppa, E.J., Kalisz, A., Sokil-Melgar, J.B., Lizzi, F.L., Liu, T., Rosado, A.L., Shao, M.C., Fair, W.R., Wang, Y., Cookson, M.S., Reuter, V.E., Heston, W.D.W.: Typing of prostate tissue by ultrasonic spectrum analysis. IEEE Transactions on Ultrasonics, Ferroelectrics, and Frequency Control 43(4), 609–619 (1996)
4. Belkin, M., Niyogi, P.: Laplacian eigenmaps for dimensionality reduction and data representation. Neural Computation 15(6), 1373–1396 (2003)
5. Wachinger, C., Yigitsoy, M., Navab, N.: Manifold Learning for Image-Based Breathing Gating with Application to 4D Ultrasound. In: Jiang, T., Navab, N., Pluim, J.P.W., Viergever, M.A. (eds.) MICCAI 2010, Part II. LNCS, vol. 6362, pp. 26–33. Springer, Heidelberg (2010)
6. Pieper, S., Lorensen, B., Schroeder, W., Kikinis, R.: The NA-MIC Kit: ITK, VTK, pipelines, grids and 3D slicer as an open platform for the medical image computing community. In: IEEE International Symposium on Biomedical Imaging: From Nano to Macro, pp. 698–701 (2006), http://www.slicer.org/
7. Hua, Y., Ahmed, H.U., Taylora, Z., Allenc, C., Emberton, M., Hawkes, D., Barratt, D.: MR to ultrasound registration for image-guided prostate interventions. Medical Image Analysis 16(3), 687–703 (2012)
8. Narayanan, R., Kurhanewicz, J., Shinohara, K., Crawford, E.D., Simoneau, A., Suri, J.S.: MRI-ultrasound registration for targeted prostate biopsy. In: IEEE ISBI, pp. 991–994 (2009)
9. Besl, P.J., McKay, N.D.: A method for registration of 3-D shapes. IEEE Transactions on Pattern Analysis and Machine Intelligence 14(2), 239–256 (1992)
10. Johnson, H.J., Harris, G., Williams, K.: BRAINSFit: Mutual information registrations of whole-brain 3D images, using the insight toolkit. The Insight Journal (2007), http://hdl.handle.net/1926/1291
11. Vapnik, V.N.: The Nature of Statistical Learning Theory. Springer, NY (1995)
12. Fan, R.E., Chen, P.H., Lin, C.J.: Working set selection using the second order information for training SVM. Machine Learning Research 6, 1889–1918 (2005)

Hierarchical Ensemble of Multi-level Classifiers for Diagnosis of Alzheimer's Disease[*]

Manhua Liu[1,2], Daoqiang Zhang[1,3], Pew-Thian Yap[1], and Dinggang Shen[1]

[1] IDEA Lab, Department of Radiology and BRIC,
University of North Carolina at Chapel Hill, USA
[2] Department of Instrument Science and Technology,
Shanghai Jiao Tong University, China
[3] Department of Computer Science and Engineering,
Nanjing University of Aeronautics and Astronautics, China
dgshen@med.unc.edu

Abstract. Pattern classification methods have been widely studied for analysis of brain images to decode the disease states, such as diagnosis of Alzheimer's disease (AD). Most existing methods aimed to extract discriminative features from neuroimaging data and then build a supervised classifier for classification. However, due to the rich imaging features and small sample size of neuroimaging data, it is still challenging to make use of features to achieve good classification performance. In this paper, we propose a hierarchical ensemble classification algorithm to gradually combine the features and decisions into a unified model for more accurate classification. Specifically, a number of low-level classifiers are first built to transform the rich imaging and correlation-context features of brain image into more compact high-level features with supervised learning. Then, multiple high-level classifiers are generated, with each evaluating the high-level features of different brain regions. Finally, all high-level classifiers are combined to make final decision. Our method is evaluated using MR brain images on 427 subjects (including 198 AD patients and 229 normal controls) from Alzheimer's Disease Neuroimaging Initiative (ADNI) database. Experimental results show that our method achieves an accuracy of 92.04% and an AUC (area under the ROC curve) of 0.9518 for AD classification, demonstrating very promising classification performance.

1   Introduction

Alzheimer's disease (AD) is an irreversible neurodegenerative disorder that leads to progressive loss of memory and cognition function. Its early diagnosis is not only challenging but also crucial for future treatment. Structural and functional brain images such as magnetic resonance images (MRI) are providing powerful imaging modalities in helping understand the neural changes related to AD [1, 2]. Recently, various

[*] This work was partially supported by NIH grants EB006733, EB008374, EB009634 and MH088520, NSFC grants (No. 61005024 and 60875030), and Medical and Engineering Foundation of Shanghai Jiao Tong University (No. YG2010MS74).

F. Wang et al. (Eds.): MLMI 2012, LNCS 7588, pp. 27–35, 2012.

classification methods have been proposed for analysis of brain images to identify the patterns of AD-related neuro-degeneration and decode the disease states [1-4].

The original neuroimaging data is too large to be directly used for classification. More importantly, not all of the neuroimaging data are relevant to disease. Thus, it is necessary to extract representative features from brain images for disease classification. For morphological analysis of brain images, multiple anatomical regions, i.e., regions of interest (ROI), are produced by grouping voxels through the warping of a labeled atlas and the regional measurements of anatomical volumes are computed as the representation features for disease classification [2]. However, the ROIs are made by prior hypotheses and the abnormal brain regions relevant to AD might not well fit to the pre-defined ROIs, thus limiting the representation power of extracted features. To alleviate this problem, the whole brain was adaptively partitioned into many regions according to the similarity and discriminability of local features and the regional features were extracted for classification [5]. Although ROI-based extraction can significantly reduce the feature dimensionality and provide robust features, some minute abnormal changes may be ignored in this method.

To overcome this limitation, voxel-wise neuroimaging features, such as grey matter (GM) probabilities, were investigated for AD diagnosis [6]. However, voxel-wise feature is of huge dimensionality, far more features than training samples, and thus their direct use for classification is not only time inefficient but also lead to low classification performance due to the large number of irrelevant and noisy features. Principal Component Analysis (PCA) was often used to reduce the feature space to the most discriminant components [7]. However, PCA is done independently from the classification task, thus it cannot always identify the disease relevant features. Another popular method is to select the most discriminative features in terms of the correlations of individual features to classification labels [3]. However, this selection method did not consider the relationships among the imaging features. Since disease-induced brain changes often happen in contiguous brain regions, the neighboring voxels to the identified features by feature selection are often jointly used for better classification [8]. In addition, it was observed that the disease-induced changes also occur in some inter-related regions, thus the correlations between different brain regions were proposed for a more accurate characterization of pathology [9]. The neuroimaging data contains rich information for disease diagnosis. Although promising results have been reported for neuroimage analysis in the above studies, it is still potentially advantageous to investigate the ensemble of multiple classifiers by making use of the rich neuroimaging information for better classification performance.

In this paper, we propose a novel classification framework for analysis of high-dimensional neuroimaging data based on the hierarchical ensemble of multi-level classifiers in a layer-by-layer fashion. First, the whole brain image is partitioned into a number of local 3D patches. Second, for each patch, two low-level classifiers are built based on the local imaging and correlation-context features, respectively. Third, the low-level classifier outputs and the statistical imaging features are integrated to build multiple high-level classifiers at different brain regions. Finally, the outputs of all high-level classifiers are combined to make the final classification. The main contributions of this paper can be summarized as: 1) A classification framework by hierarchical ensemble of multi-level classifiers is proposed to gradually transform the high-dimensional imaging features into more and more compact representations.

Thus, the large-scale classification problem is hierarchically decomposed into a set of easy-to-solve small-scale problems. 2) The rich imaging and correlation-context features of the whole brain image are extracted and gradually integrated into a hierarchical framework for more efficient and accurate classification. 3) The local spatial contiguity of the brain regions is gracefully considered by using a hierarchical spatial pyramid structure built from local patches to large brain regions.

2   Method

Although our proposed classification framework makes no assumption on a specific neuroimaging modality, the T1-weighted MR brain images are used for demonstrating its performance. Pre-processing of the images was performed before using them for classification. Specifically, all T1-weighted MR images are first skull-stripped and cerebellum-removed after a correction of intensity inhomogeneity [10]. Then, each image is segmented into three brain tissues: gray matter (GM), white matter and cerebrospinal fluid. Finally, all the tissues are spatially normalized onto a standard space by a mass-preserving deformable registration algorithm [11]. The spatially-normalized GM volumes, i.e., GM densities, are used as the imaging features. Fig. 1 shows the flow chart of the proposed hierarchical ensemble classification algorithm, which consists of 4 main steps: patch extraction, construction of low-level classifiers, high-level classifications and final ensemble, as detailed below.

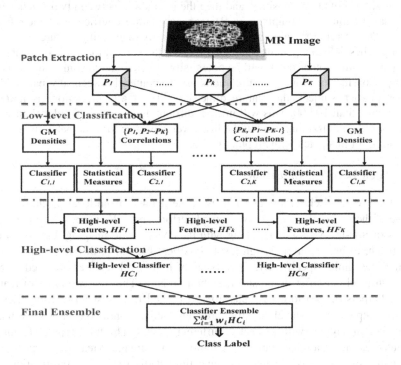

Fig. 1. The flow chart of the proposed hierarchical ensemble classification algorithm

2.1   Patch Extraction

Given a MR brain image and patch size $w{\times}w{\times}w$, to extract the discriminative local patches, we first perform the t-test on each voxel of the training image set to select the voxels with large group difference (i.e., with the p-values of t-test smaller than 0.05). For each selected voxel, we compute the mean of the p-values in its local neighborhood of size $w{\times}w{\times}w$. All selected voxels are sorted in ascending order of their mean p-values. The first 3D patch is extracted to be centered at the voxel with the smallest mean p-value, followed by the second patch at the voxel with the second smallest mean p-value. The new patch also should have less than 50% overlap with the previous extracted patches, i.e., the distance between the centers of any two patches is larger than $w/2$. Finally, by repeating above steps until all selected voxels are visited, we can get K local patches of size $w{\times}w{\times}w$, denoted as $P = \{P_1, \dots, P_k, \dots, P_K\}$.

2.2   Construction of Low-Level Classifiers

For each patch P_k, we use its two low-level features to build the respective low-level classifiers $C_{1,k}$ and $C_{2,k}$. The first low-level classifier $C_{1,k}$ is simply built using the local imaging features as mentioned above. Since the disease-induced structural changes may also occur in several inter-related regions, the second low-level classifier $C_{2,k}$ is constructed with the correlation-context features, which can capture more information about the AD pathology. Each patch is first represented by a feature vector consisting of its GM densities, and then the interaction between two patches within the same subject is computed as Pearson correlation coefficient of their feature vectors. The correlation value measures the similarity of imaging features between a pair of patches. When a patient is affected by AD, the correlation value of a particular brain patch with another patch will be potentially affected due to some factors such as atrophy. Considering that the correlations are computed between any pair of local patches in each subject, the feature dimensionality of all correlations is $K{\times}(K\text{-}1)$, usually more than 10,000. This will make it difficult to train a single global classifier. Thus, for effective training, we build a low-level classifier for each patch by using the correlations of this patch with all other patches.

2.3   High-Level Classification

Since the low-level classifiers are built with the features from local patch, direct ensemble of these classifiers may have limited performance. We propose to combine the outputs of low-level classifiers, along with the coarse-scale imaging features in each local patch, to build multiple high-level classifiers located at different brain regions for final ensemble. Specifically, three types of high-level features are used to build each high-level classifier in the specified brain region. The first two types of features are the outputs of two low-level classifiers $C_{1,k}$ and $C_{2,k}$. Instead of using class labels, the outputs of low-level classifier are computed as continuous values, evaluating the prediction degrees with respect to different classes. The third type of features is computed as the mean and standard deviation of the imaging features in each patch. Although these coarse-scale features have limited discriminative information, they can achieve high robustness to noise and are useful for high-level classification.

Similar to the process of patch extraction, the high-level classifiers are constructed to consider the variant discriminability of different brain regions. We first order the local patches in terms of the classification accuracies of the low-level classifiers built on local imaging features. The first high-level classifier is centered at the local patch with the highest classification accuracy and the high-level features from its neighboring patches in a certain brain region are combined to construct the high-level classifier. The size of brain region is optimized by evaluating the classification accuracy on different sizes of brain regions. After the first high-level classifier, the second and other subsequent high-level classifiers are similarly constructed one by one, with their respective brain regions partially overlapped. Finally we can obtain a set of high-level classifiers on different brain regions, i.e., $HC = \{HC_1, \dots, HC_j, \dots, HC_M\}$.

It is worth noting that our proposed ensemble classification method is not limited to any particular choice of classifier model. Some standard classifiers, such as SVM and Adaboost decision trees, can be used to build the base classifiers. We choose SVM classifier as the base classifier and implement it using MATLAB SVM toolbox. SVM constructs a maximal margin hyperplane by mapping the original features with a kernel function. For the low-level classifier, its probability output is used as the input of high-level classifier as mentioned above.

2.4   Final Ensemble

Ensemble of the M high-level classifiers is performed by weighted voting to make the final decision. The ensemble classifier is generally superior to the single classifier when the predictions of component classifiers have enough diversity [12]. In our case, the high-level classifiers are trained on the features of different brain regions, thus giving a certain degree of diversity for improved ensemble classification. In the case of allowing overlap among the brain regions, the discriminating capacities of high-level classifiers are correlative. Thus, it is important to select a subset of high-level classifiers with larger discriminating capacity for ensemble. Although exhaustive search of all possible combinations allows obtaining an optimal subset of high-level classifiers for ensemble, it is computationally expensive as the number of classifiers increases. Greedy approach focuses on adding or removing a specific classifier at each time for maximizing the improvement of ensemble performance [13], thus taking less computational cost. In this paper, we employ a forward greedy search strategy to select a subset of high-level classifiers for ensemble. However, this classifier selection is performed on the training set and thus may not be optimal for the testing set. To improve the generalization, we divide the training set into 10 folds, and in each fold a subset of classifiers is selected with the forward greedy search. The selection frequency of each classifier is computed over all folds, indicating the likelihood of the respective high-level classifier to improve the ensemble accuracy. Thus, it can be treated as its weight in the final ensemble. Specifically, for a test sample x, the weighted sum of the prediction outputs of high-level classifiers is computed to make the final decision:

$$D(x) = sign\left(\sum_{j=1}^{M} w_j\, PC_j(x)\right) \tag{1}$$

where $PC_j(x)$ is the prediction output of the j-th high-level classifier HC_j for the test sample x, and w_j is the weight assigned to the j-th high-level classifier, i.e., the selection frequency by forward greedy search strategy.

3   Experimental Results

The data used for evaluation of the proposed classification algorithm were taken from the ADNI database (www.loni.ucla.edu/ADNI). We use T1-weighted MR brain imaging data from the baseline visits of 427 ADNI participants including 198 AD (Males:52%, MMSE:23.3±2.0, Age:75.7±7.7) and 229 normal controls (NC) (Males:52%, MMSE:29.1±1.0, Age:76.0±5.0) for evaluation. The preprocessing of the T1-weighted MR images was performed as described in Section 2. After spatial normalization, the GM densities were smoothed using a Gaussian kernel to improve signal-to-noise ratio and down-sampled to 64×64×64 voxels for experiments. To evaluate the classification performance, we use a 10-fold cross-validation strategy to compute the classification accuracy (ACC) measuring the proportion of correctly classified subjects among the whole population, as well as the sensitivity (SEN), i.e., the proportion of AD patients correctly classified, and the specificity (SPE), i.e., the proportion of NCs correctly classified. Each time, one fold of the data set was used for testing, while the other remaining 9 folds were used for training. The training set was split further into training and validation parts for parameter tuning.

We conducted two experiments to investigate the effectiveness of the proposed hierarchical ensemble classification algorithm. The first experiment was conducted to compare the efficacy of different features in classification. Our proposed algorithm integrated three types of features, i.e., statistical measures (SM), GM-based classifier outputs (GCO), and correlation-based classifier outputs (CCO), all extracted from each patch to build the high-level classifiers. To investigate the efficacy of these features, we compared the classification accuracies with respect to different combinations of these features as shown in Table 1. We can see that the use of all three types of features by our proposed method can improve the classification performance.

Table 1. Comparison of classification performances on using different features

Features	ACC (%)	SEN (%)	SPE (%)
Statistical Measures (SM)	85.25	83.39	86.86
GM-based classifier outputs (GCO)	90.16	88.87	91.26
Correlation-based classifier outputs (CCO)	89.70	89.42	89.92
SM + GCO	91.11	89.45	92.53
SM + CCO	90.87	88.42	93.00
GCO + CCO	90.88	89.42	92.11
SM + GCO + CCO	**92.04**	**90.92**	**92.98**

The second experiment was conducted to test the effectiveness of the proposed hierarchical ensemble classification framework. We compared the performance of the proposed method to other two possible classification methods. The first possible classification method is to use PCA to transform the high-dimensional GM densities to a low-dimensional feature space, from which a single classifier is constructed. The dimensionality of the reduced feature space is determined via the 10-folds cross validation on the training set. The second classification method is to directly ensemble the decisions of all low-level classifiers using the weighted voting. The weight assigned to each classifier is determined using the same strategy as in our proposed method. The classification results are shown in Table 2, with the respective ROC curves given in Fig. 2. These results indicate that the ensemble of multiple classifiers can perform better than the single classifier, and the hierarchical ensemble of multi-level classifiers can further improve the classification performance.

Table 2. Comparison of three classification methods

Classification methods	ACC (%)	SEN (%)	SPE (%)	AUC
Single classifier	86.43	83.89	88.64	0.9289
Ensemble of low -level classifiers	89.70	86.89	92.11	0.9390
Our proposed method	**92.04**	**90.92**	**92.98**	**0.9518**

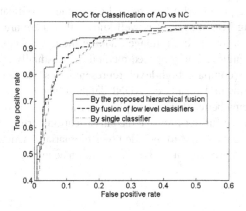

Fig. 2. ROC curves of three classification methods

Furthermore, we compared the results of the proposed method with some recent results reported in the literature that are also based on MRI data of ADNI subjects. In particular, three methods are compared in Table 3. In [1], the linear program boosting method was proposed to incorporate the spatial smoothness of features into the learning process with a regularization. In [4], ten methods, including five voxel-based methods, three cortical thickness based methods and two hippocampus based methods, are compared with the linear SVM classifier. The best result, i.e., using voxel-wise GM features, is provided in Table 3. In [2], the volumetric features from 93 ROIs was used to build a single SVM classifier for classification. These results further validate the efficacy of our proposed method in AD classification.

Table 3. Comparison of the classification accuracies reported in the literature

Methods	Subjects	ACC (%)	SEN (%)	SPE (%)
Hinrichs et al. 2009 [1]	183 (NC+AD)	82.00	85.00	80.00
Cuingnet et al. 2011 [4]	162NC+137AD	88.58	81.00	95.00
Zhang et al. 2011[2]	52NC+51AD	86.20	86.00	86.30
Proposed method	229NC+198AD	**92.04**	**90.92**	**92.98**

For a better understanding of the AD-related brain regions, we picked out the most discriminative patches based on the hierarchy of classifiers. We first select the high-level classifier with the highest accuracy, from which we choose the patches that give higher accuracy in low-level classification. We found that most of these patches were located at the brain regions such as hippocampus, parahippocampal gyrus and amygdala, which are all consistent with those reported in the literature [2, 4].

4   Conclusion

In this paper, we have presented a hierarchical ensemble classification algorithm for diagnosis of AD using MR images. It is well known that there are rich imaging features extracted from the whole brain image, making the task of constructing a robust global classifier challenging. The proposed method can gradually aggregate low-level imaging features into compact high-level representations via building multi-level classifiers. Our experimental results on ADNI database show that ensemble of multiple classifiers performs better than the single classifier and hierarchical ensemble of multi-level classifiers can further improve the classification performance. In the future work, we will extend our method to include other biomarkers acquired from multiple modalities for further improvement of the classification accuracy in diagnosis of AD.

References

1. Hinrichs, C., Singh, V., Mukherjee, L., Xu, G., Chung, M.K., Johnson, S.C.: Spatially augmented LPboosting for AD classification with evaluations on the ADNI dataset. Neuroimage 48, 138–149 (2009)
2. Zhang, D., Wang, Y., Zhou, L., Yuan, H., Shen, D.: Multimodal classification of Alzheimer's disease and mild cognitive impairment. Neuroimage 55, 856–867 (2011)
3. Davatzikos, C., Fan, Y., Wu, X., Shen, D., Resnick, S.M.: Detection of Prodromal Alzheimer's Disease via Pattern Classification of MRI. Neurobiol Aging (2006) (epub.)
4. Cuingnet, R., Gerardin, E., Tessieras, J., Auzias, G., Lehericy, S., Habert, M.O., Chupin, M., Benali, H., Colliot, O.: Automatic classification of patients with Alzheimer's disease from structural MRI: a comparison of ten methods using the ADNI database. Neuroimage 56, 766–781 (2011)
5. Fan, Y., Shen, D., Gur, R.C., Gur, R.E., Davatzikos, C.: COMPARE: Classification of Morphological Patterns Using Adaptive Regional Elements. IEEE Trans. Med. Imaging 26, 93–105 (2007)

6. Ishii, K., Kawachi, T., Sasaki, H., Kono, A.K., Fukuda, T., Kojima, Y., Mori, E.: Voxel-based morphometric comparison between early- and late-onset mild Alzheimer's disease and assessment of diagnostic performance of z score images. American Journal of Neuroradiology 26, 333–340 (2005)

7. Davatzikos, C., Resnick, S.M., Wu, X., Parmpi, P., Clark, C.M.: Individual patient diagnosis of AD and FTD via high-dimensional pattern classification of MRI. Neuroimage 41, 1220–1227 (2008)

8. Vemuri, P., Gunter, J.L., Senjem, M.L., Whitwell, J.L., Kantarci, K., Knopman, D.S., Boeve, B.F., Petersen, R.C., Jack Jr., C.R.: Alzheimer's disease diagnosis in individual subjects using structural MR images: Validation studies. Neuroimage 39, 1186–1197 (2008)

9. Zhou, L., Wang, Y., Li, Y., Yap, P.T., Shen, D.: Hierarchical Anatomical Brain Networks for MCI Prediction: Revisiting Volumetric Measures. Plos One 6, e21935 (2011)

10. Sled, J.G., Zijdenbos, A.P., Evans, A.C.: A nonparametric method for automatic correction of intensity nonuniformity in MRI data. IEEE Trans. Med. Imaging 17, 87–97 (1998)

11. Shen, D., Davatzikos, C.: Very high resolution morphometry using mass-preserving deformations and HAMMER elastic registration. Neuroimage 18, 28–41 (2003)

12. Brown, G., Wyatt, J., Harris, R., Yao, X.: Diversity creation methods: a survey and categorisation. Information Fusion 6, 5–20 (2005)

13. Ruta, D., Gabrys, B.: Classifier selection for majority voting. Information Fusion 6, 63–81 (2005)

Dense Deformation Reconstruction via Sparse Coding[*]

Yonghong Shi[1], Guorong Wu[2], Zhijian Song[1], and Dinggang Shen[2]

[1] Digital Medical Research Center, Shanghai Key Lab of MICCAI,
Fudan University, Shanghai, 200032, China
{yonghong.shi,zjsong}@fudan.edu.cn
[2] Department of Radiology and Biomedical Research Imaging Center
University of North Carolina, Chapel Hill, NC 27510
{grwu,dgshen}@med.unc.edu

Abstract. Many image registration algorithms need to interpolate dense deformations from a small set of sparse deformations or correspondences established on the landmark points. Previous methods generally use a certain pre-defined deformation model, e.g., B-Spline or Thin-Plate Spline, for dense deformation interpolation, which may affect the final registration accuracy since the actual deformation may not exactly follow the pre-defined model. To address this issue, we propose a novel leaning-based method to represent the to-be-estimated dense deformations as a linear combination of sample dense deformations in the pre-constructed dictionary, with the combination coefficients computed from sparse representation of their respective correspondences on the same set of landmarks. Specifically, in the training stage, for each training image, we register it to the selected template by a certain registration method and obtain correspondences on a fixed set of landmarks in the template, as well as the respective dense deformation field. Then, we can build two dictionaries to, respectively, save the landmark correspondences and their dense deformations from all training images at the same indexing order. Thus, in the application stage, after estimating the landmark correspondences for a new subject, we can first represent them by all instances in the dictionary of landmark correspondences. Then, the estimated sparse coefficients can be used to reconstruct the dense deformation field of the new subject by fusing the corresponding instances in the dictionary of dense deformations. We have demonstrated the advantage of our proposed deformation interpolation method in two applications, i.e., CT prostate registration in the radiotherapy and MR brain registration in the neuroscience study. In both applications, our learning-based method can achieve higher accuracy and potentially faster computation, compared to the conventional method.

---

[*] This research was supported by the grants from National Institute of Health (No. 1R01 CA140413, R01 RR018615 and R44/43 CA119571). This work was supported by the grants from National Natural Science Foundation of China (No. 60972102), National Key Technology R&D Program (No. 2012BAI14B05 and Science and Technology Commission of Shanghai Municipality grant (No. 08411951200).

F. Wang et al. (Eds.): MLMI 2012, LNCS 7588, pp. 36–44, 2012.

1   Introduction

Dense deformation interpolation is a common problem in medical image registration [1]. For example, in the feature-based registration, a set of landmarks is often first automatically determined, i.e., by robust feature matching [2], for identifying anatomical correspondences. Then, the dense deformation field is interpolated from those landmark correspondences, in order to map every point in the subject image to the template image. Similarly, in the image-guided radiation therapy for prostate cancer treatment [3], anatomical correspondences on the boundary landmarks can be determined manually by physicist, or automatically by the correspondence-based deformable segmentation method [4]. Then, to transfer the dose plan defined in the planning image onto the treatment image, it also needs a dense deformation interpolation method to estimate deformation on each non-landmark point within the prostate.

To deal with this deformation interpolation problem, many methods have been proposed, i.e., by parameterizing the dense deformation field with some pre-defined models [5-7]. Thin-plate spline (TPS) is one of the most popular deformation interpolation methods used in both computer vision and medical imaging areas, which provides the deterministic solution with minimal bending energy for the interpolated dense deformation field [7]. Although accurate interpolation could be achieved when using a large number of landmarks, its computational burden will be also significantly increased. On the other hand, the actual dense deformations on anatomical structures might not exactly follow the pre-defined models in TPS, thus probably affecting the interpolation accuracy.

To this end, we propose a novel leaning-based method to accurately reconstruct the dense deformation field from a small set of correspondences estimated on the landmarks. Our main idea is to estimate the dense deformation field by looking for a sparse combination of similar deformation instances from the dictionary, which has been pre-learned from the training images. The key in our method is to build two paired dictionaries: one high-dimensional dictionary for saving dense deformation fields (called as *deformation dictionary*), and another low-dimensional dictionary for saving the respective landmark correspondences (called as *correspondence dictionary*). Thus, the combination coefficients used to fuse the dense deformation instances in the *deformation dictionary* for a new subject can be efficiently estimated from the sparse representation of this subject's landmark correspondences by all the correspondence instances in the *correspondence dictionary*. Specifically, in the training stage, each training image is carefully registered with the template image to obtain the dense deformation field for constructing the *deformation dictionary*, as well as the associated correspondences on the template landmarks for constructing the *correspondence dictionary*. It is worth noting that, for each training image, it has one instance (deformation field) in the *deformation dictionary* and another instance (landmark correspondences) in the *correspondence dictionary*, which are arranged with the same indexing order in the two dictionaries. In the application stage, two particular steps are taken to determine the dense deformation field for the testing image with estimated correspondences on the landmarks. First, we seek for the sparse representation of its landmark correspondences from the correspondence dictionary. Second, we calculate the dense deformation field by fusing the deformation instances in the deformation dictionary according to the sparse coefficients estimated in the first step.

To demonstrate the advantages of our novel learning-based deformation interpolation method, we apply it to deformable registration of both CT prostate images and MR brain images, respectively. Specifically, in deformable registration of CT prostate image during the radiotherapy of prostate cancer, the two paired dictionaries include the instances from not only different patients but also the previous treatment images of the current subject under treatment. Then, after determining the landmark correspondences along the prostate boundary by a deformable surface model for the current subject, the dense deformations for all image points can be immediately interpolated by sparse coding from the two paired dictionaries. Moreover, we have successfully integrated our deformation interpolation method with a feature-based registration algorithm [2] to speed up the registration of MR brain images. Specially, by looking up the correspondence dictionary with the tentatively-estimated correspondences in the middle (or even early) stage of registration, the final dense deformation field from template to subject can be immediately reconstructed from the final deformation instances included in the deformation dictionary. In both applications, our learning-based interpolation method achieves better performance in interpolation accuracy and potential registration speed, compared with a widely-used interpolation method, TPS.

2   Method

The goal of deformable registration is to align subject image S with template image T. In many applications, a small number of landmarks or key points will be determined in the template image by either manual delineation or automated key point detector [4]. A long column vector x can be used to record the coordinates of all P template landmarks. For warping subject S to template, we need to estimate its dense deformation field $y_D(S)$, based on the established correspondences $y_L(S)$ for P template landmarks x. Here, $y_L(S)$ and $y_D(S)$ are both column vectors as well. In this paper, we propose a learning-based method to estimate the dense deformation field $y_D(S)$ from the discrete correspondence vector $y_L(S)$, as detailed below.

2.1   Efficient Deformation Interpolation via Sparse Representation

Given the template image T, a number of training images $I = \{I_m | m = 1, ..., M\}$ will be carefully registered with T, thus obtaining the deformation instances $\{y_D(I_m) | m = 1, ..., M\}$, where $y_D(I_m)$ is the column vector of dense deformation field directed from the template to the training image I_m. Also, we can obtain the correspondence vector $y_L(I_m)$ from P landmarks x in the template image T to the training image I_m. It is worth noting that the definition of correspondence instance y_L may vary in different applications, as we will show in Section 2.2.

Dictionary Construction: Both deformation dictionary and correspondence dictionary are simultaneously constructed, with the same indexing order for the training images, such as $A_D = [y_D(I_m)]$ $(m = 1, ..., M)$ and $A_L = [y_L(I_m)]$ $(m = 1, ..., M)$, where A_D and A_L denote the matrices with each column representing $y_D(I_m)$ and $y_L(I_m)$, respectively. Since the dimensionality of each correspondence vector $y_L(I_m)$ is usually much smaller than the dimensionality of the deformation vector $y_D(I_m)$, we can find a good representation for the correspondence vector $y_L(S)$ of subject image S, from a sufficient number of instances in the dictionary A_L, as described below.

Sparse Representation of Correspondence Vector: Here, we seek for a linear combination of the underlying correspondence vector $y_L(S)$ from dictionary A_L by estimating the weight vector $w = [w_1, w_2, \ldots, w_M]'$, where each w_m indicates the contribution of correspondence instance $y_L(I_m)$ in representation of $y_L(S)$ [8]. Inspired by the discriminative power of l_1-norm in face recognition and multi-task learning, we further apply the l_1-norm upon the weight vector w to require selecting only a small number of most representative instances $y_L(I_m)$ in the dictionary A_L to represent $y_L(S)$, which falls into the well-known LASSO (Least Absolute Shrinkage and Selection Operator) problem [9]. Thus, the objective function can be given as:

$$\hat{w} = \underset{w}{\text{argmin}} \|A_L w - y_L(S)\|_2^2 + +\rho \|w\|_2^2 + \lambda \|w\|_1, \tag{1}$$

where the scale ρ is the regularization parameter for the squared l_2-norm, and λ is the l_1-norm regularization parameter. They are a ratio lying in the interval [0, 1]. They will be specified in different applications empirically [10]. Here, the weight vector w is called as sparse coefficients in our method. For fulfilling registration accuracy, we first partition the image into several parts, and then build the over-completed dictionaries on each part. Finally, the objective function is optimized by using the Euclidian-project based method in SLEP software package [10].

Prediction of Dense Deformation from Sparse Coefficients: The key novelty in our method is the use of strong correlation between the low-dimensional correspondence instances and the high-dimensional deformation instances, included in two paired dictionaries A_L and A_D, respectively. Then, after obtaining the sparse coefficients w from Eq. (1), we can use it to fuse the deformation instances in the dictionary A_D for effectively predicting the dense deformation field $y_D(S)$ for the subject S as given below:

$$y_D(S) = A_D \cdot w, \tag{2}$$

2.2   Two Applications

Our learning-based deformation interpolation method can be applied widely to many medical imaging problems. Here, we select the deformable registration of CT prostate images and MR brain images as two examples to demonstrate the performance of our proposed method.

Deformable Registration of Daily CT Prostate Images: In adaptive radiation therapy of prostate cancer, the prostate boundaries in each treatment images of one patient, as well as their correspondences to the prostate boundaries in the planning day image, can be automatically produced by a deformable surface model [4]. Then, for efficiently transforming the treatment plan designed in the planning image to the treatment image, the dense deformations on all image points need to be accurately estimated, which can be done by our proposed method.

Specifically, in this application, the template landmarks x denotes the vertex nodes of prostate boundary surface built on the planning image of the current patient. Vector $y_L(S)$ denotes the correspondences of x estimated by the deformable surface model on the current treatment image S.

The correspondence instances and deformation instances in the paired dictionary A_L and A_D in this application can be obtained from the images of other training patients, as well as the previous treatment image of the current patient.

Thus, given the correspondences $y_L(S)$ on the prostate boundary in the current treatment image S, the dense deformation field $y_D(S)$ can be efficiently estimated by first computing the sparse coefficients w in Eq. 1 and fusing the deformation instances in the dictionary A_D according to Eq. 2. Particularly, in the initial treatment stage when no previous treatment image is collected from the current patient, the dictionary is built only from other training patients. With progress of treatment, more and more treatment images of the current patient are included into the dictionary. The instances from the previous treatment images of the current patient will play an increasing critical role in sparse representation and deformation interpolation, which is consistent with the similar strategies used in other longitudinal image studies [3].

Deformable Registration of MR Brain Images: In the feature-based deformable registration [2], the procedures of correspondence detection and dense deformation interpolation are alternatively performed in estimating deformation pathway from template image to subject image. Due to the potential large inter-subject variations, the entire deformation pathway has to be iteratively estimated, which often leads to slow registration.

Our proposed deformation interpolation method can be incorporated into the feature-based deformable registration algorithm to improve the registration accuracy and speed. Our main idea is to stop the registration algorithm in a given stage of registration, and then efficiently estimate the final dense deformation field by taking those approximately-estimated correspondences on landmarks as the reference to look up the correspondence dictionary. The assumption in this application is that those approximately-estimated correspondences can be regarded as (approximate) low-dimension representation of final dense deformation field. Therefore, this application is more challenging than the previous application in CT prostate image registration, because correspondences here are not completely satisfied. Actually, these correspondences, obtained in the given stage of registration, need to be further refined in the conventional deformable registration method. But with our proposed method, we can choose to accurately and quickly estimate the final dense deformation field from approximately-estimated correspondences as described below.

First, we use a deformable registration method to align M training images onto the template and thus obtain M dense deformation instances $y_D(I_m)$ (directed from template to the training images), for constructing the deformation dictionary A_D. Second, for each training image I_m, we use its correspondences estimated at the given stage of registration as its particular correspondence instance $y_L(I_m)$ to construct the correspondence dictionary A_L. After constructing these two paired dictionaries, our method can be integrated into the conventional feature-based registration method for improving the registration performance. Specifically, for the subject S, its registration with template will be stopped in the given stage of registration, for obtaining the approximately-estimated landmark correspondences $y_L(S)$. Then, the sparse coefficients w can be estimated by Eq. 1 to find the sparse representation of $y_L(S)$ from all correspondence instances in A_L. Finally, the dense deformation field $y_D(S)$ for the subject S can be further obtained by fusing the deformation instances in A_D w.r.t. the estimated sparse coefficients w using Eq. 2.

3 Experiments

Experiment on CT Prostate Images: The performance of our proposed method is evaluated on serial prostate CT images of 24 patients. Most patients have up to 12 scanned images, with image size of $512 \times 512 \times 61$ and voxel size of $1 \times 1 \times 3mm^3$. Due to the lack of ground truth, we use the interpolation result by TPS as the reference to measure the residual error between dense deformation field by our method and that by TPS. In order to evaluate the importance of patient-specific information in this application, we specifically construct the two sets of paired dictionaries: one set uses only the population information from other training patients to construct A_L and A_D(namely Population Sparse Coding (*PSC*)), and another set uses not only the population information but also patient-specific information of current subject to construct A_L and A_D (namely Population+Longitudinal Sparse Coding (*PLSC*)). Specially, we use at least 70 images (including planning and treatment images) from 6 patients as training data to build the dictionaries for *PSC* and *PLSC* methods, respectively. In addition, all previous treatment images of the current subject are also included into the dictionaries for the *PLSC* method. Here, the regularization parameter $\rho = 0.0005$ and $\lambda = 0.0005$.

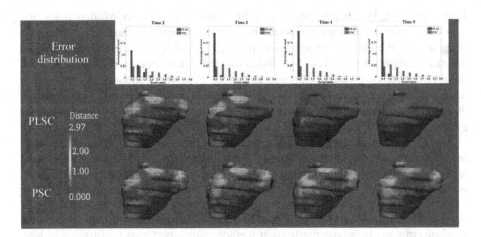

Fig. 1. The distribution of residual errors at different treatment images by using *PSC* or *PLSC* is shown on row 1st. The spatial mapping of residual errors on prostate surfaces is shown on row 2nd (PLSC) and 3rd (PSC), respectively.

The 1st row in Fig. 1 shows the residual error distributions by *PSC* (red) and *PLSC* (blue) methods. Apparently, the error distributions are similar in *PSC* across different treatment days, while the residual errors are significantly reduced in *PLSC* after more and more treatment images of current subject are included. We can also find similar observations in the visualized spatial maps of residual errors on prostate surfaces in the 2nd (PLSC) and 3rd (PSC) row in Fig. 1, respectively. The results in Fig. 1 demonstrate that: (1) the performance of *PLSC* is much better than that of the *PSC* because of progressively including the patient-specific instances into the dictionaries. Actually, the instances selected for sparse representation in the *PLSC* method are mostly coming from the previous treatment images of the current subject, which validates the discriminative power of our learning-based method in selecting similar instances to represent information in the new treatment image. (2) The *PLSC* method can achieve the residual error of less than 1.0mm which indicates the comparable interpolation result w.r.t. TPS.

Table 1. Comparison of residual errors for all the images of 24 patients between *PSC* and *PLSC* methods. (Unit: mm)

Method	Mean±Std	Minimum	Median	Maximum
PSC	1.37±0.96	0.0045	1.13	4.99
PLSC	0.21±0.17	0.0009	0.16	2.47

Furthermore, Table 1 shows the overall residual errors along the prostate boundary (5mm inward/outward prostate boundary) for all images of the 24 patients, since this area is critical for radiation therapy. It can be observed that the average error is 0.21mm for the *PLSC*, which is much lower than 1.37mm by the *PSC*. Also, the maximum error by using *PLSC* is 2.47mm, which is smaller than 4.99mm by *PSC*.

Experiment on MR Brain Images: In this application, 232 deformation fields and respective brain images are simulated by a learning-based method [11]. Then, we integrate our deformation interpolation method with a state-of-the-art feature based deformable registration method, by constructing the correspondence dictionary A_L with the approximately-estimated landmarks at a given stage of registration, as explained in Section 2.2. We use 80 simulated deformation fields to construct the dictionaries and any 30 deformation fields selected from the rest 152 deformation fields as ground-truth for evaluation. Here, the regularization parameter $\rho = 0.0005$ and $\lambda = 0.0005$.

Fig. 2 compares the performance of our method (blur line) and TPS (red line) used in the feature-based method at any given stage of registration. Given the approximately-estimated landmark correspondences at the given stage of registration, we can either use TPS or our learning-based method to interpolate the dense deformation field. Since we have the ground-truth, we can compare the residual error between ground-truth and the estimated deformation field point by point. The average residual error by the whole registration method, which performs registration in low, middle, and high resolutions, is 0.62mm indicated by green arrow in Fig. 2. If we stop the registration in the first stages of high resolution and use the landmark correspondences estimated at those stages, such as the 5th, 10th and 15th iterations, to interpolate the final dense deformation field, the average residual errors are 0.64mm, 0.59mm and 0.57mm by our method and 0.93mm, 0.84mm and 0.81mm by TPS, respectively. Intuitively, the landmark correspondences will gradually become more and more accurate as the registration progresses. Therefore, if we evaluate on landmark correspondences estimated in the middle stage (the 25th iteration) of high-resolution registration, the average residual error can be further reduced to 0.55mm by our method and 0.78mm by TPS. The results in Fig. 2 indicate: (1) our method can give more accurate results at any given stage by comparing with TPS no matter in the low, middle and high resolution of a registration process. (2) Our method can converge to accurate results during the first stages in high resolution, while the feature-based method obtains comparable results until finishing the total iteration. (3) Our method saves the running time apparently.

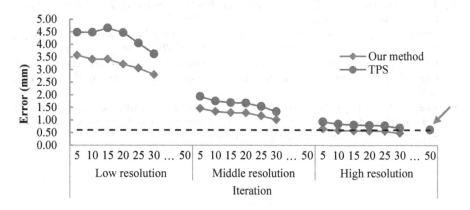

Fig. 2. The distribution of residual errors at any given stage of registration by our method and TPS, respectively

4   Conclusion

We have presented a novel learning-based method for accurate deformation interpolation from a small set of discrete anatomical correspondences. Specifically, we estimate the dense deformation field by fusing the most similar instances in the deformation dictionary, by using the sparse coefficients obtained from the sparse representation of low-dimensional landmark correspondences. Our method has been successfully applied to deformable registration of daily CT prostate images and also MR brain images, achieving more accurate registration performance at faster registration speed.

References

1. Hajnal, J.V., Hill, D.L.G., Hawkes, D.J.: Medical Image Registration (Biomedical Engineering Series). CRC Press (2001)
2. Shen, D., Davatzikos, C.: HAMMER: Hierarchical attribute matching mechanism for elastic registration. IEEE Transactions on Medical Imaging 21(11), 1421–1439 (2002)

3. Shi, Y., Liao, S., Shen, D.: Learning Statistical Correlation for Fast Prostate Registration in Image-guided Radiotherapy. Medical Physics 38, 5980–5991 (2011)
4. Fen, Q., Foskey, M., Chen, W., Shen, D.: Segmenting CT Prostate Images Using Population and Patient-specific Statistics for Radiotherapy. Medical Physics 37, 4121–4132 (2010)
5. Rueckert, D., Sonoda, L.I., Hayes, C., Hill, D.L.G., Leach, M.O., Hawkes, D.J.: Nonrigid Registration Using Free-Form Deformations: Application to Breast MR Images. IEEE Transactions on Medical Imaging 18(8), 712–721 (1999)
6. Wu, G., Yap, P.T., Kim, M., Shen, D.: TPS-HAMMER: Improving HAMMER Registration Algorithm by Soft Correspondence Matching and Thin-plate Splines Based Deformation Interpolation. NeuroImage 49, 2225–2233 (2010)
7. Bookstein, F.L.: Principal Warps: Thin-Plate Splines and the Decomposition of Deformations. IEEE Transactions on Pattern Analysis and Machine Intelligence 11(6), 567–585 (1989)
8. Turkan, M., Guillemot, C.: Image Prediction Based on Neighbor Embedding Methods. IEEE Transaction on Image Processing 99, 1–11 (2011)
9. Tibshirani, R.: Regression Shrinkage and Selection via the Lasso. Journal of the Royal Statistical Society. Series B (Methodological) 58(1), 267–288 (1996)
10. Liu, J., Ye, J.: Efficient Euclidean Projections in Linear Time. In: Proceedings of the 26th International Conference on Machine Learning, Montreal, Canada. ACM, New York (2009)
11. Xue, Z., Shen, D., Karacali, B., Stern, J., Rottenberg, D., Davatzikos, C.: Simulating Deformations of MR Brain Images for Validation of Atlas-based Segmentation and Registration Algorithms. Neuroimage 33, 855–866 (2006)

Group Sparsity Constrained Automatic Brain Label Propagation

Shu Liao, Daoqiang Zhang, Pew-Thian Yap, Guorong Wu, and Dinggang Shen

Department of Radiology and BRIC, University of North Carolina at Chapel Hill
liaoshu.cse@gmail.com

Abstract. In this paper, we present a group sparsity constrained patch based label propagation method for multi-atlas automatic brain labeling. The proposed method formulates the label propagation process as a graph-based theoretical framework, where each voxel in the input image is linked to each candidate voxel in each atlas image by an edge in the graph. The weight of the edge is estimated based on a sparse representation framework to identify a limited number of candidate voxles whose local image patches can best represent the local image patch of each voxel in the input image. The group sparsity constraint to capture the dependency among candidate voxels with the same anatomical label is also enforced. It is shown that based on the edge weight estimated by the proposed method, the anatomical label for each voxel in the input image can be estimated more accurately by the label propagation process. Moreover, we extend our group sparsity constrained patch based label propagation framework to the reproducing kernel Hilbert space (RKHS) to capture the nonlinear similarity of patches among different voxels and construct the sparse representation in high dimensional feature space. The proposed method was evaluated on the NA0-NIREP database for automatic human brain anatomical labeling. It was also compared with several state-of-the-art multi-atlas based brain labeling algorithms. Experimental results demonstrate that our method consistently achieves the highest segmentation accuracy among all methods used for comparison.

1 Introduction

Automatic and accurate human brain labeling plays an important role in medical image analysis, computational anatomy, and pathological studies. Multi-atlas based image segmentation [1–4] is one of the main categories of methods for automatic human brain labeling. It consists of two main steps, namely the registration step, and the label fusion step. In the registration step, atlases (i.e., images with segmentation groundtruths) are registered to the image to be segmented. The corresponding segmentation groundtruth of each atlas is also registered to the image to be segmented accordingly. In the label fusion step, the registered segmentation groundtruths of atlases are mapped and fused to estimate the corresponding label map of the image to be segmented. In this paper, we mainly focus at the label fusion step.

F. Wang et al. (Eds.): MLMI 2012, LNCS 7588, pp. 45–53, 2012.

There are many novel label fusion strategies proposed in the literature [5–9] for multi-atlas based image segmentation. For instance, the majority voting (MV) scheme assigns each voxel of the image to be segmented the label which appears most frequently at the same voxel position across all the registered atlas images. The simultaneous truth and performance level estimation (STAPLE) [9] scheme iteratively weights the contribution of each atlas based on an expectation maximization approach. Sabuncu et al. [7] proposed a novel probabilistic framework to capture the relationship between each atlas and the input image.

Recently, Rousseau et al. [4] proposed a novel label fusion method for automatic human brain labeling based on the non-local mean principle and patch based representation. More specifically, each reference voxel in the input image is linked to each voxel in atlas images based on their patch based similarity. Then, voxels in atlas images within a small neighborhood of the reference voxel are served as candidate voxels to estimate the label of the reference voxel. This method has several attractive properties: First, it does not require non-rigid image registration between atlases and input image [4]. Second, it allows one to many correspondences to select a set of good candidate voxels for label fusion. However, it also has several limitations: (1) Candidate voxels which have low patch similarity with the reference voxel will still contribute in label propagation. (2) The dependency among candidate neighboring voxels with the same anatomical label is not considered.

Therefore, we are motivated to propose a new group sparsity constrained patch based label propagation framework. Our method estimates the sparse coefficients to reconstruct the local image patch of each voxel in the input image from patches of its corresponding candidate voxels in atlas images, and then use the estimated coefficients as graph weights to perform label propagation. Candidate voxels have low patch similarity with the reference voxel in the input image can be effectively removed by the sparsity constraint. The group sparsity is also considered to capture the dependency among candidate voxels with the same anatomical label. Moreover, we extend the proposed framework to the reproducing kernel Hilbert space (RKHS) to capture the nonlinear similarity of the patch based representations. Our method was evaluated on the NA0-NIREP database and compared with several state-of-the-art label fusion methods. Experimental results show that our method achieves the highest segmentation accuracy among other methods under comparison.

2   Group Sparsity Constrained Patch Based Label Propagation

The general label propagation framework [4] can be summarized as follows: Given N atlas images I_i and their corresponding label maps L_i $(i = 1, ..., N)$ registered to the input image I_{new}, the label at each voxel position $\boldsymbol{x}$ in I_{new} can be estimated by Equation 1:

$$L_{new}(\boldsymbol{x}) = \frac{\sum_{i=1}^{N} \sum_{\boldsymbol{y} \in \mathcal{N}_i(\boldsymbol{x})} w_i(\boldsymbol{x}, \boldsymbol{y}) L_i(\boldsymbol{y})}{\sum_{i=1}^{N} \sum_{\boldsymbol{y} \in \mathcal{N}_i(\boldsymbol{x})} w_i(\boldsymbol{x}, \boldsymbol{y})}, \tag{1}$$

where $\mathcal{N}_i(\boldsymbol{x})$ denotes the neighborhood of voxel $\boldsymbol{x}$ in image I_i, which is defined as the $W \times W \times W$ subvolume centered at $\boldsymbol{x}$. $w_i(\boldsymbol{x}, \boldsymbol{y})$ is the graph weight reflecting the relationship between voxels $\boldsymbol{x}$ in I_{new} and $\boldsymbol{y}$ in I_i, which also determines the contribution of voxel $\boldsymbol{y}$ in I_i during the label propagation process to estimate the anatomical label for $\boldsymbol{x}$. L_{new} is the estimated label probability map of I_{new}.

It should be noted that $L_i(\boldsymbol{y})$ is a vector of $[0, 1]^M$ denoting the proportion of each anatomical label at voxel $\boldsymbol{y}$, and M is the total number of anatomical labels of interest in the atlases. Therefore, $L_{new}(\boldsymbol{x})$ is a M dimensional vector with each element denoting the probability of each anatomical label assigned to voxel $\boldsymbol{x}$. Similar to [4], the final anatomical label assigned to each voxel $\boldsymbol{x}$ will the determined as the one with the largest probability among all the elements in $L_{new}(\boldsymbol{x})$.

In [4], the graph weight $w_i(\boldsymbol{x}, \boldsymbol{y})$ is estimated based on the patch based similarity between voxels $\boldsymbol{x}$ and $\boldsymbol{y}$ by Equation 2:

$$w_i(\boldsymbol{x}, \boldsymbol{y}) = \begin{cases} \Phi\left(\dfrac{\sum_{\boldsymbol{x}' \in P_{I_{new}}(\boldsymbol{x}), \boldsymbol{y}' \in P_{I_i}(\boldsymbol{y})}(I_{new}(\boldsymbol{x}') - I_i(\boldsymbol{y}'))^2}{2K\alpha}\right), & \text{if } \boldsymbol{y} \in \mathcal{N}_i(\boldsymbol{x}); \\ 0, & \text{otherwise.} \end{cases} \quad (2)$$

Where K is the patch size, α is the smoothing parameter. $P_{I_{new}}(\boldsymbol{x})$ and $P_{I_i}(\boldsymbol{y})$ denote the $K \times K \times K$ image patches of images I_{new} and I_i centered at voxel $\boldsymbol{x}$ and $\boldsymbol{y}$, respectively. Φ is the smoothing kernel function. In this paper, the heat kernel with $\Phi(x) = e^{-x}$ is used similar to [4].

However, based on the graph weight defined by Equation 2, candidate voxels with low patch similarity to the reference voxel will still contribute in label propagation, which can lead to fuzzy label probability map and affect the segmentation accuracy as will be confirmed in our experiments. Therefore, we are motivated to estimate the graph weight $w_i(\boldsymbol{x}, \boldsymbol{y})$ based on the sparse coefficients to reconstruct the local patch of each voxel $\boldsymbol{x}$ in I_{new} from patches of its corresponding candidate voxels $\boldsymbol{y}$ in I_i such that candidate voxels with low patch similarity can be automatically removed due to the sparsity constraint. More specifically, for each voxel $\boldsymbol{x}$ in I_{new}, its patch can also be represented as a $K \times K \times K$ dimensional column vector, denoted as $\boldsymbol{f_x}$. For each voxel $\boldsymbol{y}$ in $\mathcal{N}_i(\boldsymbol{x})$, we also denote its corresponding patch as a $K \times K \times K$ dimensional column vector $\boldsymbol{f_y^i}$ $(i = 1, ..., N)$ and organize them into a matrix $\mathbf{A}$. Then, the sparse coefficient vector $\beta_{\boldsymbol{x}}$ for voxel $\boldsymbol{x}$ is estimated by minimizing Equation 3:

$$E(\beta_{\boldsymbol{x}}) = \frac{1}{2}||\boldsymbol{f_x} - \mathbf{A}\beta_{\boldsymbol{x}}||_2^2 + \lambda||\beta_{\boldsymbol{x}}||_1, \quad \beta_{\boldsymbol{x}} \geq 0 \quad (3)$$

where $|| \cdot ||_1$ denotes the L1 norm to enforce the sparsity constraint to the reconstruction coefficient vector $\beta_{\boldsymbol{x}}$. Minimizing Equation 3 is the constrained L1-norm optimization problem (i.e., Lasso) [10], and the optimal solution $\beta_{\boldsymbol{x}}^{opt}$ to minimize Equation 3 can be estimated by Nesterov's method [11]. Then, the graph weight $w_i(\boldsymbol{x}, \boldsymbol{y})$ can be set to the corresponding element in $\beta_{\boldsymbol{x}}^{opt}$ with respect to $\boldsymbol{y}$ in image I_i.

However, the graph weight estimated by Equation 3 still treats candidate voxels as independent instances during the label propagation process without encoding the prior knowledge of whether they are belonging to the same anatomical group. As stated in [12], without considering this prior knowledge can lead to significant representation power degradation. Therefore, we also enforce the group sparsity constraint in the proposed framework. More specifically, suppose voxels $\boldsymbol{y}$ in $\mathcal{N}_i(\boldsymbol{x})$ belonging to C ($C \leq M$) different anatomical structures based on $L_i(\boldsymbol{y})$. Then, the patch based representation of all the voxels $\boldsymbol{y}$ in $\mathcal{N}_i(\boldsymbol{x})$ belonging to the jth ($j = 1, ..., C$) anatomical structure form the matrix $\mathbf{A}_j$, with the corresponding reconstruction coefficient vector $\boldsymbol{\beta}_{\boldsymbol{x}}^j$. Therefore, matrix $\mathbf{A}$ in Equation 3 can be represented as $\mathbf{A} = [\mathbf{A}_1, \mathbf{A}_2, ..., \mathbf{A}_C]$, and $\boldsymbol{\beta}_{\boldsymbol{x}} = [(\boldsymbol{\beta}_{\boldsymbol{x}}^1)^T, (\boldsymbol{\beta}_{\boldsymbol{x}}^2)^T, ..., (\boldsymbol{\beta}_{\boldsymbol{x}}^C)^T]^T$. Thus, the objective energy function by incorporating the group sparsity constraint can be expressed by Equation 4:

$$E(\boldsymbol{\beta}_{\boldsymbol{x}}) = \frac{1}{2}||\boldsymbol{f}_{\boldsymbol{x}} - \mathbf{A}\boldsymbol{\beta}_{\boldsymbol{x}}||_2^2 + \lambda||\boldsymbol{\beta}_{\boldsymbol{x}}||_1 + \sum_{j=1}^{C} \gamma_j ||\boldsymbol{\beta}_{\boldsymbol{x}}^j||_2, \quad \boldsymbol{\beta}_{\boldsymbol{x}} \geq 0. \tag{4}$$

Where γ_j denotes the weight with respect to the jth anatomical structure, and $||\cdot||_2$ denotes the L2 norm.

3 Group Sparsity Constrained Patch Based Label Propagation in Kernel Space

Kernel methods have attractive property that they can capture the nonlinear relationship of patches of different voxels in the high dimensional feature space. It is shown in [13] that kernel-based sparse representation method can further improve the recognition accuracy for the application of face recognition. Therefore, we are motivated to extend the group sparsity constrained patch based label propagation framework to the reproducing kernel Hilbert space (RKHS).

More specifically, given a nonlinear mapping function ϕ which can map the original patch based representation $\boldsymbol{f}_{\boldsymbol{x}}$ of each voxel $\boldsymbol{x}$ in the high dimensional feature space as $\phi(\boldsymbol{f}_{\boldsymbol{x}})$, the objective energy function expressed by Equation 4 for group-sparse-patch based representation is converted to Equation 5:

$$E(\boldsymbol{\beta}_{\boldsymbol{x}}) = \frac{1}{2}||\phi(\boldsymbol{f}_{\boldsymbol{x}}) - \phi(\mathbf{A})\boldsymbol{\beta}_{\boldsymbol{x}}||_2^2 + \lambda||\boldsymbol{\beta}_{\boldsymbol{x}}||_1 + \sum_{j=1}^{C} \gamma_j ||\boldsymbol{\beta}_{\boldsymbol{x}}^j||_2, \quad \boldsymbol{\beta}_{\boldsymbol{x}} \geq 0. \tag{5}$$

Based on the kernel theory, the product between two mapped samples $\phi(\boldsymbol{f}_{\boldsymbol{x}})$ and $\phi(\boldsymbol{f}_{\boldsymbol{y}})$ in the high dimensional feature space can be represented by a kernel function κ, where $\kappa(\boldsymbol{f}_{\boldsymbol{x}}, \boldsymbol{f}_{\boldsymbol{y}}) = (\phi(\boldsymbol{f}_{\boldsymbol{x}}))^T(\phi(\boldsymbol{f}_{\boldsymbol{y}}))$. Then, Equation 5 can be rewritten as Equation 6:

$$\begin{aligned} E(\boldsymbol{\beta}_{\boldsymbol{x}}) &= \frac{1}{2}||\phi(\boldsymbol{f}_{\boldsymbol{x}}) - \phi(\mathbf{A})\boldsymbol{\beta}_{\boldsymbol{x}}||_2^2 + \lambda||\boldsymbol{\beta}_{\boldsymbol{x}}||_1 + \sum_{j=1}^{C} \gamma_j ||\boldsymbol{\beta}_{\boldsymbol{x}}^j||_2. \\ &= \frac{1}{2}\kappa(\boldsymbol{f}_{\boldsymbol{x}}, \boldsymbol{f}_{\boldsymbol{x}}) + \frac{1}{2}(\boldsymbol{\beta}_{\boldsymbol{x}})^T \mathbf{G}(\boldsymbol{\beta}_{\boldsymbol{x}}) - (\boldsymbol{\beta}_{\boldsymbol{x}})^T V(\boldsymbol{x}) \\ &\quad + \lambda||\boldsymbol{\beta}_{\boldsymbol{x}}||_1 + \sum_{j=1}^{C} \gamma_j ||\boldsymbol{\beta}_{\boldsymbol{x}}^j||_2, \quad \boldsymbol{\beta}_{\boldsymbol{x}} \geq 0. \end{aligned} \tag{6}$$

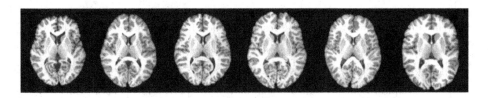

Fig. 1. Exemplar images from the NA0-NIREP database

Where $\mathbf{G}$ is the gram matrix with $\{\mathbf{G}\}_{ij} = \kappa(\mathbf{u}_i, \mathbf{u}_j)$, where $\mathbf{u}_i$ denotes the ith column of matrix $\mathbf{A}$. $\mathbf{V}(\mathbf{x})$ is a vector with $\{\mathbf{V}(\mathbf{x})\}_i = \kappa(\mathbf{u}_i, \mathbf{x})$. Equation 6 can also be optimized by Nesterov's method [11] besides additionally computing $\mathbf{G}$ and $\mathbf{V}(\mathbf{x})$. In this paper, the Gaussian radial basis function kernel is adopted, with $\kappa(\mathbf{u}_i, \mathbf{u}_j) = \exp(-\tau||\mathbf{u}_i - \mathbf{u}_j||^2)$.

4   Experimental Results

In this section, we evaluate our method for automatic brain labeling on the NA0-NIREP database [14]. The NA0-NIREP database has 16 3D brain MR images, among which eight are scanned from male adults and eight are scanned from female adults. Each image has been manually delineated into 32 gray matter regions of interest (ROIs). The images were obtained in a General Electric Signa scanner at 1.5T, with the following protocol: SPGR/50, TR 24, TE 7, NEX 1 matrix 256 × 192, FOV 24 cm. All the images were aligned by the affine transformation with the FLIRT toolkit [15] as the preprocessing step. Exemplar images of the NA0-NIREP database before registration are shown in Figure 1.

The following parameter settings were adopted for the proposed method: A small patch size $3 \times 3 \times 3$ was adopted, and the searching neighborhood size was set to $5 \times 5 \times 5$. The same patch size and searching neighborhood size were adopted for the conventional patch based label propagation method in [4] under comparison. λ was set to 10^{-4} in Equations 3, 4, 5 and 6. The kernel parameter τ was set to $1/64$ by cross validation, and the weight γ_j in Equations 4, 5, and 6 was set to 1 for each anatomical structure.

The Dice ratio was adopted as the quantitative measure. It is defined as $D(A, B) = (2|A \cap B|)/(|A| \cup |B|)$, where A and B denote the regions of a specific type of anatomical structure of the estimated label map and the groundtruth, and $|\cdot|$ denotes the number of voxels within an image region. Half of the images were randomly selected from the 16 images as atlases, and the remaining half of the images were served as the testing images. The experiment was repeated for 10 times, and the average Dice ratio obtained for each ROI by using the majority voting (MV) scheme, STAPLE [9], the conventional patch based label propagation (CPB) method [4], and the proposed group-sparse-patch based label propagation method in the reproducing kernel Hilbert space (GSP + RKHS) are listed in Table 1 with respect to the left and right hemispheres of brain.

Table 1. The average Dice ratio (in %) of different brain ROIs obtained by using different label fusion approaches with respect to the left and right hemispheres of brain on the NA0-NIREP database. The highest Dice ratio for each ROI is bolded.

Brain ROIs (left/right)	MV	STAPLE [9]	CPB [4]	GSP + RKHS
Occipital Lobe	52.3 - 54.8	59.7 - 62.8	74.9 - 79.1	**79.2 - 83.7**
Cingulate Gyrus	58.8 - 60.4	60.9 - 63.7	71.5 - 73.6	**77.3 - 79.2**
Insula Gyrus	62.4 - 66.1	63.6 - 65.7	75.3 - 78.2	**81.4 - 83.6**
Temporal Pole	57.4 - 62.9	60.7 - 62.8	74.3 - 78.5	**79.3 - 83.5**
Superior Temporal Gyrus	46.7 - 45.2	50.9 - 52.4	65.4 - 67.5	**75.2 - 75.4**
Infero Temporal Region	56.3 - 58.4	58.6 - 57.2	74.1 - 77.3	**81.5 - 81.8**
Parahippocampal Gyrus	62.7 - 66.6	60.3 - 62.4	75.3 - 77.4	**78.7 - 81.2**
Frontal Pole	59.2 - 60.5	57.4 - 62.0	78.4 - **81.6**	**79.0** - 80.8
Superior Frontal Gyrus	49.6 - 52.3	52.7 - 54.8	71.8 - 72.5	**77.3 - 78.6**
Middle Frontal Gyrus	51.9 - 54.2	53.5 - 56.7	68.3 - 71.4	**75.3 - 77.6**
Inferior Gyrus	46.9 - 45.2	48.7 - 52.4	66.4 - 68.8	**73.3 - 72.5**
Orbital Frontal Gyrus	58.3 - 59.0	58.5 - 61.7	**78.4** - 79.5	78.2 - **80.3**
Precentral Gyrus	33.6 - 35.5	36.7 - 35.9	65.4 - 67.6	**70.4 - 71.8**
Superior Parietal Lobule	39.6 - 44.3	48.2 - 48.8	64.0 - 68.3	**71.4 - 72.7**
Inferior Parietal Lobule	46.2 - 47.8	49.7 - 52.3	67.2 - 71.5	**72.4 - 74.8**
Postcentral Gyrus	33.5 - 34.6	39.7 - 42.5	53.1 - 58.0	**59.3 - 62.9**

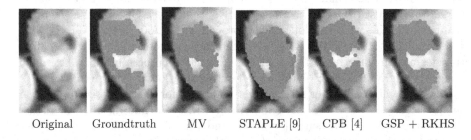

Original   Groundtruth   MV   STAPLE [9]   CPB [4]   GSP + RKHS

Fig. 2. Typical segmentation results for the parahippocampal gyrus anatomical structure on the left hemisphere of the brain using different label fusion approaches

It can be observed from Table 1 that our method (GSP + RKHS) achieves the highest segmentation accuracy among all the methods under comparison almost at all the ROIs, which reflects the effectiveness of the proposed method.

To visualize the segmentation accuracy of the proposed method, Figure 2 shows a typical segmentation result for the parahippocampal gyrus in the left hemisphere brain with different approaches. The segmentation groundtruth is also given in the second column in Figure 2 for reference. It can be observed from Figure 2 that the segmentation result obtained by our method is the closest to the groundtruth, which implies the high segmentation accuracy of our method.

Moreover, to further analyze the contribution of each component of the proposed method, Figure 3 shows the average Dice ratios of the 32 ROIs obtained by using the proposed method with only the global sparsity constraint defined

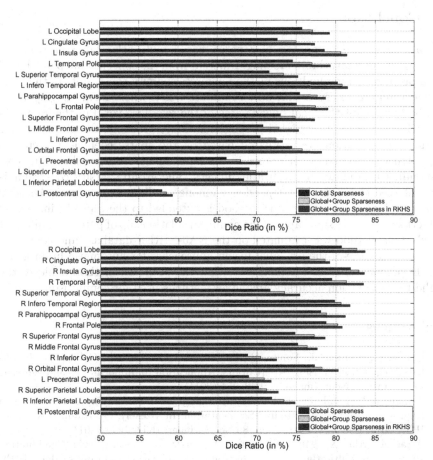

Fig. 3. The average Dice ratio for each anatomical structure obtained by the proposed method with only the global sparsity constraint, with both the global and group sparsity constraints, and with both the global and group sparsity constraints in the reproducing kernel Hilbert space, respectively, on the NA0-NIREP database.

by Equation 3, with both the global and group sparsity constraints defined by Equation 4, and with both the global and group sparsity constraints defined in the kernel space as expressed by Equation 5. It can be observed from Figure 3 that by enforcing the group sparsity constraint, the segmentation accuracy (i.e, with 74.7% overall Dice ratio) can be improved compared with using only the global sparsity constraint only (i.e., with 73.3% overall Dice ratio), which reflects the importance of incorporating the representation power of groups of input variables as stated in [12]. Mover, by extending the group-sparse-patch based label propagation framework to the nonlinear kernel space, the segmentation accuracy can be further improved (i.e., with 76.6% overall Dice ratio).

5 Conclusion

In this paper, we propose a new patch based multi-atlas label propagation method for automatic brain labeling. Different from the conventional patch based label propagation method, our method enforces sparsity constraints in the label propagation process such that only candidate voxels whose local image patches can best represent the local image patch of the reference voxel in the input image will contribute during label propagation. More precisely, the graph weights for label propagation are estimated based on the sparse coefficient vector to reconstruct the patch of each voxel in the input image from patches of its corresponding candidate voxels in atlas images. The group sparsity constraint is also enforced to capture the dependency among candidate voxels with the same anatomical label. Moreover, our method is extended to the reproducing kernel Hilbert space (RKHS) to capture the nonlinear relationship of patches of different voxels. Our method was evaluated on the NA0-NIREP database and compared with several state-of-the-art label fusion approaches for automatic brain labeling. Experimental results demonstrate that the proposed method achieves the highest segmentation accuracy among all methods used for comparison.

References

1. Coupe, P., Manjon, J., Fonov, V., Pruessner, J., Robles, M., Collins, D.: Patch-based segmentation using expert priors: Application to hippocampus and ventricle segmentation. NeuroImage 54, 940–954 (2011)
2. Asman, A.J., Landman, B.A.: Characterizing Spatially Varying Performance to Improve Multi-atlas Multi-label Segmentation. In: Székely, G., Hahn, H.K. (eds.) IPMI 2011. LNCS, vol. 6801, pp. 85–96. Springer, Heidelberg (2011)
3. Artaechevarria, X., Munoz-Barrutia, A., Ortiz-de Solorzano, C.: Combination strategies in multi-atlas image segmentation: Application to brain mr data. IEEE TMI 28, 1266–1277 (2009)
4. Rousseau, F., Habas, P., Studholme, C.: A supervised patch-based approach for human brain labeling. IEEE TMI 30, 1852–1862 (2011)
5. Rohlfing, T., Russakoff, D., Maurer, C.: Performance-based classifier combination in atlas-based image segmentation using expectation-maximization parameter estimation. IEEE TMI 23, 983–994 (2004)
6. Heckemann, R., Hajnal, J., Aljabar, P., Rueckert, D., Hammers, A.: Automatic anatomical brain mri segmentation combining label propagation and decision fusion. NeuroImage 33, 115–126 (2006)
7. Sabuncu, M., Yeo, B., van Leemput, K., Fischl, B., Golland, P.: A generative model for image segmentation based on label fusion. IEEE TMI 29, 1714–1729 (2010)
8. van Rikxoort, E., Isgum, I., Arzhaeva, Y., Staring, M., Klein, S., Viergever, M., Pluim, J., van Ginneken, B.: Adaptive local multi-atlas segmentation: Application to the heart and the caudate nucleus. MedIA 14, 39–49 (2010)
9. Warfield, S., Zou, K., Wells, W.: Simultaneous truth and performance level estimation (staple): An algorithm for the validation of image segmentation. IEEE TMI 23, 903–921 (2004)
10. Tibshirani, R.: Regression shrinkage and selection via the lasso. Journal of the Royal Statistical Society: Series B 58, 267–288 (1996)

11. Nesterov, Y.: Introductory Lectures on Convex Optimization: A Basic Course. Kluwer Academic Publishers (2004)

12. Yuan, M., Lin, Y.: Model selection and estimation in regression with grouped variables. Journal of the Royal Statistical Society: Series B 68, 49–67 (2006)

13. Gao, S., Tsang, I.W.-H., Chia, L.-T.: Kernel Sparse Representation for Image Classification and Face Recognition. In: Daniilidis, K., Maragos, P., Paragios, N. (eds.) ECCV 2010, Part IV. LNCS, vol. 6314, pp. 1–14. Springer, Heidelberg (2010)

14. Christensen, G.E., Geng, X., Kuhl, J.G., Bruss, J., Grabowski, T.J., Pirwani, I.A., Vannier, M.W., Allen, J.S., Damasio, H.: Introduction to the Non-rigid Image Registration Evaluation Project (NIREP). In: Pluim, J.P.W., Likar, B., Gerritsen, F.A. (eds.) WBIR 2006. LNCS, vol. 4057, pp. 128–135. Springer, Heidelberg (2006)

15. Jenkinson, M., Bannister, P., Brady, M., Smith, S.: Improved optimization for the robust and accurate linear registration and motion correction of brain images. NeuroImage 17, 825–841 (2002)

Sparse Patch-Guided Deformation Estimation for Improved Image Registration

Minjeong Kim, Guorong Wu, and Dinggang Shen

Department of Radiology and BRIC, University of North Carolina at Chapel Hill

Abstract. This paper presents a novel patch-guided initial deformation estimation framework for improving performance of the existing registration algorithms. It is challenging for the registration algorithm to directly align two images with large anatomical shape difference, when no good initial deformation is provided. Inspired by the patch-based multi-atlases segmentation method, we propose to estimate the initial deformation between two images (under registration) in a patch-by-patch fashion. Specifically, after obtaining the sparse representation for each local patch in the subject by using the training patches in the over-complete dictionary that include both patches and their associated deformations from the training images, the initial deformation for each local subject patch can be predicted by those estimated sparse coefficients. More specifically, after registering all training images to the template in the training stage, the following three steps can be used to register any given subject image. *First*, for each key point in the subject, we can construct a coupled dictionary from the nearby patches in the training images and their associated deformations, and can then use this dictionary to seek for sparse representation of the respective subject patch. The estimated sparse coefficients can be used to fuse the associated deformations in the dictionary, for estimating the initial deformation for the respective subject key point. *Second*, after estimating the initial deformations on a small number of key points in the subject, thin-plate spline (TPS) can be applied to interpolating the dense deformation field. *Finally*, we can apply any existing deformable registration method (with reasonable performance) to estimate the remaining deformation from the template to subject. Experimental results on both simulated and real data show that our patch-guided deformation estimation framework can allow for more accurate registration than the direct use of the original methods for registration.

1 Introduction

Deformable image registration has been widely used in many neuroscience and clinical studies, i.e., to quantitatively measure inter-group structural differences or identify abnormalities in the disease-affected brains. Although numerous registration methods have been proposed in the last decades, it still remains challenging to register images with large anatomical differences.

Instead of directly estimating deformation pathway between template and subject images, the learning-based methods [1, 2] have been recently proposed to predict the initial deformation for bringing the template very close to the subject. In this way, the

F. Wang et al. (Eds.): MLMI 2012, LNCS 7588, pp. 54–62, 2012.

remaining (small) deformation can be more effectively estimated by any existing registration algorithm. Although advanced regression model was used in these learning-based methods to predict the initial deformation, i.e., through the step of correlating the statistical deformation model with brain appearance model, its main limitation is the use of global model for representing the whole brain deformations (i.e., using a global PCA to build the statistical deformation model for the entire deformation fields), thus local deformations might not be well captured. Moreover, these methods are often lack of the ability for incremental learning, since the training dataset is generally fixed and the inclusion of new training samples will have to re-train the entire method.

Inspired by the recent success of patch-based multi-atlases labeling methods [3, 4], we propose a sparse patch-guided deformation estimation framework to augment the performance of the existing registration methods, by specially providing a good initial deformation field. The important assumption in our method is that *if a patch in the subject is locally similar to the patches in the training images, its deformation to the template will be similar to the deformations pre-estimated for those training patches*. We also assume that, given a sufficient number of training images, each local patch in the subject image can be well represented by a sparse combination of similar patches in the training images [5].

In this paper, we propose a novel patch-guided deformation estimation framework to predict a good initial deformation between template and subject images. Specifically, in the training stage, a large number of training images are carefully registered to a selected template. In the application stage, for a given subject image to be registered, a small number of key points are first selected. Then, for each subject key point, its own over-complete dictionary will be adaptively constructed by including all possible nearby patches from the training images, as well as their associated deformations (pre-estimated). This coupled dictionary can be used to sparsely represent the underlying patch of this subject key point, and those estimated sparse coefficients can be further used to fuse the associated deformations for producing a good local deformation for this subject key point. Next, after estimating local deformations for all key points in the subject image, we can apply TPS to efficiently interpolate the dense deformation field, which can be finally used as a good initialization for the subsequent registration by any existing registration methods (with reasonable performance). Experimental results on both simulated and real data show that our sparse patch-guided deformation estimation framework can achieve higher registration accuracy than any other methods under comparison.

2   Method

2.1   Overview of Sparse Patch-guided Deformation Estimation Framework

Unlike most previous registration methods that tried to directly estimate the deformation u^S (black arrow in Fig. 1) from template image T to subject image S, we predict an initial deformation u_I^S (dashed blue arrow in Fig. 1) to bring T close to S, thus making the subsequent registration much easier by just needing to refine the remaining (small) deformation u_R^S (solid blue arrow in Fig. 1). As mentioned earlier, the previous learning-based registration methods often intended to predict u_I^S based on a statistical deformation model for the whole brain image, which may fail to capture the local characteristics of deformations.

We introduce here a novel patch-based approach for adaptively predicting the initial deformation u_I^S as illustrated in Fig. 1. Specifically, in the training stage, a number of training images are first carefully registered with a selected template T. Thus, we know the deformation fields of these training images to the template (as shown in the red box of Fig. 1). Then, for any given subject image, its registration to the template image can be completed by the following three steps. **(1)** M key points are first selected automatically in the subject image S, and denoted as $X^S = \{x_j^S | j = 1, ..., M\}$. Then, we construct a coupled (patch-deformation) local dictionary for each subject key point x_j^S, by including all possible nearby patches from the training images and their associated deformations. Finally, the initial deformation on each subject key point can be predicted via the patch-based sparse representation as detailed in the next subsection. **(2)** With estimation of local deformations for all subject key points, we apply TPS interpolation to obtain the initial dense deformation field u_I^S by considering all these subject key points X^S as the source point set and their estimated local deformations as the target point set. **(3)** We can finally obtain the complete deformation field u^S by concatenating the initial dense deformation field u_I^S with the remaining deformation u_R^S estimated by a selected existing registration algorithm. In the following, we will detail the dictionary construction in Section 2.2 and the initial deformation prediction in Section 2.3, respectively.

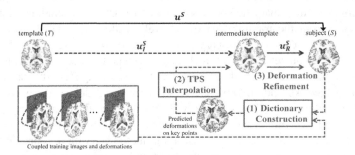

Fig. 1. Illustration of the proposed registration method by sparse patch-guided deformation estimation

2.2   Dictionary Construction on Subject Key Points

To construct the dictionary for each subject key point, N training images $L = \{L_i | i = 1, ..., N\}$ are first linearly registered with the template T. Then, we use a conventional deformable registration algorithm to carefully register each training image L_i with the template and finally estimate its deformation field f_i to the template. It is worth noting that any existing deformable registration algorithms with reasonable registration performance (even with the guidance of manual landmarks) [6, 7] can be used for the training purpose. In the application stage, for registering a new subject image S to the template T, we first also linearly align it to the template T and then select a set of key points X^s in the linearly-aligned subject image S by (a) using Canny edge detector to obtain edge points and (b) further setting a threshold on the gradient magnitude of Canny edge points to select M key points with largest edge responses in the subject S. Compared with the total number of points in the whole brain image (e.g., ~1 million), M is usually much smaller (i.e., 20,000~30,000), thus greatly reducing computational complexity.

Here, we use $P_S(x_j^S)$ to denote the particular local image patch in the subject S, centered at a key point $x_j^S \in X^S \subset \Omega_S$. Similarly, we use $P_{L_i}(y)$ to denote a candidate local patch in the i-th training image L_i, centered at the point $y \in \Omega_{L_i}$. Here, patches $P_S(x_j^S)$ and $P_{L_i}(y)$ are both represented as the column vectors. For each subject key point x_j^S under consideration, its over-complete coupled dictionary $D(x_j^S)$ can be constructed, as illustrated with the red box in the middle of Fig. 2, by incorporating all possible candidate image patches $P_{L_i}(y)$ from all training images L as well as their associated deformations $f_{L_i}(y)$ at the center point y.

Patch pre-selection is further performed, since it is important to reduce the computational burden and improve the prediction accuracy by excluding the irrelevant patches from the dictionary. The criterion γ for patch pre-selection is specially defined between $P_S(x_j^S)$ and $P_{L_i}(y)$ as follows:

$$\gamma\left(P_S(x_j^S), P_{L_i}(y)\right) = [2\mu_x\mu_y/(\mu_x^2+\mu_y^2)] \times [2\sigma_x\sigma_y/(\sigma_x^2 + \sigma_y^2)], \tag{1}$$

where μ_x and σ_x are the intensity mean and standard deviation in the local patch $P_S(x_j^S)$, and μ_y and σ_y are the intensity mean and standard deviation in the local patch $P_{L_i}(y)$, respectively. To save the computational time, we construct the dictionary within a certain search neighborhood n. Then, the definition of the local dictionary $D(x_j^S)$ at the subject key point x_j^S can be given as:

$$D(x_j^S) = \left\{\left(P_{L_i}(y), f_{L_i}(y)\right) \mid y \in n(x_j^S),\ i = 1, \dots, N,\ \gamma\left(P_S(x_j^S), P_{L_i}(y)\right) > \Gamma\right\}, \tag{2}$$

where Γ is the threshold used in patch pre-selection. Only if the value γ is greater than Γ, patch $P_{L_i}(y)$ will be included in the dictionary. After this pre-selection procedure, we assume that there are Q elements in particular dictionary $D(x_j^S)$.

In the next section, we will explain how to use the sparse representation method to seek for the linear combination of image patches in the dictionary $D(x_j^S)$ to best represent the image patch $P_S(x_j^S)$ in the subject, and then use the obtained sparse coefficients to fuse the associated deformations and predict the initial deformation on the subject key point x_j^S.

2.3   Deformation Prediction by Sparse Representation

Given the local dictionary $D(x_j^S)$ for each subject key point x_j^S, we seek for the sparse representation for its local image patch $P_S(x_j^S)$, which can be formulated as a well-known least absolute shrinkage and selection operator (LASSO) problem.

Specifically, we first assemble all Q local image patches (represented as column vectors) in the dictionary into a matrix $A(x_j^S) = [P_{L_i}(y)]$. With the same order, we can also arrange their associated deformations $f_{L_i}(y)$ into a matrix $D(x_j^S) = [f_{L_i}(y)]$. Then, a weighting vector of sparse coefficients $w(x_j^S)$ (which is a column vector with length Q) is defined to describe the contribution of each dictionary element in representing the subject patch $P_S(x_j^S)$. We further apply the l_1-norm on the weighting vector $w(x_j^S)$ to require using only a small number of similar patches in the dictionary to represent patch $P_S(x_j^S)$, for making our patch-based method robust to the outliers. Mathematically, the objective function of estimating sparse coefficients $w(x_j^S)$ at each subject key point x_j^S can be formulated as:

$$\widehat{w}(x_j^S) = \operatorname{argmin}_w \left\| A(x_j^S) \cdot w(x_j^S) - P_S(x_j^S) \right\|^2 + \lambda \left\| w(x_j^S) \right\|_1, \; s.t. \; w(x_j^S) > 0, \qquad (3)$$

where λ is a parameter controlling the strength of l_1-norm regularization. This objective function can be optimized by the Euclidian-projection based method as described in [8].

After obtaining the sparse coefficients $w(x_j^S)$, the initial deformation on the subject key point x_j^S can be predicted as:

$$u_I^S(x_j^S) = D(x_j^S) \cdot \widehat{w}(x_j^S). \qquad (4)$$

The demonstration of estimating the sparse coefficient $w(x_j^S)$ and predicting the initial deformation $u_I^S(x_j^S)$ are illustrated in the right panel of Fig. 2.

To further improve the performance of sparse representation, the size of local image patch $P_S(x_j^S)$ is adaptively determined according to the local image content. Intuitively, the patch size should be small at the areas with rich edge information (e.g., cortical area) in order to capture the complex local structural features, while the relatively large image patch should be used at the uniform regions (e.g., whiter matter regions) in order to make the image patch as distinctive as possible. Here, we use the Octree technique to efficiently partition the whole brain into a set of blocks, where the size of each block is adaptive to the local image content. Thus, for each subject key point x_j^S, we can adopt its associated block size (determined in Octree-based partition) as the patch size to construct the dictionary and seek for the sparse representation.

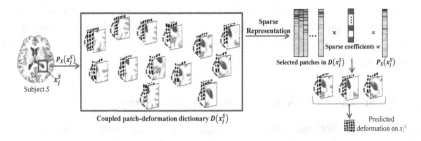

Fig. 2. Deformation prediction on a subject key point, via sparse patch-based representation

3   Experimental Results

We use HAMMER software (http://www.nitrc.org/projects/hammer_suite) available in NITRC for generating the training deformation fields and also for comparison, although any other existing deformable registration methods (with reasonable performance) can also be applied here. We also compared our result with a state-of-the-art regression-model-based deformation prediction method [2], which is re-implemented by us.

3.1   Deformation Prediction on Simulated Data

We used the algorithm proposed in [9] to generate 10 simulated brain images to serve as a ground-truth for evaluation. The mean magnitude of the ground-truth deformation fields was set to 6 mm during simulation. Then, we applied the two prediction methods, i.e., the regression-model-based deformation prediction method (which uses global statistical model) [2] and our proposed patch-based method to predict the initial deformation fields for the simulated images. By comparing the overall residual deformation error between the predicted initial deformation fields and the ground-truth ones, we can quantitatively measure the prediction error. Note that the residual deformation could be further estimated by applying the existing deformable registration algorithm such as HAMMER. The obtained average deformation errors were 2.46 mm by the regression-model-based method, and 2.01 mm by our proposed method. To inspect the deformation prediction performance in local brain structures, we further measure the averaged residual deformation errors on 93 ROIs defined on the template. As a result, our proposed prediction method achieved comparable performance in 37 ROIs, and much lower deformation errors on 56 ROIs, where the maximum improvement is 2.2 mm, compared to the regression-model-based method. This result indicates that our method can better initialize the registration than the regression-model-based method, especially for the cases with large simulated deformations (e.g., 6 mm).

3.2   Deformation Prediction on Real Data

In the training stage, we estimated the deformation fields for 50 images with respect to the template (Fig. 3a) by using HAMMER. These 50 training images were randomly selected from a MR brain image database, consisting of elderly brains aged from 65 to 80. To evaluate the quality of the initial deformations estimated by the two prediction methods, i.e., the regression-model-based method and our proposed method, we used 20 new images (not used for training) in the testing stage to examine how close each of these two methods can warp the template to the subject images (see Fig. 3). In our method, the patch size was adaptively determined by Octree-based partition, which varies between $3\times3\times3$ mm^3 and $11\times11\times11$ mm^3. Through visual inspection on Fig. 3, our method (Fig. 3d) can estimate the initial deformation for bringing template closer to the respective subject images, compared to the regression-model-based method (Fig. 3c). To quantitatively evaluate their performance, we compute the Dice overlap ratio on white matter (WM), gray matter (GM), and ventricular cerebrospinal fluid (VN) between the warped templates and the respective target subjects. Compared to the regression-model-based method, which achieved overlap ratios of 71.7%, 61.3%, and 74.2% for WM, GM and VN, respectively, our method obtained higher overall scores (73.3%, 62.8%, and 79.5% for WM, GM, and VN, respectively). This comparison shows that our proposed method can achieve better performance in predicting the initial deformations than the regression-model-based method on real images.

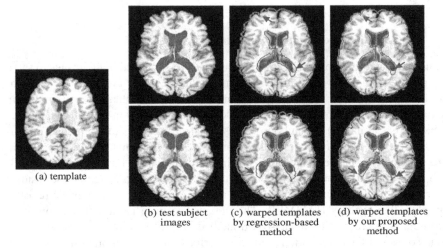

(a) template

(b) test subject
images

(c) warped templates
by regression-based
method

(d) warped templates
by our proposed
method

Fig. 3. Demonstration of aligning template to 2 subject images (b), by predicting initial deformation using regression-model-based method (c) and our proposed method (d), respectively. Compared to the target subject images (b), the warped templates by our proposed method are more similar (i.e., pointed by red arrows) to the target subject images than those by the regression-model-based method. For visual comparison, we overlaid the outlines of the whole brain and ventricle outlines for the subject images onto the respective warped templates.

3.3   Prediction and Registration Performance on LONI LPBA40 Dataset

The LONI LPBA40 dataset [10] consists of 40 subjects, each with 54 manually-labeled ROIs. After selecting one individual image as the template, we used remaining 20 subjects for training and another 19 subjects for testing. To evaluate the predication accuracy, the template image was first warped towards the 19 test subjects by applying the initial deformations predicted by the regression-model-based method and our proposed, respectively. Then, the Dice ratios for all ROIs of 19 warped template images, yielded by those two methods, were computed for comparison. The obtained average Dice ratios were 54.9% by the regression-model-based method, and 58.4% by our proposed method. Specifically, our proposed method achieved higher overlap scores for 33 among 54 ROIs (with the maximum improvement of 7.3%) than the regression-model-based method.

The residual deformations for the 19 subjects were further estimated by HAMMER. Finally, the registration results were compared with the original registration method without deformation prediction, i.e., HAMMER, in terms of the averaged tissue overlap ratio for each ROI. Our proposed method obtained higher averaged Dice overlap ratio (72.3%) than HAMMER (71.1%). In Fig. 4, we show the Dice overlap ratio for each ROI for HAMMER and our proposed method, thus indicating our framework yields better registration performance (in terms of higher tissue overlap ratios) for most of ROIs than HAMMER.

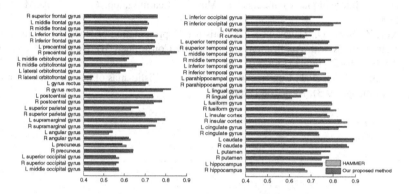

Fig. 4. Averaged overlap ratios of aligned ROIs by HAMMER and our proposed method

4   Conclusion

A novel patch-guided deformation prediction framework has been proposed for improving registration performance of the existing registration algorithms. Specifically, the initial deformation for a new subject can be directly estimated using a sparse representation of the subject-adaptive over-complete patch dictionary which includes both local image patches and their associated deformations learned from a set of training images. Experimental results show that, the use of our esitmated initial deformaiton allows for obtaining of higher registration accuracy, compared to the direct use of original registration method, or through the regression-model-based deformation estimation method. Future work includes testing our proposed methods on more other registration algorithms such as the B-spline based registration method.

References

1. Tang, S., et al.: RABBIT: rapid alignment of brains by building intermediate templates. Neuroimage 47(4), 1277–1287 (2009)
2. Kim, M., et al.: A General Fast Registration Framework by Learning Deformation-Appearance Correlation. IEEE Transactions on Image Processing 21(4), 1823–1833 (2012)
3. Rousseau, F., et al.: A Supervised Patch-Based Approach for Human Brain Labeling. IEEE Transactions on Medical Imaging 30(10), 1852–1862 (2011)
4. Coupé, P., et al.: Patch-based segmentation using expert priors: Application to hippocampus and ventricle segmentation. NeuroImage 54(2), 940–954 (2011)

5. Zongben, X., Jian, S.: Image Inpainting by Patch Propagation Using Patch Sparsity. IEEE Transactions on Image Processing 19(5), 1153–1165 (2010)
6. Vercauteren, T., et al.: Diffeomorphic demons: Efficient non-parametric image registration. NeuroImage 45(1, suppl.1), S61–S72 (2009)
7. Shen, D., Davatzikos, C.: HAMMER: Hierarchical attribute matching mechanism for elastic registration. IEEE Transactions on Medical Imaging 21(11), 1421–1439 (2002)
8. Liu, J., Ye, J.: Efficient Euclidean projections in linear time. In: Proceedings of the 26th Annual International Conference on Machine Learning, pp. 657–664. ACM, Montreal (2009)
9. Xue, Z., Shen, D., Davatzikos, C.: Statistical Representation of High-Dimensional Deformation Fields with Application to Statistically-Constrained 3D Warping. Medical Image Analysis 10(5), 740–751 (2006)
10. Shattuck, D.W., et al.: Construction of a 3D probabilistic atlas of human cortical structures. NeuroImage 39(3), 1064–1080 (2008)

Computer-Aided Detection of Aneurysms in 3D Time-of-Flight MRA Datasets

Santiago Suniaga[1], Rene Werner[2], Andre Kemmling[3], Michael Groth[3], Jens Fiehler[3], and Nils Daniel Forkert[1]

[1] Department of Computational Neuroscience, University Medical Center Hamburg-Eppendorf
[2] Institute of Medical Informatics, University of Lübeck
[3] Department of Diagnostic and Interventional Neuroradiology, University Medical Center Hamburg-Eppendorf

Abstract. The visual detection of aneurysms in 3D angiographic datasets is very time-consuming and error-prone. Depending on the individual experience, up to 40% of all aneurysms are missed in the diagnostic routine. The aim of this work is to present a computer-aided method for the automatic detection of aneurysm candidates in 3D MRA datasets. In this approach, the cerebrovascular system is automatically segmented in a first step and used for identification of vessel endpoints, which are used as an initial aneurysm candidate sample. In a following step, a number of morphological and structural parameters are calculated for each candidate. Finally, a support vector machine (SVM) is applied for reducing the number of aneurysm candidates based on the extracted parameters. The proposed method was evaluated based on 20 Time-of-Flight MRA datasets of patients with an aneurysm using linear as well as radial basis function kernels for SVM training. Leave-one-out cross validation revealed that the linear kernel SVM leads to better results, achieving a sensitivity of 100% and a concurrent false-positive rate of 3.86. In conclusion, the proposed method may help to improve and speed-up the aneurysm screening in clinical practice.

1 Introduction

The cerebral stroke is one of the most common diseases in the western hemisphere leading to death and severe neurological deficits [1]. The cerebral stroke is caused by a hypoperfusion of brain tissue due to an occlusion of an artery in approximately 80% of all cases. The remaining 20% of all strokes are caused by an acute bleeding due to a rupture of a blood vessel. These ruptures mainly occur at cerebrovascular malformations such as arteriovenous malformations or aneurysms [2].

A major problem of cerebrovascular malformations is that there are usually no specific symptoms associated with these vascular pathologies. Therefore, such malformations are most often diagnosed by incidental findings. However, especially aneurysms are quite challenging to detect if not explicitly looking for one.

F. Wang et al. (Eds.): MLMI 2012, LNCS 7588, pp. 63–69, 2012.

Previous studies have demonstrated that 21-40% of all aneurysms may be missed during diagnostic screening depending on the education and experience of an observer [3]. One reason for this is that especially small aneurysms are difficult to differentiate from healthy blood vessels such that a lot of training is required for this task. Nevertheless, an accurate aneurysm screening using standard visualization techniques like the display of the MRA datasets in orthogonal views or maximum intensity projections is very time-consuming and may easily require several minutes making a general aneurysm screening for each patient dataset not suitable for the clinical routine.

The objective of this work is to present a method for the automatic detection of aneurysm candidates, which are presented to the clinicians for final decision. Therefore, the main requirement for this method is to detect aneurysms with a sensitivity of 100% while the number of false-positive detected aneurysms should be as low as possible in order to enable a reduction of the screening time in the diagnostic routine.

2   Material and Methods

2.1   MR Imaging

Twenty Time-of-Flight (TOF) MRA datasets of patients with a diagnosed cerebral aneurysm were available for the development and evaluation of the proposed approach. All TOF MRA datasets were acquired on a 1.5 Tesla Sonata MR scanner (Siemens, Erlangen, Germany) without contrast agent using a single axial slab sequence, TR=36 ms, TE=6, and a flip angle of 25 with a field-of-view of $150 \times 200 \times 64$ mm^3 and a spatial resolution of $0.4 \times 0.4 \times 0.8$ mm^3.

Time-of-Flight MRA datasets exhibit a high blood-to-background contrast and are therefore frequently used in the clinical routine for a non-invasive examination of the cerebrovascular system and following detection of aneurysms.

2.2   Methodical Assumption

The proposed method for the automatic detection of aneurysms in 3D TOF MRA datasets is based on a number of assumptions, which are as follows:

1. Aneurysms are bulges in the blood vessel wall and therefore represent a structural vessel end.
2. Aneurysms exhibit relative small distances from the corresponding centers to the nearest bifurcation. Furthermore, aneurysms are represented by a local thickening of the vessel radius.
3. Aneurysms exhibit a, roughly approximated, blob structure and no typical vessel structure.
4. Aneurysms exhibit high surface curvatures in the neck area.

Based on these assumptions, several parameters are extracted from the 3D TOF MRA image sequences in this work, which are then used for the automatic detection of aneurysms. The filter and methods used for this purpose are described in more detail in the following section.

2.3   Extraction of Parameters

The first step of the proposed method for the automatic detection and localization of aneurysms is the segmentation of the cerebrovascular systems from a given TOF MRA dataset. In this work, a fully automatic segmentation method combining intensity as well as shape information derived from the multi-scale vesselness filter [4] using fuzzy-logic within a level-set framework [5] was applied. This approach was selected due to its ability to extract very small as well as malformed vessels at high precision.

An automatic 3D thinning algorithm is then used to extract the 3D centerline from the extracted cerebrovascular segmentation, which allows identifying and localizing bifurcations and vascular endpoints. Therefore, the iterative thinning technique proposed by Lee et al. [6] was used in this work. After calculation of the 3D skeleton, vessel ends can be easily identified using a voxel-wise neighborhood analysis. A vessel endpoint is defined by a centerline voxel that has exactly one neighboring centerline voxel. The detected vessel endpoints serve as an initial sample of aneurysm candidates (assumption 1).

Likewise, the 3D centerline can also be used for the detection of bifurcations. Here, a bifurcation is defined by a centerline voxel that has more than two neighboring centerline voxels. Using this information, the minimal distance of each aneurysm candidate to the next bifurcation in its vicinity can be calculated and used as a parameter for classification purposes. Furthermore, the cerebrovascular segmentation is also used to calculate the vessel radius corresponding to each aneurysm candidate. Therefore, the minimal distance of each candidate to the next non-segmented voxel is estimated and also used as a parameter for the automatic detection of aneurysms (assumption 2).

In a next step, a generalized multi-scale vesselness filter [7] (blobness filter) is used to enhance blob-like structures in the 3D TOF MRA datasets. The standard vesselness filter [4] enhances tubular structures by voxel-wisely calculating and analyzing the corresponding Hessian matrix. Tubular structures can be enhanced by making use of the assumption that the Hessian matrix of such structures exhibits one eigenvalue close to zero and two strong negative eigenvalues. In contrast to the standard vesselness filter, the blobness filter enhances structures that exhibit strong negative values for all three eigenvalues of the Hessian matrix. By calculating the blobness and vesselness parameter images, two more parameters are available for each candidate, whereas it is assumed that an aneurysm exhibits low vesselness and high blobness values (assumption 3).

The final step of the parameter extraction is the application of the 3D Förstner filter [8] to the TOF MRA dataset, which is used to enhance structures that exhibit high surface curvatures. Due to the fact that high surface curvatures are expected in particular at the aneurysm neck, a gray value dilation using a $3 \times 3 \times 3$ kernel is performed based on the calculated Förstner parameter image. This is supposed to ensure that the detected aneurysm candidates, which are mostly located in the center of an aneurysm, are also represented by high Förstner values (assumption 4).

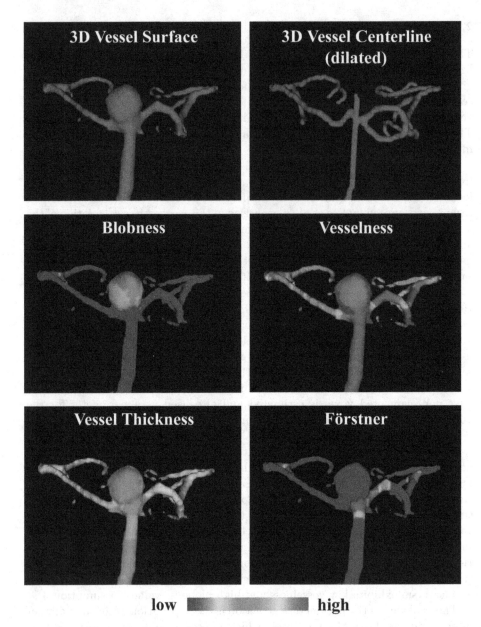

Fig. 1. 3D visualization of an aneurysm with color-coded display of the extracted parameters

2.4   Aneurysm Candidate Classification

Depending on the coverage of a MRA dataset up to 600 initial aneurysm candidates may be found for one patient. This problem can be ascribed to the fact that several artificial vessel ends are detected, in particular at small vessels, due to partial volume effects. Therefore, the aim of the last step of the proposed method is to reduce the number of initial aneurysm candidates based on the extracted parameters (bifurcation distance, vessel thickness, blobness value, vesselness value, Förstner value) to enable a realistic application in clinical practice. For this purpose, a support vector machine (SVM) [9] was used in this work for classification of the initial aneurysm candidates. For training as well as evaluation purposes, an experienced neuroradiology expert identified all aneurysms candidates that correspond to real aneurysms in the given database of 20 TOF MRA datasets. After training of the SVM using the gold-standard definitions and the six corresponding parameter values, the generated classification model can be used to reduce the number of aneurysm candidates.

3   Evaluation and Results

The proposed method was evaluated based on the 20 clinical TOF MRA datasets. Due to the rather small dataset available, leave-one-out cross validations were performed in order to enable a sufficient training of the SVM and to obtain unbiased results. Here, each dataset to be classified, consisting of all initial detected and classified aneurysm candidates and corresponding parameters, was excluded from the corresponding SVM training for generation of the classification model. The SVMs were trained using a linear as well as a radial basis function (RBF) kernel to compare the performance of both approaches. The vesselness filter used for segmentation as well as for parameter extraction was calculated using five sigma log-scales ($\sigma \in [0.25, 1.5]$). Likewise, the blobness filter was also calculated using five sigma log-scales ($\sigma \in [0.5, 5.0]$). The gamma parameter for the RBF kernel was set to 0.05.

The number of initially detected aneurysm candidates ranged between 107 and 541 (mean: 330), which had to be classified, for the datasets evaluated in this study. Overall, considerable differences were found between SVM classifications using linear and RBF kernels. In general, the linear kernel SVM performed considerably better compared to the RBF kernel SVM. More precisely, the RBF kernel SVM lead to a sensitivity of 90% (18/20 aneurysms were detected) and a false-positive rate of 13.57. In contrast to this, the application of the SVM with linear kernel lead to a sensitivity of 100% (20/20 aneurysms were detected) and a comparably lower false-positive rate of only 3.86. In general, all false-positive findings were located at vessels exhibiting high surface curvatures and windings.

4   Discussion

Several methods for the automatic detection of aneurysms in 3D MRA image sequences have been proposed in the past. Lauric, for example, proposed a method that utilizes the Writhe number to detect aneurysms [10]. The Writhe number measures how strong a curve twists and coils. An evaluation based on ten MRA datasets revealed that this method is capable of detecting aneurysms with a sensitivity of 100% and a false-positive rate of 5.3.

A completely different approach was, for example, presented by Hentschke et al. [11]. In this approach, aneurysm candidates are identified using thresholding of the blobness parameter image. The number of aneurysm candidates is then reduced in a post-processing step using a k-means cluster algorithm and application of a rule base. The evaluation based on twenty MRA datasets revealed a sensitivity of 94% and a false-positive rate of 8.0 for this method.

Another approach was proposed by Yang et al. [12]. In this approach, the cerebrovascular system is segmented in a first step. After this, the corresponding 3D centerline is computed based on the extracted segmentation and used to determine the different vessel parts and corresponding endpoints, which serve as an initial sample of aneurysm candidates. This sample is further extended using thresholding of a blobness parameter image. Finally, the candidate sample is reduced again using a rule base. The evaluation was performed based on 287 MRA datasets and showed that this method is capable of detecting aneurysms with a sensitivity of 96% and false-positive rate of 11.6.

The method presented in this work combines all relevant parameters that have been used in previous studies within one approach. The first results of this approach suggest that by this it is possible to detect aneurysms with a sensitivity comparable to the results of previous detection methods. However, the main benefit of the presented approach is a considerable lower false-positive rate.

Nevertheless, it has to be mentioned that, like in most previous studies, only saccular aneurysms have been used in this study for evaluation of the automatic detection approach. Therefore, the proposed method needs to be evaluated based on a broader basis. For this reason, the database is currently extended with more image sequences. In particular, datasets of aneurysms exhibiting a fussiform structure are of special interest for future evaluations. Apart from this, it is planned to evaluate the method based on other imaging modalities such as 3D rotational angiographies. Furthermore, more analyses regarding the optimal SVM kernel function and corresponding parameters, if required, are necessary as this evaluation has shown that the choice of the kernel function has a crucial impact to the classification results. Hence, one reason for the comparably worse results of the RBF kernel SVM may be that the gamma parameter is not yet optimized. Apart from this, overfitting may be another potential explanation for this observation.

In conclusion, the first results suggest that the proposed method is capable of detecting aneurysms with high sensitivity and concurrent low false-positive rate and may help to improve and speed-up the aneurysm screening in clinical practice.

References

1. Donnan, G.A., Fisher, M., Macleod, M., Davis, S.M.: Stroke. The Lancet 371, 1612–1623 (2008)
2. Thrift, A.G., Dewey, H.M., Macdonell, R.A., et al.: Incidence of the Major Stroke Subtypes - Initial Findings From the North East Melbourne Stroke Incidence Study (NEMESIS). Stroke 32(8), 1732–1738 (2001)
3. Okahara, M., Kiyosue, H., Yamashita, M., et al.: Diagnostic accuracy of magnetic resonance angiography for cerebral aneurysms in correlation with 3D-digital subtraction angiographic images: a study of 133 aneurysms. Stroke 33(7), 1803–1808 (2002)
4. Sato, Y., Nakajimaothers, S., Shiraga, N., et al.: Three-dimensional multi-scale line filter for segmentation and visualization of curvelinear structures in medical images. Med. Image Anal. 2(2), 143–168 (1998)
5. Forkert, N.D., Säring, D., Illies, T., et al.: Direction-Dependent Level Set Segmentation of Cerebrovascular Structures. In: Dawant, B.M., Haynor, D.R. (eds.) Image Processing, SPIE Medical Imaging 2011, vol. 7962, pp. 3S1–3S (2011)
6. Lee, T., Kashyap, R.L., Chu, C.: Building skeleton models via 3-D medial surface/axis thinning algorithms. CVGIP: Graph. Models Image Process. 56(6), 462–478 (1994)
7. Antiga, L.: Generalizing vesselness with respect to dimensionality and shape. The Insight Journal (2007)
8. Förstner, W., Gülch, E.: A fast operator for detection and precise location of distinct points, corners and centres of circular features. In: ISPRS Intercommission Workshop Interlaken, pp. 281–305 (1987)
9. Joachims, T.: Making large-scale support vector machine learning practical. In: Schölkopf, B., Burges, C., Smola, A. (eds.) Advances in Kernel Methods, pp. 169–184. MIT Press, Cambridge (1999)
10. Lauric, A.: Automated Detection and Classification of Intracranial Aneurysms based on 3D Surface Analysis. PhD Thesis, Tufts University (2010)
11. Hentschke, C.M., Beuing, O., Nickl, R., Tonnies, K.D.: Automatic cerebral aneurysm detection in multimodal angiographic images. In: Nuclear Science Symposium and Medical Imaging Conference, pp. 3116–3120 (2011)
12. Yang, X., Blezek, D.J., Cheng, L.T.: Computer-aided detection of intracranial aneurysms in MR angiography. J. Digit. Imaging 24(1), 86–95 (2011)

Data Driven Constraints for the SVM

Sune Darkner[1] and Line H. Clemmensen[2]

[1] Univrsity of Copenhagen, Dpt. of Computer Science
[2] Technical University of Denmark, DTU Informatics

Abstract. We propose a generalized data driven constraint for support vector machines exemplified by classification of paired observations in general and specifically on the human ear canal. This is particularly interesting in dynamic cases such as tissue movement or pathologies developing over time. Assuming that two observations of the same subject in different states span a vector, we hypothesise that such structure of the data contains implicit information which can aid the classification, thus the name data driven constraints. We derive a constraint based on the data which allow for the use of the ℓ_1-norm on the constraint while still allowing for the application of kernels. We specialize the proposed constraint to orthogonality of the vectors between paired observations and the estimated hyperplane. We show that imposing the constraint of orthogonality on the paired data yields a more robust classifier solution, compared to the SVM i.e. reduces variance and improves classification rates. We present a quantitative measure of the information level contained in the pairing and test the method on simulated as well as a high-dimensional paired data set of ear-canal surfaces.

Keywords: SVM, Regularization, Kernels, Classifier design, Shape.

1 Introduction

The structure of data and the way data is collected often contains information on covariances in feature space or a more direct linkage between observations, such as a pairing of observations. We present an extension of support vector machines (SVM) which embed data specific knowledge into the SVM in general. Specifically, for paired observations a constraint is presented that enforces orthogonality of the vectors spanned by paired observations and the estimated hyperplane. To arrive at the constraint we present a general framework for adding constraints based directly on the data to the SVM in the primal formulation and derive the dual formulation. We show that, for a general constraint based directly on data, selecting the appropriate formulation, the constraint can be formulated as inner products of the input space. Thus, kernels can be applied to expand the solution space to various and more complex spaces e.g. polynomials, without making an explicit feature representation [1]. The support vector machine (SVM) was introduced in [2] and builds on theory for the optimal separating hyperplane [14]. SVMs are most known for their use in classification problems but other uses such

F. Wang et al. (Eds.): MLMI 2012, LNCS 7588, pp. 70–77, 2012.

as regression have been proposed [6,11]. The SVM for regression has been modified to embrace the LASSO constraint for regression [9] but has in this form not been generalized to classification. Other extensions includes different loss functions of the residual [6], or the doubly regularized SVM as a classification version of the elastic net regression [15, 16]. These extensions have not been formulated with kernels added in the dual formulation. In [5], the discriminative direction in an SVM was defined to be the direction which moves a point towards the other class while introducing as little irrelevant change as possible with respect to the classifier function. We present constraints based directly on data and therefore use additional information contained in the data, formulated as inner products and we can apply kernels to obtain non-linear classifiers. In particular, for paired observations imposing orthogonality between the data pair vector and the separating hyperplane reduces the variance of the model. We show that when such a pairing of data exists, the bias/variance trade-off ensures more robust results, while the classification error is statistically comparable to, or better than that of an ordinary SVM. We test the approach on synthetic data and use it to examine shape differences in ear canals with movement of the mandible or the head [3] .

2   Data-Driven Constraint

We derive the SVM formulation with the generalized data-driven constraints and then specialize to a constraint of orthogonality between the separating hyperplane and the paired observations, and introduce an estimate of the pairing noise to indicate model correctness. To embed pairing information into the framework of the SVM we add a regularization term and a penalty function which we choose to be the as it does not weigh outliers as heavily as the ℓ_2-norm. The ℓ_1-norm is preferred as we desire to regularize according to the trend of the data. The SVM formulation is extended with an ℓ_1-norm of $\beta^t \mathbf{A}$ added ($\|\beta^t \mathbf{A}\|_1$), where $\mathbf{A}$ is a $p \times m$ matrix, and where m is the number of explicit constraints on β which is the normal vector to the separating hyperplane. The ℓ_1-norm is not smooth thus, letting $\delta \geq \beta^t \mathbf{A} \geq -\delta$ and minimizing with respect to δ, where δ is a vector of positive constants δ_k. This gives a suitable formulation of the dual problem and ensures that the kernel trick can be applied. We write:

$$\min \frac{1}{2}\|\beta\|^2 + \gamma \sum_{i=1}^{n} \xi_i + \lambda \sum_{k=1}^{m} \delta_k \quad \text{s.t.} \begin{cases} -\delta_k \leq \beta^t \mathbf{a}_k, & \delta_k \geq \beta^t \mathbf{a}_k \quad \forall k \\ y_i(\mathbf{x}_i^t \beta + \beta_0) \geq 1 - \xi_i, & \xi_i \geq 0 \; \forall i \end{cases} \quad (1)$$

where $\mathbf{x}_i$ denotes observation i and is a $1 \times p$ vector, $y_i \in \{-1, 1\}$ is the class indicator for observation i, and ξ_i denotes the amount of misclassification for observation i. Additionally, $\mathbf{a}_k$ denotes the kth column of $\mathbf{A}$, and γ and λ are positive constants. With the Lagrange primal formulation we minimize

$$\frac{1}{2}\|\beta\|^2 + \gamma \sum_{i=1}^{n} \xi_i + \lambda \sum_{k=1}^{m} \delta_k - \sum_{k=1}^{m} \rho_k(\beta^t \mathbf{a}_k + \delta_k) +$$

$$\sum_{k=1}^{m} \rho_k'(\beta^t \mathbf{a}_k - \delta_k) - \sum_{i=1}^{n} \alpha_i[y_i(\mathbf{x}_i^t \beta + \beta_0) - (1 - \xi_i)] - \sum_{i=1}^{n} \mu_i \xi_i \quad (2)$$

Differentiating (2) with respect to β, β_0, ξ_i, δ_k and δ'_k and equating to zero, the following is obtained

$$\beta = \sum_{i=1}^{n} \alpha_i y_i \mathbf{x}_i + \sum_{k=1}^{m} \rho_k \mathbf{a}_k - \sum_{k=1}^{m} \rho'_k \mathbf{a}_k, \ 0 = \sum_{i=1}^{n} \alpha_i y_i, \alpha_i = \gamma - \mu_i, 0 = \lambda - \rho_k - \rho'_k \tag{3}$$

as well as the positivity constraints $\alpha_i, \mu_i, \xi_i \geq 0 \ \forall i$ and $\rho_k, \rho'_k, \delta_k \geq 0 \ \forall k$. By insertion of (3) in (2) we get the dual objective function, i.e.

$$\max \sum_{i=1}^{n} \alpha_i - \frac{1}{2} \sum_{i=1}^{n} \sum_{j=1}^{n} \alpha_i \alpha_j y_i y_j \mathbf{x}_i^t \mathbf{x}_j - \sum_{k=1}^{m} \sum_{i=1}^{n} \alpha_i y_i (\rho'_k - \rho_k) \mathbf{x}_i^t \mathbf{a}_k$$

$$+ \frac{1}{2} \sum_{k=1}^{m} \sum_{l=1}^{m} (\rho'_k - \rho_k)(\rho'_l - \rho_l) \mathbf{a}_k^t \mathbf{a}_l \tag{4}$$

subject to $0 \leq \alpha_i \leq \gamma$, $\sum_{i=1}^{n} \alpha_i y_i = 0$ and $\rho'_k + \rho_k = \lambda$ yields the desired result. Additional to (3) the Karush-Kuhn-Tucker (KKT) conditions [8] are given as:

$$\rho_k(\beta^t \mathbf{a}_k + \delta_k) = 0, \ \rho'_k(\beta^t \mathbf{a}_k - \delta_k) = 0, \ \alpha_i[y_i(\mathbf{x}_i^t \beta + \beta_0) - (1 - \xi_i)] = 0,$$
$$\mu_i \xi_i = 0, \text{ and } y_i(\mathbf{x}_i^t \beta) - (1 - \xi_i) \geq 0. \tag{5}$$

From (5) it is seen that the points on the margin ($\alpha_i = 0$) can be used to calculate β_0. The hyperplane is written as (for centered data, where $\beta_0 = 0$)

$$f(\mathbf{x}) = \sum_{i=1}^{n} \alpha_i y_i \mathbf{x}^t \mathbf{x}_i + \sum_{k=1}^{m} (\rho'_k - \rho_k) \mathbf{x}^t \mathbf{a}_k \quad . \tag{6}$$

If $\mathbf{A}$ is defined in the input space $\mathbf{x}$, that is $\mathbf{A} = \mathbf{XB}$, where $\mathbf{X}$ is a matrix representing all observations, then $\mathbf{x}^t \mathbf{a}_k$ is an inner product. Since kernels are applicable to all inner products of the input space $\mathbf{x}$, kernels can be applied such that non-linear separations can be obtained (also known as the *kernel trick*), otherwise the feature space of the kernel $\phi(\mathbf{x})$ must be explicitly known. When the constraint on β is not a function of $\mathbf{x}$ it is desirable to know the feature space explicitly in order to add a meaningful constraint. A special case is when $\mathbf{A} = \mathbf{I}$; corresponding to an elastic net formulation of [15, 16] where both the Ridge (ℓ_2-norm [7]) and the LASSO (ℓ_1-norm [12]) constraints are added.

2.1   General Constraints

In general the matrix $\mathbf{A}$ can be any matrix, it can form the derivatives of β like in Fused Lasso [13], it can perform feature selection with $\mathbf{A} = \mathbf{I}$ under the ℓ_1-norm [16] or it can be dependent on data. However, when $\mathbf{A}$ is independent of data, the kernel trick cannot be applied. When the matrix $\mathbf{A}$ is dependent on the data $\mathbf{x}$ then $\mathbf{A}^t \mathbf{A}$ can be written as purely inner products of the data and therefore the kernel trick is applicable, i.e. $\mathbf{A} = \mathbf{XB}$, where $\mathbf{B}$ is some $n \times m$ matrix. It is important to consider whether the introduced constraint is meaningful in kernel space.

2.2   Constraints for Paired Observations

Consider data with two classes of paired observations, also called matched points. Matched points are: an observation in one class which has a natural pairing with an observation in the second class, thus not independent. An example is the same individual observed at two stages of a disease progression. We assume the pairing is known apriori. Separating the two classes with a traditional clustering methods or classifiers [4,6] the information about the pairing is not exploited. The mean maximum margin classifier [10] resembles the ℓ_2-norm on the constraint on the vectors formed by the observations, i.e. a maximum likelihood estimate using the ℓ_2-norm, however, we estimate the weighted median as we use ℓ_1-norm and the length of the vectors formed by the observation pairs in the kernel space. In addition we estimate β as a part of the optimization problem and not just as the mean as in the simple case of the mean maximum margin classifier. Specifically for the orthogonality constraint (OC) we set $\mathbf{A} = (\mathbf{X_1} - \mathbf{X_2})$, where $\mathbf{X_1}$ and $\mathbf{X_2}$ are matched points sets. The hyperplane for the OC-SVM using ℓ_1-norm is given by

$$f(\mathbf{x}) = \sum_{i=1}^{n} \alpha_i y_i \mathbf{x}^t \mathbf{x}_i + \sum_{k=1}^{n/2} (\rho'_k - \rho_k) \mathbf{x}^t (\mathbf{x_1}_k - \mathbf{x_2}_k) \ . \tag{7}$$

The optimization problem is expressed in terms of inner products in the input space, and therefore the kernel trick can be applied. The inner product emphasizes large angles and gives weight to outliers, i.e. directions which are far from orthogonal to the separating hyperplane making the ℓ_1-norm preferable. As $\|\beta\|$ is similar for all pairings, the length of $\mathbf{a}$ acts like a weight where large differences in terms of distance between observations are weighted proportionally to this distance. To circumvent this, the directional vectors of $\mathbf{A}$ could be normalized. However, we hypothesize that large deformations in the ear canals actually affects comfort from wearing hearing aids and it is of interest to put more emphasis on these individuals specifically. To evaluate the quality of the constraint, i.e. obtain an estimate of the pairing noise, we compute the standard deviation of the difference vectors between the paired observations. This is normalized with the within class standard deviation for each variable, making it comparable across the simulations. This indicate the model correctness, if the OC-SVM is applicable for the given data. The measure is defined as $\sigma_{pairing} = \frac{2}{p} \sum_{j=1}^{p} \frac{std(A_j)}{(std(X_{1j}) + std(X_{2j}))}$.

3   Experiments

The performance of the OC-SVM was tested on synthetic as well as real data and compared to the performance of the standard SVM. The synthetic data serves to visualize the performance of the OC-SVM as well as to test the performance for various numbers of observations and dimensions. Finally the methods were tested on 172 ear canal impression scans from 67 individuals.

3.1 Synthetic Data

The synthetic data was generated from a normal distribution with standard deviation one (group one). To simulate the coherence between the two groups, all points in group one were translated by $3\,p^{-0.5}$ along each axis in the positive direction (group two). p is the dimension of the input space. Noise with standard deviations $\sigma = 0.0, 0.3, 0.6$ and 0.9 was added to group two, called the *pairing noise* in the following. As the pairing noise is increased, the information that the OC-constraint relies on deteriorates. Figure 1 shows the distribution of the two generated classes in 2D for 1000 data points in each class, with no pairing noise added, and pairing noise of standard deviation 0.9. To illustrate the OC-SVM, the separating lines for the SVM and the OC-SVM are plotted in two dimensions; see Figure 1. It show that the OC-SVM reduces the rotational variance of the solution, but introduces a small bias, i.e. the hyperplanes shift parallel. A simualtion study was conducted to test the performance of OC-SVM in comparison to SVM. Here, 1000 paired samples were generated from which the training and test sets were drawn. To properly test the method the regularization parameters were changed such that the standard SVM estimates the optimal separating hyperplane including all samples. To reduce the number of parameters we found $\lambda = \gamma \cdot 0.10$ using leave-one-out cross-validation [6]. Samples were generated in 2, 5, 10, 100, 500, 1000 and 10000 dimensions and the models were built on 2, 5, 10, 50 and 100 paired samples for each dimension. The experiment was repeated 100 times for each combination, where the SVM and the OC-SVM were built on the same samples. The training error and the test error were measured for each method and a hypothesis of the test error being

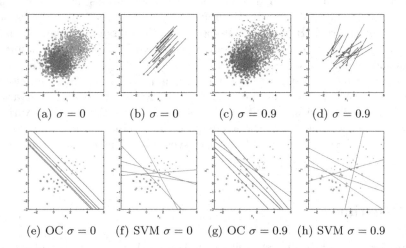

(a) $\sigma = 0$ (b) $\sigma = 0$ (c) $\sigma = 0.9$ (d) $\sigma = 0.9$

(e) OC $\sigma = 0$ (f) SVM $\sigma = 0$ (g) OC $\sigma = 0.9$ (h) SVM $\sigma = 0.9$

Fig. 1. (a-d)The synthetic data with added pairing noise to the translation from group one to group, and 40 samples with the vectors between each paired sample. (e-h) The difference between the OC-SVM (e & g) and the SVM (f & h) on six outcomes of simulated data sets. The distance between the groups is 3 ($3\sqrt{0.5}$ in each direction).

equal for the two methods was tested. The solutions of the OC-SVM had far less variance than the normal SVM, thus the variance over 100 solutions was reduced 80% compared to the variations of the solutions from the SVM. The simulations showed that the added information in general gave much more stability to the OC-SVM compared to the SVM. Expectedly, when the noise of the pairing is large, $\sigma = 0.9$, the gain in stability was neglectable. In the simulation, the OC-SVM gave significantly lower misclassification rates when the number of observations was the same as the number of dimensions and down to around 1/10 including simulations with pairing noise.

3.2   Ear Data

The purpose of the collected ear data is to examine and quantify shape changes and survey the resulting influences on comfort for hearing aid user. This is particularly important if the ear exhibits a large change due to jaw movement, information which is not passed along with the impression. The variation between individual ears is much larger than the deformation separating two positions from the same individual, thus the chance of a better than random overall classification rate is small. As benchmark, audiologists are not capable of classifying a single impression as open or closed mouth. [3] showed that every impression pair exhibits a significant change from open to closed mouth, but only 10-20% of these patients experience comfort problems. The impressions were obtained from each individuals right ear; one with closed mouth, one with open mouth and one with the head turned to the left. The impressions were made by the same audiologist to ensure consistency and scanned by the same operator on a 3D-laser scanner. Figure 2 shows the resulting surface scan of an ear impression. The data analyzed consists of 42 triplet pairs of impressions for the three settings: open mouth, closed mouth and turning the head, plus an additional 25 pairs for the open and closed mouth (67 pairs in total for open and closed mouth setting). All impressions were registered [3] giving 4356 points of correspondence in 3D thus each ear is represented as a 13068 dimensional vector. We permuted the order of the observations 500 times and each time trained on the first $n - 2$ impressions and tested the last two, one from each class, thereby obtaining measures of classification rates, variance in the model, and significance of improvement. This was performed for classification between open mouth and closed mouth

(a) 2 perspectives   (b) Difference

Fig. 2. Typical example of an ear impression from two perspectives and an example of the difference map between an open and a closed mouth impression

and closed mouth and turning of the head. The average normalized estimated pairing noise was $\sigma_{pairing} = 0.02$ thus the OC-SVM contained sufficient prior knowledge. Between open and closed mouth, the average training errors were 0% for the SVM and 38% for the OC-SVM. Both the SVM and the OC-SVM had average test errors of 40% indicating that the SVM overfit the training data to a much higher degree than the OC-SVM. The most important result is that none of the large deformations capable of causing physical discomfort were mis-classified. For the majority of the misclassifications the deformations were small (> 0.7 mm). Comparing the average variance of the results obtained with the OC-SVM and SVM respectively shows that the additional constraint reduced the variance of the normalized β by 50%. The overall average variances were $1.16 \cdot 10^{-5}$ and $7.00 \cdot 10^{-6}$ for the SVM and the OC-SVM, respectively. Further-more the variance of the estimates of the intercept for the OC-SVM is 100 times lower than the SVM, and the variation in the length of the parameter vector is 3000 times lower than that of the SVM. From the resulting normal vector to the separating hyperplane, the ear canal and the shape of Concha Cymba seemed to have importance in the classification. The general areas which change when the mouth is opened are thus also the ear canal and the Concha Cymba. Additionally, we applied the OC-SVM to distinguish between closed mouth im-pressions and turning of the head impressions. The results showed that the SVM had an average correct test classification of 67% and the OC-SVM around the same. However, the formulation provided above allows us to use kernels. When we applied a polynomial kernel of degree 2, we increased the average test classi-fication success by an additional 3% to roughly 70% for the OC-SVM only. We also tried to apply the OC-constraint under the ℓ_2-norm but were not able to achieve classifications better than random.

4 Conclusion

A classification model based on the SVM with additional constraints based on knowledge of data has been derived. For the constraint of orthogonality on paired ear data, the variance of the separating hyperplane was reduced by up to 50%, leading to more robust solutions. For the open-closed mouth case the majority of the potentially problematic cases where identified. For the turning of the head the kernel trick was applied with a decrease in classification error of 3% as a result. In both cases the performance of the OC-SVM was equally good or better compared to the SVM. This is of great importance, in particular when few observations are available and the variance in general is known to be high due to the curse of dimensionality. Furthermore, the classification rates for the OC-SVM proved to be significantly better or comparable to those of the ordinary SVM. For the OC-SVM the paired observations were automatically weighted according to the Euclidian length of the difference vector between the paired observations. That is, paired observations with large differences have a higher weight in the constraint of orthogonality than paired observations with subtle differences. In extension to this, a general framework for adding data-specific constraints to the

SVM was derived in this paper. The framework makes it easy to use, underlying a priori knowledge of data to obtain robust solutions for classification problems. The framework may also be used to obtain other desired properties, such as sparseness or correlation between variables.

References

1. Aizerman, M., Braverman, E., Rozonoer, L.: Theoretical foundations of the potential function method in pattern recognition learning. Automation and Remote Control 25, 821–837 (1964)
2. Boser, B., Guyon, I., Vapnik, V.: A training algorithm for optimal margin classifiers. In: Fifth Annual Workshop on Computational Learning Theory, pp. 144–152 (1992)
3. Darkner, S., Larsen, R., Paulsen, R.R.: Analysis of Deformation of the Human Ear and Canal Caused by Mandibular Movement. In: Ayache, N., Ourselin, S., Maeder, A. (eds.) MICCAI 2007, Part II. LNCS, vol. 4792, pp. 801–808. Springer, Heidelberg (2007)
4. Duda, R.O., Hart, P.E., Stork, D.G.: Pattern Classification. John Wiley & Sons (2001)
5. Golland, P.: Discriminative direction for kernel classifiers. In: NIPS, pp. 745–752 (2001)
6. Hastie, T., Tibshirani, R., Friedman, J.: The Elements of Statistical Learning. Springer (2001)
7. Hoerl, A.E., Kennard, R.W.: Ridge regression: Biased estimation for nonorthogonal problems. Technometrics 12, 55–67 (1970)
8. Karush, W.: Minima of Functions of Several Variables with Inequalities as Side Constraints. Master's thesis, Univ. of Chicago (1939)
9. Li, F., Yang, Y., Xing, E.: From lasso regression to feature vector machine. In: Weiss, Y., Schölkopf, B., Platt, J. (eds.) Advances in Neural Information Processing Systems 18, pp. 779–786. MIT Press, Cambridge (2006)
10. Schölkopf, B., Smola, A.J.: Learning with Kernels: Support Vector Machines, Regularization, Optimization, and Beyond. MIT Press (2002)
11. Shawe-Taylor, J., Cristianini, N.: Kernel Methods for Pattern Analysis. Cambridge University Press, UK (2004)
12. Tibshirani, R.: Regression shrinkage and selection via the lasso. J. R. Statist. Soc. B 58(1), 267–288 (1996)
13. Tibshirani, R., Saunders, M., Rosset, S., Zhu, J., Knight, K.: Sparsity and smoothness via the fused lasso. J. R. Statist. Soc. B 1(67), 91–106 (2006)
14. Vapnik, V.: The Nature of Statistical Learning Theory, 2nd edn. Springer, New York (1999)
15. Wang, L., Zhu, J., Zou, H.: The doubly regularized support vector machine. Statistica Sinica 16, 589–615 (2006)
16. Zou, H., Hastie, T.: Regularization and variable selection via the elastic net. J. R. Statist. Soc. B 67(pt. 2), 301–320 (2005)

Towards Improving the Accuracy of Sensorless Freehand 3D Ultrasound by Learning

Juliette Conrath and Catherine Laporte

Dept. of Electrical Engineering, École de technologie supérieure, Montreal, Canada
juliette.conrath.1@ens.etsmtl.ca, catherine.laporte@etsmtl.ca

Abstract. Sensorless freehand 3D ultrasound (US) exploits the correlation between pairs of images in order to track the rigid motion of the US probe without an external position sensor. Conventionally, in-plane motion is compensated by maximizing image correlation. Out-of-plane motion is then estimated using a calibrated model of elevational speckle decorrelation. This approach is prone to systematic error due to interactions between the effects of in-plane and out-of-plane motion components on speckle decorrelation. This paper proposes to establish an error correction model using relevance vector regression and a database of image pairs with known probe motion. Preliminary results on synthetic US image pairs show a statistically significant reduction in mean target registration error, illustrating the promise of the new approach.

1 Introduction

Freehand 3D ultrasound (US) is a protocol for acquiring 3D US data using a conventional 2D probe swept manually over the area of interest. The freehand protocol offers a wider field of view than dedicated 3D probes, while exploiting 2D technology widely and cheaply available in the clinic. In order to reconstruct volumes from 2D images, it is necessary to know their relative positions. Typically, this is achieved by tracking the probe using an optical or electromagnetic position sensor. This decreases the unique flexibility intrinsic to US imaging and has somewhat limited widespread use of the technique [17].

An alternative is to track probe motion using the images themselves. Since in freehand 3D US, probe motion is primarily elevational, one can exploit speckle decorrelation for this purpose [2,16]. Indeed, due to the finite width of the US beam, speckle patterns in nearby images are correlated. Under Rayleigh scattering conditions, a one-to-one, probe-specific relationship exists between image correlation and elevational translation which can be used for tracking. For perfectly aligned parallel frames, this method is very accurate. It can also be adapted to work accurately outside Rayleigh scattering conditions [3,13].

Unfortunately, freehand motion does not produce pure elevational translations of the probe. Thus, in-plane motion and out-of-plane rotations must also be estimated. Housden et al. [6] do this by first compensating in-plane motion using a correlation-based image registration algorithm and then computing out-of-plane motion by combining elevational translation estimates at different image

F. Wang et al. (Eds.): MLMI 2012, LNCS 7588, pp. 78–85, 2012.

locations. However, this leads to systematic inaccuracies, particularly when the probe trajectory differs significantly from a pure elevational translation.

Indeed, in-plane motion and out-of-plane rotations act as nuisance motions for decorrelation-based probe tracking by further decorrelating the speckle patterns in a manner not predicted by the elevational speckle decorrelation model. This corrupts out-of-plane motion estimates. The accuracy of in-plane motion estimates is also compromised. Although common similarity measures provide fairly accurate registration for pure translational in-plane motion [1,5], it is well known that speckle decorrelation caused by out-of-plane motion affects their reliability. Moreover, due to particularities of the US image formation process, rotational motion also decreases the reliability of both image similarity-based registration methods and decorrelation-based out-of-plane motion tracking techniques [9,14]. Previous approaches towards addressing these problems rely on external sensors [7,10] or registration to another imaging modality [11].

In this paper, we hypothesize that a solution to this problem can be learned by studying the behaviour of conventional image registration and speckle decorrelation methods on synthetic image sequences with known probe motion and characteristics similar to those expected in a real freehand 3D scan. The proposed overall methodology is illustrated in Fig. 1. First, a database of synthetic US

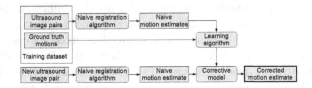

Fig. 1. Block diagram of the proposed learning-based approach

image pairs is generated with varied, known probe motions. A block correlation-based tracking algorithm similar to [6] is applied to these data (section 2). The resulting motion estimates and corresponding ground truth motions are then used to train an error correction model (section 3). Improved motion estimates can then be obtained for new image pairs, as illustrated by preliminary experiments on synthetic images (section 4).

2 Block Correlation-Based Image Registration

Our goal is to estimate the rigid probe motion between a reference image and a moving image in an US image sequence. Fig. 2 (left) shows the coordinate system. Motion is decomposed into in-plane components, i.e. translations along the x and y axes, and rotation about the z axis (θ_z), and out-of-plane components, i.e. translation along the z axis and rotations about the y and x axes (θ_y and θ_x, respectively). This section describes an image-based tracking method based

Fig. 2. Coordinate system (left) and subdivision of images into 10×10 patches (right)

on separate in-plane and out-of-plane registration steps. It is similar in spirit to [16,5,6]. The output of this method is what we hope to improve using learning.

In order to limit the influence of external factors when evaluating our new approach, we make the following assumptions throughout the paper: (1) There is no physiological motion, i.e. decorrelation results only from probe motion. This assumption is implicit in sensor-based tracking methods. (2) The images consist entirely of fully developed speckle, or elevational motion estimates have been corrected using adaptive techniques such as [3,13]. (3) The image planes do not intersect each other. Solutions for intersection detection have been proposed in [6,12] and could be eventually be implemented in our approach.

To enable out-of-plane motion estimation, a depth-dependent, transducer-specific elevational speckle decorrelation model is first calibrated [20]. To this end, the image plane is divided into n non-overlapping patches (Fig. 2, right). During calibration, a speckle phantom is scanned at fixed regular elevational intervals and the normalized cross-correlation between pairs of corresponding patches is measured. A piecewise linear decorrelation curve (Fig. 3, right) is then fitted to these measurements and associated with each patch.

After calibration, new pairs of images can be registered both in-plane and out-of-plane. The images are divided into the same n patches as for calibration, and the motion between two images is described as a set of 3D translation vectors associated with each patch center. Each patch-wise 3D translation vector is comprised of two in-plane components (in x and y) and one out-of-plane component (in z). These are computed using the normalized cross-correlation array between corresponding patches on the moving and reference images:

$$\rho(u,v) = \frac{\sum_{x,y}[f(x,y) - \bar{f}_{u,v}][g(x-u, y-v) - \bar{g}]}{(\sum_{x,y}[f(x,y) - \bar{f}_{u,v}]^2 \sum_{x,y}[g(x-u, y-v) - \bar{g}]^2)^{0.5}}, \qquad (1)$$

where (u,v) is the potential offset in (x,y), g is the patch to register, $\bar{g}$ is its mean intensity, f is the corresponding zone on the reference image and $\bar{f}_{u,v}$ is its mean intensity under the window containing the patch positioned at (u,v).

From $\rho(u,v)$, we compute two pieces of information for each patch : (1) the position of the maximum value, which provides an approximation to its in-plane translations in the x and y directions, and (2) the maximum value itself, which is used to estimate its elevational translation z via the decorrelation curve established by calibration. The process is illustrated in Fig. 3. To localize the required

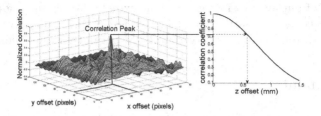

Fig. 3. 3D translation estimation from normalized cross-correlation measures on a single image patch

normalized cross-correlation peak to sub-pixel precision, we use a fast frequency domain up-sampling technique [4]. The rigid motion parameters x, y, z, θ_z, θ_y, θ_x are then estimated from the point correspondences defined by the resulting n 3D translation vectors using a conventional Procrustes alignment procedure [21].

This approach is somewhat inaccurate as it does not account for the mutual influences of the different types of motion on the correlation measurements. However, these inaccuracies are largely systematic: they arise from the peculiarities of the US image formation process. Thus, it is not unreasonable to expect that a model can be trained to account for some of these phenomena, as explained next.

3   Learning-Based Correction of Registration Errors

Applying the algorithm of section 2 to a database of synthetic image pairs provides data for studying its (mis-)behaviour and inferring the relationship between the estimated probe motion and the true probe motion (known by design). A relevance vector machine (RVM) [19] was chosen for this purpose, as it typically provides both sparse and accurate regression models.

Our task requires a multi-dimensional output (one dimension for each motion parameter to be corrected). Thus, we use the multivariate extension of RVMs proposed in [18]. In this framework, the relationship between the true motion parameters, $\mathbf{x} = \{x, y, z, \theta_x, \theta_y, \theta_z\}$ and those estimated using the algorithm of section 2, $\hat{\mathbf{x}} = \{\hat{x}, \hat{y}, \hat{z}, \hat{\theta}_x, \hat{\theta}_y, \hat{\theta}_z\}$ is modeled as a linear combination of Gaussian basis functions centered at each of the input points, listed in ϕ:

$$\mathbf{x} = \mathbf{W}\phi(\hat{\mathbf{x}}) + \epsilon, \tag{2}$$

where $\mathbf{W}$ is a matrix of weights associated with the different basis functions and output variables and ϵ is a zero-mean Gaussian noise vector with diagonal covariance matrix $\mathbf{S}$. As in the original RVM formulation [19], assuming a Gaussian prior for the weights (with diagonal covariance matrix $\mathbf{A}$) reduces the number of relevant basis functions to a small number, thereby yielding a sparse and generalizable regression model. In the multivariate extension [18], the optimization of $\mathbf{W}$, $\mathbf{S}$ and $\mathbf{A}$ is performed such as to compute a single set of relevance vectors for the entire set of output dimensions. To some extent, this accounts for possible correlations between the output variables. We found this to improve accuracy when compared to using one mono-variate RVM per output dimension.

4   Experiments

To evaluate the potential of our method, we generated a large number of synthetic US sequences with known probe trajectories using Field II [8]. A virtual fully developed speckle phantom was used for all sequences and scanned with a virtual 3.5 MHz linear transducer. The resulting RF vectors were envelope detected, log-compressed and scan-converted to simulate acquisition by a clinical scanner. This created B-mode images of 300×450 pixels, which were then decompressed using the algorithm of [15].

One sequence of 100 B-scans was created using pure elevational translation of the probe by increments of 0.1 mm. This sequence was used to find elevational decorrelation curves for each of a grid of 10×10 image patches, as described in section 2. A preliminary study showed that the number of patches has little incidence on the results, and 10×10 seems to give the best overall results.

A dataset of 400 image pairs was then prepared to test the proposed learning-based algorithm. A random rigid transformation was used to move the virtual probe in each sequence and recorded as ground truth. z was exponentially distributed with a mean of 0.15 mm, x and y were Gaussian-distributed with mean 0 mm and standard deviation 0.15 mm, and the rotation parameters $\theta_x, \theta_y, \theta_z$ were Gaussian-distributed with mean $0°$ and standard deviation $0.1°$. Image pairs with intersections were then removed from the dataset, providing a usable database of 290 non intersecting image pairs. These distributions were chosen based on the assumption of slow, mostly elevational probe motion which would typically occur in a freehand 3D scan with high frame rate.

A block correlation-based estimate of probe motion (section 2) was computed for each image pair. The multivariate RVM describing the relationships between these estimates and the ground truth transformations was trained using the publicly available MATLAB implementation of [18]. Five-fold cross-validation was performed on the 290 image pair database. Probe motion estimates obtained before and after learning-based correction were compared to the ground truth using the mean target registration error (mTRE) evaluated at the image patch centers. Fig. 4 (right) shows a box plot of the cross-validation mTRE before and after learning-based correction for the 290 random motion sequences. These results show a substantial reduction in mTRE after learning-based correction, which was revealed to be statistically significant ($p < 0.001$) by a paired t-test. The variance of the global error also appears to be greatly reduced by the proposed method. Fig. 4 (left) shows box plots of the error on each of the motion components, where the error is defined as the difference between the estimated value and the ground truth value. These results show that improvement in overall registration (i.e. in the mTRE) largely results from reduction of the errors in z. This motion component is most frequently over-estimated by the block

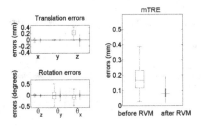

Fig. 4. Results obtained for the 290 6 DOF image pairs. Box plots of the errors on each of the motion components (left) and of the mTRE (right) obtained with and without learning (thin and wide boxes, respectively).

correlation-based registration approach, which incorrectly attributes all image decorrelation to out-of-plane motion, whereas it is partially caused by the in-plane motion components (in particular, θ_z). Improvements in the variance of the error are also observed for the rotational out-of-plane components θ_x and θ_y, indicating that the learning-based correction yields more reliable results.

To further assess the behaviour of the learning-based approach, it was tested on more image pairs with constrained motion. 104 image pairs with purely translational motion components in the range [0.1, 0.5] mm (in x, y and z) were generated, as well as 125 image pairs with only in-plane motion components in the range [0.1, 0.5] mm (in x, y) and [0.1, 1.0]° (in θ_z). The results are shown in box plot form in Fig. 5(a,b). The learning-based approach correctly tends to decrease the estimate of z in order to compensate for the block correlation-based algorithm's tendency to produce over-estimates in the presence of decorrelation induced by in-plane motion. Since the width of the elevational decorrelation curve varies with depth, over-estimates of z also vary with depth when no learning is used, causing incorrect estimates of tilt (θ_x). These are well corrected by the learning-based regression model. In specific cases (Fig. 5 (a)), the learning-based error correction model slightly overcompensates for over-estimates of z.

While these results are very encouraging, there are motions for which learning-based correction does not perform as well. In particular, Fig. 5 (c) shows the results of an experiment where the algorithms were applied to 10 image pairs generated with fixed $z = 0.4$ mm and increasing probe tilt (θ_x). In this case, the block correlation-based algorithm incorrectly interprets the tilting motion as elevational translation, and the learned model, in turn, corrects z well, but lacks information to correctly recover θ_x. While this situation represents a minority of cases (much better results are obtained in the general 6 degree of freedom case, see Fig. 4), there is room for improvement. One potential path lies in the use of multiple speckle decorrelation models, calibrated for different fixed tilting angles, such as were described in [7]. In our framework, these could be used to obtain multiple block correlation-based motion estimates and provide the learning algorithm with additional information related to θ_x.

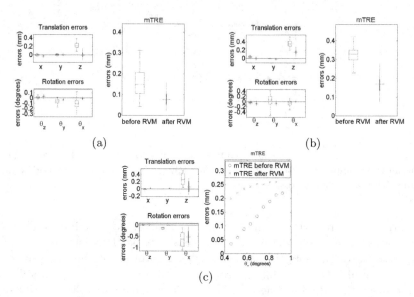

Fig. 5. Errors on each of the motion components (left) and mTRE (right) obtained before and after learning (wide and thin boxes, respectively) on sequences with (a) only translational motion, (b) only in-plane motion and (c) fixed elevational translation and varying tilt (rotation about the x axis).

5   Conclusions

We described a learning-based error correction method for improving the tracking accuracy of block correlation-based sensorless freehand 3D US. Our results show that the proposed method significantly reduces the over-estimation of out-of-plane motion that occurs using conventional block correlation-based methods, with large improvements in mTRE over a large dataset of image pairs with varied motions. However, there remains some inaccuracies in the presence of tilting motion. Future work will aim towards disambiguation of the z and θ_x motion components, generalisation of the approach to arbitrary transducers, experiments on real imagery and extension to non-Rayleigh scattering conditions.

Acknowledgment. This work was funded by NSERC.

References

1. Bohs, L.N., Trahey, G.E.: A novel method for angle independent ultrasonic imaging of blood flow and tissue motion. IEEE T. Biomed. Eng. 38(3), 280–286 (1991)
2. Chen, J.-F., et al.: Determination of scan-plane motion using speckle decorrelation: theoretical considerations and initial test. Int. J. Imaging Syst. Technol. 8(1), 38–44 (1997)

3. Gee, A.H., et al.: Sensorless freehand 3D ultrasound in real tissue: speckle decorrelation without fully developped speckle. Med. Image Anal. 10(2), 137–149 (2006)
4. Guizar-Sicairos, M., et al.: Efficient subpixel image registration algorithms. Opt. Lett. 33(2), 156–158 (2008)
5. Housden, R.J., et al.: Sub-sample interpolation strategies for sensorless freehand 3D ultrasound. Ultrasound Med. Biol. 32(12), 1897–1904 (2006)
6. Housden, R.J., et al.: Sensorless reconstruction of unconstrained freehand 3D ultrasound data. Ultrasound Med. Biol. 33(3), 408–419 (2007)
7. Housden, R.J., et al.: Rotational motion in sensorless freehand three-dimensional ultrasound. Ultrasonics 48(5), 412–422 (2008)
8. Jensen, J.A.: Field: a program for simulating ultrasound systems. In: Proc. Nordic-Baltic Conf. Biomedical Imaging, vol. 4, pp. 351–353 (1996)
9. Kallel, F., et al.: Speckle motion artifact under tissue rotation. IEEE T. Ultrason. Ferr. 41(1), 105–122 (1994)
10. Lang, A., et al.: Fusion of electromagnetic tracking with speckle-tracked 3D freehand ultrasound using an unscented Kalman filter. In: Proc. SPIE Med. Imaging, vol. 7265, pp. 72651A-1–72651A-12 (2009)
11. Lang, A., et al.: Multi-modal registration of speckle-tracked freehand 3D ultrasound to CT in the lumbar spine. Med. Image Anal. 16, 675–686 (2012)
12. Laporte, C., Arbel, T.: Combinatorial and probabilistic fusion of noisy correlation measurements for untracked freehand 3D ultrasound. IEEE T. Med. Imaging 27(7), 984–994 (2008)
13. Laporte, C., Arbel, T.: Learning to estimate out-of-plane motion in ultrasound imagery of real tissue. Med. Image Anal. 15, 202–213 (2011)
14. Li, P.-C., et al.: Tissue motion and elevational speckle decorrelation in freehand 3D ultrasound. Ultrason. Imaging 24, 1–12 (2002)
15. Prager, R.W., et al.: Decompression and speckle detection for ultrasound images using the homodyned k-distribution. Patt. Recogn. Lett. 24, 705–713 (2003)
16. Prager, R.W., et al.: Sensorless freehand 3-D ultrasound using regression of the echo intensity. Ultrasound Med. Biol. 29(3), 437–446 (2003)
17. Prager, R.W., et al.: Three dimensional ultrasound imaging. P. I. Mech. Eng. H 24(2), 193–223 (2010)
18. Thayananthan, A., Navaratnam, R., Stenger, B., Torr, P., Cipolla, R.: Multivariate Relevance Vector Machines for Tracking. In: Leonardis, A., Bischof, H., Pinz, A. (eds.) ECCV 2006. LNCS, vol. 3953, pp. 124–138. Springer, Heidelberg (2006)
19. Tipping, M.E.: Sparse Bayesian learning and the relevance vector machine. J. Machine Learning Research 1, 211–244 (2001)
20. Tuthill, T.A., et al.: Automated three-dimensional US frame positioning computed from elevational speckle decorrelation. Radiology 209(2), 575–582 (1998)
21. Umeyama, S.: Least-squares estimation of transformation parameters between two point patterns. IEEE T. Pattern Anal. 13(4), 376–380 (1991)

A Novel 3D Joint MGRF Framework for Precise Lung Segmentation

Behnoush Abdollahi[1,2], Ahmed Soliman[1], A.C. Civelek[3], X.-F. Li[3],
G. Gimel'farb[4], and Ayman El-Baz[1,*]

[1] BioImaging Laboratory, Bioengineering Department, University of Louisville,
Louisville, KY, USA
[2] Department of Computer Engineering and Computer Science, University of
Louisville, Louisville, KY, USA
[3] Radiology Department, University of Louisville, Louisville, KY, USA
[4] Department of Computer Science, University of Auckland, Auckland, New Zealand
aselba01@louisville.edu

Abstract. A new framework implemented on NVIDIA Graphics Processing Units (GPU) using CUDA for the precise segmentation of lung tissues from Computed Tomography (CT) is proposed. The CT images, Gaussian Scale Space (GSS) data generation using Gaussian Kernels (GKs), and desired maps of regions (lung and the other chest tissues) are described by a joint Markov-Gibbs Random Field (MGRF) model of independent image signals and interdependent region labels implemented on GPU. The initial segmentation from the original and the generated GSS CT images is based on the Linear Combination of Discrete Gaussian (LCDG) models; The initial segmentation is obtained from the original and the generated GSS CT images; then they are iteratively refined using a parallel MGRF model implemented on GPU with analytically estimated potentials. Finally, these initial segmentations are fused together using a Bayesian fusion approach to get the final segmentation of the lung region. Experiments on eleven real data sets based on Dice Similarity Coefficient (DSC) metric confirms the high accuracy of the proposed approach. The execution time results show that our algorithm takes about three seconds which is about 10^3 times faster when compared to a naive single threaded implementation on CPU.

1 Introduction

Lung cancer is the leading cause of cancer death in the USA. The most recent statistics showed that in 2011, 156,940 Americans died from lung cancer, which accounts for 27% of all cancer deaths in the USA [1]. Early diagnosis can improve the effectiveness of treatment and increase the patient's chance of survival. Segmentation of the lung tissues from CT images is a crucial step in developing any non-invasive Computer-Assisted Diagnostic (CAD) system for early diagnosis of

---

* Corresponding author.

F. Wang et al. (Eds.): MLMI 2012, LNCS 7588, pp. 86–93, 2012.

lung cancer. Lung tissue, in CT images, appears as dark regions. Thus, this contrast between the lung and chest is the basis for the majority of the segmentation schemes; however some lung tissues such as arteries, veins, bronchi, bronchioles, and lung nodules (if they exist) have gray-levels very close to the chest tissues. This overlap of the chest and some of the lung signals must be differentiated in order to achieve an accurate segmentation of the lung tissue.

In the literature, many techniques were developed for lung segmentation in CT images. Hu et al. [2] proposed an optimal gray level thresholding technique to select a threshold value based on the unique characteristics of the data set; then morphological operations are used to fill the holes that can be missed in the initial threshold-based segmentation. A segmentation-by-registration scheme was proposed by Sluimer et al. [3] for the automated segmentation of the pathological lung in CT. Deformable boundary models such as active contours (snakes), level sets, or geodesic active contours are also used to segment the lung region from CT images. Snakes can extract a region of interest (ROI) or locate an object boundary. Itai et al. [4] extracted the lung region with a 2D parametric deformable model using the lung borders as an external force. A 2D geometric active contour (Silveira et al. [5]) was initialized at the boundary of the chest region, and then it was automatically split into two regions representing the left and right lungs. Won et al. [6] segmented the lung region with a 2D geodesic active contour using the prior information about the lung area as a stopping criterion rather than the border of the lung as the external force. The main drawbacks of the deformable model-based segmentation are the excessive sensitivity to initialization and the inability of traditional external forces (e.g., based on edges, gray levels, etc.) to capture natural inhomogeneity in the lung regions. As a result, it is hard to provide an adequate guidance to the deformable model to achieve accurate segmentation. Additional details about lung segmentation techniques are in the survey by Sluimer et al. [7]. In recent years, many works in the field of medical image analysis have started utilizing GPUs in problems with heavy computations. Yu et al. [8] presented an improved Gibbs sampling method on GPU to accelerate motif finding, which is an important problem in bioinformatics that requires more and more computational capabilities due to high computational complexity of motif finding. To the best of our knowledge, this is the first work that implements Gibbs distribution as a texture model based on MGRF on CUDA to be used in image processing field.

This paper details the CT images, generated GSS data, and desired maps of regions by a parallel joint MGRF model of independent image signals, implemented using CUDA, that accounts for the spatial interactions between region labels (see Fig. 1). We follow a parallel programming approach in the implementation of the joint MGRF model. Recently, the GSS theory has received a lot of attention due to its solid mathematical framework of analysis of 2D/3D data in the spatial domain. We use three different scales of 3D GKs (see Fig. 3) to reduce the inhomogeneity that exists in chest CT images. Fig. 2 demonstrates an example of the original and smoothed CT images using the 3D GKs. As demonstrated in Fig. 1, the original image data and the generated GSS data are

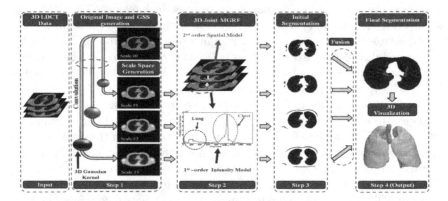

Fig. 1. The proposed framework for lung segmentation from CT images

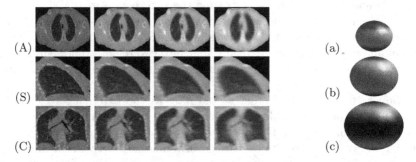

Fig. 2. Original and smoothed CT images using 3D GKs shown in Fig. 3. Results projected onto 2D axial (A), sagittal (S), and coronal (C) planes for visualization. The first column represents the original CT images; the second column represents the smoothed CT images using the 3D GK in Fig. 3(a); the third column represents the smoothed CT images using the 3D GK in Fig. 3(b); and the fourth column represents the smoothed CT images using the 3D GK in Fig.3(c).

Fig. 3. Three different scales of 3D GKs

segmented by the LCDG-models, and the segmentations are iteratively refined by a parallel MGRF model implemented on GPU with analytically estimated potentials. Finally, these initial segmentations are fused together by a Bayesian fusion approach to get the final segmentation of the lung regions.

2   Methods

2.1   Joint Markov-Gibbs model of CT Lung Images

Let $\mathbf{R} = \{(i, j, z) : 1 \leq i \leq I, 1 \leq j \leq J, 1 \leq z \leq Z\}$ be a finite arithmetic grid, $\mathbf{Q}$ be the set of integer gray levels, $\mathbf{K}$ be the set of region labels, and $\mathbf{g} : \mathbf{R} \rightarrow \mathbf{Q}$ and $\mathbf{m} : \mathbf{R} \rightarrow \mathbf{K}$ be a grayscale image and its region map, respectively.

The MGRF model of images is given by a joint probability distribution of CT images and the desired region maps $P(\mathbf{g}, \mathbf{m}) = P(\mathbf{m})P(\mathbf{g}|\mathbf{m})$. Here, $P(\mathbf{m})$ is an unconditional distribution of maps and $P(\mathbf{g}|\mathbf{m})$ is a conditional distribution of images, given the map. The Bayesian maximum *a posteriori* estimate of the map $\mathbf{m}$ ($\mathbf{m}^* = \arg\max_{\mathbf{m}} L(\mathbf{g}, \mathbf{m})$), given the image $\mathbf{g}$, maximizes the log-likelihood function:

$$L(\mathbf{g}, \mathbf{m}) = \log P(\mathbf{g}|\mathbf{m}) + \log P(\mathbf{m}) \tag{1}$$

The model demonstrated in Eq. 1 will be used for both original and GSS data images. In this work, we focus on accurate identification of the spatial model of the lung voxels ($P(\mathbf{m})$), and the intensity distribution of the lung tissue ($P(\mathbf{g}|\mathbf{m})$).

2.2   Spatial Interaction Model of CT Images

In line with a generic MGRF with voxel pair interactions [9], we restrict the neighborhood of interactions to be the nearest 26 voxels; by symmetry, they are independent of region orientations. Let $\mathbf{V}_a = \{V_a(k, k') = V_{a,\text{eq}}$ if $k = k'$ and $V_a(k, k') = V_{a,\text{ne}}$ if $k \neq k'$: $k, k' \in \mathbf{K}\}$ denote bi-valued Gibbs potentials describing symmetric pairwise interactions of type $a \in \mathbf{A} = \{\text{hvdc}, \text{hvdu}, \text{hvdl}\}$ between the region labels, where hvdc, hvdu, and hvdl are the closest symmetric horizontal-vertical-diagonal three-fold interactions in the current slice, the upper slice, and the lower slice, respectively. Let $\mathbf{N}_{\text{hvdc}} = \{(\pm1, 0, 0), (0, \pm1, 0)\}$, $\mathbf{N}_{\text{hvdu}} = \{(0, 0, 1), (\pm1, \pm1, 1)\}$, and $\mathbf{N}_{\text{hvdl}} = \{(0, 0, -1), (\pm1, \pm1, -1)\}$ be subsets of inter-voxel offsets for the 26-neighborhood system. Then the Gibbs probability distribution of region maps is as follows:

$$P(\mathbf{m}) \propto \exp\left(\sum_{(i,j,z) \in \mathbf{R}} \sum_{a \in \mathbf{A}} \sum_{(\xi,\eta,\zeta) \in \mathbf{N}_a} V_a(m_{i,j,z}, m_{i+\xi,j+\eta,z+\zeta}) \right) \tag{2}$$

To identify the MGRF model described in the above equation, we use Maximum Likelihood Estimation (MLE) to estimate the Gibbs Potentials $\mathbf{V}$.

$$V_{a,\text{eq}} = \frac{K^2}{K-1}\left(f'_a(\mathbf{m}) - \frac{1}{K} \right), \quad V_{a,\text{ne}} = \frac{K^2}{K-1}\left(f''_a(\mathbf{m}) - 1 + \frac{1}{K} \right) \tag{3}$$

where $f'_a(\mathbf{m})$ and $f''_a(\mathbf{m})$ are the relative frequencies of equal and non-equal pairs, respectively, of the labels in all the equivalent voxel pairs $\{((i, j, z), (i + \xi, j + \eta, z + \zeta)) : ((\xi, \eta, \zeta) \in \mathbf{N}_a\}$. In this paper we introduce a new analytical maximum likelihood estimation for the Gibbs potentials (see the supplementary material for the complete proof).

2.3   Intensity Model of CT Lung Images

Let q be in $\mathbf{Q}$. The discrete Gaussian is defined as the probability distribution $\Psi_\theta = (\psi(q|\theta) : q \in \mathbf{Q})$ on $\mathbf{Q}$ such that $\psi(q|\theta) = \Phi_\theta(q + 0.5) - \Phi_\theta(q - 0.5)$ for $q = 1, \ldots, Q-2$, $\psi(0|\theta) = \Phi_\theta(0.5)$ and $\psi(Q-1|\theta) = 1 - \Phi_\theta(Q-1.5)$, where $\Phi_\theta(q)$ is the cumulative Gaussian function with the parameter θ. The empirical gray level distribution for CT images is closely approximated using Linear Combination of Discrete Gaussians (LCDG) with C_p positive and C_n negative components:

$$p_{\mathbf{w},\Theta}(q) = \sum_{r=1}^{C_\mathrm{p}} w_{\mathrm{p},r} \psi(q|\theta_{\mathrm{p},r}) - \sum_{l=1}^{C_\mathrm{n}} w_{\mathrm{n},l} \psi(q|\theta_{\mathrm{n},l}) \tag{4}$$

where all the weights are non-negative, and their sum equals to one. A sequential EM-based algorithm is adapted to solve for the parameters of the LCDG intensity model [9,10].

2.4   Bayesian Fusion of Initial Segmentation Results

The Bayesian fusion method can be applied to fuse the segmentation results from different classifiers under one condition; that each classifier's output is expressed by a posterior probability. Outputs of N classifiers are fused by computing the average of their posterior probability as follows:

$$P_F(q \in k|\mathbf{g}) = \frac{1}{N} \sum_{\tau=1}^{N} P_\tau(q \in k|\mathbf{g}); k \in \mathbf{K} \tag{5}$$

The final decision for each pixel to be classified as lung or other tissues will be based on the new estimated posterior probability P_F.

2.5   Parallel MGRF Implementation and the Proposed Segmentation Framework

The calculation of the Gibbs probability described in section 2.2 for each pixel in the image is independent from other pixels and can be performed in parallel on GPU threads. Our GPU implementation of the MGRF is an iterative algorithm. At each iteration only all the pixels of one 2D image ($m \times n$) of the 3D CT are taken into consideration and hence $m \times n$ threads work concurrently to calculate the Gibbs probability for each pixel. Threads are organized in a 32×32 grid of blocks of size 16×16 threads. Each thread in a block accesses all the 26-neighborhood pixels. When the LCDG results from each scale are obtained, they are transferred to the GPU iteratively. After the Gibbs distribution for each scale is achieved the revised maps will be copied back to the CPU to be fused.

The whole iterative segmentation process is as follows:

- ○ **Input:** Read the original 3D CT data and generate the smoothed CT data in scale space by convolving the original image with the 3D GKs.
- ○ **Initialization:** For the original and the smoothed CT images, find an initial map by the voxelwise Bayesian maximum *a posteriori* classification of a given image after initial estimation of K LCDG-models of signals of each object class represented by one of the dominant modes.
- ○ **Iterative refinement:** Transfer the initial map of the original and smoothed CT data to GPU to refine the maps by iterating following two steps in parallel: (I) estimate the potential values for the region map model, and (II) re-collect the empirical gray level densities for the current regions, re-approximate these densities, and update the map. The results are copied back to the CPU.

○ **Output:** The final map for the original and the smoothed CT images are fused together using Eq. 5 to get the final segmentation of the lung regions.

3   Experimental Results and Conclusions

Experiments were conducted on eleven data sets with the CT images acquired with a multi-detector GE Light Speed Plus scanner (General Electric, Milwuakee, USA) with the following scanning parameters: slice thickness of 2.5 mm reconstructed every 5 mm, scanning pitch 1.5, 140 KV, 100 MA, and F.O.V 36 cm. The size of each 3D data set is $512 \times 512 \times 390$. The CT images contain two classes $(K = 2)$: darker lung tissue and the brighter chest region. A typical 3D CT and its smoothed 3D images using $33 \times 33 \times 5$ GK, and their final marginal estimated distributions are shown in Fig. 4. The step-by-step estimation of the marginal density function of the lung and the chest, at each scale, is included in the supplementary material. The detailed 3D segmentation results are in Fig. 5.

Experimental results are acquired from running the algorithm on both CPU and GPU/CUDA. Regarding the CPU implementation, the algorithm is tested on a platform with four Intel DualCore 3.33 GHz CPU with 48 GB of RAM.

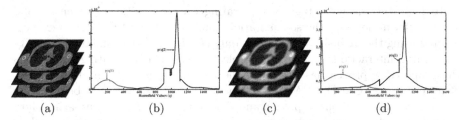

Fig. 4. A typical 3D CT and smoothed 3D data using $33 \times 33 \times 5$ Gaussian kernel (a,c), and final estimated marginal pdf of chest and lung at two scales (b,d)

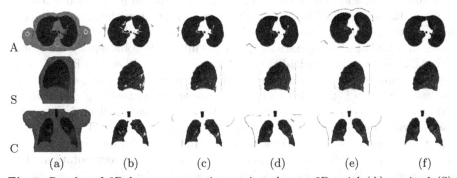

Fig. 5. Results of 3D lung segmentation projected onto 2D axial (A), sagittal (S), and coronal (C) planes for visualization: 2D profiles of the original CT images (a), segmentation of the original CT (b), segmentation of the smoothed CT using GK with size $9 \times 9 \times 5$ (c), segmentation of the smoothed CT using GK with size $17 \times 17 \times 5$ (d), segmentation of smoothed CT using GK with size $33 \times 33 \times 5$ (e), and our final segmentation (f). Note that the false positive error shown in green and false negative error shown in yellow with respect to ground truth (radiologist segmentation).

Fig. 6. The ROC curves for intensity only (red), intensity and spatial (green), and intensity and spatial in GSS (blue)

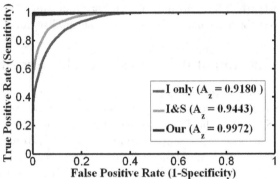

All the GPU implementations are executed on an NVIDIA Tesla M2090 GPU card installed on a Linux machine with a 3.4 GHz AMD Phenom II X4 965 processor, and 16 GB RAM. Each data set is executed five times on both CPU and GPU and the average is saved for each case. Our method took 3.436 seconds that shows about 10^3 times speedup when compared to the naive single threaded implementation that took 160.203 minutes on the CPU.

To highlight the advantage of integrating the GSS with the intensity and spatial information into the segmentation approach, the test CT data were segmented using the intensity information only ($I only$) and the combined intensity and spatial interactions ($I\&S$) [11]. Table 1 shows that integrating the GSS in the proposed approach has improved the results of the segmentation, as evidenced by the largest DSC. Moreover, the statistical paired t-tests between the mean DSCs values of our approach and that of (I) and ($I\&S$) approaches show a significant difference between our approach and other approaches (p-values less than 0.05), as shown in Table 1. These results highlight the advantages of using the GSS in addition to the intensity and the spatial interaction features. To verify the strength of our approach over current algorithms, we compare our proposed method to three state-of-the-art algorithms: IT followed by a sequence of morphological operations (IT) [2], Multiple Resolution Segmentation (MRS) [12], deformable model-based on Gradient Vector Flow (GVF) [13], and a segmentation-by-registration approach which is proposed by Sluimer et al. [3]. The low accuracy of [3] is due to the large variability in the lung region from subject to subject. Some factors such as patient's age, pathological tissues, and local deformation due to breathing cause misalignment in the CT images that cannot be handled only by 3D global registration. This misalignment during the registration step affects on the final accuracy of the lung segmentation. Our approach shows the best segmentation accuracy (the largest DSC), as shown in Table 1. Moreover, this increment is statistically significant according to the statistical paired t-test on the DSCs of the comparable approaches. These results highlight the advantages and strengths of the proposed approach.

Furthermore, we evaluated our approach using Receiver Operating Characteristic (ROC) statistics, which tests the sensitivity of the method against the selection of the operating points (the classification threshold). Fig. 6 clearly demonstrates that our segmentation method has achieved an improved performance, evidenced by the greatest area under the ROC curve ($A_z = 0.9972$).

Our experiments show that, using different sizes of 3D GKs, the proposed identification of the parallel MGRF model, for original and smoothed CT images, exhibits promising results in segmenting the lung region from CT images. Our future work will focus on developing a likelihood that will enable us estimate the number and sizes of GKs that will lead to accurate lung segmentation.

Table 1. Comparison of segmentation accuracy as measured by DSC of our method to six other approaches. Note that the results of our segmentation algorithm are obtained using the original CT and four GKs.

DSC	Segmentation algorithm						
	Our	I only	I & S	IT	MRS	GVF	[3]
Min.	**0.937**	0.578	0.634	0.613	0.539	0.692	0.77
Max.	**0.971**	0.742	0.883	0.891	0.750	0.941	0.85
Mean	**0.960**	0.632	0.783	0.816	0.613	0.848	0.81
St.dev.	**0.011**	0.091	0.078	0.091	0.054	0.087	0.069
p-value		0.0001	0.0001	0.0001	0.0001	0.0001	0.0001

References

1. Siegel, R., Ward, E., et al.: Cancer statistics, 2011 CA Cancer J. Clin. (2011)
2. Hu, S., Hoffman, E., Reinhardt, J.: Automatic lung segmentation for accurate quantitation of volumetric x-ray CT images. IEEE TMI 20, 490–498 (2001)
3. Sluimer, I., Prokop, M., van Ginneken, B.: Toward automated segmentation of the pathological lung in CT. IEEE TMI 24, 1025–1038 (2005)
4. Itai, Y., Hyoungseop, K., et al.: Automatic segmentation of lung areas based on snakes and extraction of abnormal areas. In: IEEE ICTAI, pp. 377–381 (2005)
5. Silveira, M., Nascimento, J., Marques, J.: Automatic segmentation of the lungs using robust level sets. In: IEEE EMBS, pp. 4414–4417 (2007)
6. Won, C., Kim, D., et al.: Lung segmentation by new curve stopping function using geodesic active contour model. IEICE Transactions, 1727–1729 (June 2006)
7. Sluimer, I., Schilham, A., et al.: Computer analysis of computed tomography scans of the lung: a survey. IEEE TMI 25, 385–405 (2006)
8. Yu, L., Xu, Y.: A parallel Gibbs sampling algorithm for motif finding on GPU. In: IEEE ISPA, pp. 555–558 (2009)
9. Farag, A., El-Baz, A., Gimelfarb, G.: Precise segmentation of multi-modal images. IEEE TIP 15(4), 952–968 (2006)
10. Schlesinger, M., Hlavac, V.: Ten lectures on statistical and structural pattern recognition. Kluwer Academic (2002)
11. El-Ba, A., Gimel'farb, G.G., Falk, R., Holland, T., Shaffer, T.: A New Stochastic Framework for Accurate Lung Segmentation. In: Metaxas, D., Axel, L., Fichtinger, G., Székely, G. (eds.) MICCAI 2008, Part I. LNCS, vol. 5241, pp. 322–330. Springer, Heidelberg (2008)
12. Bouman, C., Liu, B.: Multiple resolution segmentation of textured images. IEEE TPAMI 13, 99–113 (1991)
13. Xu, C., Prince, J.L.: Snakes, shapes, and gradient vector flow. IEEE TPAMI 7, 359–369 (1998)

Nonlinear Discriminant Graph Embeddings for Detecting White Matter Lesions in FLAIR MRI

Samuel Kadoury[1], Guray Erus[2], and Christos Davatzikos[2]

[1] Ecole Polytechnique de Montreal, Montreal, Canada
[2] SBIA, Dept. of Radiology, University of Pennsylvania, Philadelphia, PA, USA

Abstract. Brain abnormalities such as white matter lesions (WMLs) are not only linked to cerebrovascular disease, but also with normal aging, diabetes and other conditions increasing the risk for cerebrovascular pathologies. Discovering quantitative measures which assess the degree or probability of WML in patients is important for evaluating disease burden, progression and response to interventions. In this paper, we introduce a novel approach for detecting the presence of WMLs in periventricular areas of the brain with a discriminant graph-embedding framework, introducing within-class and between-class similarity graphs described in nonlinear manifold subspaces to characterize intra-regional compactness and inter-regional separability. The geometrical structure of the data is exploited to perform linearization and canonical kernalization based on fuzzy-matching principles of 876 normal tissue patches in 73 subjects, and tested on patches imaging both WML (263) and healthy areas (133) in 33 subjects with diabetes. Experiments highlight the advantage of introducing separability between submanifolds to learn the studied data and increase the discriminatory power, with detection rates over 91% in true-positives, and the importance of measuring similarity for specific pathological patterns using kernelized distance metrics.

1 Introduction

The prevalence of cerebral white matter lesions (WMLs) has been extensively studied for the past decade in the elderly population, patients with cardiovascular risk factors or from patients with central nervous system disorders, including cerebrovascular disease and dementia. The development of targeted biologic markers correlating the extent of WML to the severity of the pathology has gained tremendous attention in order to improve both the diagnosis and prognosis possibilities of patients who are susceptible to cardiovascular symptoms.

Towards this end, precise measurements of such pathology from magnetic resonance imaging (MRI), and more importantly measuring the evolution of a pathology over time, becomes a crucial aspect for detecting and monitoring the disease, as well as for evaluating the risk of progression. While a number of protocols are being researched to best visualize these lesions, WML are shown

F. Wang et al. (Eds.): MLMI 2012, LNCS 7588, pp. 94–102, 2012.

as hyperintense regions in fluid-attenuated inversion recovery (FLAIR) T2 images. Consequently, clarity of the lesions located in periventricular areas is increased in FLAIR images compared with other images [1]. Automatization of T2-hyperintense lesion detection is desirable not only with regard to time and cost effectiveness, but also constitutes a prerequisite to minimize user bias.

Although there have been some approaches to segment multiple sclerosis lesions from FLAIR images using classification techniques (SVM, fuzzy, kNN, Bayesian) [2], few have attempted to describe each pathological pattern as a deviation from normal brain images along a simplified manifold structure, allowing the computation of an appropriate distance between individuals and each pathological pattern. The definition of an optimal space for the comparison of different populations was already addressed by linear dimensionality reduction techniques. Unfortunately, they typically fail to capture complex high-dimensional data where the underlying structure resides in a nonlinear space, such as in the brain cortex which bares strong variability [3, 4]. Manifold learning techniques intrinsically take under consideration the inherent geometry to assess physiological or morphological anatomy [5–7], which allows relevant comparison of individuals to the studied population through a low-dimensional Euclidean map. While they show promise, they suffer in handling outliers and multiple anatomical regions by assuming that the data resides on a single continuous manifold. A convenient way of dealing with both spatial anatomical "variations" and pathological "deviations" inside a single region is exploiting the geometrical structure and local information to maximize the discriminatory power in high order data [8].

We introduce a novel framework based on graph embeddings which extends manifold learning techniques to help differentiate brain lesions and normal tissue in various periventricular regions (PVR) of the brain using high order data structures. Grassmanian correlation kernels are used to treat the manifold as a Euclidean vector space to estimate similarity as principle angles and handle outsider instances. Within-class and between-class similarity graphs described in nonlinear manifold subspaces are used to characterize intra-regional compactness which establishes the patterns of normal appearances and inter-regional separability to distinguish between multiple critical areas. The originality of our method resides in the training of multiple healthy tissue areas to detect the presence of WML in test images, and the definition of a physiological difference from normal images within manifold space. We present detection results on FLAIR MRI scans of elderly patients with diabetes obtained in a clinical study.

2   Methods

The computation of the pathologic deviation from normality, which is measured as a distance between unseen image patches and a given healthy brain population, consists of three steps: (1) generating the Gram matrix using Grassmanian kernel functions from a set of training images, (2) constructing the within and between similarity graphs according to locally linear embeddings (LLE) using a

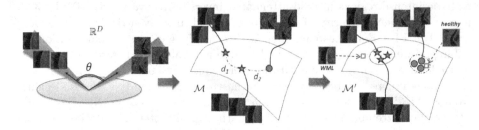

Fig. 1. Illustration of the manifold-based white matter lesion detection method, where the concept of principle angles between images represented in high-dimensional space $\mathbb{R}^D$ is applied. Images are embedded as points in a Grassmanian manifold space $\mathcal{M}$ where point to point classification is possible. Grassmanian kernels are used to increase the discriminatory power by mapping points in a new subspace $\mathcal{M}'$ to estimate the deviation of unseen samples from a learned healthy tissue distribution.

recently proposed fuzzy block matching measure, (3) perform supervised non-linear manifold learning to obtain the optimal projection matrix. The output projection matrix maps unseen images on the single nonlinear manifold in order to classify as healthy or in presence of WML. Fig. 1 illustrates the workflow.

2.1 Grassmanian Kernels

Given N labelled periventricular images $\boldsymbol{I}_i$ of dimension D, we create the training set of m-dimensional points $\mathbb{X} = \{(\boldsymbol{X}_i, l_i)\}_{i=1}^N$ from the underlying manifold $\mathcal{M}$ using SVD over the image-set, where $\boldsymbol{X}_i \in \mathbb{R}^{D \times m}$ and $l_i \in \{1, 2, \ldots, C\}$, with C denoting the number of periventricular brain regions. The similarity between two points on the manifold $(\boldsymbol{X}_i, \boldsymbol{X}_j)$ is measured as a combination of two Grassmannian kernels defined in the Hilbert Space such that:

$$\mathbb{K}_{i,j} = \alpha_1 k_{i,j}^{[proj]}(\boldsymbol{X}_i, \boldsymbol{X}_j) + \alpha_2 k_{i,j}^{[CC]}(\boldsymbol{X}_i, \boldsymbol{X}_j) \tag{1}$$

with $\alpha_1, \alpha_2 \geq 0$. The projection kernel defined as $k_{i,j}^{[proj]} = \|\boldsymbol{X}_i^T \boldsymbol{X}_j\|_F^2$ determines the largest canonical correlation value based on the cosine of principal angles between two sets. The second, denotes canonical correlation Grassmanian kernel:

$$k_{i,j}^{[CC]} = \max_{\mathbf{a}_p \in \text{span}(\boldsymbol{X}_i)} \max_{\mathbf{b}_q \in \text{span}(\boldsymbol{X}_j)} \mathbf{a}_p^T \mathbf{b}_q \tag{2}$$

subject to $\mathbf{a}_p^T \mathbf{a}_p = \mathbf{b}_p^T \mathbf{b}_p = 1$ and $\mathbf{a}_p^T \mathbf{a}_q = \mathbf{b}_p^T \mathbf{b}_q = 0$, $p \neq q$. This kernel is positive definite since $z^T \mathbb{K} z > 0$ such that $\forall z \in \mathbb{R}^n$ as shown in [8], and well-defined since singular values of $\boldsymbol{X}_1^T \boldsymbol{X}_2$ are equal to $\boldsymbol{R}_1^T \boldsymbol{X}_1^T \boldsymbol{X}_2 \boldsymbol{R}_2$, with $\boldsymbol{R}_1, \boldsymbol{R}_2 \in Q(o)$, indicating orthonormal matrices of order o. This makes the kernel invariant to various representation of the subspaces. With each kernel describing different features of the brain patches, the combination allows to cover a wider spectrum of the distribution and improve the discriminatory accuracy.

2.2   Graph-Embedding Framework

Let $G = (\boldsymbol{X}, \boldsymbol{W})$ be an undirected similarity graph, with the collection of vertices $\boldsymbol{X}$ connected by edges, and the symmetric matrix $\boldsymbol{W} \in \Re^{N \times N}$ with elements describing the relationships between the vertices. The diagonal matrix $\boldsymbol{D}$ and the Laplacian matrix $\boldsymbol{L}$ are defined as $\boldsymbol{L} = \boldsymbol{D} - \boldsymbol{W}$, with $\boldsymbol{D}(i,i) = \sum_{j \neq i} \boldsymbol{W}_{ij} \forall i$. The task at hand is to maximize a measure of discriminatory power by mapping the underlying data $\boldsymbol{X}$ into a vector space $\boldsymbol{Y}$, while preserving similarities between data points in the high-dimensional space. Discriminant graph-embedding aims to maintain these similarities according to graph preserving criterion, which in the case of LLE [9] are included in M, which is a sparse and symmetric $N \times N$ matrix, with I as identity:

$$\sum_i \|Y_i - \sum_j M(i,j)Y_j\|^2 = Y^T(I - M)^T(I - M)Y \qquad (3)$$

$$= \underset{Y^T T = 1}{\operatorname{argmin}} Y^T(\boldsymbol{D} - \boldsymbol{W})Y$$

Within and between Similarity Graphs: The local geometrical structure of $\mathcal{M}$ can be modeled by building a within-class similarity graph $\boldsymbol{W}_w$ and a between-class similarity graph $\boldsymbol{W}_b$. When constructing the discriminant LLE graph, manifold elements $\boldsymbol{X}$ are partitioned into these two difference classes. The intrinsic graph G is first created by assigning edges only to vertices $\boldsymbol{X}$ of the same class. The local reconstruction coefficient matrix $M(i,j)$ can be acquired by minimizing the objective function as:

$$\min_M \sum_{j \in \mathcal{N}_w(i)} \|\boldsymbol{X}_i - M(i,j)\boldsymbol{X}_j\|^2 \sum_{j \in \mathcal{N}_w(i)} M(i,j) = 1 \ \forall i \qquad (4)$$

with $\mathcal{N}_w(i)$ as the neighborhood of size k_1, within the same PVR as point i. Each sample is therefore reconstructed only from images of the same region. As shown in Eq.(3), the local reconstruction coefficients are incorporated in the within-class similarity graph, such that the matrix $\boldsymbol{W}_w$ is defined as:

$$W_w(i,j) = \begin{cases} (M + M^T - M^T M)_{ij}, & \text{if } \boldsymbol{X}_i \in \mathcal{N}_w(\boldsymbol{X}_j) \text{ or } \boldsymbol{X}_j \in \mathcal{N}_w(\boldsymbol{X}_i) \\ 0, & \text{otherwise} \end{cases} \qquad (5)$$

Conversely, the between-class similarity matrix $\boldsymbol{W}_b$ represents the statistical properties to be avoided in the optimization process and used as a high order constraint. Distances between samples in different PVRs are computed as:

$$W_b(i,j) = \begin{cases} 1/k_2, & \text{if } \boldsymbol{X}_i \in \mathcal{N}_b(\boldsymbol{X}_j) \text{ or } \boldsymbol{X}_j \in \mathcal{N}_b(\boldsymbol{X}_i) \\ 0, & \text{otherwise} \end{cases} \qquad (6)$$

with $\mathcal{N}_b$ containing k_2 neighbors having different class label from the ith sample. The objective is mapping points from $\mathcal{M}$ to a new manifold $\mathcal{M}'$, ie. $\boldsymbol{X}_i \to \boldsymbol{Y}_i$, by mapping connected healthy samples in $\boldsymbol{W}_w$ as close as possible to the class cluster, while moving different brain areas of $\boldsymbol{W}_b$ as far as possible from one another. This results in optimizing the following objective functions:

$$f_1 = \min \frac{1}{2} \sum_{i,j} (\boldsymbol{Y}_i - \boldsymbol{Y}_j)^2 W_w(i,j) \qquad (7)$$

$$f_2 = \max \frac{1}{2} \sum_{i,j} (\boldsymbol{Y}_i - \boldsymbol{Y}_j)^2 W_b(i,j) \qquad (8)$$

Local Image Similarity Measure: To create the neighborhoods $\mathcal{N}_w$ and $\mathcal{N}_b$ for each image patch, we adopt an approach similar to a fuzzy block matching method which avoids the constraint of a strict one-to-one pairing [10] and captures local similarties. One can assume over the image domain $\mathbb{R}^D$, a weighted graph w_{ij} that links together pixels $\mathbf{x}$ of the input image $\boldsymbol{I}_i$ and pixels $\mathbf{y}$ of the image $\boldsymbol{I}_j$ with a weight $w_{ij}(\mathbf{x}, \mathbf{y})$, which is computed as follows:

$$w_{ij}(\mathbf{x}, \mathbf{y}) = \frac{1}{Z_{ij,\mathbf{x}}} e^{-\frac{\sum_{\mathbf{x}' \in P_{I_i}(\mathbf{x}), \mathbf{y}' \in P_{I_j}(\mathbf{y})} (I_i(\mathbf{x}') - I_j(\mathbf{y}'))^2}{2m\beta\sigma^2}} \qquad (9)$$

where $P_{I_i}(\mathbf{x})$ is an arbitrary ROI in image $\boldsymbol{I}_i$, centered at pixel $\mathbf{x}$ and the parameter $Z_{ij,\mathbf{x}}$ is a constant of normalization such as: $\forall \mathbf{x} \in \mathbb{R}^D, \sum_{\mathbf{y} \in \mathbb{R}^D} w_{ij}(\mathbf{x}, \mathbf{y}) = 1$; m is the number of pixels in the region $P_{I_i}(\mathbf{x})$; σ is the standard deviation of the noise and β is a smoothing parameter ($\beta = 0.5$). This weighted graph w_{ij} is a representation of non-local interactions between the input image $\boldsymbol{I}_i$ and the image $\boldsymbol{I}_j$ of the training dataset. In the context of periventricular image regions in the brain, the location of the brain structures is not highly variable and it is then not desirable to go through the entire image domain to find a good match. In this work, we constrain the search of non-local structures by using a limited number of pixels around $\mathbf{x}$: $w = \{w(\mathbf{x}, \mathbf{y}), \forall \mathbf{x} \in \mathbb{R}^D, \mathbf{y} \in \mathcal{S}(\mathbf{x})\}$, where $\mathcal{S}(\mathbf{x})$ is the surrounding region of the pixel $\mathbf{x}$. The size of the considered surrounding region $\mathcal{S}$ is linked to the variability in the periventricular region. Hence, a binary similarity measure is defined as: $d_{\mathbb{R}^D}(\boldsymbol{I}_i, \boldsymbol{I}_j) = \sum_{\forall \mathbf{x} \in I_i, \mathbf{y} \in \mathcal{S}_{I_j}(\mathbf{x})} \max_j w_{ij}(\mathbf{x}, \mathbf{y})$, thereby reflecting the global interactions between $\boldsymbol{I}_i$ and $\boldsymbol{I}_j$ by summing the most significant weights for each surroundings $\mathcal{S}$ in $\boldsymbol{I}_j$.

2.3   Supervised Manifold Learning

The last step consists of determining the optimal projection matrix by simultaneously maximizing class separability and preserving interclass manifold property. By assuming that points on the manifold are known as similarity measures given by the Grassmanian kernel $\mathbb{K}_{i,j}$ from Eq.(1), a linear solution can be defined, ie., $\boldsymbol{Y}_i = (\langle \alpha_1, \boldsymbol{X}_i \rangle, \dots, \langle \alpha_r, \boldsymbol{X}_i \rangle)^T$ with $\alpha_i = \sum_{j=1}^{N} a_{ij} \boldsymbol{X}_j$. Defining the coefficient $\boldsymbol{A}_l = (a_{l1}, \dots, a_{lN})^T$ and kernel $\boldsymbol{K}_i = (k_{i1}, \dots, k_{iN})^T$ vectors, the output can be described as $\boldsymbol{Y}_i = \langle \alpha_l, \boldsymbol{X}_i \rangle = \boldsymbol{A}_l^T \boldsymbol{K}_i$. The minimization of Eq.(7) becomes:

$$f_1 = \sum_i \mathbf{A}_i^T \mathbf{K}_i \mathbf{K}_i^T \mathbf{A}_i^T W_w(i,i) - \sum_{i,j} \mathbf{A}_i^T \mathbf{K}_j \mathbf{K}_i^T \mathbf{A}_i^T W_w(i,j)$$

$$= \mathbb{A}^T \mathbb{K} \mathbf{D}_w \mathbb{K}^T \mathbb{A} - \mathbb{A}^T \mathbb{K} \mathbf{W}_w \mathbb{K}^T \mathbb{A} \qquad (10)$$

$$= \mathbb{A}^T \mathbb{K} \mathbf{L}_w \mathbb{K}^T \mathbb{A}$$

given Eq. (3). Here, $\mathbb{A} = [\mathbf{A}_1 | \mathbf{A}_2 | \ldots | \mathbf{A}_r]$ and $\mathbb{K} = [\mathbf{K}_1 | \mathbf{K}_2 | \ldots | \mathbf{K}_N]$. Similarly, the maximization of the between-class graph is defined as $f_2 = \mathbb{A}^T \mathbb{K} \mathbf{L}_b \mathbb{K}^T \mathbb{A}$, with $\mathbf{L}_b = \mathbf{D}_b - \mathbf{W}_b$. By combining f_1 and f_2, the optimal projection matrix $\mathbb{A}^*$ is acquired from the optimization of the function:

$$\mathbb{A}^* = \operatorname*{argmax}_{\mathbb{A}} \mathbb{A}^T \mathbb{K} \mathbf{L}_b \mathbb{K}^T \mathbb{A} - h\mathbb{A}^T \mathbb{K} \mathbf{L}_w \mathbb{K}^T \mathbb{A} \qquad (11)$$

which is obtained by the eigenvalue decomposition method and h is a Lagrangian multiplier. For any query image $\mathbf{X}_q$, a manifold representation $\mathbf{V}_q = \mathbb{A}^T \mathbf{K}_q$ is obtained using the kernel function and mapping $\mathbb{A}$. The class label l_q is first resolved by the class label of $y^* = \min_{i=1}^N \| \mathbf{V}_q - \mathbf{Y}_i \|^2$. The deviation is then calculated by the L^2 distance to the median of the healthy ventricular region l_q.

3   Experiments and Results

Data images used in this study were obtained from a diabetic population of 106 elderly patients. The patient mean age was 60 ± 4.7 (range $54 - 77$, median 59). Forty-nine were female and 57 were male. MRIs from two clinical scanners (Philips Achieva 3T; GE Discovery 3T) were performed during the baseline period on enrollment into the study (TR = 8000, TE = 100). All participant exams consisted of transaxial T1-w, T2-w, proton-density (PD), and FLAIR scans. All scans except T1-w were performed with a 3-mm slice thickness, no slice gap, a 240×240mm field of view and a 256×256 matrix. From the FLAIR images, 12 periventricular locations were identified and for each of these locations, 39×39 image patches were extracted from 73 normal cases to train the model and from 33 patients for testing purposes. Ground-truth lesions from the test images were manually segmented by an expert rater and classified as healthy or with WMLs according to the lesion load. From the 396 test patches, 263 were classified as healthy (no lesion load) and 133 in presence of WML. All images were nonlinearly co-registered to a template using HAMMER [11].

Fig. 2 illustrates some results from the fuzzy block matching method used to select the closest PVR in the training set when creating the between-class ($\mathcal{N}_b$) and within-class ($\mathcal{N}_w$) neighborhoods. The process would identify the most similar samples outside of the current region. We then tested the robustness of the PVR classification step, used as prerequisite to find WMLs. Training patches from all 12 PVR were embedded in the continuous nonlinear manifold, and each query image patch was mapped onto $\mathcal{M}'$ using the kernelized function. The PVR assigned to the query was determined from the closest sample's class (L^2 norm). The PVR classification accuracy was of 98.6% for all 396 testing patches.

Table 1. Classification results for the presence of WMLs in periventricular regions

	Temporal lobe			Frontal lobe			Parietal lobe			All PVR		
	SVM	LLE	**DLLE**	SVM	LLE	**DLLE**	SVM	LLE	**DLLE**	SVM	LLE	**DLLE**
Sensitivity tp/(tp+fn)	0.68	0.90	**0.95**	0.63	0.82	**0.88**	0.63	0.88	**0.94**	0.65	0.86	**0.91**
Specificity tn/(tn+fp)	0.88	0.97	**0.99**	0.90	0.98	**0.98**	0.93	0.98	**0.98**	0.90	0.98	**0.98**
Overall accuracy	0.82	0.95	**0.98**	0.80	0.92	**0.95**	0.83	0.95	**0.97**	0.81	0.94	**0.96**

Fig. 2. Results of between-class neighborhood assignments in 3 query images using weighted block matching, selecting highest similarity samples outside current PVR

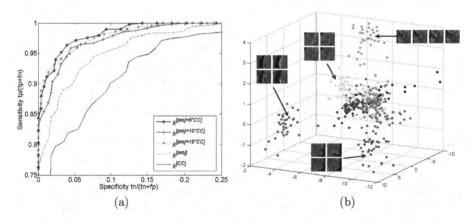

(a)   (b)

Fig. 3. (a) Comparison in ROC curve accuracy using 3 types of canonical correlation kernels. (b) Resulting 3D manifold embedding of testing images from all 12 PVR.

The optimal size was found at $k_1 = 10$ for within-class neighborhoods ($\mathcal{N}_w$), and $k_2 = 5$ for between-class neighborhoods ($\mathcal{N}_b$). The optimal manifold dimensionality was set at $d = 6$, when the trend of the nonlinear residual reconstruction error curve stabilized for the entire training set. Fig. 3a shows the ROC curves when using different types of kernels ($k^{[CC]}, k^{[proj]}, k^{[CC+proj]}$), illustrating the increased accuracy using the combined kernel ($\alpha_1 = 1, \alpha_2 = 5, h = 1$), which suggests each are extracting complementary features from the dataset. A 3D embedding of the computed manifold is represented in Fig. 3b, showing the group of testing image patches provided by multiple PVR in a single continuous manifold structure. Table 1 presents results for SVM (nonlinear RBF kernel), LLE and the proposed method in each ventricular area, with regard to sensitivity and specificity measures. By defining a manifold-specific distance to the healthy cluster which indicates the presence of WML, the total detection rate was of 91.7% from all 396 test images, with a false positive rate of 1.6%. These indicate that the graph-discriminant framework offers the highest diagnostic accuracy, and considerably outperforms SVM. The 8.3% of missed cases represents test images with small lesions.

4   Discussion and Future Work

Our main contribution consists in describing healthy brain regions from FLAIR images in a discriminant nonlinear graph embedding with Grassmanian manifolds to detect white matter lesions. A fuzzy block matching is implemented as a non-local similarity measure to select local neighborhoods, while intrinsic and penalty graphs measure similarity within healthy tissue samples and different brain regions, respectively, to differentiate WMLs in an anatomically correct subspace. A combination of canonical correlation kernels creates a secondary manifold to simplify the deviation estimation from normality, improving WML detection accuracy compared to LLE. Experiments show the need of nonlinear embedding of the learning data, and the relevance of the proposed method for stratifying different stages of WML progression. In the context of multiple sclerosis, the method can improve for the early detection of the disease with promising classification rates based on ground-truth knowledge. Future work will improve the deviation metric using high-order tensorization and investigate into fully automated WML segmentation for monitoring and therapy applications.

References

1. Bakshi, R., Ariyaratana, S., Benedict, R., Jacobs, L.: Fluid-attenuated inversion recovery magnetic resonance imaging detects cortical and juxtacortical multiple sclerosis lesions. Arch. Neurol. 58, 742–748 (2001)
2. Mortazavi, D., Kouzani, A., Soltanian-Zadeh, H.: Segmentation of multiple sclerosis lesions in MR images: a review. Neuroradiology 54, 299–320 (2012)
3. Lao, Z., Shen, D., Liu, D., et al.: Computer-assisted segmentation of white matter lesions in 3D MR images using SVM. Acad. Radio. 15, 300–313 (2008)
4. Schmidt, P., Gaser, C., Arsic, M., et al.: An automated tool for detection of FLAIR-hyperintense white-matter lesions in Multiple Sclerosis. Neuroimage 59, 3774–3783 (2012)
5. Duchateau, N., De Craene, M., Piella, G., Frangi, A.F.: Characterizing Pathological Deviations from Normality Using Constrained Manifold-Learning. In: Fichtinger, G., Martel, A., Peters, T. (eds.) MICCAI 2011, Part III. LNCS, vol. 6893, pp. 256–263. Springer, Heidelberg (2011)
6. Aljabar, P., Wolz, R., Srinivasan, L., et al.: A combined manifold learning analysis of shape and appearance to characterize neonatal brain development. IEEE Trans. Med. Imaging 30, 2072–2086 (2011)

7. Gerber, S., Tasdizen, T., Fletcher, P., Joshi, S., Whitaker, R.: Manifold modeling for brain population analysis. Med. Image Anal. 14, 643–653 (2010)
8. Harandi, M., Sanderson, C., et al.: Graph embedding discriminant analysis on grassmannian manifolds for improved image set matching. In: CVPR, p. 2705 (2011)
9. Roweis, S., Saul, L.: Nonlinear dimensionality reduction by locally linear embedding. Science 290, 2323–2326 (2000)
10. Rousseau, F., Habas, P., Studholme, C.: Human brain labeling using image similarities. In: CVPR, pp. 1081–1088 (2011)
11. Shen, D., Davatzikos, C.: HAMMER: hierarchical attribute matching mechanism for elastic registration. IEEE Trans. Med. Imaging 21, 1421–1439 (2002)

Use of Pattern-Information Analysis in Vision Science: A Pragmatic Examination

Mathieu J. Ruiz[1,2], Jean-Michel Hupé[2], and Michel Dojat[1]

[1] GIN - INSERM U836 & Université J. Fourier, 38700 La Tronche, France
{mathieu.ruiz, michel.dojat}@ujf-grenoble.fr
[2] CerCo - CNRS UMR 5549 & Université de Toulouse, 31300 Toulouse, France
{jean-michel.hupe}@cerco.ups-tlse.fr

Abstract. MultiVoxel Pattern Analysis (MVPA) is presented as a successful alternative to the General Linear Model (GLM) for fMRI data analysis. We report different experiments using MVPA to master several key parameters. We found that 1) different feature selections provide similar classification accuracies with different interpretation depending on the underlying hypotheses, 2) paradigms should be created to maximize both Signal to Noise Ratio (SNR) and number of examples and 3) smoothing leads to opposite effects on classification depending on the spatial scale at which information is encoded and should be used with extreme caution.

Keywords: Machine Learning, SVM, Neurosciences, Brain.

1 Introduction

MVPA is presented as a successful alternative to GLM. It outperforms GLM for detecting low SNR brain activation [1], [2], [3] while yielding similar results on data correctly analyzed by GLM [3], [4]. Thanks to methodologists´ efforts, various toolboxes are today freely available, offering a simple, friendly user interface to novices for processing with MVPA. In parallel, some brain researches give the naïve impression that it is simple to obtain outstanding results using MVPA. In this paper, we report different experiments we performed using MVPA to better understand the effects of several key parameters on our data analysis and consequently our final interpretation. We focus on three methodological points that, if better mastered, will help neuroscientists make the right choices for a proper use of MVPA:

- **Feature selection** is of paramount importance to avoid the curse of dimensionality: the use of too many features compared to the set of available examples leads to a bad hyperplane computation and then hampers class separation. In many studies, features are selected in Regions Of Interest (ROIs) defined in independent experiments. Most of the time, a second feature selection inside those ROIs is required: for instance voxels are selected based on T values obtained by a GLM [1], [2], [5]. This leads to an additional (implicit) hypothesis about the data and prevents generalization to the whole ROI. We propose an alternative method.

F. Wang et al. (Eds.): MLMI 2012, LNCS 7588, pp. 103–110, 2012.

- **The example set size** is a problem in fMRI experiments because few examples (typically ≤100) can be acquired compared to the number of voxels per acquisition (typically ≥10^5). Moreover, Rapid Event-Related Paradigms (RERP), i.e. an Inter Stimulus Interval (ISI) ≤ Hemodynamic Response Function (HRF) peak (about 6s), provide less examples for classification compared to Block Paradigms (BP). From the psychophysics point of view RERP should nevertheless be preferred because they are less cognitively biased than BP. RERP prevent subjects from habituating to the stimuli, mind wandering or being less attentive. We explored methods to increase the number of examples provided by RERP, either by discretizing parameter estimates or by performing supplementary sessions.

- **Spatial smoothing** of the data is customary in GLM analyses in order to increase SNR and reinforce the normality of the voxels distribution. Oppositely since MVPA relies on information stored in activation patterns, smoothing could blur subtle differences between patterns and may better be avoided. We explored the effects of the kernel size of spatial smoothing on the classification accuracy.

2   Materials and Methods

Subjects

Data were collected on two subjects (MR and JMH, authors) during two different sessions each. MR performed twice the same orientation session (S1-O1 and S1-O2). JMH performed an orientation session (S2-O) and a color session (S2-C).

Protocol

Orientation and color sessions contained 4 stimulation conditions, with respectively oriented bars or color concentric sinusoidal gratings visual stimuli, with an additional fixation-only condition for the HRF return to the baseline. Similarly to [6], each condition lasted 1.5s, appeared 6 times and was randomly distributed. ISI was randomly set to 3, 4.5 or 6s.

o *Oriented bars*: Stimuli were black and white sinusoidal gratings taking one out of 4 possible orientations (0, pi/2, pi/4 and 3pi/4 rad.) and displayed within a circular 4.5deg. radius aperture. They were projected on a neutral gray background (CIE xyY=0.32, 0.41, 406). At the center of the screen, a dark gray dot (0.45deg. radius) had to be fixated for the whole duration of the experiment.

o *Color concentric sinusoidal gratings:* Stimuli were similar to [6]. They subtended a maximum 5deg. radius with a square wave luminance profile alternating (1.2 cycles/deg.) between one out of four colors (red, green, blue and yellow) and isoluminant gray. Colors were approximately equalized in luminance using a classical flicker experiment.

o *Attentional task*: Each subject performed a one-back task to maintain his attentional workload constant throughout the experiment. Letters (A, T, O, M and X) appeared one at a time over the central dot in a pseudorandom order. Letters were 1deg. wide, lasted 1s with an ISI of 300ms. The subject had to press a button when the same letter appeared twice in a row (ten times in a run).

MRI Acquisition

We acquired structural and EPI functional images on a Philips 3T Achieva whole body scanner using an 8-channel head coil. For structural image we used a T1-3D FFE sequence (TR/TE: 25/15ms, flip angle: 15deg., acquisition matrix: 180x240x256 (x, y, z), BW=191Hz/pixel, and total measurement time=9min40s). Functional images were acquired using a gradient-echo EPI sequence (TR/TE: 2500/30ms, flip angle: 80deg., acquisition matrix: 80x80, 38 adjacent slices, spatial resolution 2.75x2.75x3mm^3). For each session, 12 functional runs were acquired containing 78 TRs. We used an eye-tracker (ASL 6000) for eye movements recording.

MR Data Processing

Standard preprocessing steps were applied to fMRI data using SPM8[1]: slice timing correction and realignment. We extracted Rigid-Head Motion Parameters (RHMPs). Anatomical T1 images were coregistered to the mean functional image. To address our methodological questions, a smoothing step could be added. We either used a 4mm, 6mm or 8mm 3D FWHM Gaussian filter. Parameter Estimate Images (PEIs, also called images of beta weights) were computed by fitting a boxcar function convolved with HRF. A GLM was created based on 12 predictors (5 conditions, subjects blinks and 6 RHMPs). PEIs discretization was modeled with 9 predictors. The first predictor was a single event; the second predictor contained the 29 other events; 1 predictor contained subjects blinks and 6 predictors were RHMPs. There were as many GLMs as there were stimulation conditions during the whole sessions (i.e. 24 x 12 runs). In order to decrease the noise in the data, PEIs were divided by the square root of the GLM residuals.

Classification

o *Classifiers*: We performed our classification analyses using a Support Vector Classification (SVC, linear kernel, C parameter default value=1) provided by the python module scikit-learn (v.0.10)[2] [7]. We also used a Recursive Feature Elimination (RFE) method that performs a feature selection through iterative classification [8]. The first classification uses all the features of the ROI; at each iteration the worst features (here 1% of the features with the lowest weights) are eliminated, until reaching the chosen final feature set size (set to 288 voxels, RFE performed around 90 iterations).

o *Examples*: PEIs were used as examples for the classifiers. The non-discretized models produced 12 PEIs per condition (or 48 examples in total). The discretized models produced 72 PEIs per condition (or 288 examples in total).

o *Cross-Validation*: We used a leave-one-run-out cross-validation procedure: a classifier was trained on 11 runs (4x11 examples) and tested on the remaining one (4 examples). The accuracy score was the average accuracy of the 12 possible classifiers. For the PEI discretization method we also computed the mean

---

[1] http://www.fil.ion.ucl.ac.uk/spm/
[2] http://scikit-learn.org/stable/

accuracy over 12 classifiers, but this time each classifier was trained over 264 examples (24x11) and tested on the 24 examples of the remaining run (examples within a run may not be fully independent so they cannot be separated to be used for training or testing).

o *Feature Selection*: We constrained our analyses inside a ROI that contained most of the visual areas with 3424 and 3313 voxels for subjects MR and JMH respectively (Fig. 1, Left). We performed a second feature selection inside those ROIs by selecting 288 voxels. We chose this number in order to reach optimal conditions when performing the classification with discretized PEIs, by having as many features as examples. Similar amounts of voxels were also used in the literature as a second feature selection [1], [2]. The second feature selection could be based on 1) the best SNR as assessed by T values of an activation contrast (all active conditions against the rest), 2) the best GLM model fitting the data as assessed by F values of all active condition pair contrasts, 3) their importance in the classification as computed by RFE, using the voxels with the best weights and 4) the bootstrap random selection of 288 voxels in the ROI (10 000 iterations).

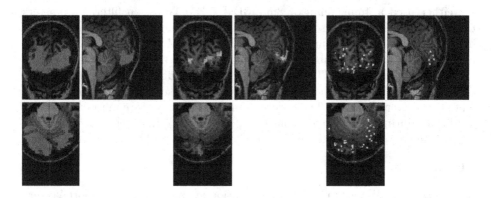

Fig. 1. Left: ROI for subject MR. Middle: voxels selected (n=288) by the best T, RFE and best F methods (red, green and blue respectively). Right: Randomly selected voxels (n=288) that gave the best performance.

3   Results

Feature Selection

In our experiments, chance level and the binomial law significance level (p=0.05) were respectively 25% (four conditions) and 36%. For orientation (S1-O1, S1-O2 and S2-O), information was robust enough (distributed and redundant) in the considered ROI, to obtain significant classification accuracy (Confidence Interval (CI) minimum=43% in average) with 288 voxels randomly selected with bootstrap as well as by using all the voxels of the ROI (Fig. 2A). All methods (but best F for S2-O) yielded classification accuracy higher than the upper

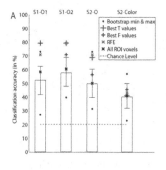 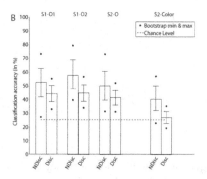

Fig. 2. A. Classification accuracy for all methods used with a 4mm kernel smoothing. B. Classification accuracy for non-discretized and discretized PEIs with a 4mm kernel smoothing. Bars denote the classification mean accuracy for 10 000 iterations with random selection of 288 voxels in the ROI. Error bars denote a 95% CI.

limit of the 95% CI of the bootstrap. Their accuracy, but S1-01, was lower or equal to the maximum accuracy provided by bootstrap method. This indicates that random selection can outperform *a priori* selection criteria. This raises the question of the population of voxels selected by each method. Clearly, (Fig. 1 Middle, Right) indicates differences both in density and localization. With bootstrap method, the best classification was obtained with highly sparse voxels. The overlap was respectively of 48%, 44% and 8% between best T/RFE, best T/best F and bootstrap/other methods (on average).

To assert the significance of these results, we shuffled the set of labels to generate incoherent patterns of information (data not shown). We obtained classification accuracy at the chance level for all methods. Note that for bootstrap method, the binomial law significance level, Bonferroni-corrected for multiple comparisons, was 54% (10000 iterations). With randomized labels, the maximum classification accuracy obtained was below (e.g. 48% for S1-O2). Compared to other methods, bootstrap 1) gives the global performance for the ROI, 2) provided in our case similar results and 3) allows for robust statistics thanks to larger samples. Only this method is considered in the following sections.

Example Set Size

We found a significant decrease (paired T-test, $p \leq 0.0001$, mean 11%) in accuracy for discretized PEIs (Fig. 2B).

We found a significant increase (paired T-test, ≤ 0.0001, 6% to the best single session) in accuracy for the combined session (Fig. 3A).

Smoothing

We found (Fig. 3B) a significant main effect of smoothing (paired t-test: $p \leq 0.0001$). Post-hoc analysis showed significant differences between all conditions (Tukey-HSD test $p \leq 0.0001$ all kernel pairs, but S2-O, 4mm vs. 8mm = $p \leq 0.01$,

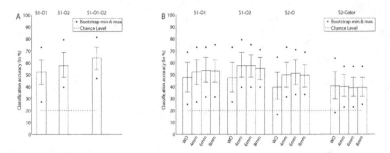

Fig. 3. A. Classification accuracy for two sessions and their combination with a 4mm kernel smoothing. B. Classification accuracy for different smoothing kernel sizes. WO: without smoothing. See Figure 2 for legend.

and S1-O2 4mm vs. 6mm not significant). For orientation sessions, 4mm kernel smoothing systematically provided a significant increase in classification accuracy compared to no blurring, while a small decrease in accuracy (0.5%) was reported when using 4mm compared to no smoothing for color session.

4 Discussion

We investigated the impact on classification accuracy of 1) feature selection 2) increasing example set size either by PEI discretization or additional sessions and 3) kernel smoothing size.

Feature Selection

MVPA requires selecting features (in our case voxels) on which classification will be performed. No feature selection (i.e. using all voxels in the brain) led to poor results (25, 23, 27 and 30% for S1-O1, S1-O2, S2-O and S2-C respectively), not significantly different from chance with the binomial law. Features can be selected through independent experiments such as retinotopic mapping but a second feature selection step can be required. It often relies on a univariate selection, like voxels with the best T values of an activation contrast [2], [9]. Such selection has been criticized because voxels with low T values can be relevant for classification [10]. It requires hypothesis about which voxels are relevant to the classification. Here we compared a bootstrap classification method with two univariate- (GLM) and a multivariate- (RFE) based feature selection in a ROI. We found that the best classification accuracy obtained with bootstrap was similar, or even higher, to accuracy obtained with the best T, F and RFE methods. However, the voxel populations selected by each method were not the same and their repartition was different. Each selected population was relevant (classification obtained by chance led to bad results) and correctly localized in grey matter (see for instance Fig. 1, Right). In consequence, feature selection method may not influence accuracy but importantly can favor a distributed or a localized interpretation of the results.

Example Set Size

Classifiers need enough examples to perform accurately. When using RERP, two solutions were proposed to increase the amount of examples: compute many estimates with low SNR [11], or perform multiple sessions [6]. Mumford et al. [11] suggested to estimate each event in a separate GLM: the first regressor is the onset of a single event; the second regressor contains onsets of all other events. They found that discretized PEIs yielded better classification accuracies than other methods when short ISI were used. At higher ISI, similar classification accuracies were found. Our results showed significant decreases in accuracy (up to 13.5%) with discretized PEIs. This might be due to a lower SNR of the PEIs because fewer events were used compared to [11]. Consequently, a large amount of examples is not enough to increase classification accuracy. In [6], 5 subjects performed 3 to 5 sessions composed of 8 to 10 event-related runs. Each type of stimulus was presented 8 times in a run, which provided them many examples while keeping well estimated PEIs. Classification accuracy was nevertheless highly different between subjects (40-70% in retinotopic V1; chance=12.5%). When using two sessions, we found only a small significant increase in accuracy (6%). First, accuracy was already high in a single session and we might have reached an upper limit. This limit could depend on information encoding (e.g. color session had poorer classification accuracy than orientation session). Second, sessions were realigned and then images interpolated which might have decreased SNR. Note that performing multiple sessions is not always possible with untrained volunteers. Based on these results, we suggest to perform many short runs in the same session, as proposed in [12] using a BP. It remains to be shown whether RERP also benefit from this method.

Smoothing

Several articles investigated smoothing effect using BP or slow ERP with various conclusions [5], [13], [14]. [13] found that to some extent high smoothing tended to provide better SVM (i.e. with fewer support vectors). Using PEIs [14] found that high smoothing led to a significant decrease in accuracy (5%). [5] reported a significant 1-1.5% increase in accuracy with high smoothing for emotional prosody classification. We tested 3 smoothing kernel sizes and found a significant increase in classification accuracy (up to 10%) for the orientation sessions with smoothing. [15] showed that classification of oriented bars came more likely from a radial bias in the periphery of V1 (bias sampling by averaging within voxel boundaries [1], [16]). The radial bias is expressed at a large scale so smoothing probably increased SNR and exacerbated the pattern. Classification accuracy of the color session was hampered by smoothing maybe because information is encoded at a fine-grained level. This would be in line with the idea that improvement due to smoothing reflects the spatial scale at which the information is encoded [5]. We therefore suggest to systematically compare classification accuracies with and without smoothing. It might increase classification accuracy and indirectly reveal how information is encoded.

Acknowledgments. This work is supported by Agence Nationale de Recherche ANR-11-BSH2-010. M. Ruiz is recipient of a PhD grant from MENRT (France).

References

1. Kamitani, Y., Tong, F.: Decoding the visual and subjective contents of the human brain. Nat. Neurosci. 8(5), 679–685 (2005)
2. Gerardin, P., Kourtzi, Z., Mamassian, P.: Prior knowledge of illumination for 3D perception in the human brain. Proc. Natl. Acad. Sci. U.S.A. 107(37), 16309–16314 (2010)
3. Reddy, L., Tsuchiya, N., Serre, T.: Reading the mind's eye: decoding category information during mental imagery. Neuroimage 50(2), 818–825 (2010)
4. Haxby, J.V., Gobbini, M.I., Furey, M.L., Ishai, A., Schouten, J.L., Pietrini, P.: Distributed and overlapping representations of faces and objects in ventral temporal cortex. Science 293(5539), 2425–2430 (2001)
5. Ethofer, T., Van De Ville, D., Scherer, K., Vuilleumier, P.: Decoding of emotional information in voice-sensitive cortices. Curr. Biol. 19(12), 1028–1033 (2009)
6. Brouwer, G.J., Heeger, D.J.: Decoding and reconstructing color from responses in human visual cortex. J. Neurosci. 29(44), 13992–14003 (2009)
7. Pedregosa, F., Varoquaux, G., Gramfort, A., Michel, V., Thirion, B., Grisel, O., Blondel, M., Prettenhofer, P., Weiss, R., Dubourg, V., Vanderplas, J., Passos, A., Cournapeau, D., Brucher, M., Perrot, M., Duchesnay, E.: Scikit-learn: Machine learning in python. J. Mach. Learn. Res. 12, 2825–2830 (2011)
8. Guyon, I., Weston, J., Barnhill, S., Vapnik, V.: Gene selection for cancer classification using support vector machines. Mach. Learn. 46(1-3), 389–422 (2002)
9. De Martino, F., Valente, G., Staeren, N., Ashburner, J., Goebel, R., Formisano, E.: Combining multivariate voxel selection and support vector machines for mapping and classification of fMRI spatial patterns. Neuroimage 43(1), 44–58 (2008)
10. Norman, K.A., Polyn, S.M., Detre, G.J., Haxby, J.V.: Beyond mind-reading: multi-voxel pattern analysis of fMRI data. Trends Cogn. Sci. 10(9), 424–430 (2006)
11. Mumford, J.A., Turner, B.O., Ashby, F.G., Poldrack, R.A.: Deconvolving BOLD activation in event-related designs for multivoxel pattern classification analyses. Neuroimage 59(3), 2636–2643 (2012)
12. Coutanche, M.N., Thompson-Schill, S.L.: The advantage of brief fMRI acquisition runs for multi-voxel pattern detection across runs. Neuroimage 61(4), 1113–1119 (2012)
13. LaConte, S., Strother, S., Cherkassky, V., Anderson, J., Hu, X.: Support vector machines for temporal classification of block design fMRI data. Neuroimage 26(2), 317–329 (2005)
14. Etzel, J.A., Valchev, N., Keysers, C.: The impact of certain methodological choices on multivariate analysis of fMRI data with support vector machines. Neuroimage 54(2), 1159–1167 (2011)
15. Freeman, J., Brouwer, G.J., Heeger, D.J., Merriam, E.P.: Orientation decoding depends on maps, not columns. J. Neurosci. 31(13), 4792–4804 (2011)
16. Kriegeskorte, N., Cusack, R., Bandettini, P.: How does an fMRI voxel sample the neuronal activity pattern: compact-kernel or complex spatiotemporal filter? Neuroimage 49(3), 1965–1976 (2010)

Human Age Estimation with Surface-Based Features from MRI Images

Jieqiong Wang[1], Dai Dai[1], Meng Li[1], Jing Hua[2], and Huiguang He[1,*]

[1] State Key Laboratory of Management and Control for Complex Systems, Institute of Automation, Chinese Academy of Sciences, Beijing, China
huiguang.he@ia.ac.cn
[2] Department of Computer Science, Wayne State University, Michigan, USA

Abstract. Over the past years, many efforts have been made in the estimation of the physiological age based on the human MRI brain images. In this paper, we propose a novel regression model with surface-based features to estimate the human age automatically and accurately. First, individual regional surface-based features (thickness, mean curvature, Gaussian curvature and surface area) from the MRI image were extracted, which were subsequently used to construct combined regional features and the brain networks. Then, the individual regional surface-based features, brain network with surface-based features and combined regional surface-based features were used for age regression by relevance vector machine (RVM), respectively. In the experiment, a dataset of 360 healthy subjects aging from 20 to 82 years was used to evaluate the performance. Experimental results based on 10-fold cross validation show that, compared to the previous methods, age estimation model with combined surface-based features can yield a remarkably high accuracy (mean absolute error: 4.6 years and root mean squared error: 5.6 years) and a significantly high correlation coefficient (r = 0.94), which is the best age estimation result as far as we know and suggests that surface-based features are more powerful than other features used in previous methods for human age estimation.

Keywords: age estimation, surface-based features, relevance vector machine.

1 Introduction

Brain development has been proved to follow a specific pattern during the normal aging process [1] which means people can predict normal age from brain development pattern. Diseases such as schizophrenia or Alzheimer's disease (AD) can change the pattern [2, 3] and consequently change the predicted age. Therefore, patients group with larger gap between the predicted brain age and the true age which can be used to help diagnose diseases. For these reasons, it is very important to estimate brain age from brain development pattern which can be obtained by MRI images.

Over the past years, voxel-based morphometry (VBM) [4] has been widely used to find the relationship between the pattern and age. Researchers have used VBM to

---

* Corresponding author.

prove that Gray matter (GM) and cerebrospinal fluid (CSF) changes with normal age [5, 6]. However, accurate quantitative measure of the relationship between brain development pattern and normal age are not given in these work.   In recent years, Ashburner et al. [7] and Franke et al. [8] tried to estimate the ages of subjects based on their brain images utilizing a relevance vector machine (RVM) with voxel-based features. However, voxel-based features have no information about brain surface gyri and sulci which are very important to age estimation because they both change significantly during the normal aging process.

Since Surface-based features obtained by reconstructed surface include the information of surface gyri (sulci) and overcome the limitation of voxel-based features, we firstly use regional surface-based features to estimate normal age in this paper. Because it has been proved that brain network is related to normal age [9].Then we constructed brain network with surface-based features and analyze its performance in age estimation. Moreover, we put different regional surface-based features together to construct combined regional features and applied combined features to predict normal age.

This paper makes several contributions. First, we are the first to apply surface-based features in age estimation and analyze surface-based features performance from different views. Second, our prediction results are the best one as far as we know which indicate that surface-based features are more sensitive to human age than voxel-based features.

2   Method

2.1   Subjects

Brain structural MRI images of healthy subjects in the train set and test set are both chosen from the available IXI database (http://www.brain-development.org/). After eliminating subjects without age information and subjects without surface-based features (errors happen during the surface reconstruction), 360 normal subjects aged 20-82 years (185 females, 175 males, mean age $\pm$ standard deviation (SD) = 47.04 ± 16.16) were used in this research.

2.2   Pipeline of Age Estimation Model

Fig 1 gives the pipeline of age estimation model. In the model, we employ different kinds of surface-based features (individual regional surface-based features, brain network with surface-based features and combined regional surface-based features) respectively in RVR with radial basis kernel. Then 10-fold cross validation (CV) is utilized to compute mean absolute error (MAE) , root mean squared error (RMSE) and correlation coefficient (*corr*). Considering the occasionality of every division, we operate 10-fold CV 10 times to measure the age estimation model by getting mean value and standard deviation of MAE, RMSE and *corr*. Details will be introduced in the following section.

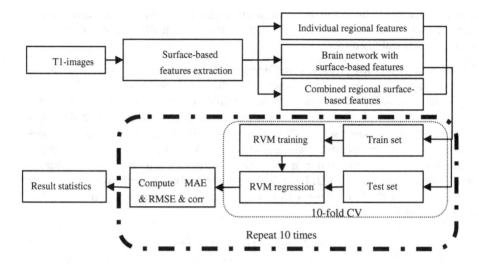

Fig. 1. Pipeline of age estimation model

2.3 Surface-Based Features Extraction

In this study, surface-based features such as cortical thickness, mean curvature, Gaussian curvature and surface area are extracted by the software FreeSurfer (v5.0.0, http://surfer.nmr.mgh.harvard.edu/). Then we calculate regional surface-based features and construct brain network and combined features with surface-based features.

Cortical Thickness. All subjects' T1-weighted images are registered with the Talairach atlas. Then intensity normalization is done to correct intensity non-uniformity [10]. The next step is the automated stripping of the skull from the intensity-normalized images [11]. Voxels are then classified as white matter or something other than white matter. After that, the cerebellum and brain stem are removed. Inner surface and outer surface are subsequently extracted. The distance between the inner surface and the outer surface gives us the thickness at each location of vertex. The result is subsequently normalized to a template to make comparison with different subjects possible.

Curvature. After the cortical surface is extracted, the two principal curvatures at every vertex of the surface are computed and noted as k_1 and k_2. In the research, mean curvature and Gaussian curvature are widely used which are defined as:

$$\text{Mean curvature}: M = \frac{1}{2}(k_1 + k_2) \tag{1}$$

$$\text{Gaussian curvature}: G = k_1 * k_2 \tag{2}$$

Individual Regional Surface-Based Features. Considering features of the vertex are sensitive to noise, the cortical surface is divided into 148 distinct cortical ROIs (Desikan-killiany atlas with 74 regions per hemisphere [12]) to obtain statistical regional features. After ROIs division, average thickness, average curvature (mean curvature and Gaussian curvature) and surface area of each ROI are all calculated as statistical regional features.

Brain Networks with Regional Surface-Based Features. A network, or graph, is typically defined as $N = (V, E)$, where V is the set of nodes and E is the set of edges. In this study, we assume a node is a ROI region and an edge is a certain similarity of regional features between a pair of node [13]. Thus each individual's network shares the same set of 148 nodes. This facilitates performing comparisons using only the weight of edges, which is measured by the kernel below. The regional features of all subjects form a $n \times E$ feature matrix, where n is the number of subjects and $E = V(V - 1)/2$. Let $ROI_k(i)$ (or $ROI_k(j)$) denote the regional feature of the i-th (or j-th) ROI of the k-th subject; then the connection weight $\omega_k(i, j)$ is defined as follow:

$$\omega_k(i, j) = \mathcal{K}\big(d_k(i, j)\big) = \exp\big(-\tfrac{d_k(i,j)}{\sigma}\big) \tag{3}$$

where $\mathcal{K}(\cdot)$ is a kernel function, $d_k(i, j) = [ROI_k(i) - ROI_k(j)]^2$ is a distance function, and $\sigma = 0.01$ is the width parameter and determines the region that the kernel function influence. The network is pruned to reduce noise: edges with weight less than 0.01 are eliminated. Moreover, principal component analysis (PCA) is applied to reduce the dimension of network features matrix.

Combined Regional Surface-Based Features. Mean curvature and Gaussian curvature are two most widely used curvature measures. Therefore we put these two regional features together to construct combined regional features. Then these two features are combined with other regional features.

2.4 Relevance Vector Regression (RVR)

Relevance vector machine (RVM) was proposed by Tipping [14] based on Bayesian estimation for classification and regression problem. Just like support vector machine (SVM), the RVM regression function is defined as:

$$f_{RVM}(\mathbf{s}) = \sum_{i=1}^{N} \alpha_i K(\mathbf{s}, \mathbf{s}_i), \tag{4}$$

where $K(.,.)$ is a kernel function, and $\mathbf{s}_i, i = 1, 2, \cdots, N$ is the surface-based features of the ith training samples.

For an input surface-based feature $\mathbf{s}$, an RVM regression models the distribution of its class label $age \in [20, 82]$ using logistic regression:

$$p(age \mid \mathbf{s}) = \frac{1}{1 + exp\big(-f_{RVM}(\mathbf{s})\big)}. \tag{5}$$

2.5 Cross Validation

In order to avoid overfitting and obtain an unbiased results of the age estimation model, 10-fold CV is used to evaluate the performance of the model. We apply the

CV framework to the age estimation model (the predicted age: p_i, the real age: r_i). Then the accuracy of age estimation accuracy can be measured by the mean absolute error and the root mean squared error:

$$\text{MAE} = \frac{1}{N}\Sigma_{i=1}^{N}|p_i - r_i|. \tag{6}$$

$$\text{RMSE} = \left[\frac{1}{N}\Sigma_{i=1}^{N}(p_i - r_i)^2\right]^{1/2}. \tag{7}$$

Besides MAE and RMSE, the correlation coefficient (*corr*) between predict age and real age is also calculated.

3   Results and Discussion

We implement three experiments in the paper. Firstly, we employ four individual regional surface-based features — regional thickness (Thick), regional mean curvature (mCurv), regional Gaussian curvature (gCurv) and surface area (surfArea) — in age estimation. Secondly, we explore performance of brain network with surface-based features. Finally, we combine different individual regional surface-based features and predict human age with the features. The experiments are performed according to Fig 1. The results are shown in Table 1, Table 2 and Table 3.

The prediction results of age estimation model with individual regional surface-based features (Table 1) show that regional thickness works best among the four regional features. This result indicates cortical thickness changes significantly during the normal aging process and supports the previous paper [15].

Table 2 shows the performance of brain networks with four different regional surface-based features. Comparing the best result of brain network (Table 2) with that of individual regional features (Table 1), even the brain networks don't perform regression well as individual regional surface-based features, it's still worthy to try since the previous work show that the brain network is related to normal age [9]. In the future, we will try more network properties such as the spatial degree distribution, average minimum path length and so on, and wish the properties can be used to improve the regression accuracy.

Table 3 shows the prediction results of the model with combined regional surface-based features. The last two columns of Table 3 show the combined feature with cortical thickness and cortical curvatures performs best. And it has been proved that surface area and cortical thickness are distinct rather than redundant features of cortical structure [16], so the relationship among the surface area, cortical thickness, and cortical curvatures need to be investigated in the future.

From the equation (1) and (2), we know that mean curvature and Gaussian curvature reflect principle curvatures in different views. This is the reason why we combine mean curvature with Gaussian curvature. Comparing the result of combined curvatures (Table 3) with that of regional curvatures (Table 1), we can see that even though single Gaussian feature perform not well, it clearly complete mean curvature's information to improve age estimation results. This phenomenon illustrates it's reasonable to combine two curvatures features.

Comparing Table1, Table 2 with Table 3, it is clear that using the combined features with two curvatures and thickness gives us the best result (MAE=4.6years RMSE=5.6years correlation=0.94). This result can be visualized in Fig 2. The prediction result of each individual is represented as a point in the figure. The blue line shows the value where predicted age matches real age. All points are very close to the blue line. This phenomenon demonstrates the predicted age and the real age are highly correlated (corr = 0.94) and proves the age estimation model with two regional curvatures and regional thickness are reliable in terms of statistics.

Table 4 compares our estimation model with previous works. Voxel-based features are used in these two works [7, 8]. From this table, we can clearly see that our model improves about 8% on MAE and 15% on RMSE. Because our model uses the same dataset and regressor as the method in [8], this result indicates that surface-based features are more sensitive to human age than voxel-based features.

Table 1. Performance of different regional features with RVR based on 10-fold cross validation. Thick: regional thickness; mCurv: regional mean curvature; gCurv: regional Gaussian curvature; surfArea: regional surface area.

(years: Mean±SD)	Thick	mCurv	gCurv	surfArea
MAE	**6.05±0.05**	7.88±0.07	11.21±0.10	10.52±0.22
RMSE	**7.37±0.03**	9.55±0.09	13.64±0.15	12.96±0.14
corr	**0.89±0.01**	0.81±0.01	0.55±0.01	0.60±0.01

Table 2. Performance of brain networks with different regional surface-based features with RVR based on 10-fold cross validation. Net: brain network.

(years: Mean±SD)	ThickNet	mCurvNet	gCurvNet	surfAreaNet
MAE	14.33±0.12	**8.38±0.03**	11.55±0.05	14.23±0.02
RMSE	17.24±0.14	**10.30±0.06**	13.74±0.06	16.18±0.02
corr	0.10±0.02	**0.77±0.01**	0.52±0.01	0.14±0.05

Table 3. Performance of different combined surface-based features with RVR based on 10-fold cross validation. A ∪ B means the combined features of feature A and feature B. 2Curv: regional mean curvature ∪ regional Gaussian curvature.

(years: Mean±SD)	2 Curv	2Curv ∪ Thick	2Curv ∪ Thick ∪ surfArea
MAE	7.47±0.09	**4.57±0.04**	5.06±0.09
RMSE	9.18±0.13	**5.57±0.04**	6.10±0.11
corr	0.82±0.01	**0.94±0.01**	0.93±0.01

Table 4. Comparing our model with state-of-the-art methods. The notation "---" represents the method doesn't give the corresponding value.

(years)	Ashburner[7]	Franke[8]	Our model
MAE	---	4.98	**4.57**
RMSE	6.5	6.73	**5.57**
Corr	0.86	0.94	0.94

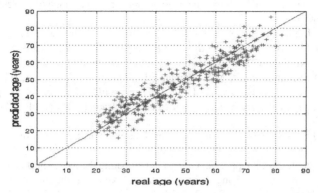

Fig. 2. Visualization of results from the age estimation model. Each point in the figure represents an individual. Both values are highly correlated (corr = 0.94). The blue line shows the value where predicted age matches real age.

4   Conclusions

In this paper, we proposed using a new kind of features — surface-based features— to estimate human age. Regional features and brain network and combined features were employed in RVR. Then 10-fold CV was applied to compute MAE , RMSE and corr to evaluate the prediction results. Experimental results show that the model with the combined feature of regional mean curvature, regional Gaussian curvature and regional thickness performs best. This model improves the prediction accuracy about 8% on MAE and 15% on RMSE by comparing with state-of-the-art methods, which illustrates surface-based features are more sensitive to human age than voxel-based features. In future work, we hope to employ our model in disease classification to help doctors make diagnosis.

Acknowledgement. This work was supported by the National Natural Science Foundation of China (61271151, 61228103), NSF (IIS-0915933, IIS-0937586, IIS-0713315) and NIH (1R01NS058802-01, 2R01NS041922-05).

References

1. Caseya, B.J., Kathleen, J.N.G., Thomas, M.: Structural and functional brain development and its relation to cognitive development. Biological Psychology 54, 241–257 (2000)
2. Davatzikos, C., Xu, F., An, Y., Fan, Y., Resnick, S.M.: Longitudinal progression of Alzheimer's-like patterns of atrophy in normal older adults: the SPARE-AD index. Brain: A Journal of Neurology 132, 2026–2035 (2009)
3. Kirkpatrick, B., Messias, E., Harvey, P.D., Fernandez-Egea, E., Bowie, C.R.: Is schizophrenia a syndrome of accelerated aging? Schizophrenia Bulletin 34, 1024–1032 (2008)

4. Ashburner, J., Friston, K.J.: Voxel-based morphometry - The methods. NeuroImage 11, 805–821 (2000)
5. Good, C.D., Johnsrude, I.S., Ashburner, J., Henson, R.N., Friston, K.J., Frackowiak, R.S.: A voxel-based morphometric study of ageing in 465 normal adult human brains. NeuroImage 14, 21–36 (2001)
6. Terribilli, D., Schaufelberger, M.S., Duran, F.L., Zanetti, M.V., Curiati, P.K., Menezes, P.R., Scazufca, M., Amaro Jr., E., Leite, C.C., Busatto, G.F.: Age-related gray matter volume changes in the brain during non-elderly adulthood. Neurobiology of Aging 32, 354–368 (2011)
7. Ashburner, J.: A fast diffeomorphic image registration algorithm. NeuroImage 38, 95–113 (2007)
8. Franke, K., Ziegler, G., Kloppel, S., Gaser, C.: Estimating the age of healthy subjects from T1-weighted MRI scans using kernel methods: exploring the influence of various parameters. NeuroImage 50, 883–892 (2010)
9. Meunier, D., Achard, S., Morcom, A., Bullmore, E.: Age-related changes in modular organization of human brain functional networks. NeuroImage 44, 715–723 (2009)
10. Dale, A.M., Fischl, B., Sereno, M.I.: Cortical surface-based analysis. I. Segmentation and surface reconstruction. NeuroImage 9, 179–194 (1999)
11. Segonne, F., Dale, A.M., Busa, E., Glessner, M., Salat, D., Hahn, H.K., Fischl, B.: A hybrid approach to the skull stripping problem in MRI. NeuroImage 22, 1060–1075 (2004)
12. Desikan, R.S., Segonne, F., Fischl, B., Quinn, B.T., Dickerson, B.C., Blacker, D., Buckner, R.L., Dale, A.M., Maguire, R.P., Hyman, B.T., Albert, M.S., Killiany, R.J.: An automated labeling system for subdividing the human cerebral cortex on MRI scans into gyral based regions of interest. NeuroImage 31, 968–980 (2006)
13. Dai, D., He, H., Vogelstein, J., Hou, Z.: Network-Based Classification Using Cortical Thickness of AD Patients. In: Suzuki, K., Wang, F., Shen, D., Yan, P. (eds.) MLMI 2011. LNCS, vol. 7009, pp. 193–200. Springer, Heidelberg (2011)
14. Tipping, M.E.: Sparse Bayesian learning and the relevance vector machine. J. Mach. Learn. Res. 1, 211–244 (2001)
15. Tamnes, C.K., Ostby, Y., Fjell, A.M., Westlye, L.T., Due-Tonnessen, P., Walhovd, K.B.: Brain maturation in adolescence and young adulthood: regional age-related changes in cortical thickness and white matter volume and microstructure. Cereb. Cortex 20, 534–548 (2010)
16. Sanabria-Diaz, G., Melie-Garcia, L., Iturria-Medina, Y., Aleman-Gomez, Y., Hernandez-Gonzalez, G., Valdes-Urrutia, L., Galan, L., Valdes-Sosa, P.: Surface area and cortical thickness descriptors reveal different attributes of the structural human brain networks. NeuroImage 50, 1497–1510 (2010)

Biomedical Images Classification
by Universal Nearest Neighbours Classifier
Using Posterior Probability

Roberto D'Ambrosio[1,3], Wafa Bel Haj Ali[3], Richard Nock[2], Paolo Soda[1],
Frank Nielsen[4], and Michel Barlaud[3,5]

[1] Universita' Campus Bio-Medico di Roma, Rome, Italy
{r.dambrosio,p.soda}@unicampus.it
[2] CEREGMIA - Université Antilles-Guyane, Martinique, France
rnock@martinique.univ-ag.fr
[3] CNRS - U.Nice, France
{belhajal,barlaud,dambrosi}@i3s.unice.fr
[4] Sony Computer Science Laboratories, Inc., Tokyo, Japan
Frank.Nielsen@acm.org
[5] Institut Universitaire de France

Abstract. Universal Nearest Neighbours (UNN) is a classifier recently
proposed, which can also effectively estimates the posterior probability
of each classification act. This algorithm, intrinsically binary, requires
the use of a decomposition method to cope with multiclass problems,
thus reducing their complexity in less complex binary subtasks. Then,
a reconstruction rule provides the final classification. In this paper we
show that the application of UNN algorithm in conjunction with a reconstruction rule based on the posterior probabilities provides a classification scheme robust among different biomedical image datasets. To this
aim, we compare UNN performance with those achieved by Support Vector Machine with two different kernels and by a k Nearest Neighbours
classifier, and applying two different reconstruction rules for each of the
aforementioned classification paradigms. The results on one private and
five public biomedical datasets show satisfactory performance.

1 Introduction

Humans are limited in their ability to distinguish similar objects and to diagnose
diseases during image interpretation because of noise and of their non-systematic
search patterns. In addition, the vast amount of image data generated by imaging
devices makes the detection of potential diseases a burdensome task, may reduce
the reproducibility and may cause oversight errors. In biomedical imaging, developments in computer vision, machine learning as well as artificial intelligence
have shown that automatic or semi-automatic image analysis may support the
physicians in different medical fields, overcoming most of the above limitations.

In this paper we focus on the challenging task of classifying biomedical images. Indeed, developing one classifier architecture with robust and satisfactory

F. Wang et al. (Eds.): MLMI 2012, LNCS 7588, pp. 119–127, 2012.

performance over different biomedical image datasets is still an open issue. Main difficulties are related to several factors, e.g. high variability of images belonging to different fields, the number of available images, the type of descriptors, etc..

Recently, some of the authors of this paper have proposed the Universal Nearest Neighbours (UNN) classifier [1]. This algorithm, intrinsically binary, requires the use of a decomposition method to cope with multiclass problems reducing these tasks into several binary subtasks. Then, a *reconstruction rule* provides the final classification [2–4]. Furthermore, it was proven that UNN classifier can effectively estimates the posterior probability of each classification act [5]. This permits us to use this information to apply reconstruction rules potentially more effective than others criteria proposed in the literature, which set the final decision using the crisp labels provided by the binary learners.

The contribution of this paper is the proposal of a new classification scheme combining UNN algorithm with a reconstruction rule based on posterior probability. To proof this claim, we have performed several tests on six different biomedical image datasets comparing UNN performance with those achieved by Support Vector Machine (SVM) with two different kernels and by a k Nearest Neighbours (kNN) classifier. Moreover, the tests were conducted applying two different reconstruction rules for each of the aforementioned classification paradigms.

2   Methods

This section first presents decomposition schemes used by UNN to address multiclass classification tasks and, second, it introduces the UNN itself.

2.1   Decomposition Methods

A classification task consists in assigning to sample $x \in \mathbb{R}^n$ a label representative of one class belonging to a set $\Omega : \{\omega_1, \omega_2, \dots, \omega_C\}$. When we are facing with a multiclass problem, we can make use of a decomposition approach reducing problem complexity in less complex binary subtasks and recombining binary classifiers outputs through a reconstruction rule.

Among the several decomposition rules proposed in literature [2, 3] we investigate the One-per-Class (*OpC*) decomposition method that reduces the original problem into C binary problems each one addressed by a dichotomizer M_c. We say that M_c is specialized in the cth class when it aims at recognizing if the sample x belongs either to the cth class or, alternatively, to any other class. Its output is 1 if $x \in \omega_c$, otherwise it is -1. For each sample x, the crisp outputs of dichotomizers are collected into the *binary profile*: $\boldsymbol{M}(x) = [M_1(x), M_2(x), \dots, M_C(x)]$. Furthermore, dichotomizers may supply other information typically related to the degree that the sample belongs (or does not belong) to the corresponding class. Such information is collected in a *reliability profile*, $\boldsymbol{\psi}(x) = [\psi_1(x), \psi_2(x), \dots, \psi_C(x)]$, whose elements measure the classification reliability on pattern x provided by each dichotomizer. Each entry varies in the interval $[0, 1]$, and a value close to 1 indicates a very reliable classification.

Table 1. The three UNN loss functions, their corresponding solutions δ_j of eq. (4) and their corresponding weights w_i updating eq. (5)

Loss function(ψ)	W_j^+	W_j^-	δ_j in eq. (4)	w_i in eq. (5)
$\exp(-x)$	$\sum_{i:j\sim_k i,\, y_{ic}y_{jc}>0} w_i$	$\sum_{i:j\sim_k i,\, y_{ic}y_{jc}<0} w_i$	$\frac{1}{2}log(\frac{W_j^+}{W_j^-})$	$w_i exp(-\delta_j y_{ic}y_{jc})$
$\log_2(1+\exp(-x))$	$\sum_{i:j\sim_k i,\, y_{ic}y_{jc}>0} w_i$	$\sum_{i:j\sim_k i,\, y_{ic}y_{jc}<0} w_i$	$log(\frac{W_j^+}{W_j^-})$	$\frac{w_i exp(-\delta_j y_{ic}y_{jc})}{1-w_i(1+exp(-\delta_j y_{ic}y_{jc}))}$
$-x+\sqrt{1+x^2}$	$\sum_{i:j\sim_k i,\, y_{ic}y_{jc}>0} w_i$	$\sum_{i:j\sim_k i,\, y_{ic}y_{jc}<0} w_i$	$\frac{2W_j^+-1}{2\sqrt{W_j^+ W_j^-}}$	$1-\frac{1-w_i+\sqrt{w_i(2-w_i)}\delta_j y_{ic}y_{jc}}{\sqrt{1+\delta_j^2 w_i(2-w_i)+2(1-w_i)\sqrt{w_i(2-w_i)}\delta_{jc}y_{ic}y_{jc}}}$

Table 2. UNN loss function and posterior probability estimators $(\hat{p}_c(x))$

Loss function name	Loss function(ψ)	$\hat{p}_c(x)$	Acronym
exponential	$\exp(-x)$	$(1+\exp(-2h_c(x)))^{-1}$	UNN(exp)
logistic	$\log_2(1+\exp(-x))$	$(1+\exp(-h_c(x)))^{-1}$	UNN(log)
Matsushita	$-x+\sqrt{1+x^2}$	$\frac{1}{2}(1+\frac{h_c(x)}{\sqrt{1+h_c(x)^2}})$	UNN(Mat)

The reconstruction rules may use both binary and reliability profiles to set the final decision. We present now two reconstruction rules for OpC: the first is a traditional implementation referred to as *Hamming decoding* (H_d), whereas the second is referred to as *MDS* rule and it has been introduced in [4]. In case of H_d, the final decision is given by $O(x) = \omega_s$, with:

$$s = argmin_i d_H(\mathbf{D}(\omega_i), \mathbf{M}(x)) \tag{1}$$

where

$$d_H(\mathbf{D}(\omega_i), \mathbf{M}(x)) = \sum_{c=1}^{C}(\frac{1-(D(\omega_i,c)M_c(x))}{2}) \quad ; \quad D(\omega_i,c) = \begin{cases} 1 & if\ i=c \\ -1 & if\ i\neq c \end{cases} \tag{2}$$

where s denotes the index of the dichotomizer setting the final output $O(x) \in \Omega$. In case of MDS, we have:

$$s = \begin{cases} \arg\max_c(M_c(x) \cdot \psi_c(x)), & if\ m \in [1, C] \\ \arg\min_c(-M_c(x) \cdot \psi_c(x)), & if\ m = 0 \end{cases} \tag{3}$$

where m is defined as $m = \sum_{c=1}^{C}[M_c(x) = 1]$, and square brackets denote the indicator function.

2.2 Universal Nearest Neighbours

Universal Nearest Neighbour (UNN) is a supervised learning algorithm that induces a leveraged kNN rule by globally minimizing a surrogate loss function in a boosting framework [1, 6–8].

Algorithm 1. Algorithm UNIVERSAL NEAREST NEIGHBORS, UNN($\mathcal{S}, \psi, k$)

Input: $\mathcal{S} = \{(x_i, y_i), i = 1, 2, ..., m, \; x_i \in \mathbb{R}^n, \; y_i \in \{-1, 1\}^C\}$, ψ strictly convex loss, $k \in \mathbb{N}_*$;

Let $\alpha_j \leftarrow 0, \forall j = 1, 2, ..., m$;
for $c = 1, 2, ..., C$ do
  Let $w \leftarrow -\nabla_\psi(0)/m$;
  for $t = 1, 2, ..., T$ do
    [**I.0**] Let $j \leftarrow \text{WIC}(\mathcal{S}, w)$;
    [**I.1**] Let $\delta_j \in \mathbb{R}$ solution of:

$$\sum_{i:j\sim_k i} y_{ic} y_{jc} \nabla_\psi \left(\delta_j y_{ic} y_{jc} + \nabla_\psi^{-1}(-w_i) \right) = 0 \; ; \tag{4}$$

    [**I.2**] $\forall i : j \sim_k i$, let

$$w_i \leftarrow -\nabla_\psi \left(\delta_j y_{ic} y_{jc} + \nabla_\psi^{-1}(-w_i) \right) \; , \tag{5}$$

    $\forall i = 1, 2, .., m$, let

$$w_i \leftarrow \frac{w_i}{\sum_{h=1}^m w_h} \; , \tag{6}$$

    [**I.3**] Let $\alpha_{jc} \leftarrow \alpha_{jc} + \delta_j$;

Output: $h_c(x_q) = \sum_{j\sim_k q} \alpha_{jc} y_{jc} \; ; \quad \forall c = 1, 2, \cdots, C$

Let denote by $\mathcal{S} = \{(x_i, y_i), i = 1, 2, ..., m, \; x_i \in \mathbb{R}^n, \; y_i \in \{-1, 1\}^C\}$ the training set. According with OpC decomposition scheme the problem is reduced into C binary classification tasks with corresponding sets of samples $\mathcal{S}^{(c)} = \{(x_i, y_{ic}), i = 1, 2, ..., m\}$. The vector of labels $y_i \in \{-1, 1\}^C$ encodes class memberships, assuming $y_{ic} = 1$ iff x_i belongs to class c and $y_{ic} = -1$ otherwise. For each problems, we learn a classifier $h_c : \mathbb{R}^n \to \mathbb{R}$ by minimizing a *surrogate risk* over $\mathcal{S}^{(c)}$ [9, 7, 8]. A surrogate risk, considered as the actual missclassification rate of h_c on the training data $\mathcal{S}$, has the following general expression:

$$\varepsilon_\mathcal{S}^\psi(h_c) \doteq \frac{1}{m} \sum_{i=1}^m \psi(y_{ic} h_c(x_i)) \; , \tag{7}$$

for some function ψ that we call a *surrogate loss*. Quantity $y_{ic} h_c(x_i) \in \mathbb{R}$ is called the multiclass *edge* of classifier h_c on example (x_i, y_{ic}).

Let $NN_k(x)$ be the set of the k nearest neighbours ($k \in \mathbb{N}^*$) of an example x. Then, the UNN classification rule , introduced in [1], is expressed as the following *weighted* kNN voting rule:

$$h_c(x) = \sum_{j \in NN_k(x)} \alpha_{jc} y_{jc} \tag{8}$$

where $\alpha_{jc} \in \mathbb{R}$ is the leveraging coefficient for example j in class c, with $j = \{1, 2, ..., m\}$ and $c = \{1, 2, ..., C\}$. Note that those coefficients are the solution of minimising the *surrogate risk* in eq. (7). Hence, eq. (8) linearly combines class labels of the k nearest with their leveraging coefficients. Eventually, one leverage coefficient (α_{jc}) per class is learned for each weak classifier (Alg.1)

We report in this paper three versions of UNN with the following losses: exponential, logistic and Matsushita, detailed in Table 1 and Table 2. For each of those functions we give the corresponding expression of δ_j, approximation to the solution of eq. (4), and w_i in eq. (5) in Table 1.

UNN may supply information related to the degree that the test sample x belongs (or not) to the corresponding class. Thus, we estimate the posterior probability $(\hat{p}_c(x))$ of decision taken by UNN on a query sample x. We report estimator's formal definition for each loss function of UNN in Table 2. The theorical approach for deriving $\hat{p}_c(x)$ from $h_c(x)$ is fully given in [5].

3 Datasets

Table 3. Summary of the used datasets

Dataset	Samples	Classes	Majority class	Minority class	features	Availability
BioCells	489	2	79.6%	20.5%	64	Private
DERM	366	6	30.6%	5.5%	33	UCI
IIFI	600	3	36.0%	31.5%	14	UCBM
Yeast	1479	9	31.3%	1.6%	8	UCI
ICPR$_{BOF}$	721	6	28.9%	8.0%	1024	ICPR2012
ICPR$_{BIF}$	721	6	28.9%	8.0%	1024	ICPR2012

We used one private and five public datasets, belonging to images classification problems of different biomedical domains. They are characterized by a large variability with respect to the number and type of features, classes and samples, allowing the assessment of the performance of classifiers in different conditions. Synthetic data about the used datasets are reported in Table 3, while a more detailed description is reported in the following:

Bio Cells (BioCells)[10]: The images were acquired by means of a fully fluorescence microscope. In biological experiments different NIS proteins mutated are expressed for putative sites of phosphorylation. The effect on the protein localization of each mutation is studied after immunostaining using anti-NIS antibodies. Immunocytolocalization analysis on 489 cells revealed 2 cell types with different subcellular distributions of NIS.

Dermatology (DERM)[11]: This is a dataset with 366 instances represented by 12 clinical features and 21 histopathological features taken from skin samples.

Indirect Immunofluorescence Intensity (IIFI) [12]: Connective tissue disease is autoimmune disorder identified by a chronic inflammatory process diagnosed by Indirect Immunofluorescence on HEp-2 substrate. The dataset consists of 14 statistical features extracted from 600 samples distributed over 3 classes.

Yeast (YEAST)[11]: This database contains information about 10 localization sites of Yeast cells. It is composed of 1484 instances represented by 8 features. We remove the endoplasmic reticulum lumen class that makes impossible perform ten-fold cross validation since it has only 5 sample.

International Conference on Pattern Recognition HEp2 Cells (ICPR): HEp2 images were acquired by means of a fluorescence microscope coupled with a 50W mercury vapor lamp. This is a dataset has 791 instances distributed over six classes. We generated two version of this dataset, $ICPR_{BOF}$ and $ICPR_{BIF}$ using two kind of descriptors: Bag of Features and BIF respectively.

4   Experiments

To proof that UNN in conjunction with MDS provides robust performance, we performed several tests on six datasets comparing UNN performance with those achieved by SVM with a linear (SVM_l) and a gaussian (SVM_{RBF}) kernels, and by a kNN classifier. According to section 2.1, compared decomposition schemes are MDS and *Hamming decoding* (H_d).

As measure of classifier performance, we compute the accuracy and the F-*measure*. The latter is defined as F-$measure = 2((Recall)^{-1} \times (Precision)^{-1})^{-1}$. *Recall* is the fraction of samples labelled as belonging to the considered class that are correctly classified, whereas *Precision* is the fraction of samples in the considered class that are correctly classified.

Experiments are performed using a 10-fold cross validation scheme. Each fold is randomly generated maintaining the a-priori distribution of the original dataset. For each fold, classifiers parameters are optimized running a 5-fold cross validation. Reported results are computed averaging out the results obtained for each fold.

4.1   Classifier Reliability

We have tested three implementations of UNN, i.e. UNN(exp), UNN(log) and UNN(Mat), using three different loss functions for the learn of leveraging kNN. Reliabilities of UNN implementations tested measured in terms of posterior probabilities $\hat{p}_c(x)$ are computed as reported in Table 2. For further details, the interested reader may refer to [5]. To estimate the posterior probabilities for SVM we use the method presented in [13]. Given a SVM decision value f for class c, we compute $\psi_c(x)$ as:

$$\psi_c(x) = \frac{1}{1 + \exp(af(x) + b)} \ , \tag{9}$$

where a and b are estimated by maximizing the log-likelihood on training samples using a five-fold cross validation.

kNN is a statistical classifier where its classification reliability is computed using the definition reported in [14]:

$$\psi_c(x) = \min[\ \max\left(1 - \frac{O_{min}}{O_{max}}, 0\right), 1 - \frac{O_{min}}{O_{min2}}\ ] \tag{10}$$

Table 4. Average values (%) of accuracy and F-measure of the different classifiers. We mark highest value (red) and the second one (green) in each row.

Metrics (%)		UNN(exp)		UNN(log)		UNN(Mat)		SVM_l		$SVMRBF$		kNN	
		MDS	H_d	MDS	H_d	MDS	H_d	MDS	H_d	MDS	H_d	MDS	H_d
BioCells	Accuracy	87.1	87.1	86.5	86.5	87.3	87.3	74.3	74.3	87.7	87.7	85.2	85.2
	F-measure	77.7	77.7	76.9	76.9	78.2	78.9	66.9	66.9	76.9	76.9	75.2	75.2
DERM	Accuracy	97.5	97.6	96.5	96.4	97.7	97.1	97.1	87.7	96.9	95.5	95.9	95.5
	F-measure	97.3	97.3	96.1	95.7	97.3	96.6	96.5	81.2	96.6	95.1	95.4	95.2
IIFI	Accuracy	69.5	69.3	68.8	69.1	70.8	68.8	67.2	66.7	71.5	67.4	70.3	68.7
	F-measure	69.0	68.5	68.4	68.4	70.3	68.0	66.8	64.8	70.3	65.5	69.6	67.7
Yeast	Accuracy	59.1	58.0	57.1	55.5	53.9	53.5	52.8	48.3	58.4	54.5	54.1	54.3
	F-measure	50.7	46.3	47.5	45.4	41.5	40.9	41.2	24.2	47.8	41.7	46.1	44.5
ICPR$_{BOF}$	Accuracy	88.1	85.3	87.1	84.6	85.9	80.5	65.4	66.0	86.3	81.6	25.1	26.6
	F-measure	87.4	84.9	86.2	83.3	85.8	81.1	72.3	55.1	85.2	79.8	21.5	21.2
ICPR$_{BIF}$	Accuracy	95.7	95.6	94.9	95.5	95.4	94.9	91.8	89.8	95.3	94.4	95.1	93.91
	F-measure	95.6	95.4	94.4	95.4	95.6	95.1	90.7	85.5	95.2	94.0	94.8	93.7

O_{min} is the distance between x and the nearest sample of the validation set, i.e. the sample determining the class, O_{max} is the highest among the values of O_{min} obtained from all samples of the output class belonging to the test set, and O_{min2} is the distance between x and the nearest sample in the validation set belonging to a class other than the output one.

4.2   Results on Biomedical Images Datasets

We report in Table 4 the classification performance provided by UNN, SVM and kNN classifiers on the six datasets. For each classification task, we report the results obtained using both MDS and H_d reconstruction rules. In order to provide a global comparison among the results, we calculate the relative performance of each experimental configurations with respect to the others (Fig. 1). For each dataset, the twelve columns with the accuracy values are sorted individually, and each classification method is assigned a rank with respect to its place among the others. The largest rank is twelve (assigned to the best method) and the lowest is one (assigned to the worst method). The six ranks for each classification method are then summed up to give a measure of the overall dominance among the methods in terms of accuracy. An analogous procedure has been carried out in case of F-measure. The analysis of data reported both in Table 4 and Fig. 1 permits us to derive the following three considerations. The first one concerns the comparison between MDS and H_d reconstruction rules. Independently of the classifier and of performance metric considered, the former improves classification results in comparison with the latter over 90%.We deem that such performance improvement is mainly due to the fact that MDS rule uses not only predicted crisps labels, as H_d does, but also the corresponding classification reliability. The second consideration focuses on UNN, observing that its performance improve using

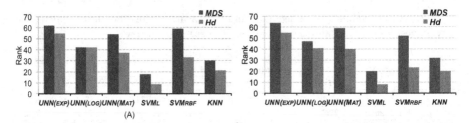

Fig. 1. Panel A and B show the rank for accuracy and F-measure respectively

posterior based reconstruction rule. Indeed, MDS scheme equals or improves UNN performance with H_d scheme in 85% of the cases, at least. For instance, focusing on ICPR$_{BOF}$ dataset, MDS improves UNN performance for all the three configurations of 2%, at least, in terms of both accuracy and F-measure. The third observation concerns how UNN performance compares with those provided by other classifiers. From a general point of view, turn our attention to Fig. 1 where we notice that the value of UNN(exp) rank is larger than the ones of other classifiers. Focusing now on recognition performance we note that UNN classifiers with MDS scheme always overcome performance of SVM with linear kernel. UNN also overcome kNN results with at least one configuration among the three tested. Comparing performance of UNN with those of SVM_{RBF} we note that results are quite similar.

5   Conclusion

In this paper we have proofed that the UNN algorithm in conjunction with a reconstruction rule based on the posterior probabilities provides a classification scheme robust among various biomedical image datasets. Indeed, this classification scheme outperforms other statistical and kernel-based classifiers. Furthermore, this reconstruction rule based on the posterior probabilities has shown larger recognition performance than a reconstruction rule based on crisp labels only.

References

1. Piro, P., Nock, R., Nielsen, F., Barlaud, M.: Leveraging k-nn for generic classification boosting. Neurocomputing 80, 3–9 (2012)
2. Allwein, E.L., et al.: Reducing multiclass to binary: a unifying approach for margin classifiers. Journal of Machine Learning Research 1, 113–141 (2001)
3. Dietterich, T.G., Bakiri, G.: Solving multiclass learning problems via error-correcting output codes. Journal of Artificial Intelligence Research 2, 263 (1995)
4. Iannelo, G., et al.: On the use of classification reliability for improving performance of the one-per-class decomposition method. DKE 68, 1398–1410 (2009)
5. D'Ambrosio, R., Nock, R., Bel Haj Ali, W., Nielsen, F., Barlaud, M.: Boosting Nearest Neighbors for the Efficient Estimation of Posteriors (April 2012)

6. Schapire, R.E., Singer, Y.: Improved boosting algorithms using confidence-rated predictions. Machine Learning Journal 37, 297–336 (1999)
7. Nock, R., Nielsen, F.: On the efficient minimization of classification-calibrated surrogates. In: NIPS*21, pp. 1201–1208 (2008)
8. Nock, R., Nielsen, F.: Bregman divergences and surrogates for learning. IEEE Trans. on Pattern Analysis and Machine Intelligence 31(11), 2048–2059 (2009)
9. Bartlett, P., Jordan, M., McAuliffe, J.D.: Convexity, classification, and risk bounds. Journal of the Am. Stat. Assoc. 101, 138–156 (2006)
10. Bel Haj Ali, W., et al.: A bio-inspired learning and classification method for sub-cellular localization of a plasma membrane protein. In: VISAPP 2012 (2012)
11. Frank, A., Asuncion, A.: UCI machine learning repository (2010)
12. Rigon, A., et al.: Indirect immunofluorescence in autoimmune diseases: Assessment of digital images for diagnostic purpose. Cytometry Part B: Clin. Cytometry 72B(6), 472–477
13. Platt, J.-C.: Probabilistic outputs for support vector machines and comparisons to regularized likelihood methods. In: Advances in Large Margin Classifiers, pp. 61–74. MIT Press (1999)
14. Cordella, L.P., et al.: Reliability parameters to improve combination strategies in multi-expert systems. Pattern Analysis & Applications 2(3), 205–214 (1999)

Simultaneous Registration and Segmentation by L1 Minimization

Pratik Shah and Mithun Das Gupta

John F. Welch Technology Center, GE Global Research, Bangalore, India
{pratik.shah,mithun.dasgupta}@ge.com

Abstract. This paper studies the problem of simultaneously registering and segmenting a pair of images despite the presence of non-smooth boundaries. We assume one of the images is well segmented by automated algorithm or user interaction. This image acts as an atlas for the segmentation process. For the remaining images in the set, we propose a novel L1 minimization based technique, which leverages the fact that the other image is not closely segmented but has a reasonably 'thin' boundary around it. The images are allowed to have non-rigid transformations amongst each other. We extend the two image formulation to multiple image registration and segmentation by introducing a low rank prior on the error matrix. We compare against rigid as well as non-rigid registration techniques. We present results on multi-modal real medical data.

1   Introduction

Simultaneous registration and segmentation of anatomical structures has garnered a lot of interest in the medical image community [1,2]. The concurrent application of registration and segmentation stems from the fact that though the underlying anatomical structure remains same, the acquired images can be very different owing to the variations in scanners, patient movements, etc. Most of these methods deal with rigid deformations taking forward the seminal work presented by Yezzi et al. [1]. [3] propose a Bayesian formulation for simultaneous inhomogeneity correction, registration, and segmentation. The registration was confined to be affine only. Recently much focus has been shifted to non-rigid deformations. [2] propose a PDE based method with the key contribution of an image matching term agnostic to absolute intensity. [4] propose a unified variational approach for image smoothing, segmentation and registration, wherein they impose pairwise registration and contour matching smoothing constraints. We propose a joint registration-segmentation formulation, where the only additional term to the registration cost is a penalty on the `area' of the region which is to be segmented `out'. By segmenting out we mean the part which does not match the region inside the atlas. In essence, if we constrain the over-segmentation present in the target image to be `thin', we can employ a sparsity prior in our cost function.

F. Wang et al. (Eds.): MLMI 2012, LNCS 7588, pp. 128–135, 2012.
© Springer-Verlag Berlin Heidelberg 2012

2   Sparsity Prior for Boundary

Consider the generic registration problem. Assume two images $I_1(x)$ and $I_2(x)$ of the same spatial resolution such that $\{x: \{a, b\} \in [N, M]\}$. Let the displacement field $u(x)$ be defined such that the following cost is minimized

$$C_{reg}(u) = \frac{1}{2} \int_{x \in [N, M]} \underbrace{(I_1(x) - I_2(x))^2 dx}_{data\ term} + \alpha \underbrace{Tr(\nabla u \nabla u^T) dx}_{continuity} \qquad (1)$$

Let the two images to be registered lie in different spatial resolutions. This situation can be handled by padding the smaller spatial resolution image by appropriate zeros such the resolutions are matched again. This can potentially lead to non-optimal cost function since the images might have many dark regions which now seem to match because of the zero padding. Another solution is to put a mask around the larger image such that only region inside the mask is used for the registration process. Let us assume that this mask is known, I_1 is the larger fixed image, I_2 is the smaller moving image and the matching should be done only within this mask. The modified data term can be written as

$$C_{data}(u) = \frac{1}{2} \int_{x \in mask} \underbrace{(I_1(x) - I_2(x - u))^2 dx}_{data\ term} + \frac{1}{2} \int_{x \notin mask} I_1(x)^2 dx \qquad (2)$$

Note the second term in Eq. 2 is independent of the displacement field u. Consequently, if the mask is known, the optimization inside the mask remains exactly same as the generic registration problem. Though for an unknown mask the optimization still remains ill-posed. This problem becomes more pronounced if the region near the boundary is deforming as well and is of similar intensity (Fig. 1). Alternatively, we can solve Eq. 2 treating mask (m) as an unknown. We impose sparsity constraint on the area of the region outside the mask m by incorporating the L_1 norm constraint. For ease of exposition we define a new term $\bar{m} \stackrel{def}{=} \{I_1(x) | x \notin m\}$.

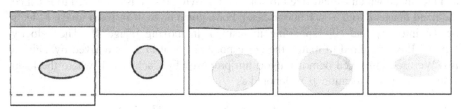

Fig. 1. From left to right: the first image I_1 is larger than the second image I_2. The red dotted box indicates the unknown mask within which the problem is simple registration. Note the yellow object and the gray bar put opposing forces on the registration cost term. Registration results: (third-fifth) Demons algorithm, 2-sided Demons and proposed method.

$$C_{reg}(u, \bar{m}) = \frac{1}{2} \int_{x \notin \bar{m}} (I_1(x) - I_2(x - u))^2 dx + \alpha Tr(\nabla u \nabla u^T) dx + \lambda |\bar{m}|_1 \quad (3)$$

Here α is the weight for the smoothness of the displacement field u and λ is the weighting for the sparsity of the area outside the mask. Further assume that we generate the image corresponding to the region outside the mask and call it the error image e. Given such a transformation the new cost function can be concisely written as

$$C_{reg}(u, e) = \frac{1}{2} \|(I_1 - e) - I_2(u)\|^2 + \lambda |e|_1 + \alpha \frac{1}{2} \|\nabla u\|^2 \quad (4)$$

We propose to solve this problem by the half quadratic method [5] which separates the discontinuous norm term from the continuous data term. Let us introduce an auxiliary variable w in the registration term, such that $w = e$. The new optimization problem which we want to solve can be written as

$$C_{reg}(u, e, w) = \frac{1}{2} \|(I_1 - w) - I_2(u)\|^2 + \alpha \frac{1}{2} \|\nabla u\|^2 + \xi \frac{1}{2} \|w - e\|^2 + \lambda |e|_1 \quad (5)$$

Eq. 5 can now be split into two sub-problems

$$C_{reg}(u, w) = \frac{1}{2} \|(I_1 - w) - I_2(u)\|^2 + \alpha \frac{1}{2} \|\nabla u\|^2 + \xi \frac{1}{2} \|w - e\|^2 \quad (6)$$

$$C_{reg}(e) = \lambda |e|_1 + \xi \frac{1}{2} \|w - e\|^2 \quad (7)$$

2.1 $C_{reg}(u, w)$ Sub-problem

Minimization w.r.t. u: The problem with respect to u is a standard registration problem. We implemented the `Demon's' registration algorithm for the non-rigid deformation estimation at each step. In registration literature, the image which moves owing to the estimated deformation is called the moving image M (I_2 in our case) and the image which is held fixed to which the moving image is compared to is called the fixed image F (($I_1 - w$) in our case). For a given point p in fixed image F, let s be the intensity and corresponding intensity r in moving image M. The velocity (optical flow) required to match the corresponding point in M is derived by Thirion [6]. We used improved demons algorithm proposed by Cachier [7], where the local velocity v_p at the location p is denoted as

$$v_p = \frac{(r - s)\nabla s}{|\nabla s|^2 + \beta^2 |r - s|^2} + \frac{(r - s)\nabla r}{|\nabla r|^2 + \beta^2 |r - s|^2} \quad (8)$$

Here, ∇ is gradient operator and β is normalization factor to balance two forces, an internal edge based force and image difference based force. The registration is achieved iteratively by minimizing local velocity at all pixels.

Minimization w.r.t. w: To estimate w, we utilize the fact that Eq. 6 is strictly convex with respect to w for fixed u, and hence a unique minimizer at each step can be computed.

$$\frac{\partial C_{reg}(u,w)}{\partial w} = 0 \Rightarrow w = \frac{\xi e + (I_1 - I_2(u))}{1 + \xi} \tag{9}$$

2.2 $C_{reg}(e)$ Sub-problem

The $C_{reg}(e)$ subproblem in Eq. 7 is an L_1 norm minimization problem. A similar problem, known as the penalty formulation, was elegantly solved in linear time by the algorithm proposed by Duchi et al. [8]. The penalty formulation is stated as, for a fixed vector v, $\min_x \frac{1}{2}\|v - x\|^2, s.t. |x|_1 \leq z$. Ignoring the trivial case where $|v|_1 \leq z$ for which the solution is $x = v$, there exists for each z a particular θ such that $\min_x \frac{1}{2}\|v - x\|^2 + \theta|x|_1$ has the same solution. The solution of this penalized formulation is directly obtained by applying the (component-wise) soft-thresholding operator [9]

$$S_\theta(v) = \text{sign}(v).\max\{0, |v| - \theta\} \quad (10)$$

The signum function $sign(c) \stackrel{\text{def}}{=} c/\|c\|$ is also defined component-wise, and by convention the elements of $sign(0)$ can be chosen arbitrarily between -1 and 1. The equivalence leads to finding θ such that $|S_\theta(v)|_1 = z$.

3   Group Segmentation

Our method can be modified to tackle a group segmentation and registration problem. Collecting the k images into a matrix $Y = [I_1, I_1 \dots I_k]$, the deformations into $U = [u_1, u_1 \dots u_k]$, the transformed atlas for matching to individual fixed image into $X = [I_a(u_1), I_a(u_2) \dots I_a(u_k)]$ and the error vectors into a matrix $E = [e_1, e_1 \dots e_k]$, we write the group problem, for k images and one atlas as $C_{grp}(U, E) = \frac{1}{2}\|(Y - E) - X\|^2 + \alpha\frac{1}{2}\|\nabla U\nabla U^T\|^2$. Without any further constraints, the group formulation is just a combination of k individual problems. For a medical application, where the images are captured with close temporal and spatial proximity, the images can be considered correlated to each other, under non-rigid transformations. We assume that the error vector obtained from one segmentation is similar to the error vectors obtained from the other images. In other words, $e_i \sim e_j, \forall i, j, \in [1, k]$. This leads to the additional group constraint $rank(E) < \rho$. Integrating the rank constraint into the framework the new cost function for the group registration becomes

$$C_{reg}(U, E) = \frac{1}{2}\|(Y - E) - X\|^2 + \alpha\frac{1}{2}\|\nabla U\nabla U^T\| + \mu rank(E) + \lambda\|E\|_1 \tag{11}$$

Applying a variable separation technique, similar to the single image case, the modified optimization can be written as two separate sub-problems

$$C(U, W) = \mu \text{rank}(W) + \frac{1}{2} \|(Y - W) - X\|^2 + \alpha \frac{1}{2} \|\nabla U \nabla U^T\| + \xi \|W - E\|^2 \quad (12)$$

$$C(E) = \xi \|W - E\|^2 + \lambda \|E\|_1 \quad (13)$$

C(E) : The minimization with respect to each error vector ei is performed similar to the case for one image.

C(U,W), wrt U : This sub-problem is the registration step and is also peformed per image.

C(U,W), wrt W: The minimization with respect to W is the most important part of the group joint registration and segmentation framework. Convex relaxation for the rank constraint was proposed by Peng at al. [10]. The rank constraint can be replaced by the nuclear norm which is the sum of the singular values $\|W\|_* \overset{\text{def}}{=} \sum_{i=1}^m \sigma_i(W)$. The modified cost function can be written as

$$C(W) = \mu \|W\|_* + \xi \|W - E\|^2 + \frac{1}{2} \|(Y - W) - X\|^2 \quad (14)$$

We adopt an accelerated proximal gradient (APL) [11] based method to solve Eq. 14. The APL technique replaces the quadratic equality constraint by a convex upper bound of it. Let us simplify the notation and contain all the constraints into one function $f(W) = \xi \|W - E\|^2 + \frac{1}{2} \|(Y - W) - X\|^2$. The simplified cost function can be written as $C(W) = \mu \|W\|_* + f(W)$. The equality constraint set $f(W)$ is convex and smooth with Lipschitz continuous gradient and hence $\|\nabla f(W_1) - \nabla f(W_2)\| \leq C_L \|W_1 - W_2\|$, where C_L is the Lipschitz constant. Instead of directly minimizing $C(W)$, APL minimizes a sequence of separable quadratic approximations to it, denoted as $Q(W, Z)$, formed at specially chosen points Z:

$$Q(W, Z) = f(Z) + \langle \nabla f(Z), W - Z \rangle + \frac{C_L}{2} \|W - Z\|^2 + \mu \|W\|_* \quad (15)$$

It can be shown that for any Z, $Q(W, Z)$ upper bounds $f(W)$. If we define $G = Z - \frac{1}{C_L} \nabla f(Z)$, then

$$\underset{W}{\arg \min} \, Q(W, Z) = \underset{W}{\arg \min} \{ \mu \|W\|_* + \frac{C_L}{2} \|W - G\|^2 \} \quad (16)$$

The solution for the particular problem can be found by iteratively evaluating the matrix G and then projecting its eigen vectors to a low ranked space spanned by the top few eigen values which are larger in magnitude than μ / C_L. For our particular problem, $C_L = 4(\xi + \lambda)$. For accelerating the general proximal gradient technique, Lin et al. [11] propose an acceleration step. This modification is achieved by starting with a large value of $\mu = \mu_0$, the weighting parameter for the norm constraint and then gradually decreasing it to some predefined floor value $\bar{\mu}$. The convergence for the APG method can be invoked for the following theorem:

Theorem 1. *Let* $F(W) = min \, \bar{\mu}\|W\|_* + \xi\|W - E\|^2 + \frac{1}{2}\|(Y - W) - X\|^2$ *Then,*
$\forall k > k_0 \stackrel{def}{=} \frac{log \, (\mu_0/\bar{\mu})}{log\frac{1}{\eta}}$

$$F(W_k) - F(W^*) \leq \frac{2C_L\|W_{k_0} - W^*\|^2}{(k - k_0 + 1)^2} \qquad (17)$$

Where, W^* *is any solution to Eq. 12,* $\mu_{k+1} = \eta\mu_k$ *and* $C_L = 4(\xi + \lambda)$.

Thus for any $\epsilon > 0$, when $\forall k > k_0 + \sqrt{\frac{2C_L\|W_{k_0}-W^*\|^2}{\epsilon}}$, we can guarantee that $F(W_k) < F(W^*) + \epsilon$.

4   Experiments and Results

For the first set of experiments, we choose two kinds of images with very different characteristics, namely: magnetic resonance (MR) images, and Lena (Fig. 2). The Lena image is deformed to generate the fixed images. The MR image is obtained from the patient scan at a different time. We quantified our algorithm performance and compared it against rigid and non-rigid registration algorithms (without the novel sparsity prior) using dice coefficient. We used area of the interested object as a metric for dice coefficient. The quantification results suggest that our approach performs consistently better than simple registration.

Circle of Willis: Carotid and vertebra-basilar arteries are the main trunk arterial lines to supply blood to brain. They form circle at the base of the brain also known as circle of Willis (COW). If any vessel is blocked or occluded or partially blocked, the circular formation of vessels makes possible to circulate blood to all higher level

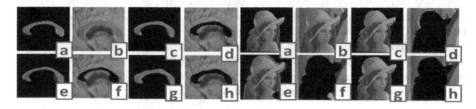

Image	rigid	nonrigid	proposed
MR	0.47389	0.7064	0.81566
lena	0.93672	0.93151	0.95857

Fig. 2. Comparison of different algorithms for segmentation and registration on 2D examples. For each image class (a) segmented atlas, (b) to be segmented image with boundary, (c,d) rigid registration: segmented and registered object, extracted background respectively, (e,f) non-rigid registration: segmented and registered object, extracted background respectively, (g,h) proposed method: segmented and registered object, extracted background respectively. Bottom Row: comparison with registration.

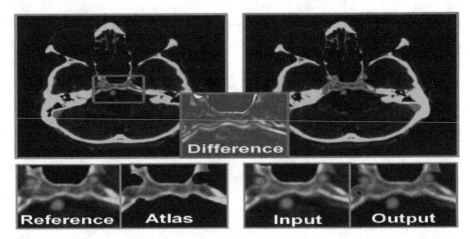

Fig. 3. Sphenoid Bone removal 2 image experiment. The blue outline images were used to create the atlas by manual segmentation. The green outline images form the output images. The red rectangle in the left most image shows the ROI which is the reference image (bottom left). The manual segmentation of the reference image generates the Atlas. The input image to the system is the ROI from the new image. The output of our method is shown in bottom right. The inset image with the brown outline shows the difference of the reference and the input image (with window leveling to show the absolute difference).

arteries (collateral circulation) and thus enables proper brain functioning1. Intra-arterial digital subtraction angiography (IADSA) is the gold standard to access the vascular pathology in intracranial region [12]. However, it provides projection based information.

CT angiography is currently widely used to visualize the vessels in 3D. Region of interest based 3D visualization either by volume rendering or Maximum intensity projection (MIP) of COW hinders by surrounded soft bone, especially sphenoid bone. Fig. 3 shows single frame result for Sphenoid bone suppression. Given the Volume of interest (VOI) for sphenoid bone and 2D atlas, our approach performs non rigid transformation on atlas to match the bone in the incoming input images. Though intracranial carotid artery is very close to bone in spatial and intensity domain, the prior of sparse deformation forced it to be out from the bone definition. The multi-image results with the MIP projection are shown in Fig. 4.

5   Conclusion and Future Work

In this work, we present a combined registration and segmentation framework, which can be used in multiple application domains. The proposed model stands out for its simplicity as well as performance. The applicability of the method is further enhanced by the fact that it has a modular structure, which enables any registration algorithm to be fed into it. We further introduce a group segmentation-registration algorithm,

---

[1] http://www.strokecenter.org/professionals/brain-anatomy/
blood-vessels-of-thebrain/

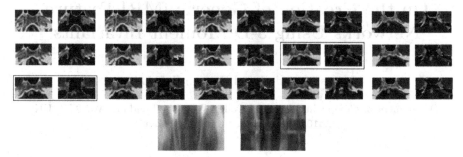

Fig. 4. Sphenoid Bone removal. Each pair of image shows the original frame and the bone removed frame. The two pairs in boxes are manually generated. The last two images show the MIP projection before and after bone removal.

which introduces a unique way of combining low norm and low rank constraints. We keep the actual evaluation of the interplay of different registration algorithms with our method as a future work.

References

1. Yezzi, A., Zollei, L., Kapur, T.: A variational framework for joint segmentation and registration. In: IEEE Mathematical Methods in Biomedical Image Analysis, pp. 44–51 (2001)
2. Wang, F., Vemuri, B.C.: Simultaneous Registration and Segmentation of Anatomical Structures from Brain MRI. In: Duncan, J.S., Gerig, G. (eds.) MICCAI 2005. LNCS, vol. 3749, pp. 17–25. Springer, Heidelberg (2005)
3. Pohl, K.M., Fisher, J., Levitt, J.J., Shenton, M.E., Kikinis, R., Grimson, W.E.L., Wells, W.M.: A Unifying Approach to Registration, Segmentation, and Intensity Correction. In: Duncan, J.S., Gerig, G. (eds.) MICCAI 2005. LNCS, vol. 3749, pp. 310–318. Springer, Heidelberg (2005)
4. Lord, N.A., Ho, J., Vemuri, B.C.: USSR: A unified framework for simultaneous smoothing, segmentation, and registration of multiple images. In: ICCV, pp. 1–6 (2007)
5. Krishnan, D., Fergus, R.: Fast image deconvolution using Hyper-Laplacian priors. In: Advances in Neural Information Processing Systems, pp. 1033–1041 (2009)
6. Thirion, J.P.: Image matching as a diffusion process: an analogy with Maxwell's demons. Medical Image Analysis, 243–260 (1998)
7. Cachier, P., Pennec, X., Ayache, N.: Fast Non Rigid Matching by Gradient Descent: Study and Improvements of the "Demons" Algorithm. Technical Report RR-3706, INRIA (1999)
8. Duchi, J., Shwartz, S.S., Singer, Y., Chandra, T.: Efficient projections onto the L1-ball for learning in high dimensions. In: ICML 2008, pp. 272–279 (2008)
9. Chambolle, A., DeVore, R.A., Lee, N.Y., Lucier, B.J.: Nonlinear wavelet image processing: Variational problems, compression, and noise removal through wavelet shrinkage. IEEE Trans. Image Processing 7, 319–335 (1996)
10. Peng, Y., Ganesh, A., Wright, J., Xu, W., Ma, Y.: Rasl: Robust alignment by sparse and low-rank decomposition for linearly correlated images. In: CVPR (2010)
11. Lin, Z., Ganesh, A., Wright, J., Wu, L., Chen, M., Ma, Y.: Fast convex optimization algorithms for exact recovery of a corrupted low-rank matrix (2009) (preprint)
12. Ghazali, R.M., Shuaib, I.L.: Comparison between 3d tof magnetic resonance angiography and intraarterial digital subtraction angiography in imaging the circle of willis. Malaysian Journal of Medical Sciences 10, 37–42 (2003)

On the Creation of Generic fMRI Feature Networks Using 3-D Moment Invariants

Loizos Markides* and Duncan Fyfe Gillies

Department of Computing, Imperial College London, London, SW7 2AZ, UK
{lm1011,d.gillies}@imperial.ac.uk

Abstract. Multi-voxel pattern analysis (MVPA) is a common technique of pattern-information fMRI, which, through the process of feature selection and subsequent classification, can aid the detection of groups of informative voxels that can be used to discriminate between competing stimuli. Networks of features have been long extracted univariately but recently researchers have turned to the development of multivariate techniques that also move from being purely mathematical, to have a more physiological meaning. In this work, we demonstrate a multivariate feature selection method that uses information encoded in the 3D spatial distribution of activated voxels at each anatomical region of the brain, in order to extract networks of informative regions that can act as generic features for running MVPA across subjects.

Keywords: pattern-information fMRI, feature selection, multi-voxel pattern analysis, ROI characterisation, 3D moments.

1 Introduction

Brain decoding operations attempt the prediction of the task that was performed by a subject at a certain time, given the respective brain activity. The primary technique used for decoding fMRI brain activation is called Multi-Voxel Pattern Analysis (MVPA), and is typically trying to generalize from a set of observed activation data, in order to make predictions about the nature of the tasks undertaken by a subject, on entirely new data. MVPA essentially seeks to apply a classifier on the fMRI data through a four step process that involves *data extraction, feature selection, training and testing of the classifier* and finally *classifier characterization*. The *feature selection* step is critical since it aims to identify the set of voxels that incorporate the maximum information for the discrimination of two competing classes of stimuli. An emerging problem with most feature selection methodologies is that they don't take into account idiosyncrasies in patterns of different individuals, and therefore, they are not reliable if used widely across subjects. In this work we present a multivariate feature selection methodology that aims to exploit locality information of voxels and achieve a higher classification accuracy while helping to maintain a physiological meaning in the extracted set of features. To accomplish that, we are using information about the shape of

---

* Corresponding author.

F. Wang et al. (Eds.): MLMI 2012, LNCS 7588, pp. 136–143, 2012.

the 3D spatial distribution of activated voxels in a set of predefined anatomical regions, in order to detect areas that have consistently diverse spatial distributions for the contrasting stimuli. The resulting networks of informative regions are then used to classify mental states across individuals.

2 Background

2.1 Feature Selection

Feature selection aims to determine the set of voxels that provides selectivity between distinct tasks. The most common methods are univariate and involve the use of the t-statistics and analysis of variance (ANOVA). T-statistics feature selection chooses voxels that exhibit significant activation for the stimuli under investigation (i.e. have a t- or a z- value above a certain threshold), while ANOVA chooses the voxels with the highest variance on their activation values over the course of the experiment. The inherent problem with univariate methods is the fact that the effective brain activations are mixed together with artefacts and their separation is difficult, while covariation patterns of the same subject are ignored. These problems are addressed by using multivariate feature selection strategies. An interesting and widely used local multivariate feature selection method is proposed by Kriegeskorte et al. [4] and tries to identify neighbourhoods that contain discriminative information by measuring the classification performance of neighbouring voxels that fall within a searchlight of predefined radius. De Martino et al. [2] were the first to suggest the combination of univariate with multivariate methods by proposing a combined approach of "univariate activation-based feature reduction and multivariate recursive SVM-based feature elimination". Moreover, Chai et al. [1] suggest a feature selection method based on mutual information among single voxels (univariate) and among patterns of voxels (multivariate), in order to reduce the dimensionality of highly informative voxels and provide a mean for measuring the functional connectivity among regions respectively. Methods like [1] and [2] that aim to reduce the feature set in order to achieve lower complexity, typically result in a set of sporadic features that might have limited physiological interpretation when compared to the full set. Therefore, in our methodology we strive to use whole brain areas as features, by removing only the non-informative but not the redundant features.

2.2 Characterisation of the Activation in a Region of Interest

In order to achieve a more accurate feature selection across subjects we need to automatically measure and compare the level of similarity between various regions of interest (ROIs) for contrasting conditions. Even though measures that solely incorporate individual voxel intensity within a ROI have been mostly utilized so far, we believe that information on how the spatial distribution of activated voxels changes within a ROI can significantly aid the feature selection process. Published methods on ROI activation characterisation can be mainly divided in two types. Type I are the ones that depend solely on registering all the subjects scans onto a standard template space and Type II are the ones that rely on correct segmentation of ROIs in native subject space. According to Pokrajac et al. [7], these categories can be further divided into the ones that incorporate spatial information and the ones that are based only on signal-intensity.

The most commonly used methodologies are of Type I and utilise signal intensity in conjunction with thresholding, where overlapping voxels across subjects above a certain threshold are considered to construct informative regions [6]. These methods are highly prone to misregistration errors, since they assume that the same voxels are located at the same coordinates for all subjects, while the normalization step usually leads to loss of crucial spatial information primarily caused by interpolation. On the other hand, methods of Type I that incorporate spatial information aim to approximate the spatial distribution of activated voxels by using either parametric or semi-parametric techniques [7].

Signal-intensity techniques of Type II involve the use of mean activation statistics like the percentage of activated voxels and mean percent signal change. These methods have an inherent advantage when comparing activations across subjects since they are independent of the spatial variability and orientation of different brain images. However, they implicitly consider the spatial locality of voxels unimportant leading to loss of information. Ng et al. [5] exhibited a way to exploit the spatial distribution of activation statistics within several manually drawn ROIs in order to achieve a more accurate discrimination among two groups of subjects, by also maintaining the advantages of mean activation statistics. In their proposed methodology, instead of attempting to approximate the actual spatial distributions (like in Type I), they make use of characteristics of the spatial distributions, in the form of second, third and fourth order moments. While traditionally-defined second order and higher moments are still prone to inter-subject registration, they formulate non-linear combinations of these metrics, in order to obtain translational, scale and rotational invariance that will help to account for the different brains shapes and sizes, as well as the orientation of the subject in the MR scanner respectively.

3   Calculation of Measures

3.1   Mean Activation Statistics

To establish a basis for the evaluation of the results of our methodology we used the percentage of activated voxels (PAV) and mean signal change (MSC).

$$PAV_\tau^{ROI} = \frac{Activated\,voxels_{t>\tau}^{ROI}}{Total\,voxels^{ROI}}, \quad MSC_\tau^{ROI} = \frac{Activated\,voxels_{t>\tau}^{ROI}}{\Sigma_{\forall ROI}\,Activated\,voxels_{t>\tau}^{ROI}}$$

The t-statistics maps were obtained by applying a t-test to each voxel, based on the BOLD signal changes that were obtained by convolving the regressors for each contrasting condition with the canonical Hemodynamic Response Function (HRF). Atlas-based segmentation of the native space was performed in order to obtain distinct masks in the native subject space for all the 68 regions of the Harvard-Oxford atlas, which is distributed as part of the FSL software. The voxel activation statistics were subsequently thresholded with a specific τ and mapped in the resulting anatomical ROIs in order to measure the PAV and MSC metrics for each region.

3.2 3D Moment Invariants

3D moment invariants were calculated in the same way as Ng et al. [5]. The proposed methodology is briefly described here. We first start by calculating the 3D moments in each of the 48 cortical and 20 sub-cortical regions, using

$$m_{pqr} = \int_{-\infty}^{+\infty} \int_{-\infty}^{+\infty} \int_{-\infty}^{+\infty} x^p y^q z^r \rho(x, y, z) dx dy dz$$

with $n = p + q + r$ being the order of the 3D moment and $\rho(x, y, z)$ being the normalized t-values of a voxel located at (x, y, z) coordinates of a ROI. To generate the ρ-values we take the positive values of the t-statistic maps and normalise their values to the range $(0,1)$. This normalization step is crucial when performing spatial analysis, in order to ensure that any overall magnitude changes do not cause any further effects in our analysis, while the negative t-values are removed because of their presently unclear interpretation.

Since we want to account for translational, scale and rotational invariance, we are not using the resulting moments directly for inference, but we need to calculate the respective 3D moment invariants. *Translational invariance* is obtained by taking the central moments:

$$\mu_{pqr} = \int_{-\infty}^{+\infty} \int_{-\infty}^{+\infty} \int_{-\infty}^{+\infty} (x - \bar{x})^p (y - \bar{y})^q (z - \bar{z})^r \rho(x, y, z) dx dy dz$$

where the centroid coordinates $\bar{x}$, $\bar{y}$, $\bar{z}$ are calculated as

$$\bar{x} = \frac{m_{100}}{m_{000}}, \quad \bar{y} = \frac{m_{010}}{m_{000}}, \quad \bar{z} = \frac{m_{001}}{m_{000}}$$

Then to obtain *scale invariance* the moments are normalized according to

$$\eta_{pqr} = \frac{\mu_{pqr}}{\mu_{000}^k} \quad with \quad k = \frac{p + q + r}{3} + 1$$

And finally, to obtain *rotational invariance*, the second, third and fourth order moments are combined in certain non-linear ways as described in [8].

$J_1 = \eta_{200} + \eta_{020} + \eta_{002}$

$J_2 = \eta_{200}\eta_{020} + \eta_{200}\eta_{002} + \eta_{020}\eta_{002} - \eta_{101}^2 - \eta_{110}^2 - \eta_{011}^2$

$J_3 = \eta_{200}\eta_{020}\eta_{002} + 2\eta_{011}\eta_{101}\eta_{110} - \eta_{002}\eta_{110}^2 - \eta_{020}\eta_{101}^2 - \eta_{200}\eta_{011}^2$

$B_3 = \eta_{300}^2 + \eta_{030}^2 + \eta_{003}^2 + 3\eta_{210}^2 + 3\eta_{201}^2 + 3\eta_{120}^2 + 3\eta_{102}^2 + 3\eta_{021}^2 + 3\eta_{012}^2 + 6\eta_{111}^2$

$B_4 = \eta_{400}^2 + \eta_{040}^2 + \eta_{004}^2 + 4\eta_{310}^2 + 4\eta_{301}^2 + 4\eta_{130}^2 + 4\eta_{103}^2 + 4\eta_{031}^2 + 4\eta_{013}^2 + 6\eta_{202}^2$

$\qquad + 6\eta_{022}^2 + 6\eta_{220}^2 + 12\eta_{112}^2 + 12\eta_{121}^2 + 12\eta_{211}^2$

The resulting five 3D moment invariants are used as indicators of the spatial distribution of the activated voxels in each ROI.

4   Materials and Methods

4.1   Imaging Data

To evaluate our methodology, we have used the dataset of Duncan et al. [3] that is distributed freely via the OpenFMRI project website under the ODC Public Domain Dedication and License v1.0. The dataset consists of 45 subjects that performed two runs of a visual one-back task with four categories of items: written words, objects, scrambled objects and consonant letter strings. In a visual one-back task, the subjects are supposed to press a button if the stimulus that they are currently viewing is the same as the previous one. In the original work by the authors of [3], two functional localiser scans were performed in order to identify word- and object- specific regions of the ventral and lateral occipito-temporal cortex, respectively. The functional ROIs were determined by using the overlapping signal intensity across subjects in conjunction with thresholding were utilized (ROI characterisation of Type I in Section 2.2.).

4.2   Approach

The pre-processing of fMRI data included brain extraction and motion correction using FSL's BET and McFlirt tools respectively. Each voxel's intensity was spatially smoothed using a Gaussian smoothing kernel with a full width at half maximum (FWHM) of 4mm. The scans from all subjects were then registered to a T1-weighted full brain anatomical image using rigid body registration. Atlas-based segmentation of the subject's native space was performed by first register-ing the T1-weighted image for each subject to the MNI-152 2mm standard with 12-parameter affine registration with FSL's Flirt tool, and subsequently using the resulting parameters to apply an inverse transformation of the Harvard-Oxford cortical and sub-cortical atlases to the subject's native space.

To obtain t-statistics maps for each condition, the General Linear Model was applied as it is implemented in FSL's FEAT tool. A t-statistic map was acquired for each of the following four conditions: 1) written words vs rest, 2) objects vs rest, 3) scrambled objects vs rest, 4) consonant letter strings vs rest. Mean activation statistics and 3D moment invariant measures were then calculated for the t-statistics map of each condition, as described in Section 3.

Since we wanted to compare ROI measures across different conditions, we ran a permutation test [5] to calculate the probability of similar measures to be drawn from the same distribution for our contrasting conditions. ROIs with $\alpha < 0.05$ were subsequently combined in one mask that was used to initialize the classification. For the actual classification process we have used linear kernel Support Vector Machines (SVM), having the percentage of correct guesses for each condition to act as a performance metric of the accuracy of classification.

For the creation of the feature masks 45-fold cross validation was performed, where the t-maps from 44 subjects where used to create the feature set, and clas-sification was ran on the remaining subject. ANOVA with $p = 0.05$ was used as an additional step prior to classification in order to filter out possible uninforma-tive voxels in the resulting feature set. In order to avoid possible within-subject peeking caused by ANOVA, 12-fold cross validation was performed, where 11 runs were used for training and one run for testing at each fold. Princeton's MVPA toolbox in Matlab was used for running the classification.

5   Results

Table 1 shows the p-values for activation differences of words versus consonant letter strings (upper) and objects versus scrambled images (lower) for 8 of the regions that exhibited interesting effects. Regions with p-values lower than 0.05 for each of our metrics express a difference in the spatial distribution of activation for the contrasting conditions and were chosen to create discriminative feature masks. Therefore, masks A and B reflect the ROIs indicated by mean activation statistics with $\tau = 3$, masks C and D reflect the ROIs indicated by mean activation statistics with $\tau = 5$, and masks E and F reflect the ROIs indicated by the 3D moment invariants statistics. Figure 1a shows a boxplot of

Table 1. P-values for activation differences of (a) words versus consonant letter strings and (b) objects versus scrambled images. Values in bold exhibit p-values with $\alpha < 0.05$ and belong to areas where the activation metrics are drawn from different distributions.

ROI	PAV		MSC		J1	J2	J3	B3	B4
	$\tau = 3$	$\tau = 5$	$\tau = 3$	$\tau = 5$					
Words versus Consonant letter strings									
SLOC	0.1122	0.4629	0.2375	0.3886	**0.0023**	0.0717	0.0753	0.2007	**0.0194**
ILOC	0.4752	0.7028	**0.0031**	0	**0.0075**	0.0535	0.2136	0.6061	0.1590
LING	0.0931	0.4355	0.4871	0.5034	0	**0.0034**	0.1887	0.2744	**0.0272**
TOFC	0.5372	0.7907	**0.0286**	**0.0035**	0.9409	0.9480	0.9524	0.9967	0.9990
OFG	**0.0161**	0.1464	0.4477	0.3149	0	0	0	**0.0005**	0
OCCP	**0.0002**	**0.0104**	0.0678	0.3170	0	0	0	0	0
LACC	0.4531	0	0.2286	0	0	0	0	0	0
RACC	0.6658	0.4757	0.3911	0.2137	0	0	0	0	0
Objects versus Scrambled Images									
SLOC	0.5474	0.6244	0.1254	**0.0013**	0.8001	0.8408	0.8846	0.0790	0.8053
ILOC	0.2708	0.5834	0.0554	0.2181	**0.0003**	**0.0008**	**0.0031**	0.2340	**0.0008**
LING	0.2393	0.6554	0.0681	0.4705	0	0	0	0	0
TOFC	0.6153	0.8348	0.9002	0.6320	**0.0106**	**0.0137**	**0.0176**	0.1572	**0.0147**
OFG	0.0667	0.3913	0.1092	0.4731	0	0	0	**0.0009**	0
OCCP	**0.0372**	0.3593	**0.0119**	0.0881	0	0	0	0	0
LACC	0.1722	0.2936	0.1347	0.3779	0.6884	0.6700	0.9999	0.8302	0.8361
RACC	0.6417	0.3694	0.6771	0.3686	0	0	0	0	0

SLOC-ILOC=Superior/Inferior Lateral Occipital, TOFC=Temporal Occipital Fusiform Cortex

OCCP=Occipital Pole, OFG=Occipital Fusiform, LING=Lingual Gyrus, LACC-RACC=Accumbens

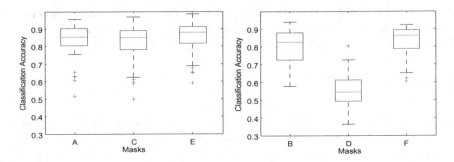

Fig. 1. a.(left) Classification Accuracy for the words versus consonant letter strings using the masks resulted from mean activation statistic with $\tau = 3$ (A) and $\tau = 5$ (C) and with 3D moment invariants (E). **b.(right)** Classification Accuracy for the objects versus scrambled images using the masks resulted from mean activation statistic with $\tau = 3$ (B) and $\tau = 5$ (D) and with 3D moment invariants (F)

the classification accuracy for the words versus consonant letter strings for all three masks A,C and E while Figure 1b shows a boxplot of the classification accuracy for the objects versus scrambled images for all three masks B,D and F. The networks of ROIs resulting from the 3D moment invariants (masks E,F) yielded better classification accuracy from the mean activation statistics of both thresholds. One might argue that the improvement on classification accuracy of our approach is limited while the univariate methods are much simpler to apply. It is therefore important to mention that the choice of threshold was done by running eleven iterations of the experiments with the τ value starting at 0 and increasing by 0.5 at every iteration. Masks A and B ($\tau = 3$) provided the highest classification accuracy out of all iterations. Moreover, mask D ($\tau = 5$) exhibited classification accuracy close to chance, most probably because several informative regions were cut out during thresholding. This illustrates the inherent sensitivity of the mean activation statistics methods on choosing the right threshold value, something that does not apply to the 3D moment invariants.

It is interesting to note that various regions exhibited a difference in spatial distribution for both pairs of contrasting conditions, meaning that the same areas can help in discriminating different tasks when used as part of different ROI networks. Moreover, while the specific values in Table 1 are unique for a randomly-chosen subject due to cross-validation, the resulting chosen networks of regions for all subjects were consistent across the experiments.

6   Conclusion

In this work we have demonstrated a methodology that successfully uses differences in the spatial distribution of positive t-statistic values, in order to create networks of discriminative regions that can act as generic features for the classification of various contrasting conditions. The uniqueness of our approach is that we can make inferences at an inter-subject level by running our analysis in the subjects' native space, something that is not possible with other widely used methodologies [2][4], which can be prone to misregistration errors when used to extract features that can classify mental states across individuals. Additionally, we have shown that our method outperforms its univariate equivalents based on mean activation statistics.

In the original analysis of the same dataset, Duncan et al. [3] attempt the detection of functional ROIs for word- and object- sensitive regions of the occipito-temporal cortex. Even though their study dealt with the analysis of fMRI data at a much finer scale and higher resolution, since they were looking for activation within a single ROI, we believe that one of the factors that caused low consistency on their inter-subject findings was the use of ROI characterisation based solely on the signal intensity of individual voxels. Since methods like the latter are massively univariate, we believe that ROI characterisation using features related to the spatial distribution instead of the signal intensity of voxels with either Type I or Type II, can be a promising candidate for functional localisation of inter-subject commonalities or differences even at this finer scale.

Our future work aims to utilise the proposed methodology in order to attempt to model inter-subject commonalities in the resulting components of decomposition of the fMRI signal across individuals with unsupervised leaning techniques in order to attempt the physiological characterisation of these components through testing for what condition differences they can actually discriminate.

References

1. Chai, B., Walther, D.B., Beck, D.M., Li, F.-F.: Exploring Functional Connectivities of the Human Brain using Multivariate Information Analysis. In: Bengio, Y., Schuurmans, D., Lafferty, J.D., Williams, C.K.I., Culotta, A. (eds.) NIPS, pp. 270–278. Curran Associates, Inc. (2009)
2. De Martino, F., Valente, G., Staeren, N., Ashburner, J., Goebel, R., Formisano, E.: Combining multivariate voxel selection and support vector machines for mapping and classification of fMRI spatial patterns. Neuroimage 43(1), 44–58 (2008)
3. Duncan, K.J., Pattamadilok, C., Knierim, I., Devlin, J.T.: Consistency and variability in functional localisers. NeuroImage 46(4), 1018–1026 (2009)
4. Kriegeskorte, N., Goebel, R., Bandettini, P.: Information-based functional brain mapping. Proceedings of the National Academy of Sciences of the United States of America 103(10), 3863 (2006)
5. Ng, B., Abugharbieh, R., Xuemei, H., McKeown, M.J.: Spatial Characterization of fMRI Activation Maps Using Invariant 3-D Moment Descriptors. IEEE Transactions on Medical Imaging 28(2), 261–268 (2009)
6. Park, H.J., Levitt, J., Shenton, M.E., Salisbury, D.F., Kubicki, M., Jolesz, F., McCarley, R.: An MRI study of spatial probability brain map differences between first-episode schizophrenia and normal controls. NeuroImage 22(3), 1231–1246 (2004)
7. Pokrajac, D., Megalooikonomou, V., Lazarevic, A., Kontos, D., Obradovic, Z.: Applying spatial distribution analysis techniques to classification of 3D medical images. Artificial Intelligence in Medicine 33(3), 261–280 (2005)
8. Sadjadi, F.A., Hall, E.L.: Three-dimensional moment invariants. IEEE Trans. Pattern Anal. Mach. Intell. 2(2), 127–136 (1980)

Description and Classification of Confocal Endomicroscopic Images for the Automatic Diagnosis of Inflammatory Bowel Disease

Sara Couceiro[1], João P. Barreto[1], Paulo Freire[2], and Pedro Figueiredo[2]

[1] Institute for Systems and Robotics, University of Coimbra, Portugal
[2] Faculty of Medicine, University of Coimbra, Portugal
and Dept. of Gastroenterology, University Hospital of Coimbra, Portugal

Abstract. Confocal Endomicroscopy (CEM) is a newly developed diagnosis tool which provides *in vivo* examination of the gastrointestinal (GI) histological architecture, avoiding the traditional biopsy . The analysis of CEM images is a challenging task for experts, since there isn't a clearly defined taxonomy of the several disease stages. We aim at building an automatic on-the-fly classifier to provide useful clinical advices for diagnosis. In this work, we propose to make a split between two main subsets of our expert-annotated database: *low* and *high probability of pathology*. We focus on segmentation techniques to extract relevant histological structures, and then encode this information in a feature vector used for classification.

Keywords: Confocal Endomicroscopy, Image Classification, Support Vector Machine.

1 Introduction

Inflammatory Bowel Disease (IBD) refers to a group of inflammatory conditions of the small intestine and the colon. Since most of the initial symptoms are undervalued by patients, IBD diseases are frequently noted at severe and chronic stages of illness. However, like in every clinical context, the diagnosis at early stages strongly increases the chances of successful treatment.

The common practice for the analysis of the histological architecture of the GI tract consists in removing the suspicious areas detected during endoscopy, and then sending them to lab analysis. Confocal Endomicroscopy (CEM) is a recently developed technique that allows the *in vivo* examination of the intestinal mucosa during ongoing endoscopy [5]. The basis behind this new diagnosis tool is the integration of a mini-confocal microscope with the distal tip of a conventional endoscope. The main advantage of the CEM over the traditional biopsy is the real-time examination of the intestinal histology, avoiding the need of tissue removal with increased risks of infection and bleeding, which require subsequent medical treatment. Unfortunately, since this is a quite recent technique, the taxonomy of CEM images has not yet been clearly defined. Physicians are still

F. Wang et al. (Eds.): MLMI 2012, LNCS 7588, pp. 144–151, 2012.

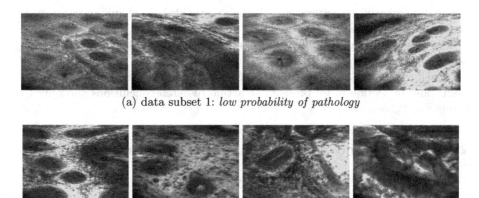

(a) data subset 1: *low probability of pathology*

(b) data subset 2: *high probability of pathology*

Fig. 1. Inter and intra class variability

exploring the complexity of these images and, even for them, their interpretation is still a challenging task [1].

This paper presents exploratory research toward building an on-the-fly automatic classification system to distinguish between two main IBD stages: *low* and *high probability of pathology*. The main challenge in this classification problem is related to the intra and inter class variability. As it is shown in Fig.1, besides the great variability between images from the same class, the differences between the two classes are not clearly evident.

In what concerns the histological architecture of the GI tract, the most evident structures are the intestinal crypts, which are responsible for the ongoing renewal of the epithelial tissue. According to experts feedback, the presence of crypts in the tissue is highly relevant to make a diagnosis. Their number, shape, appearance and distribution over the tissue are determinant to distinguish between the disease stages. Therefore, we focus on segmentation and description of these intestinal structures to detect abnormalities in the tissue.

Due the novelty of the CEM technique, the classification of the CEM images has not been very explored yet. Relevant references can be found in [1, 2], where André *et al* propose a content-based retrieval approach to perform classification of endomicroscopic images from an expert-annotated database. It starts by describing images using bi-scale dense Scale-Invariant Feature Transform (SIFT) features [8], that are quantized into visual words using k-means clustering. The classification is then performed by querying an image database with a histogram of visual words and retrieving the most similar images from the database. This approach requires large amounts of storage space, which may become unfeasible for large database sizes.

Unlike André's works [1, 2], that blindly apply techniques developed for conventional perspective cameras, we build our system based on the physicians interpretation of CEM images. We rely on tissue's histological properties to create a real-time classification system to assist doctors during endoscopy, while segmenting relevant structures and, therefore, provide helpful guidances for medical imaging analysis.

The paper outline is as follows: Section 2 describes the image segmentation scheme used to locate crypts in the tissue. In section 3, we refer to the chosen approach to face the classification task. Section 4 contains the experiments and discussion. In section 5, we present the actual research conclusions and refer to future work goals.

2   Detection and Segmentation of Crypts in CEM Images

Due to the great appearance variability of crypts, their segmentation is not a trivial task. As it can be observed in Fig. 1, crypts are irregular structures with markedly different texture patterns, and contour boundaries that are often poorly defined. In many cases, it is very difficult to accurately locate the exact frontier that separates the interior and exterior areas of a crypt, since there is a soft transition between these two s.

We propose an algorithm for the detection and segmentation of crypts that comprises three main steps, which are further explained in 2.1, 2.2 and 2.3. We start by performing the detection of crypts' centers by searching for local maxima in an energy of image symmetry (Fig.2(a)). Then, in the segmentation stage, we use a canny filter to locate the contours of these structures and fit an ellipse to the edge points (Fig. 2(b)). As we can see from Fig. 2(a) and 2(b), the detection step, not only catches the real centers of the crypts, but also several points that effectively denote symmetric structures in the image, but do not correspond to any crypt. Since there is no obvious solution to immediately discard the false detections, we decided to follow a strategy of overdetection. Centers detector is tuned to catch every high symmetric location, and the segmentation process is fully carried for all the detected keypoints. In the last stage (Fig. 2(c)), we use a binary Support Vector Machine (SVM) discriminator that will decide if each segmented corresponds to a crypt.

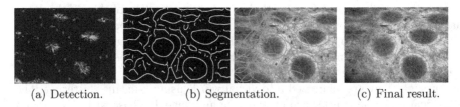

(a) Detection.   (b) Segmentation.   (c) Final result.

Fig. 2. Detection and Segmentation of Crypts in CEM images

2.1   Detection of Crypts' Centers Based on Symmetry Energy

Despite crypts great variability, their shapes range from circular to elongate, reminding elliptical structures, which are symmetric objects. We rely on this symmetry property of the crypts to identify them in intestinal tissue images.

Like in [7], we explore the bilateral symmetry of the local intensity levels of the image signal, by using a frequency-based approach. The extraction of local frequency information is done through a multi-resolution wavelet analysis, by using a bank of filters tuned at different scales. We use log-Gabor wavelets to obtain amplitude and phase information from the image signal [7].

The location of crypts centers is performed by computing local maxima of the symmetry energy (Fig. 3(a)).

2.2   Crypts' Shape Segmentation

Due to the elliptical shape of crypts, the most natural segmentation approach is to find an ellipse around each one of the detected keypoints. This is done by searching for boundary points around the center of the crypt and then fit a conic to them. The algorithm herein described was inspired and adapted from [10].

We first apply a Canny edge detector [3] over the original image signal to extract strong intensity transitions. Since the Canny algorithm relies on image local derivatives, it is highly sensible to noisy image data. To improve the final output of the Canny detector, we blur the image with a Gaussian kernel that is tuned to preserve crypts boundaries and eliminate other (irrelevant) image details. For each detected keypoint, we perform a radial search of boundary points, as proposed in [10]. We consider a searching circular patch in the original image whose center is the detected keypoint, and whose radius is large enough to include the whole crypt. The patch is mapped into a polar image by changing from Cartesian coordinates $\mathbf{x} = (x, y)^{\mathsf{T}}$ to polar coordinates $\chi = (\rho, \theta)^{\mathsf{T}}$. The ρ-dimension is scanned from the left to the right to find positive responses of the Canny filter, as show in Fig.3(b). Fig.3(c) shows the detected transitions mapped back from the polar space to the original Cartesian space. The parameters of the ellipse that best fits the detected edge points are determined using a RANdom SAmple Consensus (RANSAC) [4,10]. The final result is shown in Fig 3(d).

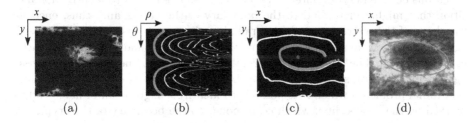

(a)   (b)   (c)   (d)

Fig. 3. Detailed steps of the detection and segmentation of a crypt in a CEM image. The search from left to right in the radial image (b) is substantially faster than in the Cartesian image (c).

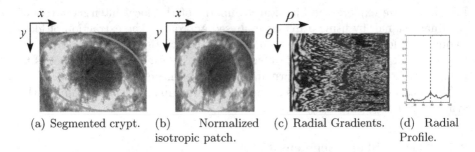

(a) Segmented crypt.   (b)   Normalized   (c) Radial Gradients.   (d) Radial
                         isotropic patch.   Profile.

Fig. 4. Normalization step followed by feature extraction

2.3   Crypts Description and SVM Discriminator

In this step, we aim at building a discriminative local description scheme to
encode crypts' appearance that enables a standard SVM classifier to distinguish
between crypts and other symmetric structures.

Before the descriptors computation, we perform a normalization step of the
segmented s to increase the resilience of the description schemes to image transformations, as shown in Fig.4. We use an affine transformation to map the segmented ellipses to equally sized circumferences. This corresponds to warp the
image to a normalized isotropic patch in which the computed descriptors will
be affine invariant by construction. This not only allows to normalize the shape
of crypts, but also to reduce the slant effect that occurs if the endoscope is not
positioned perpendicularly to the tissue surface during image acquisition.

We start by trying the SIFT descriptor [8] and texture analysis methods like
Histogram Moments, Gray Level Co-occurence Matrix (GLCM) and Laws Energy [9], which have already been employed in the past in the context of medical
image classification. In addition, we experiment with a specifically created radial
descriptor, that uses image gradients for capturing small intensity and texture
variations between crypts' interior and exterior s. The idea is to identify a transition that might correspond to the boundary of the crypts and, thus, encode
the shape of these structures. Such a radial gradient profile is obtained by averaging the gradient magnitude values over 360 degrees around the center of each
crypt (Fig.4(c)). The descriptor is normalized using the L2-norm for robustness
against image contrast and brightness changes [8]. Fig.4(d) shows the normalized radial profile, in which it is possible to identify a slight peak of magnitude,
marked by the dashed line, which corresponds to the boundary of the crypt.

3   Classification

As pointed out by medical experts, the spatial organization of crypts in CEM
images is highly discriminative to distinguish between disease stages. Therefore,
we propose to split the data into two main subsets: subset 1, in which there is
a certain patterned arrangement of crypts, and subset 2, in which the tissue's

appearance is closer to a disordered stage. From a medical diagnosis point-of-view, this corresponds to a division between images with low (set 1) and high (set 2) probability of pathology. The diagnosis is accomplished by a standard SVM classifier that decides to which set the input image belongs. The SVM is applied on a feature vector that encodes the number of crypts in each image, provided by the crypts detector, and their arrangement in the tissue (*lattice*), computed using Delaunay Triangulation.

4 Experimental Validation

4.1 Dataset Specifications and Cross-Validation Scheme

Our expert-annotated database contains a total of 192 CEM images, collected from 18 patients using a Pentax CEM device with a field-of-view (FOV) of 475 μm. The images are distributed over the two subsets as follows: 88 (46%) belonging to subset 1 and 104 (54%) to subset 2. Both in the SVM discriminator stage of crypts detection and in the binary SVM image classifier, we use the RBF kernel and 10-fold cross-validation to classify the whole dataset. The SVM parameters σ (spread of RBF kernel) and C (regularization term) were adjusted using a two-layer grid-search, as proposed in [6].

4.2 Evaluation of Crypts Detection and Segmentation

The success of centers detection is evaluated by quantifying the proportion of correctly detected centers. Thus, a local maxima is only accepted as a true detection if it is close enough to a real center. Both in subsets 1 and 2, we achieve high detection recalls (0.99). However, since we follow an overdetection approach, the precision values are very low (0.33 and 0.07 in subsets 1 and 2, respectively).

The success of the segmentation is quantified by metrics that compare the segmentation curves computed from crypts detector with the expert annotations. The criteria used in this comparison is based in the overlap area, the distance between the centers and the difference between the rotation angles. The segmentation algorithm performs quite well in subset 1, with a percentage of correctly segmented crypts of 78%, but falls short in subset 2, in which its performance is only about 42%. This is related to the tissue's appearance of the dataset images. In the first subset, there is a certain patterned arrangement of crypts. Besides, these structures show a more regular shape and their contours have stronger intensity transitions than in subset 2, which improves the canny's response.

In the SVM discrimination step, we compare the proposed radial gradient descriptor with textures features [9] and the SIFT descriptor [1,2,8]. The results are shown in Fig. 5. Our descriptor clearly outperforms the texture features and has very similar performance to the SIFT descriptor, with the advantage of being much simpler and easier to compute. It is also quite interesting to observe that, when using all the evaluated features, the precision of the detector increases (by reducing the number of spurious detections), but the recall is slightly decreased.

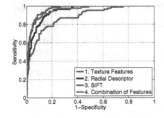

	ACC	SE	SP	PRC
1	0.80	0.80	0.80	0.37
2	0.86	0.86	0.86	0.47
3	0.89	0.88	0.89	0.55
4	0.92	0.73	0.94	0.67

Fig. 5. SVM Discriminator Scores. The graph shows a Receiver Operating Characteristic (ROC) curve obtained from one of the 10-fold cross validation rounds and the table shows the values of Accuracy (ACC), Sensitivity (SE), Specificity (SP) and Precision (PRC) computed by averaging the results over the rounds.

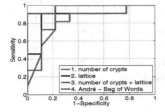

	ACC	SE	SP	PRC
1	0.83	0.86	0.80	0.83
2	0.86	0.85	0.88	0.90
3	0.89	0.90	0.88	0.90
4	0.71	0.82	0.58	0.71

Fig. 6. Image Classification Scores. The graph shows a ROC curve obtained from one of the 10-fold cross-validation rounds and the table shows the values of Accuracy (ACC), Sensitivity (SE), Specificity (SP) and Precision (PRC) computed by averaging the results over the rounds.

4.3   Image Classification Evaluation

In the image classification stage, we compare the features we proposed based on experts interpretation of CEM images with SIFT descriptor [1,2,8]. The results are shown in Fig. 6. As proposed in [1,2], we quantize SIFT features into visual words and enconde them in image histograms. Then, instead of performing the retrieval, we use these histograms to train the SVM classifier. In the available dataset, our descriptor provides higher scores than André's. We consider this result quite satisfactory, since we are using conceptually simpler features, which reflect experts clinical evaluation of the GI histological appearance.

5   Conclusion

This paper presents preliminary research toward building an on-the-fly CEM image classification system, based on the physicians interpretation of the histological architecture of the GI tract, while segmenting relevant structures in the tissue and, thus, provide useful imaging analysis information. Given the complexity of the classification problem and the small size of the available dataset, we consider the current results encouraging toward further research. The current image classifier's performance shows that the histological appearance of

CEM images provide reliable information to train a discriminative and robust classifier. However, some technical improvements still need to be carried out to improve the crypts detector results. Currently, we are conducting research toward the enhancement of the discriminative power of the features used in the SVM discriminator. We aim at developing specific crypts descriptors to increase the SVM discrimination precision while maintaining high recall rates (Fig. 5). Future research directions will also focus on the improvement of the RANSAC-based segmentation both in terms of computational time and accuracy.

References

1. André, B., Vercauteren, T., Buchner, A.M., Wallace, M.B., Ayache, N.: A Smart Atlas for Endomicroscopy using Automated Video Retrieval. Medical Image Analysis 15(4), 460–476 (2011)
2. André, B., Vercauteren, T., Perchant, A., Buchner, A.M., Wallace, M.B., Ayache, N.: Introducing Space and Time in Local Feature-Based Endomicroscopic Image Retrieval. In: Caputo, B., Müller, H., Syeda-Mahmood, T., Duncan, J.S., Wang, F., Kalpathy-Cramer, J. (eds.) MCBR-CDS 2009. LNCS, vol. 5853, pp. 18–30. Springer, Heidelberg (2010)
3. Canny, J.: A Computational Approach to Edge Detection. IEEE Trans. Pattern Anal. Mach. Intell. 8(6), 679–698 (1986)
4. Fischler, M.A., Bolles, R.C.: Random sample consensus: a paradigm for model fitting with applications to image analysis and automated cartography. Commun. ACM 24(6), 381–395 (1981)
5. Hoffman, A., Goetz, M., Vieth, M., Galle, P.R., Neurath, M.F., Kiesslich, R.: Confocal laser endomicroscopy: technical status and current indications. Endoscopy 38(12), 1275–1283 (2006)
6. Hsu, C.-W., Chang, C.-C., Lin, C.-J.: A practical guide to support vector classification. Technical report, Department of Computer Science, National Taiwan University (2003)
7. Kovesi, P.: Symmetry and Asymmetry from Local Phase. In: Sattar, A. (ed.) Canadian AI 1997. LNCS, vol. 1342, pp. 2–4. Springer, Heidelberg (1997)
8. Lowe, D.G.: Distinctive image features from scale-invariant keypoints. Int. J. Comput. Vision 60(2), 91–110 (2004)
9. Manavalan, R., Thangavel, K.: Evaluation of textural feature extraction methods for prostate cancer trus medical images. International Journal of Computer Applications 36(12), 33–39 (2011)
10. Melo, R., Barreto, J.P., Falcao, G.: A new solution for camera calibration and real-time image distortion correction in medical endoscopy-initial technical evaluation. IEEE Trans. Biomed. Engineering 59(3), 634–644 (2012)
11. Sivic, J., Zisserman, A.: Video google: A text retrieval approach to object matching in videos. In: ICCV, pp. 1470–1477 (2003)

A Localized MKL Method for Brain Classification with Known Intra-class Variability

Aydın Ulaş[1,*], Mehmet Gönen[2], Umberto Castellani[1], Vittorio Murino[1,3],
Marcella Bellani[4], Michele Tansella[4], and Paolo Brambilla[5]

[1] Department of Computer Science, University of Verona (UNIVR), Verona, Italy
mehmetaydin.ulas@univr.it
[2] Aalto University, Department of Information and Computer Science, Finland
[3] Istituto Italiano di Tecnologia (IIT), Genova, Italy
[4] Dpt Public Health & Community Medicine, Psychiatry, ICBN, UNIVR, Italy
[5] IRCCS "E. Medea" Scientific Institute, Udine, Italy

Abstract. Automatic decisional systems based on pattern classification methods are becoming very important to support medical diagnosis. In general, the overall objective is to classify between healthy subjects and patients affected by a certain disease. To reach this aim, significant efforts have been spent in finding reliable biomarkers which are able to robustly discriminate between the two populations (i.e., patients and controls). However, in real medical scenarios there are many factors, like the gender or the age, which make the source data very heterogeneous. This introduces a large intra-class variation by affecting the performance of the classification procedure. In this paper we exploit how to use the knowledge on heterogeneity factors to improve the classification accuracy. We propose a *Clustered Localized* Multiple Kernel Learning (CLMKL) algorithm by encoding in the classication model the information on the clusters of apriory known stratifications.

Experiments are carried out for brain classification in Schizophrenia. We show that our algorithm performs clearly better than single kernel Support Vector Machines (SVMs), linear MKL algorithms and canonical Localized MKL algorithms when the gender information is considered as apriori knowledge.

Keywords: brain imaging, magnetic resonance imaging, computer-aided diagnosis, localized multiple kernel learning, schizophrenia.

1 Introduction

Advanced pattern recognition methods have demonstrated their growing importance in the medical domain for the definition of new decisional systems able to support medical diagnosis. In particular, in neuroscience the use of brain classification methods represents a recent and relevant trend aiming at discriminating healthy subjects from patients having a certain mental disorder [13,17]. This leads to a two-class classification problem that is addressed by using for instance

---

* Strada Le Grazie 15, 37134, Verona, VR, Italy.

F. Wang et al. (Eds.): MLMI 2012, LNCS 7588, pp. 152–159, 2012.

discriminative learning methods like Support Vector Machine (SVM). However, in practical situations the performance of classifiers are highly affected by intra-class variations. For instance in brain classification there is a general diversity of the brain properties between male and female (in both patients and controls). In this paper, we propose a new brain classification method which encodes explicitly the known intra-class variability into the classification model. To this aim, we benefit from recently proposed *localized Multiple Kernel Learning* (LMKL) [8] approaches. In LMKL, the idea is to define a decision function whose parameters depend on the input data, i.e., *localized* information. In practice, similar to classifier selection [19,12], the localized estimates are used to select or combine kernels [8]. In our work, we specialize this approach to design a new model which embeds the information on the clusters of a pre-defined data stratification (i.e., male and female). Instead of adopting a *sample-specific* localization like in [8], we introduce a *cluster localized* approach to set up the combination scheme. The difference of our method from LMKL is that instead of letting the algorithm choose the partitioning, we use apriori partitioning based on expert knowledge. We call our method *Clustered Localized Multiple Kernel Learning* (CLMKL). In this fashion, according to the spirit of Multiple Kernel Learning (MKL) methods [9], we learn a separate combination of input kernels for each cluster.

MKL methods have been recently proposed on the medical domain to detect Alzheimer's disease [10,6]. In Castro et al. [4], a recursive composite kernel method is applied for schizophrenia. In these works, MKL approach was employed to integrate/select different factors of the disease. Note that also our MKL formulation can deal naturally with different sources of information as shown in the experiments. We evaluate our method on brain classification for Schizophrenia detection. Several experimental configurations are evaluated as well as a comparison with other MKL classification methods by showing a clear improvement of our method. Our method allows to train all data in different clusters together, thus avoiding the reduction of training examples and over-training. This can clearly be seen when we compare our method with separating the clusters and training/testing a single model for each cluster.

The paper is organized as follows: in Section 2, we introduce the MKL framework and our methodology, we show our experiments and results in Section 3 and we conclude in Section 4.

2   Methodology

2.1   Multiple Kernel Learning

The assumption behind kernel methods is to transform linearly unseparable data into a higher dimensional (possibly with infinite dimension) space where it is possible to separate the classes linearly [18]. The support vector machine (SVM) in this sense is a discriminative classifier which is based on the theory of structural risk minimization proposed for binary classification problems. Given a sample of N training instances $\{(\boldsymbol{x}_i, y_i)\}_{i=1}^{N}$ where $\boldsymbol{x}_i$ is the D-dimensional input vector and $y_i \in \{-1, +1\}$ is its class label, SVM finds the linear discriminant with the maximum margin in the feature space induced by a mapping function $\Phi \colon \mathbb{R}^D \to \mathbb{R}^S$. Considering the dual formulation with the "kernel trick", the discriminant function can be rewritten as

$$f(\boldsymbol{x}) = \sum_{i=1}^{N} \alpha_i y_i k(\boldsymbol{x}_i, \boldsymbol{x}) + b$$

where $k \colon \mathbb{R}^D \times \mathbb{R}^D \to \mathbb{R}$ is called the *kernel function* (similarity between instances of data) and $\boldsymbol{\alpha}$ denotes the dual variables corresponding to each training sample.

There are several kernel functions successfully used in the literature, such as the linear kernel, the polynomial kernel, and the Gaussian kernel. Selecting the kernel function and its parameters is an important issue in training. Generally, a separate validation set is used to choose the best performing kernel among a set of kernels. Recently, multiple kernel learning (MKL) methods have been proposed [2,15], which learn a combination k_η instead of selecting a specific kernel and its corresponding parameters. The simplest way is to combine the kernels as a weighted sum which corresponds to the linear MKL:

$$k_\eta(\boldsymbol{x}_i, \boldsymbol{x}_j; \boldsymbol{\eta}) = \sum_{m=1}^{P} \eta_m k_m(\boldsymbol{x}_i, \boldsymbol{x}_j)$$

with $\eta_m \in \mathbb{R}$. Different versions of this approach differ in the way they put restrictions on the kernel weights: [2,15,16]. This is similar to classifier combination [14] in the sense that instead of choosing a single classifier, we select a set of classifiers and let the algorithm do the picking. MKL can be used for selecting/combining a set of different kernels which correspond to different notions of similarity or can be used to combine different sources of information probably with different dimensions which in our case correspond to different parts of the brain. In this work, we compare our method with RBMKL and SMKL, where RBMKL denotes the rule-based MKL algorithm that trains an SVM with the mean of the combined kernels [5], SMKL is the iterative algorithm of [16] that uses projected gradient updates and trains single-kernel SVMs at each iteration.

2.2   Our Method

Given a set of base classifiers, the idea behind classifier combination [14] is to find a function to accurately combine the decisions of individual base classifiers. Classifier selection [19,12] is different than classifier combination in the sense that the combination is also based on the input data point through a gating function [11]. In a similar setting, Gönen and Alpaydın [8] propose a data-dependent formulation called localized multiple kernel learning (LMKL) that combines kernels using weights calculated from a gating model where the gating model $\eta_m(\cdot \,|\, \cdot)$, parameterized by $\mathbf{V}$, assigns a weight to the feature space obtained with $\Phi_m(\cdot)$. Then the combined kernel matrix is represented as

$$k_\eta(\boldsymbol{x}_i, \boldsymbol{x}_j) = \sum_{m=1}^{P} \eta_m(\boldsymbol{x}_i | \mathbf{V}) k_m(\boldsymbol{x}_i, \boldsymbol{x}_j) \eta_m(\boldsymbol{x}_j | \mathbf{V}).$$

This gating function can be formulated to be learned from the data so that the similarity is computed using multiple kernels where the kernel weights not only depend on kernel functions but on the input data. This can be done in an unsupervised way using the stratifications in the training data but in some applications the stratification of input data can be known apriori. For instance in medical applications the population can be subdivided into males and females. The crucial step is to formulate a good gating function to incorporate this apriori information and in this work we propose a gating function in order to take into account the knowledge of *intra*-class variability. In a medical application, the overall aim is the classification between healthy subjects and patients affected by a certain disease (i.e., two-class classification). In particular, we want the gating function to behave differently w.r.t. the gender (i.e., two apriori known subject stratifications). With this idea in mind, we embed the apriori clustering information and we formulate the following gating function based on softmax:

$$\eta_m(\boldsymbol{x}|\mathbf{V}) = \sum_{c=1}^{K} \delta_c(c_{\boldsymbol{x}}) \frac{\exp(v_c^m)}{\sum_{h=1}^{P} \exp(v_c^h)} \qquad \forall m \qquad (1)$$

where $\mathbf{V} = \{v_1^m, v_2^m, \dots, v_K^m\}_{m=1}^{P}$ are the weights (v_i^m is the weight if ith cluster and mth kernel), K is the number of clusters, $c_{\boldsymbol{x}}$ denotes the cluster of $\boldsymbol{x}$, and $\delta_c(c_{\boldsymbol{x}})$ is the Kronecker delta where $\delta_c(c_{\boldsymbol{x}}) = 1$ if $c_{\boldsymbol{x}} = c$, and 0 otherwise. We will refer to our method as CLMKL throughout the text. With this formulation, we get a constant set of weights for each cluster (gender). When the similarity between a data point and another one within the same cluster is computed, the same weights are used. But, this effect is reduced when the similarity is computed between two data points belonging to different clusters. For example, if the weight of a kernel is 0, when we compute the similarity between two data points belonging to two different clusters, this kernel is ignored. Only the kernels with nonzero weights contribute to the computation of similarities between inter-cluster data points. The gating model parameters are computed using alternating optimization: first, the kernel weights are fixed and the SVM parameters are estimated by standard solvers (i.e., libSVM), second, the SVM parameters are fixed and kernel weights are estimated by a gradient descent procedure. The two steps are iterated until convergence (starting from a random initialization of the weights). The gating function is chosen in order to enforce the weights to be in the interval between 0 and 1.

3   Experiments and Results

3.1   Data Set

The study population used in this work consists of 42 patients (21 male, 21 female) who were being treated for schizophrenia and 40 controls (19 male, 21 female) with no DSM-IV axis I disorders and had no psychiatric disorders among first-degree relatives. Diagnoses for schizophrenia were corroborated by the clinical consensus of two psychiatrists. T1 weighted structural MRI scans were acquired with a 1.5 Tesla machine and to minimize biases and head motion, restraining foam pads were used. The original image size is 384x512x144; these images are then rotated and realigned to a resolution of 256x256x192. After this alignment, they were segmented into specific brain regions called Regions of Interest (ROIs) manually by experts following a specific protocol for each ROI [3]. In this work, we use three ROIs from the two hemispheres of the brain summing upto a total of six different brain regions: Dorsolateral prefrontal cortex (*ldlpfc* and *rdlpfc*), Entorhinal Cortex (*lec* and *rec*), and Thalamus (*lthal* and *rthal*) which are found to be impaired in schizophrenic patients.

Preprocessing. After the alignment and ROI tracing, DARTEL [1] tools within SPM software [7] was used to pre-process the data. Initially, images are segmented into grey and white matter in *Native* and *DARTEL imported* spaces. The DARTEL imported images have lower resolution than the original images but are used to spatially align to standard MNI atlas. In the second step, DARTEL template generation is applied which creates an average template from the input data while simultaneously aligning white and grey matter. In this step, the flowfields of the registration are also computed which will be used to segment the MNI space normalized images into ROIs. In the final step, the DARTEL template is used to spatially normalize all images into standard MNI space. In this way, smoothed (12 mm Gaussian), and Jacobian scaled grey matter images are constructed which is general practice in neuroimaging applications.

Feature extraction. The images at the end of the preprocessing pipeline are the intensity probability maps which are then used to construct the features for our classification experiments. Since we already have ROI segmented source images, using the flow fields computed in the second step of preprocessing; we create the intensity maps for every subject and ROI instead of extracting a single set of features for the whole brain. Since the ROIs have different bounding boxes, the sizes of these images are not the same for all subjects. By applying thresholding at 0.2 level, we compute histograms of probability maps for every subject and ROI. Number of bins in each histogram is chosen to be 40 which showed the best performance in our experiments. As a result, we have a data set of six different ROIs, 82 subjects with a feature vector of size 40 which we apply our classification pipeline.

3.2   Experiments

In our first set of experiments, we show how our algorithm behaves when presented with only one data source. We compare CLMKL with SVM which is the single SVM on the feature set, CONCAT which is the concatenation of the feature and the gender information and LMKL mentioned in Section 2. We used linear kernels as base kernels in all our experiments because the number of parameters to optimize is fewer. We use a Leave-One-Out (LOO) validation scheme by training

Table 1. Accuracies on schizophrenia detection data set using one data source only

ROI	SVM	CLMKL	CONCAT	LMKL
ldlpfc	54.88	**73.17**	54.88	65.85
rdlpfc	70.73	**76.83**	70.73	70.73
lec	71.95	**81.71**	73.17	74.39
rec	67.07	**74.39**	69.51	69.51
lthal	70.73	**79.27**	78.05	71.95
rthal	71.95	**74.39**	69.51	68.29

all the methods using all but one data point (x_i) and testing if we can get the correct classification on x_i. We do this for all x_i and the percentage of correct classifications over all subjects is the accuracy which we report in all our tables. We can see the accuracies for single data source in Table 1. Our method is always the most accurate method and better than single SVMs, the concatenation and the canonical LMKL.

In our second set of experiments, we combine all the ROIs to see the effect of our algorithm compared to other MKL algorithms, the concatenation of features, and the results of separately training the male and female subjects. We can see the results in Table 2. CONCAT shows the accuracy of a linear SVM when the features of all ROIs are concatenated. This time we can clearly see the advantage of our method. We obtain the best results when we use CLMKL, which uses the apriori clustering information without depending on the input data point. This makes sense because as the number of parameters increase, it gets harder to optimize and LMKL may be stuck in a local minima. We can deduce two results from this table. We can see that our method includes the gender information in terms of apriori knowledge and has better accuracy than the linear MKL methods and single SVMs. Second, when we divide the data into male/female subsets and train accordingly, we increase accuracy (male/female separated accuracies are better than training male/female together because the anatomic similarities make it easier to classify the same gender) but not as much as CLMKL. This is what we expect because the number of subjects in the training set gets smaller, but this is also why our method is superior to other MKL methods and canonical localized algorithms.

Table 2. Accuracies on schizophrenia detection data set using all ROIs

Method	Together	Male	Female
SVM	71.95	75.00	76.19
RBMKL	71.95	82.50	71.43
SMKL	71.95	85.00	71.43
CONCAT	69.51		
LMKL	73.17		
CLMKL	**90.24**		

Table 3. Accuracies on schizophrenia detection data set by adding gender information.

Method	w/o gender	w/ gender
CONCAT	69.51	70.73
RBMKL	71.95	69.51
SMKL	71.95	69.51
CLMKL	**90.24**	

To be fair, we also include the gender information as another data source (kernel) and compare the accuracy of CLMKL also with this case. We can see from Table 3 that also in this case CLMKL is superior to other methods. What we observe from this table is that when we add the gender as another data source to the classification system, it becomes important and can change the model significantly. In the SMKL and RBMKL cases, we see that this creates a problem and the accuracies actually decrease.

4   Conclusions

In this paper we benefit from the knowledge of heterogenity factors in order to deal with intra-class variability and therefore improve the performance of automatic medical decisional systems.

We propose a new *localized* Multiple Kernel Learning algorithm which takes into account the information on the clusters of a known subject stratification. We evaluate our CLMKL method on a dataset of Schizophrenic patients and healthy controls by showing a substantial improvement of our approach in comparison to several other methods. In particular, the gender factor was considered as prior information in order to properly encode the variability between male and female. Even when a single data source is considered, our CLMKL shows improvements over classical SVM algorithms. Moreover, we observe a further improvement of our method when data from multiple sources is considered (in our case different ROIs of the brain). The strength of our method also shows when we compare our method with the models trained/tested on male/female separated data. Our method allows to train all data together, thus avoiding small number of subjects and overfitting.

Our future work will address the exploitation of other known heterogenity factors like age, education level, and other meta information coming from the subject's interview. Moreover, the method can be evaluated on other features coming from other image modalities.

References

1. Ashburner, J.: A fast diffeomorphic image registration algorithm. Neuroimage 38(1), 95–113 (2007)
2. Bach, F., Lanckriet, G., Jordan, M.: Multiple kernel learning, conic duality, and the smo algorithm. In: ICML 2004, pp. 41–48 (2004)

3. Baiano, M., Perlini, C., Rambaldelli, G., Cerini, R., Dusi, N., Bellani, M., Spezzapria, G., Versace, A., Balestrieri, M., Mucelli, R.P., Tansella, M., Brambilla, P.: Decreased entorhinal cortex volumes in schizophrenia. Schizophr. Res. 102(1-3), 171–180 (2008)
4. Castro, E., Martínez-Ramon, M., Pearlson, G., Sui, J., Calhoun, V.: Characterization of groups using composite kernels and multi-source fMRI analysis data: Application to schizophrenia. NeuroImage 58(2), 526–536 (2011)
5. Cristianini, N., Shawe-Taylor, J.: An Introduction to Support Vector Machines and other Kernel-based Learning Methods. Cambridge University Press (2000)
6. Filipovych, R., Resnick, S.M., Davatzikos, C.: Multi-Kernel Classification for Integration of Clinical and Imaging Data: Application to Prediction of Cognitive Decline in Older Adults. In: Suzuki, K., Wang, F., Shen, D., Yan, P. (eds.) MLMI 2011. LNCS, vol. 7009, pp. 26–34. Springer, Heidelberg (2011)
7. Friston, K., Ashburner, J., Kiebel, S., Nichols, T., Penny, W. (eds.): Statistical Parametric Mapping: The Analysis of Functional Brain Images. Academic Press (2007)
8. Gönen, M., Alpaydın, E.: Localized multiple kernel learning. In: ICML 2008, pp. 352–359 (2008)
9. Gönen, M., Alpaydın, E.: Multiple kernel learning algorithms. JMLR 12, 2181–2238 (2011)
10. Hinrichs, C., Singh, V., Xu, G., Johnson, S.: Predictive markers for AD in a multimodality framework: An analysis of MCI progression in the ADNI population. NeuroImage 55(2), 574–589 (2011)
11. Jacobs, R.A., Jordan, M.I., Nowlan, S.J., Hinton, G.E.: Adaptive mixtures of local experts. Neural Computation 3, 79–87 (1991)
12. Kang, H.J., Doermann, D.: Selection of classifiers for the construction of multiple classifier systems. In: ICDAR 2005, vol. 2, pp. 1194–1198 (2005)
13. Kawasaki, Y., Suzuki, M., Kherif, F., Takahashi, T., Zhou, S.Y., Nakamura, K., Matsui, M., Sumiyoshi, T., Seto, H., Kurachi, M.: Multivariate voxel-based morphometry successfully differentiates schizophrenia patients from healthy controls. NeuroImage 34(1), 235–242 (2007)
14. Kuncheva, L.I.: Combining pattern classifiers: methods and algorithms. Wiley-Interscience (2004)
15. Lanckriet, G., Cristianini, N., Bartlett, P., Ghaoui, L.E., Jordan, M.: Learning the kernel matrix with semidefinite programming. JMLR 5, 27–72 (2004)
16. Rakotomamonjy, A., Bach, F., Canu, S., Grandvalet, Y.: SimpleMKL. JMLR 9, 2491–2521 (2008)
17. Ulaş, A., Duin, R., Castellani, U., Loog, M., Mirtuono, P., Bicego, M., Murino, V., Bellani, M., Cerruti, S., Tansella, M., Brambilla, P.: Dissimilarity-based detection of schizophrenia. International Journal of Imaging Systems and Technology 21(2), 179–192 (2011)
18. Vapnik, V.N.: Statistical Learning Theory. John Wiley and Sons (1998)
19. Woods, K., Philip Kegelmeyer Jr., W., Bowyer, K.: Combination of multiple classifiers using local accuracy estimates. IEEE TPAMI 19(4), 405–410 (1997)

Supervised Image Segmentation across Scanner Protocols: A Transfer Learning Approach

Annegreet van Opbroek[1], M. Arfan Ikram[2], Meike W. Vernooij[2],
and Marleen de Bruijne[1,3]

[1] Biomedical Imaging Group Rotterdam, Departments of Medical Informatics and
Radiology, Erasmus MC - University Medical Center Rotterdam, The Netherlands
[2] Departments of Epidemiology and Radiology, Erasmus MC - University Medical
Center Rotterdam, The Netherlands
[3] Department of Computer Science, University of Copenhagen, Denmark

Abstract. Supervised classification techniques are among the most powerful methods used for automatic segmentation of medical images. A disadvantage of these methods is that they require a representative training
set and thus encounter problems when the training data is acquired e.g.
with a different scanner protocol than the target segmentation data. We
therefore propose a framework for supervised biomedical image segmentation across different scanner protocols, by means of transfer learning.
We establish a transfer learning algorithm for classification, which can
exploit a large amount of labeled samples from different sources in addition to a small amount of samples from the target source. The algorithm
iteratively re-weights the contribution of training samples from these different sources based on classification by a weighted SVM classifier. We
evaluate this technique by performing tissue classification on MRI brain
data from four substantially different scanning protocols. For a small
number of labeled samples from a single image obtained with the same
protocol, the proposed transfer learning method outperforms classification on all available training data as well as classification based on the
labeled target samples only. The classification errors for these cases can
be reduced with up to 40 percent compared to traditional classification
techniques.

1 Introduction

Supervised classification techniques are commonly used in automatic segmentation of biomedical images. A major drawback of these methods is that they
require a sufficiently large training set from a similar distribution as the images
to be segmented. This means that in practice these techniques often cannot be
applied to data obtained with a different scanning protocol, scanner, or image
modality, without establishing a new, usually manually annotated dataset.

Common methods to cope with differences between training and test distributions are based on exploiting similarities between training and test data, e.g.
by embedding the physics of the image acquisition process in the segmentation
framework [1], and using prior tissue probability maps to identify new training

F. Wang et al. (Eds.): MLMI 2012, LNCS 7588, pp. 160–167, 2012.
© Springer-Verlag Berlin Heidelberg 2012

samples from target data [2]. Another approach is to use unsupervised clustering methods on the target source [3–5].

In this article we present a new approach to the problem of learning automatic classification across scanners, which can reduce the effort of re-training, by transferring knowledge from different scanners. Our method relies on a relatively new area of machine learning, called *Transfer Learning* [6]. Transfer learning copes with cases where distributions, feature spaces and/or tasks differ between training and test data, as opposed to traditional machine learning techniques where these are assumed to be the same between training and testing.

As a proof of concept we investigate whether transfer learning can improve between-scanner segmentation performance in a basic voxelwise classification segmentation framework. Hereto we establish a transfer learning method that makes use of a large amount of *different-distribution* training samples, which come from different sources than the target data, in addition to a relatively small amount of *same-distribution* samples from the target distribution. Our method relies on iteratively weighting these different-distribution samples according to classification-outcome of a weighted support vector machine (SVM) classifier on all available training data. This way, the suitable different-distribution samples are selected, which help regularize the classification and thus reduce the problems related to the small sample size of the same-distribution data.

2   A Transfer Learning Approach to Classification

We make use of a small amount of labeled data from the target source, which we will call the same-distribution training data, denoted by $T_s = \{x_i^s, y_i^s\}_{i=1}^{N_s}$, where N_s represents the number of same-distribution training samples x_i^s, with corresponding labels y_i^s. Apart from T_s we also have a large amount of training data from other sources, which may have different distributions. This different-distribution training data is denoted by $T_d = \{x_i^d, y_i^d\}_{i=1}^{N_d}$, where N_d is the total number of different-distribution training samples x_i^d, with labels y_i^d (typically $N_d \gg N_s$), so that there is a total training set $T = T_d \cup T_s$. Our algorithm iteratively calculates a weighted SVM classifier c_t from all available training data, which is then used to determine a new weight vector w^{t+1} for all training samples. Samples from T_d that contradict labeled same-distribution data may be misclassified by the trained classifier. In the next round these samples will receive a lower weight, and will thus have less influence on the decision boundary. The weighting of the different-distribution training samples is achieved by multiplication with $\beta^{|1-\delta(c_t(x_i^d), y_i^d)|}$, where $\delta(c(_t x_i^d), y_i^d)$ denotes the Kronecker delta.

The value for β is taken as $\beta = 1/(1 + \sqrt{2 \ln N_d / N_{\mathrm{it}}})$, as determined for the TrAdaBoost algorithm [7], which is also based on iteratively reweighting same-distribution training samples. Here N_{it} denotes the total number of iterations performed. Thus, when more iterations are performed the reduction of weights in one iteration diminishes. An initial weight vector w^1 for respectively the different- and same-distribution samples gives each of the different-distribution training samples a weight $\frac{R}{N_d}$ and the same-distribution training

Table 1. Our transfer learning algorithm in pseudo code

Input:	Output:
T, N_s, N_d, N_{it},R	classifier for test data $c_{N_{it}}$

set $\beta = 1/(1 + \sqrt{2 \ln N_d/N_{it}})$

set $w_i^1 = \begin{cases} \frac{R}{N_d} & \text{for } i = 1, 2, \ldots, N_d \\ \frac{1}{N_s} & \text{for } i = N_d + 1, \ldots, N_d + N_s \end{cases}$

For $t = 1, 2, \ldots, N_{it}$

Normalize $\boldsymbol{w}^t = \frac{\boldsymbol{w}^t}{\sum_{j=1}^{N_d+N_s} w_j^t}$,

Calculate Classifier c_t from T and $\boldsymbol{w}^t$

Update $w_i^{t+1} = w_i^t \beta^{|1-\delta(c_t(\boldsymbol{x}_i^d), y_i^d)|}$,   for $i = 1, 2, \ldots, N_d$

end

samples a weight $\frac{1}{N_s}$, so that R ($R \geq 0$) denotes the ratio between the total weight of the T_d samples and the total weight of the T_s samples. The algorithm is summarized in Table 1.

2.1 Weighted Support Vector Machine Classification

For classification we use a *weighted support vector machine*, as provided by LIB-SVM [8]. In this weighted SVM every training sample $\boldsymbol{x}_i$ is given a weight $w_i^t \geq 0$ that describes the importance of the sample, so that a training sample with a high weight is more important to classify correctly. The objective function for the optimal classifier $c_t(\boldsymbol{x}) = \boldsymbol{V} \cdot \boldsymbol{x} + v_0$ by weighted SVM reads

$$\min_{\boldsymbol{V}} \tfrac{1}{2} \boldsymbol{V} \cdot \boldsymbol{V} + C \sum_{i=1}^{N} w_i^t \xi_i \tag{1}$$

$$\text{s.t.} \quad \boldsymbol{V}^T \boldsymbol{x}_i + v_0 \geq 1 - \xi_i \quad \text{for } y_i = +1$$

$$\boldsymbol{V}^T \boldsymbol{x}_i + v_0 \leq -1 + \xi_i \quad \text{for } y_i = -1$$

$$\xi_i \geq 0 \quad\quad i = 1, 2, \ldots, N \ .$$

Also, as in regular SVM the trade-off parameter C can be determined with cross-validation.

3 Experiment: MRI Brain Tissue Segmentation

We consider the application of MRI brain tissue segmentation by voxelwise classification on images acquired with a certain scanner, for which no manual labels are yet available. Since manual segmentation is time consuming only a very small amount of voxels in a single image is labeled, to train a classification scheme for the remainder of images. In addition to these same-distribution training samples, a larger amount of manually labeled samples from different patients made with a variety of scanners, are already available from other studies. We evaluate whether our transfer learning algorithm can outperform traditional classification.

Data Description. We use annotated MRI brain data from four different sources, which display a large amount of variation in intensity and tissue contrast:

1. 6 T1-weighted images from the Rotterdam Scan Study [9] made with a 1.5T GE scanner with $0.49 \times 0.49 \times 0.80$ mm^3 voxel size
2. 12 HASTE-Odd images (inversion time = 4400 ms, TR = 2800 ms, TE = 29 ms) from the Rotterdam Scan Study [9] made with a 1.5T Siemens scanner with $1.25 \times 1 \times 1$ mm^3 voxel size
3. 18 T1-weighted images from the Internet Brain Segmentation Repository (IBSR) [10] with $0.94 \times 0.94 \times 1.5$ mm^3 voxel size
4. 20 T1-weighted images from the IBSR, 10 from a 1.5T Siemens scanner, 10 from a 1.5T GE scanner, both with $1 \times 3.1 \times 1$ mm^3 voxel size

Slices from one image of the four different sources are shown in Fig. 1.

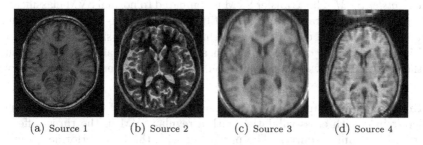

(a) Source 1   (b) Source 2   (c) Source 3   (d) Source 4

Fig. 1. Slices of images from the four different sources

For the Haste-Odd the images are inverted so that CSF has lowest intensity and WM the highest, as in the T1-weighted images. All 56 images are corrected for non-uniformity in intensity with the N3 method [11] within a mask, and then normalized so that the voxels between the 4th and the 96th intensity percentile are mapped between 0 and 1. For all images expert segmentations for white matter (WM), gray matter (GM), and cerebrospinal fluid (CSF) are available for training and testing. Some images also have expert segmentations for white matter lesions; these voxels are included in the WM class.

Experimental Setup. A set of cross-validation experiments is performed. All four sources are in turn used as the test source, while the other three sources are used to extract different-distribution training data. As training and test samples voxels are randomly selected within the manually annotated brain mask. As different-distribution training data, 1 500 samples per source are randomly selected from the different images. Same-distribution training data is sampled from a single image from the test source, where we start by adding one same-distribution sample from every class, and subsequently add more samples randomly distributed over the classes to generate learning curves to analyze the classification performance as a function of the number of same-distribution training samples.

The learning curves are created by testing on 4 000 randomly selected samples from each test source image that is not used for training, resulting in a total of 20 000 to 76 000 test samples, depending on the amount of images in the source. This gives a reliable estimation of the classification performance on whole images, but is computationaly less expensive. We repeat the experiment for every test source image as same-distribution training source, and determine average classification accuracy per image. In addition, to compare to brain tissue segmentation results reported in the literature, full image segmentation is performed at $N_s = 20$.

A total of four features are used for classification, consisting of the image intensity plus three spatial features which give the x, y, and z coordinates of the voxel as a fraction of the total dimensions of the brain. The features within each source are normalized to zero mean and unit standard deviation. From now on we will refer to the transfer learning algorithm with the weighted SVM classifier as a *Transfer SVM*. The Transfer SVM is compared to normal SVM classification both on all available training data $(T_s \cup T_d)$ and on the same-distribution training data (T_s) alone. In all classification schemes the SVM classifier is extended to a multiclass classifier by one-vs-one classification, which overall gives better results on the data than one-vs-rest classification. All SVM classifiers use a linear kernel.

Parameter Selection. The SVM parameter C for each of the four experiments is determined with cross-validation with a regular SVM in the three different-distribution training sources. The parameter with the best performance in the three sources is selected. The total number of iterations of the transfer learning algorithm is set to $N_{it} = 20$, which is sufficient for convergence in all cases.

For each number of same-distribution training samples the parameter R that determines the balance between the initial weights of the different- and same-distribution samples in the Transfer SVM is determined with cross-validation with the Transfer SVM on the data from the three different-distribution sources. In turn each source is selected as target source to extract labeled same-distribution samples and test data, while the other two sources are used to extract different-distribution training data. The best R is then determined by averaging between the three sources. The resulting R is around 5 for three same-distribution training samples, but falls off exponentially to $R \approx 1$ for 200 same-distribution training samples.

Results. In Fig. 2 the learning curves for each of the four experiments are shown. In all experiments we see that for a small number of same-distribution training samples (between 3 and 40 in Fig. 2(b), and a broader range for the other three experiments) the Transfer SVM outperforms both the SVM on all

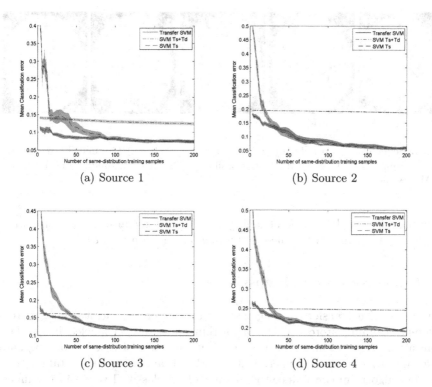

Fig. 2. Mean classification errors and 95%-confidence intervals for our transfer learning SVM, the conventional SVM on $T_d \cup T_s$, and the SVM on T_s, all with a linear kernel. The test source consist of (a) Source 1, (b) Source 2, (c) Source 3, (d) Source 4, the different-distribution training data comes from the three remaining sources.

training data $T_s + T_d$ and the SVM on the labeled same-distribution data T_s only. When more same-distribution training samples are available the SVM classifier on T_s converges to the Transfer SVM and might even perform slightly better. For a very small amount of same-distribution training data the SVM classifier on all available training samples performs best in two of the four cases. In these cases the Transfer SVM seems to give too little weight to the different-distribution training samples, which results in a classifier that does not outperform the SVM on $T_s + T_d$.

Fig. 3 shows an example of segmentations from Source 1 obtained by the three methods for 20 same-distribution training samples. The Transfer SVM classifier produces a good segmentation with a classification error of 6.7%. The segmentation of the SVM $T_s + T_d$ classifier undersegments WM and CSF and gives an error of 9.3%, while the SVM T_s classifier oversegments the CSF, resulting in an error of 14.0%. According to the learning curve in Fig. 2(a) the number of labeled same-distribution training samples needed for the SVM T_s classifier to produce a similar result lies around $N_s = 80$. Thus, in this case transferring knowledge

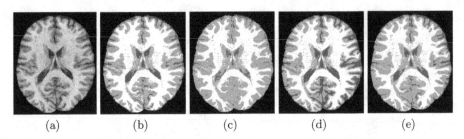

(a)	(b)	(c)	(d)	(e)

Fig. 3. Segmentation results on Source 1 for $N_s = 20$. (a) Original T1 image, (b) manual segmentation, (c) SVM $T_s + T_d$ classifier, (d) SVM T_s classifier, and (e) Transfer SVM classifier.

from the different-distribution training samples with a transfer classifier reduces the costs on labeling new same-distribution data with a factor 4.

4   Conclusion and Discussion

We presented a transfer learning method to segment biomedical images from different scanning protocols. Our algorithm makes use of labeled image data from a variety of scanners, on top of a small amount of labeled training data from the target scanner. Experiments on MRI brain tissue segmentation show that our algorithm can reduce the amount of misclassified voxels in the image with up to 40%. To do this, the algorithm exploits already available training data from different scanners and weights them according to correspondence with the training data from the target scanner. With our algorithm just a few manually annotated samples in a single image obtained with a new protocol are sufficient to retrain the method and provide much better results than a classifier trained on different- or same-distribution data alone. Our transfer learning algorithm has proved to be capable of handling data from four drastically different sources, with different pulse sequence parameters and different slice thickness in different orientations.

To allow direct comparison of different learning algorithms, we have in this work focused on segmentation based on voxelwise classification. This framework could be used as the basis for a more advanced brain tissue segmentation algorithm including e.g. regularization, atlas based priors, and modeling of partial volume effect. To give an indication of the performance of our segmentation method in comparison with the current state of the art, we compare the performance reported for nine methods in [3] applied to the IBSR dataset with 20 subjects. For $N_s = 20$ our method reports a mean Jaccard index on the 20 images of 0.15 for CSF, 0.68 for GM, and 0.61 for WM. The best of the 9 algorithms in [3] reports coefficients of 0.10 for CSF, 0.68 for GM, and 0.69 for WM. Three methods in [3] report coefficients higher than 0.61 for WM, but our algorithm outperforms all methods based on CSF scores, and all but one on GM scores. Also, when N_s is increased our method performs even better.

Even though the focus of the experiments in this paper is on MRI brain tissue segmentation, the proposed method is general and we expect it to be useful in many other applications where classification is used, such as voxel classification in other areas, brain structure segmentation, and computer aided diagnosis.

To conclude, the experiments give a strong indication that supervised image segmentation techniques can benefit from different-distribution training data, in a transfer learning setting. This way, the large amount of (publicly) available annotated data from previous studies can be used to segment images with relatively large differences in imaging protocols, which forms an important step towards application in a clinical setting.

References

1. Fischl, B., Salat, D., van der Kouwe, A., Makris, N., Ségonne, F., Quinn, B., Dale, A.: Sequence-independent segmentation of magnetic resonance images. Neuroimage 23, S69–S84 (2004)
2. Cocosco, C., Zijdenbos, A., Evans, A.: A fully automatic and robust brain MRI tissue classification method. Medical Image Analysis 7(4), 513–527 (2003)
3. Mayer, A., Greenspan, H.: An adaptive mean-shift framework for MRI brain segmentation. IEEE Transactions on Medical Imaging 28(8), 1238–1250 (2009)
4. Grabowski, T., Frank, R., Szumski, N., Brown, C., Damasio, H.: Validation of partial tissue segmentation of single-channel magnetic resonance images of the brain. NeuroImage 12(6), 640–656 (2000)
5. Van Leemput, K., Maes, F., Vandermeulen, D., Suetens, P.: Automated model-based tissue classification of MR images of the brain. IEEE Transactions on Medical Imaging 18(10), 897–908 (1999)
6. Pan, S., Yang, Q.: A survey on transfer learning. IEEE Transactions on Knowledge and Data Engineering 22(10), 1345–1359 (2010)
7. Dai, W., Yang, Q., Xue, G., Yu, Y.: Boosting for transfer learning. In: Proceedings of the 24th International Conference on Machine Learning, pp. 193–200. ACM (2007)
8. Chang, C., Lin, C.: Libsvm: a library for support vector machines. ACM Transactions on Intelligent Systems and Technology (TIST) 2(3), 27 (2011)
9. Hofman, A., Breteler, M., Van Duijn, C., Janssen, H., Krestin, G., Kuipers, E., Stricker, B., Tiemeier, H., Uitterlinden, A., Vingerling, J., et al.: The Rotterdam Study: 2010 objectives and design update. European Journal of Epidemiology 24(9), 553–572 (2009)
10. Worth, A.: The Internet Brain Segmentation Repository (IBSR)
11. Sled, J., Zijdenbos, A., Evans, A.: A nonparametric method for automatic correction of intensity nonuniformity in MRI data. IEEE Transactions on Medical Imaging 17(1), 87–97 (1998)

Learning to Locate Cortical Bone in MRI

Gerardo Hermosillo, Vikas C. Raykar, and Xiang Zhou

Siemens Medical Solutions USA, Inc.
51 Valley Stream Parkway, Malvern, PA 19355, USA

Abstract. Automatic analysis of MR images requires the correct identification of the various tissues within them. Cortical bone is the most challenging tissue to identify in MR. We present an algorithm to automatically
predict the cortical bone locations from whole-body MR Dixon images. Our
algorithm combines local information from MR with global information
borrowed from exemplar patients with co-registered MR and CT images.
The local information is calculated using a classifier trained to discriminate bone from soft tissue using new multi-image template features. The
global information is incorporated by retrieving annotated bone maps of
the exemplars using a new, non-rigid registration algorithm. We combine
the local and global information by an iterative filtering precedure.

Keywords: whole-body MR imaging, template features, sparse logistic
regression, non-rigid registration.

1 Introduction

Segmenting an MR-image into different tissue classes is a necessary step for
quantitative analysis in applications such as bone metastasis detection and tissue
mass quantification. This can be done by direct segmentation methods or by
registering the MR image with an annotated atlas and using the atlas to identify
the tissue classes. Our focus is on automatically segmenting cortical bone in
MR, which is the most challenging tissue to identify. While segmentation based
approaches work reasonably well for other tissues, it is hard to distinguish bone
from soft-tissue based on the local MR intensities alone. On the other hand,
atlas based approaches are well constrained and are usually employed to avoid
leaks in segmentation but the segmentation obtained may not be very accurate
due to errors in registration. In this paper, we propose a hybrid algorithm that
combines a learning based segmentation approach with atlas based registration.
Our algorithm is designed to work with opposed phase MR imaging sequences,
which is a technique used to characterize masses that contain both fat and
water on a cellular level [5]. This sequence is typically used in abdominal and
pelvic imaging to diagnose adrenal and renal neoplasms, hepatic steatosis, and
fat containing tumors. Specifically, we use the MR dual-echo Dixon T1 image
sequence which allows for inline computation of fat and water images. Four
contrasts are available from this single acquisition: in-phase (standard T1), out-
of-phase, fat, and water.

F. Wang et al. (Eds.): MLMI 2012, LNCS 7588, pp. 168–175, 2012.
© Springer-Verlag Berlin Heidelberg 2012

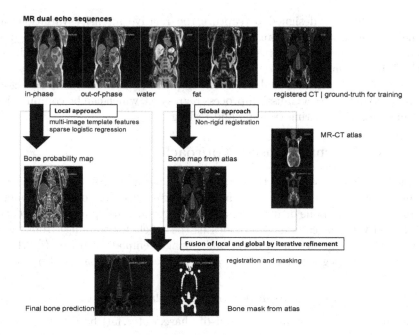

Fig. 1. *Overview of the approach* The proposed algorithm is designed to combine both local and global information using two orthogonal paradigms. The local information is predicted using a learning based approach and the global information is borrowed from a co-registered MR-CT atlas.

Figure 1 gives an overview of our approach. The local information is predicted based on the observed MR image sequences and the global information is borrowed from a co-registered MR-CT atlas. We use a binary classifier trained to discriminate bone from soft tissue to generate a bone probability map. The binary classifier is trained using a set of co-registered MR and CT images from the same patient as ground truth. It uses novel multi-image template features (§ 2.1) and a sparse logistic regression classifier (§ 2.2) to select only a sparse set of templates. We use non-rigid registration (§ 3) to retrieve an annotated bone map of an MR-CT exemplar. The deformation obtained by this step is applied to the CT image to provide an estimate of the cortical bone locations. The final algorithm combines the local and global information by an iterative filtering procedure (§ 4).

A combination of local pattern recognition and atlas registration method was earlier proposed in [3]. Our algorithm differs from this work in the following aspects: (a) Most of the results in [3] were presented for human brain scans with some preliminary results on one whole-body animal dataset. In contrast, our algorithm is validated of a set of 16 human whole body sequences (§ 5). (b) Our method of combining the local and global information is quite different from that used in [3], where the authors use the atlas registration result as a prior for Gaussian-process regression. (c) We propose a set of new multi-image template

features that are designed to capture the relative intensity variations across
the four images rather than the local intensity variations in one image alone.
Our features are robust across different patients since they do not explicitly use
the MR intensity values. (d) The final sparse linear classifier uses only a small
subset of these features and hence is computationally efficient. The algorithm
proposed in [3] uses a Gaussian-process regression, which can be computationally
demanding both during training and testing.

2   The Learning Based Approach

In this section we describe the learning based approach. At each voxel we compute a set of features and then apply a linear classifier to predict whether a
voxel belongs to bone or not. The classifier is trained using a set of co-registered
MR and CT images (which provides us the labels for training) from the same
patient. The classifier uses novel multi-image template features (§ 2.1) and a
sparse logistic regression classifier (§ 2.2) to select only a sparse set of templates.

2.1   Multi-image Template Cosine Similarity Features

For any voxel, let $i = [\text{in-phase}, \text{out-of-phase}, \text{water}, \text{fat}]$ be a four dimensional
vector of image intensities across multiple images, where each element is the MR
intensity value in the in-phase, out-of-phase, water, and the fat image respectively. Our proposed feature value is computed via the cosine similarity of x with
a pre-defined binary template t (for example $t = [1, 0, 0, 1]$), that is,

$$f(i,t) = \cos(\theta) = \frac{i \cdot t}{\|i\|\|t\|}. \tag{1}$$

By varying the template t we can exhaustively generate a set of features which
capture all possible variations in the MR intensities across the four images.
If we use two levels in the template (either 0 or 1) then we have a total of
$d = 2^4 - 1 = 15$ templates (ignoring the null template $t = [0,0,0,0]$) to generate
our features. The templates are normalized to have unit norm.

Since MR intensities are always positive and the template value is either 0
or 1, all the features lie in the range 0 to 1. The cosine of the angle between x
and t determines whether two vectors are pointing in roughly the same direction. In essence, each feature is capturing the direction of the variation of the
intensities across the four images. For example the feature $f(x, [0,0,0,1])$ is high
if the intensity in the fat channel is higher relative to the intensity in the other
three channels. We have intentionally used the cosine similarity so that the final
feature value *does not depend on the actual intensities* of the voxels, because
MR sequences (unlike CT images) lack a standard image intensity scale and
hence can lead to potential over-fitting and generalization problems if features
are designed based on the actual intensity values.

More fine grained variations across multiple images can be captured with
templates having multiple levels. In general if we have M images and K levels
for the template (from 0 to $K - 1$) we have a total of $M^K - 1$ templates.

2.2   Sparse Logistic Regression

Given the set of features $\mathbf{x} = [f(i, t_1), \ldots, f(i, t_d)]$ which correspond to the cosine similarity with the d templates, the probability that the voxel is a bone is written as a logistic sigmoid acting on the linear classifier, that is, $\Pr[y = 1|\mathbf{x}, \mathbf{w}] = \sigma\left(\mathbf{w}^\top \mathbf{x}\right)$, where $\mathbf{w}$ is the d-dimensional weight vector to be learnt. The logistic sigmoid link function is defined as $\sigma(z) = 1/(1 + e^{-z})$.

Given a set of n training instances $\mathcal{D} = \{\mathbf{x}_i, y_i\}_{i=1}^n$, the maximum likelihood (ML) estimate for $\mathbf{w}$ maximizes the log-likelihood of the parameters, that is, $\widehat{\mathbf{w}}_{\mathrm{ML}} = \arg\max_{\mathbf{w}} \log p(\mathcal{D}|\mathbf{w})$. Define $p_i = p(y_i = 1|\mathbf{x}_i, \mathbf{w}) = \sigma\left(\mathbf{w}^\top \mathbf{x}_i\right)$–the probability that the ith instance $\mathbf{x}_i$ is positive. Assuming that the training instances are independent the log-likelihood can be written as

$$l(\mathbf{w}) = \log p(\mathcal{D}|\mathbf{w}) = \sum_{i=1}^n y_i \log p_i + (1 - y_i) \log(1 - p_i). \tag{2}$$

The ML solution in practice can exhibit over-fitting. This can be addressed by using a prior on $\mathbf{w}$ and then finding the *maximum a-posteriori* (MAP) solution. In order to promote sparsity we impose a Laplace prior (with a common scale parameter γ) on each parameter w_i, that is, $p(w_i|\gamma) = (\sqrt{\gamma}/2) \exp\left(-\sqrt{\gamma}|w_i|\right)$. We also assume that individual weights in $\mathbf{w}$ are independent and hence the overall prior is the product of the priors for each component, that is,

$$p(\mathbf{w}|\gamma) = \prod_{i=1}^d p(w_i|\gamma) = \left(\frac{\sqrt{\gamma}}{2}\right)^d \exp\left(-\sqrt{\gamma}\|\mathbf{w}\|_1\right), \tag{3}$$

where $\|\mathbf{w}\|_1 = \sum_{i=1}^d |w_i|$ is the l_1-norm. Once we observe the training data $\mathcal{D}$ we update the prior to compute the posterior $p(\mathbf{w}|\mathcal{D})$, which can be written as follows (using Bayes's rule)–$p(\mathbf{w}|\mathcal{D}, \gamma) \propto p(\mathcal{D}|\mathbf{w})p(\mathbf{w}|\gamma)$. The mode of the posterior–the *maximum a-posteriori* (MAP) estimate is given by $\widehat{\mathbf{w}}_{\mathrm{MAP}} = \arg\max_{\mathbf{w}} p(\mathbf{w}|\mathcal{D}, \gamma) = \arg\max_{\mathbf{w}} [\log p(\mathcal{D}|\mathbf{w}) + \log p(\mathbf{w}|\gamma)]$. Substituting for the log likelihood (Eq. 2) and the prior (Eq. 3) we have $\widehat{\mathbf{w}}_{\mathrm{MAP}} = \arg\max_w L(\mathbf{w})$, where

$$L(\mathbf{w}) = \left[\sum_{i=1}^N y_i \log p_i + (1 - y_i) \log(1 - p_i)\right] - \sqrt{\gamma}\|\mathbf{w}\|_1. \tag{4}$$

The terms which do not depend on $\mathbf{w}$ have been omitted. We optimize this function based on the bound optimization approach with a component-wise update procedure proposed in [4].

3   The Registration Based Approach

We use a nonrigid registration algorithm to compute a deformation field that aligns the in-phase images from the subject and the atlas. Applying the same deformation to the atlas CT yields our cortical bone map. Before the non-rigid registration, we find a global translation by optimizing the global cross-correlation using fast Fourier transform.

To introduce notations, we are looking for ϕ such that: $I_1(\mathbf{x}) \sim I_2(\phi(\mathbf{x}))$, where $I_1 : \mathbb{R}^3 \to \mathbb{R}$ is the image used as reference, $I_2 : \mathbb{R}^3 \to \mathbb{R}$ is the one to be registered and $\sim$ denotes *correspondence*. In this setting, the unknown is a deformation field $\phi : \mathbb{R}^3 \to \mathbb{R}^3$ that provides correspondent locations in I_2 of locations defined in I_1.

We present a new diffeomorphism-building strategy within a conjugate gradient maximization of the local cross-correlation as defined in [2]. The standard approach described in [1] can be summarized by the following algorithm, given an initial deformation ϕ_0:

$$\begin{cases} \phi^* = \phi_0 \circ \phi_1 \circ \phi_2 \circ \cdots \circ \phi_\infty \\ \phi_k = id + \epsilon \left. \dfrac{\partial}{\partial \phi} S(I_1, I_2 \circ \phi) \right|_{\phi = \phi_0 \circ \phi_1 \circ \phi_2 \cdots \circ \phi_{k-1}} \end{cases}, \tag{5}$$

where S is the similarity measure, $\epsilon > 0$ is small enough to guarantee the invertibility of ϕ_k, id denotes the identity mapping and ϕ_∞ represents ϕ_n for some n large enough to attain convergence criteria. This algorithm can also be stated using pseudo-code as follows:

Set $i = 0$ and $\phi^* = \phi_0$.

While a stopping criterion is not reached:

compute S between I_1 and $I_2^i \equiv I_2 \circ \phi^*$,

compute the gradient of S with respect to a small deformation of I_2^i,

add a fraction of this gradient to id in order to form ϕ_{i+1},

set $\phi^* = \phi_i \circ \phi_{i+1}$ and increment i by one.

Instead, we propose a more efficient algorithm:

$$\begin{cases} \phi^* = \phi_0 \circ \delta_1^{-1} \circ \delta_2^{-1} \circ \cdots \circ \delta_\infty^{-1}, \\ \delta_k = id + \epsilon \left. \dfrac{\partial}{\partial \delta} S(I_1 \circ \delta, I_2 \circ \phi_0 \circ \delta_1^{-1} \circ \delta_2^{-1} \circ \cdots \circ \delta_{k-1}^{-1}) \right|_{\delta = id} \end{cases}, \tag{6}$$

which corresponds to the following pseudo-code:

Set $i = 0$ and $\phi^* = \phi_0$.

While a stopping criterion is not reached:

compute S between I_1 and $I_2^i \equiv I_2 \circ \phi^*$,

compute the gradient of S with respect to a small deformation of I_1,

add a fraction of this gradient to id in order to form δ_{i+1},

invert δ_{i+1} to produce δ_{i+1}^{-1},

set $\phi^* = \phi_i \circ \delta_{i+1}^{-1}$ and increment i by one.

The advantage of this algorithm is that the gradient of S with respect to a small deformation of I_1 involves only estimating the gradient of the fixed reference image I_1. This vector map is *the same* during the whole optimization process. Also, the gradient of I_1 is computed only at the sampling grid points and therefore no interpolation in necessary. Finally, although it may seem that the additional step of inverting δ_{i+1} could increase the computational cost, in fact δ_{i+1} is always a very small deformation and therefore the inverse of δ_{i+1} is well approximated by $id - (\delta_{i+1} - id)$. Combined with the conjugate gradient approach, this algorithm achieves at least one order of magnitude speed up as compared to the algorithms described in [1,2]. The iterative hybrid system described in § 4 solves 6 different registration problems in under 3 minutes.

4   The Hybrid Approach

The learning and registration approaches are orthogonal. The former is such that the true positive bone locations that are predicted are perfectly positioned within the MR space, but a lot of false positives from tissue boundaries are included in the prediction since it does not exploit global structure. On the other hand, the registration approach explicitly models the shape of all bones and the spatial relationship between them, but the positioning of this model may not be accurate due to errors in registration. We describe an iterative procedure that combines these approaches in an attempt to extract the good properties of each, thus maintaining the perfect location of the true positives while eliminating a large number of false positives with global information. More specifically, we iterate the following steps:

1. We first register the subject MR image to the atlas MR and bring the atlas CT into the subject MR space.
2. A bone mask is generated by computing the distance map to bone locations in the atlas CT and considering only locations that are sufficiently close to bone. The distance threshold is initially set to 10 mm.
3. The mask is then applied to the classifier prediction to eliminate some of the false positives. The same masking procedure is applied to the classifier prediction on the atlas image.
4. Now we register these masked predictions from the subject and the atlas and re-generate the atlas CT with the new deformation. This allows the registration to focus more on the bone.
5. We then reduce the distance threshold used to compute the mask.

The above steps are repeated until the distance parameter reaches 2 mm. At steady state, the masked prediction and the masked atlas should match.

5   Results

We validated our algorithm on a database of 16 MR/CT sequences. For each patient, we register the CT image to the MR in-phase image via non-rigid registration and then threshold it at 276 HU. This serves as our ground truth for validating the predicted bone map. Since the registration is not perfect our ground truth is noisy. However, the ground truth CT images were visually reviewed and were considered to be of sufficient quality for initial quantitative evaluation. Figure 2 illustrates our proposed algorithm on one of the testing cases. The top panel (top two rows) shows the full field of view while the bottom panel (bottom two rows) shows a zoomed-in section around the hip. For each

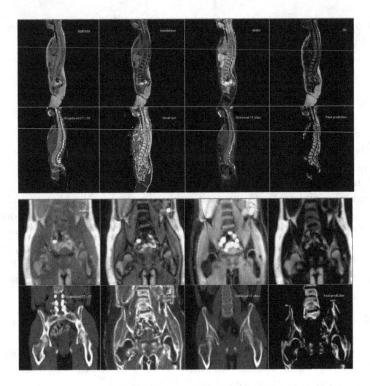

Fig. 2. Illustration of our proposed cortical bone segmentation algorithm (see § 5)

panel the top row shows the four MR images (in-phase, out-of-phase, water, and fat) and the bottom row shows from left to right: the registered CT (ground truth), the initial classifier prediction, the atlas CT brought to the MR space by registration and the final prediction. As mentioned earlier, there are some errors due to registration which are visible in the lower part of the spine in the CT image (first column). The pure learning based approach (second column) fails to distinguish between cortical bone and the tissue boundaries. Most of the false positives can be effectively eliminated by combining it with the registration based approach (last two columns). Our algorithm returns a bone map, which is the probability that the given location is cortical bone. Hence for quantitative evaluation we plot the Receiver Operating Characteristic (ROC) curve and compute the partial area under the ROC curve (pAUC) from 0 to 0.15. The ROC curve plots the sensitivity along the y-axis and false positive rate along the x-axis. The sensitivity is the fraction of bone voxels detected by the algorithm and the false positive rate is the fraction of voxels wrongly classified as bone. Figure 3 shows the ROC plots for the 8 cases for which ground truth was available. The remaining 8 cases were visually evaluated and the results were consistent with the 8 cases with ground truth. Each plot overlays the ROC for the initial prediction (dashed red line) and the final prediction (solid black line). As expected, masking the initial prediction via iterative refinement significantly

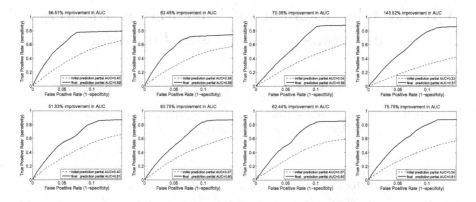

Fig. 3. Quantitative evaluation via ROC plots for eight different cases (see § 5)

improves the performance across all cases. The improvements in pAUC ranged from 52% to 144% across the nine cases, with an average of 73%.

6   Conclusions and Future Work

In this paper we proposed an algorithm to segment cortical bone from MR images by combining both local and global information. Our algorithm exhibits reasonable performance and may be useful for applications that require the knowledge of cortical bone locations such as the evaluation of bone metastasis from MR. Our future work will aim at identifying the key elements that affect performance in some specific applications of our system.

References

1. Chefd'hotel, C., Hermosillo, G., Faugeras, O.: Flows of diffeomorphisms for multimodal image registration. In: International Symposium on Biomedical Imaging. IEEE (2002)
2. Hermosillo, G., Chefd'hotel, C., Faugeras, O.: Variational methods for multimodal image matching. International Journal of Computer Vision 50(3), 329–343 (2002)
3. Hofmann, M., Steinke, F., Scheel, V., Charpiat, G., Farquhar, J., Aschoff, P., Brady, M., Scholkopf, B., Pichler, B.J.: MRI-Based Attenuation Correction for PET/MRI: A Novel Approach Combining Pattern Recognition and Atlas Registration. Journal of Nuclear Medicine 49, 1875–1883 (2008)
4. Krishnapuram, B., Carin, L., Figueiredo, M.A.T., Hartemink, A.J.: Sparse multinomial logistic regression: Fast algorithms and generalization bounds. IEEE Transactions on Pattern Analysis and Machine Intelligence 27(6), 957–968 (2005)
5. Merkle, E.M., Nelson, R.C.: Dual Gradient-Echo In-Phase and Opposed-Phase Hepatic MR Imaging: A Useful Tool for Evaluating More Than Fatty Infiltration or Fatty Sparing. Radiographics 26(5), 1409–1418 (2006)

Quality Classification of Microscopic Imagery with Weakly Supervised Learning

Xinghua Lou, Luca Fiaschi, Ullrich Koethe, and Fred A. Hamprecht

HCI, IWR, University of Heidelberg, Speyererstr. 6, 69115, Germany
http://hci.iwr.uni-heidelberg.de/MIP/

Abstract. In this post-genomic era, microscopic imaging is playing a crucial role in biomedical research and important information is to be discovered by quantitatively mining the resulting massive imagery databases. To this end, an important prerequisite is robust, high quality imagery databases. This is because defect images will jeopardize downstream tasks such as feature extraction and statistical analysis, yielding misleading results or even false conclusions. This paper presents a weakly supervised learning framework to tackle this problem. Our framework resembles a cascade of classifiers with feature and similarity measure designed for both global and local defects. We evaluated the framework on a database of images and obtained a 96.9% F-score for the important normal class. Click-and-play open source software is provided.

1 Introduction

Modern biomedical research heavily relies on large scale experiments and controlling the quality of the resulting data is crucial for any meaningful analysis. Whereas this problem has been investigated thoroughly for "-omic" techniques such as microarray [13], there has not been sufficient work on controlling the quality of microscopic imagery databases [15], despite the significant role imaging techniques are playing in this post-genomic era. Existing approaches depend on manual inspection via visualization or semi-automated processing [5,1]. However, the increasing scale and resolution of biomedical experiments such as high-content screening (HCS) [4] and high-resolution 3D connectomic data [8] has raised urgent demand for scalable quality control approaches. We are seeking for automated, efficient method for detecting defect images from large scale image databases. Image defects can occur during sample preparation, such as debris contamination, and also during image acquisition, such as out-of-focus [5,1]. They will jeopardize downstream tasks including registration, segmentation, tracking as well as statistical analysis. Usually defect images are rare and exhibit large variability of appearance. For example, w.r.t. normal images (Fig. 1A and E), defects can occur at the full image scale due to out-of-focus (Fig. 1B, D and F), also at particular regions within an image due to debris contamination (Fig. 1C, G and H).

Many challenges arise for quality control in large scale microscopic imagery databases. Firstly, supervised learning algorithms (support vector machine, random forest, etc.) [6] becomes inapplicable in practice. Because the rareness of

F. Wang et al. (Eds.): MLMI 2012, LNCS 7588, pp. 176–183, 2012.

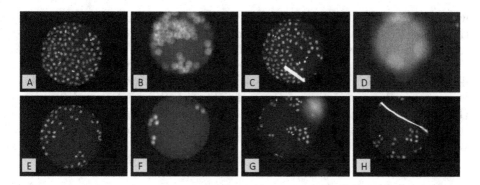

Fig. 1. Examples of normal and defect images in a high-content screening imagery database: A and E - normal images; B, D and F - out-of-focus; C, G and H - debris

defect images makes it too time consuming to collect sufficient training samples, which may require manual screening of the entire dataset. Secondly, it is also difficult to directly model the defects because of the large variability in scale and appearance [1]. Finally, the increasing quantity and resolution of images in such databases prohibit any manual inspection and filtering, and require algorithmic scalability as well as support of parallel computing [5].

We present a framework to address this important problem and we pursue two goals: low labeling efforts and high scalability. We cast this problem as an outlier detection problem [3] (i.e. defect images as outliers) and chose to develop our framework based on the one-class SVM [18]. Briefly, one class SVM only requires training samples from the normal class and, in some projected space by kernalization, it finds the most compact "ball" to enclose those samples. Test samples outside this ball (i.e. the decision boundary) will be classified as outliers.

Several outlier detection algorithms have been proposed in the literature, such as statistical models [7], distance measure [9], density estimation [2] or space partition [11]. We opt to choose one-class SVM for its capability of implicit feature projection via the kernel trick [19], which is frequently needed when handling image data. On the contrary, for example, isolation forest [11] partitions the original feature space by decision trees and determines outliers as those samples with a short path to the root. Despite their high scalability, they are restricted to the original feature space and extension by kernalization is not obvious. This encounters problems when handling image features, which are usually histograms, and which require kernalized similarity measure (e.g. earth mover's distance based [17]).

2   Defects in Microscopic Images: Global vs. Local

We group common causes for image defects into two classes, depending on whether they affect the image globally or locally. A typical cause for global defect is out-of-focus imaging and typical examples of regional defects such as debris contamination (e.g. hair) [1]. We handle these two types of defects differently with appropriate features and similarity measure, which allows for predicting three classes (normal, globally defect and regionally defect) even when training samples are only provided for the normal class.

For handling global defect, one important motivation is that it must be reflected in the statistics drawn from the entire image. For example, the formation of images is the convolution of the real light with the point spread function (PSF). When out-of-focus occurs, the PSF becomes wider, and this can be seen from the intensity histogram drawn from the entire image (e.g. Fig. 2A vs. Fig. 2B).

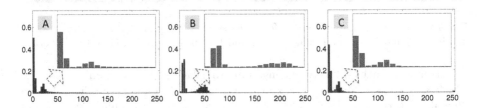

Fig. 2. Examples of the intensity histograms of normal and defect images. From left to right, the histograms corresponding to image A to C in Fig. 1. The red histogram inside is the zoomed view showing the intensity range of interest (between 0 and 64).

The task becomes more difficult when regional defects occur, because they exhibit considerable variability in scale, position and shape. A global statistic is no longer informative, e.g. Fig. 2A (normal) very similar to Fig. 2C (regional defect), and extracting information from fine regional details becomes necessary. In addition, regional defects show significant variability in appearance, implying the requirement for more features to achieve the required discriminative power.

3   Classification by One-Class SVM Cascade

To exploit the characteristics of global and regional defects and handle these two classes properly, we propose the quality classification framework shown in Fig. 3. Briefly, stage one operates on the full image level and aims at filtering out globally defect images. Stage two and three work on patch level, coupled to form a coarse-to-fine procedure for detecting regional defects. The overall framework resembles a cascade of one-class SVM classifiers.

3.1   Global Out-of-Focus Detection by Histogram Comparison

To efficient compare two images with different focus, various methods have been proposed in the computer vision community for natural image deblurring (see [12] and references therein). We follow the same intuition – out-of-focus blurring mainly affects the high frequency part (e.g. texture details) of an image. In particular, we build a histogram of the Gaussian gradient magnitude to capture

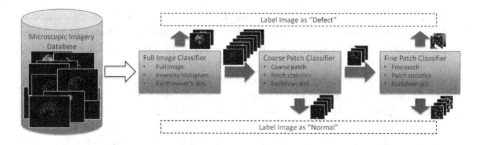

Fig. 3. Workflow of the proposed one-class SVM cascade. Red and green arrows indicate the flow of detected outlier and normal images/patches, respectively.

the high frequency part of an image. This histogram is used as the input feature for constructing the first one-class SVM that detects out-of-focus images. In particular, we first normalize the histogram and kernalize it using earth mover's distance (EMD) [17]. EMD describes the efforts required for transporting probability mass from one distribution (i.e. normalized histogram) to the other, and has proven superior to the Euclidean distance measure [17] (though the later is computationally much cheaper). Formally, given two normalized histograms (h_i and h_j), the kernel for out-of-focus detection is

$$K^{\mathrm{EMD}}(h_i, h_j) = \exp(-\lambda^{\mathrm{EMD}} EMD(h_i, h_j)) \tag{1}$$

Here, λ^{EMD} adjusts the scale of the EMD response. Note that, in order to have a valid kernel for one-class SVM, the histogram must be normalized [14].

3.2   Regional Defect Detection from Patch Statistics

We have already shown the need for finer level analysis: regional defects are not possible to capture from full image statistics. Moving from image level to patch level is not direct: unlike out-of-focus, regional defects can occur at any location and scale, and exhibit arbitrary appearance. Also, one has to consider the increasing complexity: hundreds of patches may need be extracted per image from a database of thousands of images yielding a new problem of size million.

We employs two techniques for regional defect detection. Firstly, we draw basic statistics from low level features and use RBF kernel for patch similarity measure. Secondly, we construct a coarse-to-fine procedure for speedup.

Low Level Features and Patch Statistics. We use low level features from to characterize the images from different aspects including texture (structure tensor), edge (gradient magnitude), and local extreme (eigenvalues of Hessian). For each feature, the following statistics are drawn from the patch: mean, standard deviation and quantiles (10%, 50% and 90%). For patch classification, we move away from histogram and EMD kernel because of its high computational cost: EMD is more expensive than Euclidean distance (for RBF kernel) by several orders of magnitude. .

On Feature Bagging and Classifier Ensembles. The high dimensional patch statistics is used as input features to the one-class SVM. Inevitably, some have no positive contribution to the patch similarity measure. Unfortunately, we cannot perform feature selection as in supervised learning. This problem is solved using feature bagging and classifier ensemble [10]. Briefly, we sample subsets of features (viz. bagging) and train a one-class SVM on each subset individually. The intuition is: important features become more influential in a lower dimensional feature subset, and accumulating votes from the ensembles brings more robustness than a single one-class SVM trained on all features.

To illustrate the improvement in discriminative power from feature bagging, we randomly sample 500 patches for each normal and defect class and plot their RBF kernel in Fig. 4. We hope to have an ideal kernel (Fig. 4A) that makes all normal samples (first 500 rows/columns) completely similar to each other and fully distinct to defect samples (the remaining rows/columns). The kernel computed using all features (Fig. 4B) does not exhibit the desired property because the important features are averaged out by the dimension of the input. This is improved when using feature bagging. We can see the improvement from the average kernel computed with bagged features (Fig. 4C): the contrast between the normal and defect samples is apparently enhanced, which implies improved discriminative power. Note that, in the context of one-class SVM, we do not have to make the defect samples all similar to each other because they can be distributed arbitrary outside the decision boundary (ball).

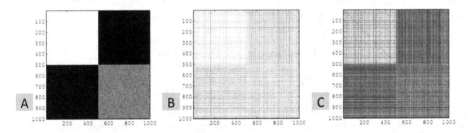

Fig. 4. Kernel matrices for 500 normal and 500 defect samples: A – ideal kernel; B – kernel using all features; C – average kernel from feature bagging

Coarse-to-Fine Filtering Procedure. Observing that a significant amount of image regions are "obviously" normal ones (such as background, regions with sparse objects), we incorporate a coarse-to-fine filtering procedure for speedup. The "fine" step (stage three in Fig. 3) operates on small patches (thus expensive). The speedup is obtained at the "coarse" step, i.e. stage two in Fig. 3, which operates on larger patches. In particular, stage two "filters out" easy normal image regions so that they can be skipped in the expensive stage three. Large patch size may average out small defect regions and produce a false normal patch. To prevent this, we made stage two more selective on determining normal images by setting a high ν value to the one-class SVM[18].

4   Experimental Results

We evaluated our framework on an image database for mammalian cell culture study. The new 9216-microwell cell array (in a 96 × 96 layout) [16] was used, yielding one image per well (Fig. 1). An automated scanning microscope was used with an overall imaging time of around 10 hours (4 seconds/image). Our approach is wrapped into a click-and-play software implementation that is available to the public[1].

It is important to select normal, training images with different characteristics (e.g. cell density, illumination, etc.) such that the training features (histograms or patch statistics) are not biased towards any particular type of normal images. Also, it is helpful to train the system incrementally. That is, starting with some training images, train and predict on a small subset of images; select representative samples from the wrongly predicted ones, add them to the training set and retrain the system. We made two rounds of incremental learning and eventually found 140 (out of 9216) training images. Overall, the framework took roughly 2.5 hours to complete the prediction on the entire dataset on a 4 core (2.8G-Hz) machine. Training time is roughly 5 minutes per stage.

We define normal images as those that are useful for our cell segmentation and counting task and generate manual ground truth accordingly. Table. 2 shows the overall detection accuracy by our framework, depicted as a confusion matrix (rows being the ground truth), and the per class precision/recall is given in Table 1. The parameter settings that yields this result are biased to more tolerance of false positive rate, because it is more costly to mistake defect images for normal images. Note that the definition of "normal" may change with the task of the analysis. For example, slightly out-of-focus images are useful for cell counting but useless for phenotype classification.

Table 1. Per class precision and recall

	Normal	Out-of-Focus	Regional
Normal	7854	146	338
Out-of-Focus	1	426	28
Regional	19	47	357

Table 2. Classification confusion matrix

	Precision	Recall	F-score
Normal	0.997	0.942	0.969
Out-of-Focus	0.688	0.936	0.793
Regional	0.494	0.844	0.623

Some examples of detected regional defects are shown in Fig. 5. Our framework shows high accuracy on detecting regional defects, even though they exhibit strong variability in size, shape, texture and other characteristics. Fig. 7 shows some errors by our framework. We notice that misdetection occurs when the regional defect is not sufficiently strong (left two images).

Fig. 6 shows the detected out-of-focus images represented by their signed distance to the classifier's decision boundary in a 96 × 96 cell array layout. Higher value indicates more severe out-of-focus error. As we can see from the prominent strip in the center, some systematic error caused the microscopy to

---

[1] http://ilastik.org/

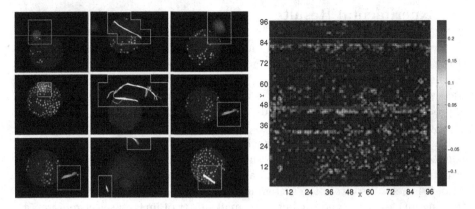

Fig. 5. Examples of regional defects found by our framework

Fig. 6. Location of out-of-focus images on 96x96 well plate

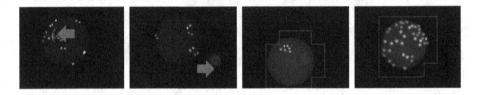

Fig. 7. Examples of errors in regional defect detection: misdetected (left two) and false positive (right two)

malfunction during the entire acquisition time for row 45 and 46. This suggests investigation and helps to avoid such systematic errors in future experiments.

Discussion: It is worth pointing out that training data preparation would be too expensive for two-class learning. Firstly, defects exhibit huge variability in appearance, which forces users to collect "defect" images by browsing through huge databases. This task is tedious and becomes more so if there are few positive (defect) images, as is desirable from the experimental point of view. Secondly, we showed the necessity of patch level classification for detecting regional defects. Two-class learning will require users to explicitly mark each defect region/patch, thus even more expensive. We avoid this excessive labeling efforts in our approach.

5   Conclusions and Outlook

This paper presents a framework for microscopic image quality control based on one class learning. We studied the distinct properties of global and local defects in microscopic images and proposed appropriate features and similarity measures for them. At the same time we show that its possible to distinguish globally and regionally defect images with a scalable cascade of one class classifiers using only training images from the normal class.

In the future, we plan to integrate our method with the automated microscopy control. This offers the advantage that the detection results can give feedback to correct image acquisition in place and in time. Also, given our generic framework, we plan to extend our method to other biomedical imaging scenarios.

References

1. Bray, M.A., Fraser, A.N., Hasaka, T.P., et al.: Workflow and Metrics for Image Quality Control in Large-Scale High-Content Screens. J. Biomol. Screening (2011)
2. Breunig, M.M., Kriegel, H.P., Ng, R.T.J., et al.: LOF: identifying density-based local outliers. ACM Sigmod Record 29(2), 93–104 (2000)
3. Chandola, V., Banerjee, A., Kumar, V.: Outlier detection: A survey. ACM Comput. Surv. (2007)
4. Echeverri, C.J., Perrimon, N.: High-throughput RNAi screening in cultured cells: a user's guide. Nat. Rev. Genet. 7(5), 373–384 (2006)
5. Goode, A., Sukthankar, R., Mummert, L., et al.: Distributed online anomaly detection in high-content screening. In: ISBI (2008)
6. Hastie, T., Tibshirani, R., Friedman, J.: The Elements of Statistical Learning. Springer Series in Statistics. Springer New York Inc., New York (2001)
7. Hero, A.O.: Geometric entropy minimization (GEM) for anomaly detection and localization. In: NIPS (2006)
8. Kaynig, V., Fischer, B., Buhmann, J.M.: Probabilistic image registration and anomaly detection by nonlinear warping. In: CVPR (2008)
9. Knox, E.M., Ng, R.T.: Algorithms for mining distance-based outliers in large datasets. In: VLDB (1998)
10. Lazarevic, A., Kumar, V.: Feature bagging for outlier detection. In: KDD (2005)
11. Liu, F.T., Ting, K.M., Zhou, Z.H.: Isolation Forest. In: ICDM (2008)
12. Liu, R., Li, Z., Jia, J.: Image partial blur detection and classification. In: CVPR (2008)
13. MAQC Consortium The MicroArray Quality Control (MAQC) project shows inter- and intraplatform reproducibility of gene expression measurements. Nat. Biotechnol. 24(9), 1151–1161 (2006)
14. Pele, O., Werman, M.: Fast and robust earth mover's distances. In: ICCV (2009)
15. Pepperkok, R., Ellenberg, J.: High-throughput fluorescence microscopy for systems biology. Nat. Rev. Mol. Cell Bio. 7(9), 690–696 (2006)
16. Reymann, J., Beil, N., Beneke, J., et al.: Next-generation 9216-microwell cell arrays for high-content screening microscopy. Bio.Techniques 47(4), 877 (2009)
17. Rubner, Y., Tomasi, C., Guibas, L.J.: A Metric for Distributions with Applications to Image Databases. In: ICCV (1998)
18. Schoelkopf, B., Platt, J.C., Shawe-Taylor, J., et al.: Estimating the support of a high-dimensional distribution. Neural. Comput. 13(7), 1443–1471 (2001)
19. Schoelkopf, B., Smola, A.J.: Learning with Kernels: Support Vector Machines, Regularization, Optimization, and Beyond. The MIT Press, Cambridge (2002)

Graph-Based Inter-subject Classification of Local fMRI Patterns

Sylvain Takerkart[1,2], Guillaume Auzias[3,1], Bertrand Thirion[4], Daniele Schön[5], and Liva Ralaivola[2]

[1] CNRS, INT (UMR 7289), Marseille, France
[2] Aix-Marseille University, LIF (UMR 7189), Marseille, France
[3] CNRS, LSIS (UMR 7296), Marseille, France
[4] INRIA-Saclay-Ile-de-France, Parietal Team, Palaiseau, France
[5] CNRS, INS (UMR 1106), Marseille, France

Abstract. Classification of medical images in multi-subjects settings is a difficult challenge due to the variability that exists between individuals. Here we introduce a new graph-based framework designed to deal with inter-subject functional variability present in fMRI data. A graphical model is constructed to encode the functional, geometric and structural properties of local activation patterns. We then design a specific graph kernel, allowing to conduct SVM classification in graph space. Experiments conducted in an inter-subject classification task of patterns recorded in the auditory cortex show that it is the only approach to perform above chance level, among a wide range of tested methods.

Keywords: fMRI, classification, graphs, kernels, inter-subject, variability.

1 Introduction

Since brain functions are considered to arise from activities distributed across networks, multivariate pattern recognition methods are adapted to study information processing in the brain. Multi-voxel pattern analysis (MVPA) of functional MRI allows to study the organization of distributed representations in the brain by using a classification framework where one attempts to predict the category of the input stimuli from the data [8]. MVPA has been largely applied within individual subjects [13].

However, because of the challenge posed by the large inter-individual variability, very few studies describe inter-subject decoding, i.e successfull prediction on data from a subject that was not part of the training set. Among these, most rely on global (i.e full-brain) analysis, using large-scale features ([12], [15]). The few studying fine-scale local patterns achieve very low inter-subject generalization performances [3], or use implicit abstract models [9]. None attempt to characterize the inter-subject *functional* variability (i.e the fact that the correlation between cortical folding and the underlying functional organization vary between subjects [4]) and use such characterization in the classification process.

F. Wang et al. (Eds.): MLMI 2012, LNCS 7588, pp. 184–192, 2012.

In this paper, we introduce a new framework specifically aimed at tackling the challenges offered by inter-subject *functional* variability by modelling its spatial properties. Our approach integrates the fact that the geometric properties of local functional features, as well as their levels of activation, can vary across subjects, under the assumption that the underlying spatial structure of the local activation pattern is consistent. We therefore design a graphical model to represent such patterns with their properties of interest: the nodes of the graphs represent small activation patches; their attributes carry the relevant features, such as their position and activation level; the edges of the graph (given by spatial adjacency) encode the spatial structure of the pattern. The classification is then performed directly in graph-space with Support Vector Machines (SVM), using a graph kernel specifically designed to take into account all properties of our graphical model. Since the topographic organization of primary sensory areas ensures the structural consistency of activation patterns across subjects, we validate our framework on fMRI data recorded in the primary auditory cortex during a tonotopy experiment [10].

This paper is organized as follows: we detail the construction of our graphical model in section 2 and the kernel design in section 3; we then describe our experiments in section 4 and present our results in section 5.

2   Graphical Model of Activation Patterns

We here describe the design of a graphical model that summarizes the information relevant to characterize a pattern a pattern of activation measured with fMRI within a contiguous *region of interest* (ROI).

Graph nodes. Assuming that the ROI admits an underlying subdivision into a set of smaller and functionally relevant sub-regions, the first step to construct our graphical model estimates a parcellation of the ROI, i.e. a partition into a set of sub-regions or *parcels* [5]. Specifically, for a contiguous ROI $\mathcal{R}$, we compute the parcellation $\mathcal{V} = \{V_i\}_{i=1}^q$ of $\mathcal{R}$, so that the q parcels verify: $\cup_{i=1}^q V_i = \mathcal{R}$ and $V_i \cap V_j = \emptyset$ whenever $i \neq j$. We use $\mathcal{V}$ as the set of vertices of our graphical model, each parcel corresponding to a node of the graph.

Nodes attributes: functional features. Let f be the real-valued function describing the BOLD activation. In a parcel V_i, the activations values $\{f(v)\}_{v \in V_i}$ are summarized to form an n-dimensional feature vector $F(V_i)$; we note $\mathcal{F}$ the $n \times q$ matrix $\mathcal{F} = [F(V_1) \cdots F(V_q)]$ of functional features, where each column i of F is $F(V_i)$. A simple example of such F, which we make use of later on, is to compute the mean activation value within a parcel.

Nodes attributes: geometric features. Let x be a coordinate system defined in $\mathcal{R}$. We summarize the geometric information of parcel V_i through a m-dimensional feature vector $X(V_i)$, computed from the locations $\{x(v)\}_{v \in V_i}$. We note $\mathcal{X}$ the $m \times q$ matrix $\mathcal{X} = [X(V_1) \cdots X(V_q)]$ of geometric features. $\mathcal{X}$ may contain information on the shape or location of the parcels.

Graph edges: structural information. The set of edges is represented by a binary adjacency matrix $A = (a_{ij}) \in \mathbb{R}^{q \times q}$, where $a_{ij} = 1$ if parcels V_i and V_j

are spatially adjacent (i.e if $\exists v_i \in V_i, \exists v_j \in V_j$ so that v_i and v_j are neighbors, for a given neighborhood definition), and $a_{ij} = 0$ otherwise. This adjacency matrix encodes the spatial structure of the activation pattern.

Full graphical model. Using these definitions, we have defined an attributed region adjacency graph [14] (hereafter noted *a-RAG*) $G = (\mathcal{V}, A, \mathcal{F}, \mathcal{X})$, which represents the fMRI activation pattern within the ROI $\mathcal{R}$ by encoding functional, geometric and structural information.

3   Kernel Design

The fully generic family of convolution kernels [7] is defined as:

$$K(G, H) = \sum_{g \subseteq G, h \subseteq H} \prod_t k_t(g, h), \tag{1}$$

where $t \in \mathbb{N}^*$ is the, usually small, number of base kernels k_t, which act on subgraphs g and h. To design a kernel for our *a-RAGs*, we need to choose the type of subgraphs, the value of t and to instantiate each base kernel k_t.

Subgraphs used to design such kernels include paths and random walks [6], tree motives [11] etc. For simplicity reasons, we will here use paths of length two; note that the definitions below are directly extendable to other choices. Given the characteristics of the *a-RAGs*, we need to define $t = 3$ elementary kernels k_f, k_g and k_s, respectively acting on functional, geometric and structural features.

Let $G = (\mathcal{V}_G, A_G, \mathcal{F}_G, \mathcal{X}_G)$ and $H = (\mathcal{V}_H, A_H, \mathcal{F}_H, \mathcal{X}_H)$ be two *a-RAGs*: we note $g_{ij} = \{i, j\}$ and $h_{kl} = \{k, l\}$ two pairs of nodes in G and H, respectively; let q_G and q_H be the number of nodes in G and H, respectively — note that q_G and q_H may be different.

Functional kernel. Kernel k_f aims at measuring the similarity of the activation in parcels of g_{ij} and h_{kl}. We therefore propose the following product (and thus positive definite) kernel

$$k_f(g_{ij}, h_{kl}) = e^{-\|F_i^G - F_k^H\|^2 / 2\sigma_f^2} \cdot e^{-\|F_j^G - F_l^H\|^2 / 2\sigma_f^2}, \tag{2}$$

where $\sigma_f \in \mathbf{R}_+^*$ and F_p^G (resp. F_p^H) is the pth column of $\mathcal{F}_G$ (resp. $\mathcal{F}_H$). Using such a product of Gaussian kernels allows dealing with the inter-subject functional variability.

Geometric kernel. The second base kernel k_g acts on the geometric features. To allow for inter-subject variability, we follow the same principle as for the functional kernel, which gives:

$$k_g(g_{ij}, h_{kl}) = e^{-\|X_i^G - X_k^H\|^2 / 2\sigma_g^2} \cdot e^{-\|X_j^G - X_l^H\|^2 / 2\sigma_g^2}, \tag{3}$$

where $\sigma_g \in \mathbf{R}_+^*$, and X_p^G (resp. X_p^H) is the pth column of $\mathcal{X}_G$ (resp. $\mathcal{X}_H$).

Structural kernel. The base kernel k_s aims at valuing the structural similarity of G and H. Since our main hypothesis is that the structure is consistent across patterns recorded in different subjects, we adopt a decision function (by opposition to the smooth functional and geometric kernels), by using the linear kernel on binary entries a_{ij}^G and a_{kl}^H of the adjacency matrices A_G and A_H, which encodes the fact that pairs g_{ij} and h_{kl} are both edges:

$$k_s(g_{ij}, h_{kl}) = a_{ij}^G.a_{kl}^H \tag{4}$$

Resulting kernel. With the definitions of k_f, k_g and k_s, we may define the resulting kernel (with parameters σ_g and σ_f):

$$K(G, H) = \sum_{i,j=1}^{q_G} \sum_{k,l=1}^{q_H} k_g(g_{ij}, h_{kl}) \cdot k_f(g_{ij}, h_{kl}) \cdot k_s(g_{ij}, h_{kl}), \tag{5}$$

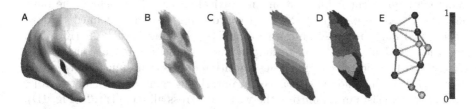

Fig. 1. Graph construction process. A. Inflated cortical surface of the right hemisphere for one subject; Heschl's gyrus is highlighted. B. A normalized activation pattern C. The two coordinates fields computed within the ROI. D. Example of parcellation with 10 parcels (arbitrary colors for illustration only). E. Example of an attributed graph: the nodes are located at the barycenter of the parcels and the color encodes the average level of activation in the parcel.

4   Real Experiment and Data Analysis

fMRI tonotopy experiment. In order to test this framework, we used a dataset that was acquired to study the tonotopic property of the human auditory cortex. This property states that neighboring neurons in the cortex respond to auditory stimuli of neighboring frequencies. This results in a spatially organized mapping of the auditory cortex. Typically higher frequencies are represented in the medial part of the primary auditory cortex (A1) while lower frequencies are represented more laterally, although recent high resolution studies suggest a more complex patterns with mirror-symmetric frequency gradients [10].

For each of the nine subjects, a T1 image was acquired (1mm isotropic voxels). Each stimulus consisted of a 8s sequence of 60 isochronous tones covering a narrow bandwidth around a central frequency f. There were five types of sequences (i.e. conditions), each one centered around a different frequency f ($f \in \{300Hz, 500Hz, 1100Hz, 2200Hz, 4000Hz\}$), with no overlap between the bandwidths covered by any two types of stimuli. Five functional sessions were acquired, each containing six sequences per condition presented in a pseudo-random order. Echo-planar images (EPI) were acquired with slices parallel to the sylvian fissure (repetition time=2.4s, voxel size=2x2x3mm, matrix size 128x128). Fieldmaps were recorded to allow EPI geometric distortion correction.

Data processing and classification. The preprocessing of the functional data, carried on in *SPM8* (`www.fil.ion.ucl.ac.uk/spm`), consisted in realignment, slice timing correction and "fieldmap" unwarping. Then, a generalized linear model was performed (in *nipy*: `nipy.sourceforge.net`) with one regressor of interest per stimulus. The weight (beta) maps of these regressors served as estimates of the response size for each stimulus. For the spatial proximity to have an anatomical meaning, one has to work on the 2D cortical surface. We therefore used *freesurfer* (`surfer.nmr.mgh.harvard.edu`) to extract the corti-cal surface from the T1 image and automatically define the primary auditory cortex (Fig. 1A) as part of Heschl's gyrus (thus defining our cortical ROI $\mathcal{R}$ in each subject). The beta maps are then projected onto the cortex, and slightly smoothed (equivalent fwhm of 3mm) in cortical space, which defines the func-tion $\{f(v)\}_{v \in \mathcal{R}}$ (Fig. 1B). A 2D local coordinates system is defined through a conformal mapping of $\mathcal{R}$ onto a rectangle [1], defining $\{x(v)\}_{v \in \mathcal{R}}$ (Fig. 1C). One then need a parcellation technique that produces homogeneous parcels. We use Ward's hierarchical clustering algorithm on anatomo-functional features $\{f(v), x(v)\}$, with an added spatial constraint: the merging criterion of two adja-cent parcels consists in minimzing the variance across all parcels [12] (Fig. 1D), and the neighboring criterion is given by the neighboring of the vertices of the cortical mesh. Finally, we define one functional feature F, the mean activation in a parcel (normalized between 0 and 1) and a 2D geometric feature vector X as the coordinates of the barycenter of each parcel.

Using the kernel trick, one can then directly perform Support Vector Clas-sification in graph space (G-SVC) to guess the class of the input stimulus (i.e the tone frequency) from a given activation pattern. In practice, the Gram ma-trix was computed with custom-designed code, and given as input to the SVC function of the *scikit-learn* python module (`scikit-learn.org`), which uses *Lib-SVM* (`www.csie.ntu.edu.tw/~cjlin/libsvm/`) to implement SVM. A leave-one-subject-out cross-validation scheme was used to measure the classification accuracy. For each fold of this cross-validation, we estimated the kernel param-eters σ_f and σ_g as the median euclidean distance between the functional and geometric (respectively) feature vectors of the parcels between all nodes of all example-graphs in the training set, which corresponds to a standard heuristic [2]. Two types of analyses were conducted. First, we performed simulations with a fixed number of nodes q for all graphs and all subjects; several simulations were conducted, with $q \in \{5, 6, 7, 8, 9, 10, 15, 20, 25, 30\}$. Second, we imposed different number of nodes for each subject, randomly taken in three intervals $I_q = [5, 13]$, $[14, 22]$ and $[5, 21]$; for each of these intervals, we ran 18 simulations with different random sets of node numbers (each time with a different q for each subject).

In order to compare the performances of our framework to vector-based meth-ods, one need to define a vertex to vertex correspondance across subjects (which is not needed with our framework). We therefore aligned the anatomy of all subjects to a standard spherical cortical space using *freesurfer* and projected the beta maps to this standard space. $\mathcal{R}$ is now common to all subjects and we can use $\{f(v)\}_{v \in \mathcal{R}}$ as a feature set. Several classification algorithms were then used, each time with several values of their respective hyper-parameters: 1) linear SVC; 2) non linear SVC, with gaussian (with $\sigma \in \{10^{-n}\}_{n \in \{-2,-1,0,1\}}$) and polynomial (of order $n \in \{2,3,4\}$) kernels; 3) k-nearest neigbors (with $k \in \{3,5,7,11,15\}$); 4) logistic regression with l_1 and l_2 regularization (with weight $\lambda \in \{10^n\}_{n \in \{2,3,4\}}$).

5   Results and Discussion

Table 1 contains the performances of our G-SVC framework vs. the different benchmark vector-based methods. The scores are the mean classification accuracies across all folds of the cross-validation; for the benchmark methods, the reported score is the highest one across simulations ran with all values of their hyper-parameters; for G-SVC, it is the mean performances across all values of q. All vector-based methods performed similarly, but none of them performed significantely above chance level (equal to 0.2 since there were five types of auditory stimuli). Our G-SVC framework was the only method to perform significantely above chance level (one sample t-test, $p < 0.05$, indicated by a $\star$), in both the left and right Heschl's gyri (HG). It also performed significantely better than the best benchmark method (linear SVC for the right HG, logistic regression for the left HG; paired t-test with matched left-out subject, $p < 0.05$; indicated by a $\diamond$). Table 2 describes the accuracy of our G-SVC depending on the number of graph nodes q. Our framework performed above chance level in all cases (one sample t-test, $p < 0.05$; $\star$), and significantely better than the best benchmark method (paired t-test, $p < 0.05$; $\diamond$) in all but two cases (left HG, $q = 10, 15$).

Table 1. G-SVC vs. benchmark methods

	G-SVC	lin. SVC	non lin. SVC	k-NN	log. reg.
right HG	**0.45**$^{\star\diamond}$	0.25	0.23	0.27	0.27
left HG	**0.36**$^{\star\diamond}$	0.26	0.24	0.25	0.24

Table 2. Influence of the number of graph nodes q in G-SVC

G-SVC q nodes	5	6	7	8	9	10	15	20	25	30
right HG	**0.48**$^{\star\diamond}$	0.45$^{\star\diamond}$	0.45$^{\star\diamond}$	0.43$^{\star\diamond}$	0.47$^{\star\diamond}$	0.43$^{\star\diamond}$	0.44$^{\star\diamond}$	**0.48**$^{\star\diamond}$	0.47$^{\star\diamond}$	0.44$^{\star\diamond}$
left HG	0.33$^{\star\diamond}$	0.37$^{\star\diamond}$	0.35$^{\star\diamond}$	0.38$^{\star\diamond}$	0.35$^{\star\diamond}$	0.35*	0.34*	0.37$^{\star\diamond}$	**0.39**$^{\star\diamond}$	0.38$^{\star\diamond}$

Results of the simulations using a randomized number of nodes q for each subject are given in Table 3. In all 108 simulations, our G-SVC framework performed above chance level (one sample t-test, $p < 0.05$, $\star$). This shows that the proposed kernel is efficient for graphs having different number of nodes. Moreover, in 80% of the simulations (86/108), it outperformed the best benchmark

Table 3. Mean G-SVC performances with variable q over 18 simulations (number that resulted in accuracy above chance level $\star$, above the best benchmark method $\diamond$)

Interval I_q	[5,13]	[14,22]	[5,21]
right HG	0.43 (18*, 18$^\diamond$)	0.45 (18*, 18$^\diamond$)	0.45 (18*, 18$^\diamond$)
left HG	0.35 (18*, 12$^\diamond$)	0.36 (18*, 9$^\diamond$)	0.36 (18*, 11$^\diamond$)

method (paired t-test, $p < 0.05$, $\diamond$). Overall, the performances are very similar to the ones obtained when the number of nodes is fixed for all subjects.

Discussion. In this paper, we designed a graphical model and a graph-kernel that allows to compare and discriminate high dimensional patterns of fMRI activation across subjects. To our knowledge, this is the first time that a graph-based pattern recognition approach is used to study local fMRI activation patterns. Specifically, we have demonstrated the power of this approach in a classification task that aims at predicting experimental variables from fMRI patterns when the classifier is trained on data from a set of subjects and its generalization performance is tested on data from a different subject.

Our G-SVC framework performed above chance level in all cases, whereas none of the benchmark methods did. This validates that this framework is appropriate to deal with inter-subject variability that is not accounted for by a state of the art group alignment, such as the one offered in *freesurfer*. However, it is important to use the anatomical information at our disposal, as was attempted in this study by *i)* working on the cortical surface, and *ii)* defining a local coordinates system within our region of interest for each subject, thus using the most of the local individual anatomy. Indeed, we also tested G-SVC using the raw three-dimensional voxel coordinates for x, and the performances (not reported here) were systematically lower.

A major asset of using a graph kernel such as the one defined here is that the graphs can have different number of nodes, without having to strictly solve a graph matching problem, i.e to assign nodes to one another across instances. This is emphasized by the results of our simulations where the number of nodes was randomly chosen and forced to be different for each subject. In those, our framework still outperformed vector-based methods, demonstrating the ability to deal with graphs with different node numbers. We also noted a few simulations where the classification accuracy was higher than with a fixed q for all subjects. This suggests that there might exist an "optimal" number of nodes for each subject and that performances could increase by adequately choosing q for each subject. We will address this in future work, for instance by using a model selection criterion (BIC, AIC etc.) in the parcellation. Another source of potential improvement lies in selecting the hyper-parameter σ_f and σ_g of the kernel in a nested cross-validation, rather than using a heuristic estimator.

6 Conclusion

We have designed a graphical model carrying functional, geometric, and structural features to represent spatial patterns. With a custom-designed graph kernel providing a natural metric, this framework seems particularly attractive to perform classification tasks in multi-subject settings, as evidenced by the conclusive results obtained here when dealing with inter-subject functional variability in fMRI data. This modelling strategy therefore opens the possibility to characterize and discriminate populations based on their functional patterns of activation.

Acknowledgment. Thanks to the CNRS Neuro-IC program for funding, and to the *Centre IRMf de Marseille* and its staff for data acquisition.

References

1. Auzias, G., Lefèvre, J., Le Troter, A., Fischer, C., Perrot, M., Régis, J., Coulon, O.: Model-Driven Harmonic Parameterization of the Cortical Surface. In: Fichtinger, G., Martel, A., Peters, T. (eds.) MICCAI 2011, Part II. LNCS (LNAI), vol. 6892, pp. 310–317. Springer, Heidelberg (2011)
2. Caputo, B., Sim, K., Furesjo, F., Smola, A.: Appearance-based object recognition using svms: which kernel should i use? In: Proc. of NIPS Workshop on Stat. Methods for Computational Experiments in Visual Processing and Computer Vision (2002)
3. Clithero, J.A., Smith, D.V., Carter, R.M., Huettel, S.A.: Within- and cross-participant classifiers reveal different neural coding of information. NeuroImage 56(2), 699–708 (2011); Multivariate Decoding and Brain Reading
4. Van Essen, D.C., Dierker, D.L.: Surface-Based and probabilistic atlases of primate cerebral cortex. Neuron 56(2), 209–225 (2007)
5. Flandin, G., Kherif, F., Pennec, X., Malandain, G., Ayache, N., Poline, J.-B.: Improved Detection Sensitivity in Functional MRI Data Using a Brain Parcelling Technique. In: Dohi, T., Kikinis, R. (eds.) MICCAI 2002, Part I. LNCS, vol. 2488, pp. 467–474. Springer, Heidelberg (2002)
6. Gärtner, T.: Exponential and geometric kernels for graphs. In: NIPS Workshop on Unreal Data: Principles of Modeling Nonvectorial Data (2002)
7. Haussler, D.: Convolution kernels on discrete structures. Technical Report UCSC-CRL-99-10, UC Santa Cruz (1999)
8. Haxby, J.V., Gobbini, M.I., Furey, M.L., Ishai, A., Schouten, J.L., Pietrini, P.: Distributed and overlapping representations of faces and objects in ventral temporal cortex. Science 293(5539), 2425–2430 (2001)
9. Haxby, J.V., Guntupalli, J.S., Connolly, A.C., Halchenko, Y.O., Conroy, B.R., Gobbini, M.I., Hanke, M., Ramadge, P.J.: A common, High-Dimensional model of the representational space in human ventral temporal cortex. Neuron 72(2), 404–416 (2011)
10. Humphries, C., Liebenthal, E., Binder, J.R.: Tonotopic organization of human auditory cortex. NeuroImage 50(3), 1202–1211 (2010)
11. Mahé, P., Vert, J.P.: Graph kernels based on tree patterns for molecules. Machine Learning 75, 3–35 (2009)

12. Michel, V., Gramfort, A., Varoquaux, G., Eger, E., Keribin, C., Thirion, B.: A supervised clustering approach for fMRI-based inference of brain states. Pattern Recognition 45(6), 2041–2049 (2012)
13. Norman, K.A., Polyn, S.M., Detre, G.J., Haxby, J.V.: Beyond mind-reading: multi-voxel pattern analysis of fMRI data. Trends in Cognitive Sciences 10(9), 424–430 (2006)
14. Pavlidis, T.: Structural pattern recognition. Springer (1977)
15. Poldrack, R.A., Halchenko, Y.O., Hanson, S.J.: Decoding the Large-Scale structure of brain function by classifying mental states across individuals. Psychological Science 20(11), 1364–1372 (2009)

Combining Multiple Image Segmentations by Maximizing Expert Agreement

Joni-Kristian Kamarainen, Lasse Lensu, and Tomi Kauppi

Machine Vision and Pattern Recognition Laboratory
Department of Information Technology
Lappeenranta University of Technology
P.O. Box 20, FI-53851 Lappeenranta, Finland
lasse.lensu@lut.fi
http://www2.it.lut.fi/mvpr/

Abstract. A common characteristic of collecting the ground truth for medical images is that multiple experts provide only partially coherent manual segmentations, and in some cases, with varying confidence. As the result, there is considerable spatial variation between the expert segmentations, and for training and testing, the "true" ground truth is estimated by disambiguating (combining) the provided segments. STAPLE and its derivatives are the state-of-the-art approach for disambiguating multiple spatial segments provided by clinicians. In this work, we propose a simple yet effective procedure based on maximizing the joint agreement of experts. Our algorithm produces the optimal disambiguation by maximizing the agreement and no priors are used. In the experimental part, we generate a new ground truth for the popular diabetic retinopathy benchmark, DiaRetDB1, for which the original expert markings are publicly available. We demonstrate performance superior to the original and also STAPLE generated ground truth. In addition, the DiaRetDB1 baseline method performs better with the new ground truth.

1 Introduction

Image databases and expert ground truth are in common use in medical imaging research. The motivation for using expert ground truth arises from the fact that a variety of imaging modalities exist for medical examinations and generally the ground truth is not provided by a device. The common solutions to get spatial ground truth estimating the true segmentation of physiological details or lesions make use of synthetic images, physical or digital phantoms related to the imaging, or involve a group of experts to perform manual or semi-automatic segmentation. For studies striving for the true expert knowledge based on the visual evaluation of real *in vivo* images, the last approach is the best option since real images are used in clinical diagnosis and no special effort must be made to validate the synthetic data. In this case, the two relevant questions are the number of experts to use and how the ambiguous information represents the "truth". However, as the number of experts for the laborious manual work increases and the experts are qualified for medical diagnosis work, their joint

F. Wang et al. (Eds.): MLMI 2012, LNCS 7588, pp. 193–200, 2012.
© Springer-Verlag Berlin Heidelberg 2012

agreement should converge to the ground truth – to the gold standard in medical diagnosis which is based on the second opinion from a peer or several peers.

In many applications, method development is driven by publicly available and commonly accepted benchmark datasets. This practice enables the evaluation and comparison of image processing methods, and assessment of the state of the art. In a wider context, the practice is in accordance with other research fields, such as biometrics, where continuously developed benchmarks set pressure for developing better methods. However, to the authors' best knowledge, only the DiaRetDB1 benchmark dataset [1] provides the original expert segmentations used to generate the combined ground truth. This is surprising as a characteristic and preferred property of medical data for research purposes is that the provided ground truth originates from multiple experts and it should be possible to validate also that. Examples are shown in Figures 1. The expert segmentations vary significantly, and therefore, the expert information must be considered more as delineations than accurate manual segmentations, and there clearly exists the need for an appropriate combining (disambiguation) procedure.

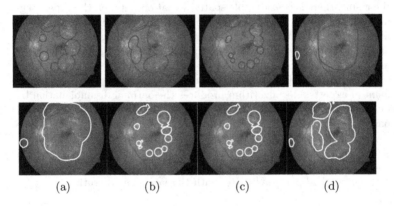

Fig. 1. 1st row: DiaRetDB1 expert markings for the lesion *Hard exudate* (red: high confidence, yellow: moderate, green: low). The disambiguated ground truth (white) produced by (a) minimal and (b) maximal confidence (Sec. 2.1). The disambiguated ground truth by (c) the proposed method and (d) STAPLE with default parameters.

For machine learning methods, the combined ground truth is required to represent the "truth" to be learned. However, it is the adopted disambiguation procedure which ultimately defines the truth. The authors of DiaRetDB1 proposed a heuristic method called "expert fusion", which has the good property that it was based on processing the whole image ensemble. The state-of-the-art approach is the STAPLE method by Warfield et al. [2] and its derivatives [3,4]. STAPLE is based on a probabilistic formulation of the segment combination problem with certain constancy priors and the Expectation-Maximization (EM) algorithm. The method performs well with toy and many true examples, but for multiple experts and varying confidences its performance is unclear. Our approach has the following good properties:

- The proposed method needs no prior models for the spatial distribution of structures or spatial homogeneity constraints.
- The proposed method does not estimate the "most likely segmentation" of a single image but the most likely segmentation of the whole image ensemble.
- The proposed method does not assume similar "behavior" of the experts, i.e., trained raters.

We propose a simple yet effective method to automatically find the optimal solution for a given data. We avoid complicated formulation requiring priors by using a simple guideline familiar to all clinicians: make the decision on a patient for which the peers (experts) jointly agree. The disambiguated ground truth corresponds to the maximal joint-agreement of experts, which is empirically demonstrated with DiaRetDB1 by presenting results superior to the original DiaRetDB1 method and STAPLE. In addition, the performance of the DiaRetDB1 baseline algorithm significantly improves when using our method.

2 Disambiguation Method

Our disambiguation method stems from the evaluation practices in medical imaging, and the main application is automatic lesion detection/segmentation. Supervised methods require example images for training, validation, and testing and to extract meaningful features multi-valued ground truth must be correctly disambiguated. We adopt the following general guidelines:

- Ground truth is combined from the markings of N experts (raters) who have independently marked the images and whose opinions are equally important.
- The markings are represented as spatial segments.
- Each segment is associated with a single confidence value (e.g., low, moderate, or high) given by the raters.
- The main evaluation procedure is *image-based*, which supports the clinical practice (cf. patient-based diagnosis).
- Pixel-wise ground truth (spatial segments) is computed from the expert markings and is represented as a binary mask (*disambiguation*). [1]
- Image-wise ground truth is constructed from the binary masks and is binary (*true/false*) whether a specific lesion or finding is present or not.
- A detection algorithm must provide a "score value" for the all lesion types in each test image.
- The scores and image-wise ground truth are used to compute a ROC curve or other characteristic values for the comparison (e.g., the equal error rate).

The receiver operating characteristic (ROC) curve is a standard evaluation procedure used in computer vision, such as in the comparison of face recognition algorithms. For medical applications, the ROC axes directly correspond to the meaningful clinical measures specificity and sensitivity, and the equal error rate (EER) is a point on the ROC curve where the specificity and sensitivity are

---

[1] Probability maps can be considered as the ideal result, but for straightforward training and testing, such masks should be finally converted into binary masks.

equal. If there is no prior knowledge of a desired sensitivity or specificity level, then the EER represents a neutral evaluation measure.

2.1   Average Expert Opinion

The input to this process is the segments marked by several medical experts, such as the four markings in Figure 1. Other marking types have also been tested, such as lesion-specific "representative points" [5], but the polygon segments seem to be the most intuitive for medical experts and result to the best performance.

The most straightforward combination procedure is averaging:

$$I_{conf_{i,j}}(x,y) = \frac{1}{N} \sum_{n=1}^{N} I_{exp_{i,j,n}}(x,y) \tag{1}$$

where $I_{conf_{i,j}}$ is the average segmentation of the input image i for the lesion type j. N is the total number of experts and $I_{exp_{i,j,n}}(x,y)$ is the segmentation mask of the nth expert. The expert segmentation masks $I_{exp_{i,j,n}}(x,y)$ are constructed from the expert images, such as the four examples in Figure 1, by filling the polygons with values of the expert-chosen confidence levels. The symbolic confidence levels converted into an ordinal scale are, for example, 0 for no marking, 1/3 for low, 2/3 for moderate, and 1 for high. The only requirement for the scale is that it is monotonically increasing. The average confidence image in (1) corresponds to the mean expert opinion in the same scale as the original annotations.

The average confidence image has two disadvantages: 1) it does not take into account the possible differences of the experts in their use of the scale and 2) for machine learning methods, the average expert segmentation does not produce binary values for foreground and background. A binary mask can be generated by thresholding the average expert segmentation image with the threshold $\tau \in [0,1]$:

$$I_{mask_{i,j}}(x,y) = \begin{cases} 1, \text{if } I_{conf_{i,j}}(x,y) \geq \tau \\ 0, \text{otherwise} . \end{cases} \tag{2}$$

The threshold parameter τ adjusts experts' joint-agreement: for $\tau \to 0$ the binary mask approaches to *set union*, and for $\tau \to 1$ to *set intersection* (see Fig. 1). If the resulting mask in (2) contains only zeros, then the image-wise ground truth is *false* for the lesion j in the image i. If any pixel is one, then the value is *true*.

In [5], the average segmentations we formally defined in (1), were implicitly used and the authors tested "plausible" confidence thresholds with their baseline method. Based on the tests, the confidence threshold was set to 0.75, which corresponds to the semantic "moderate confidence" in their scale. However, the baseline method undesirably tied the training and evaluation together. As a consequence, their selection of the moderate average confidence is questionable.

2.2   Optimal Expert Opinion by Maximizing Mutual Agreement

The approach here is based on the following intuitive principle: "The ground truth should optimally represent the mutual agreement of all experts". A performance measure for the mutual agreement is needed. The performance depends only on the two factors: the *experts' markings* $I_{exp_{i,j,n}}$ and *ground truth* (g_t), and without loss of generality it is expected to output a real number

$$\text{perf} : \left\{ I_{exp_{i,j,n}}, g\_t_{i,j} \right\} \to \mathbb{R} \ . \tag{3}$$

$\{\cdot\}$ is used to denote that the performance is computed for a set of rated images. The definition reminds of the chicken-and-egg dilemma since the ground truth is inferred from the expert markings $I_{exp_{i,j,n}}$ using (1) and (2). This is justifiable since the true ground truth is a latent variable which should be inferred from the markings of the $n = 1, \ldots, N$ experts which are constant and the only inference variable is the threshold τ in (2). Generation of the image-wise ground truth is straightforward: if any of the pixels in $I_{mask_{i,j}}(x, y)$ for the lesion j is non-zero, the image is labeled to contain that lesion. A detection ROC curve can be automatically computed from the image-wise ground truth and image scores computed from the expert images. ("confidence score" in [6]). For the image-wise expert scores, we adopt the *summax rule*: pixel confidences of $I_{exp_{i,j,n}}$ are sorted, and 1% of the highest values are summed. We choose the average equal error rate (EER point on the ROC curve) as our performance measure in (3), which can now be given in the more explicit form:

$$\text{perf}(\{I_{exp_{i,j,n}}\}, \{g\_t_{i,j}\}) = \frac{1}{N} \sum_{n} \text{EER}\left(\{summax_{1\%}(I_{exp_{i,j,n}})\}, \{I_{mask_{i,j}}(x, y; \tau)\}\right). \tag{4}$$

A single EER value is computed for each expert n and over all images (i), and then the expert-specific EER values are summed for the lesion j.

The summax rule can be justified as a robust maximum rule by the multiple classifier theory [7], and the EER measure can be replaced with any other measure, for example, with a given sensitivity or specificity level. The only factor which affects the performance in (4) is the threshold τ which is used to form the ground truth. To maximize the mutual agreement, we should seek for the most appropriate threshold $\hat{\tau}$ which provides the highest average performance (EER) over all experts - the optimal disambiguation threshold. In addition, instead of a single threshold $\hat{\tau}$, separate thresholds $\hat{\tau}_j$ are selected for each lesion since different lesion types may significantly differ by their visual detectability. The optimal ground truth is ultimately equivalent to searching the optimal threshold:

$$\hat{\tau}_j \leftarrow \underset{\tau_j}{\text{argmin}} \ \frac{1}{N} \sum_{n} EER(\cdot, \cdot) \ . \tag{5}$$

The most straightforward approach to realize the *argmin* step is to iteratively test all possible values of τ from 0 to 1. The values can be enumerated from the expert confidence and converted to integers for numerical stability. Equation (5) maximizes the performance for each lesion type over all experts ($\sum_n$). The optimal thresholds $\hat{\tau}_j$ are lesion specific and they are guaranteed to produce the maximal mutual expert agreement according to the performance measure *perf*.

3   Results

We empirically test our method with the DiaRetDB1 dataset downloaded from http://www2.it.lut.fi/project/imageret/ which to the authors' best knowledge is the only database which provides also the original expert markings. STAPLE here represents the state-of-the-art and was downloaded from http://crl.med.harvard.edu/software/STAPLE/.

DiaRetDB1 [1] has recently become an important database for evaluating diabetic retinopathy detection algorithms. The database contains dedicatedly selected retinal images divided into fixed sets of training and test images both containing a representative set of *normal findings*, and from mild to severe non-proliferative findings including *microaneurysms* (MA), *haemorrhages* (HA), *hard exudates* (HE) and *soft exudates* (SE). A detailed description is available in [1].

3.1   Disambiguation

We report the performance using the EER which is justified since no auxiliary/prior information on the risks or penalties for false negatives or false positives is available. EER represents a "balanced error point" in the ROC curve and allows comparison to the previous works.

The results for DiaRetDB1 are presented in Table 1. It is noteworthy that the original confidence threshold (0.75) in [5] is not optimal for any of the lesion types, and is clearly incorrect for haemorrhages (HA, 0.60) and microaneurysms (MA, 0.10). The underlined values in the table are the best achieved performances. The average performance for all lesion types significantly varies depending on the threshold.

To compare our approach to the state-of-the-art, we combined the expert masks using the STAPLE algorithm described in [2,3,4]. The STAPLE algorithm

Table 1. Expert-specific equal error rate (EER) and the average EER performances for DiaRetDB1. EER for the different confidence thresholds τ_j reported and the algorithm found optimal values underlined. The last three rows are the results of the STAPLE algorithm and with the masks generated by using different confidence levels (S1: 0.25, S2: 0.75, S3: 1.00).

	Haemorrhage (HA)					Hard exudate (HE)					Microaneurysm (MA)					Soft exudate (SE)				
τ	e1	e2	e3	e4	Joint	e1	e2	e3	e4	Joint	e1	e2	e3	e4	Joint	e1	e2	e3	e4	Joint
.00	0.17	0.17	0.14	0.09	0.14	0.29	0.12	0.05	0.07	0.13	0.04	0.22	0.22	0.12	0.15	0.45	0.17	0.23	0.11	0.24
.10	0.12	0.12	0.12	0.06	0.10	0.26	0.09	0.05	0.02	0.11	0.03	0.20	0.22	0.11	__0.14__	0.42	0.10	0.19	0.07	0.20
.20	0.08	0.08	0.07	0.02	0.07	0.25	0.07	0.05	0.05	0.10	0.17	0.20	0.25	0.10	0.18	0.42	0.07	0.17	0.07	0.18
.30	0.07	0.07	0.02	0.02	0.05	0.24	0.05	0.05	0.05	0.09	0.17	0.17	0.18	0.07	0.15	0.32	0.05	0.08	0.08	0.13
.40	0.07	0.07	0.02	0.02	0.05	0.18	0.05	0.06	0.06	0.09	0.20	0.15	0.18	0.09	0.16	0.29	0.06	0.08	0.08	0.13
.50	0.05	0.05	0.05	0.05	0.05	0.16	0.03	0.06	0.06	0.08	0.22	0.11	0.16	0.12	0.15	0.26	0.09	0.09	0.09	0.13
.60	0.02	0.05	0.02	0.02	__0.03__	0.16	0.03	0.06	0.06	0.08	0.20	0.16	0.14	0.18	0.17	0.16	0.11	0.11	0.11	0.12
.70	0.03	0.06	0.05	0.05	0.05	0.16	0.03	0.06	0.06	0.08	0.20	0.20	0.10	0.18	0.17	0.07	0.14	0.13	0.14	0.12
.75	0.03	0.06	0.05	0.05	0.05	0.16	0.03	0.06	0.06	0.08	0.20	0.20	0.10	0.18	0.17	0.07	0.14	0.13	0.14	0.12
.80	0.09	0.06	0.08	0.11	0.09	0.03	0.07	0.03	0.07	__0.05__	0.15	0.18	0.18	0.18	0.17	0.09	0.09	0.12	0.13	__0.11__
.90	0.09	0.06	0.08	0.11	0.09	0.03	0.07	0.03	0.07	__0.05__	0.16	0.17	0.16	0.21	0.17	0.09	0.09	0.12	0.13	__0.11__
1.0	0.12	0.12	0.12	0.16	0.13	0.03	0.07	0.03	0.08	0.06	0.21	0.21	0.21	0.21	0.21	0.10	0.10	0.11	0.14	__0.11__
S1	0.07	0.07	0.02	0.02	0.05	0.27	0.09	0.02	0.02	0.10	0.17	0.17	0.18	0.07	0.15	0.35	0.05	0.12	0.08	0.15
S2	0.07	0.07	0.02	0.02	0.05	0.20	0.02	0.07	0.05	0.09	0.19	0.16	0.19	0.07	0.15	0.29	0.06	0.08	0.08	0.13
S3	0.05	0.05	0.05	0.05	0.05	0.16	0.03	0.06	0.06	0.08	0.21	0.10	0.18	0.10	0.15	0.20	0.10	0.10	0.10	0.13

Table 2. The minimum, maximum, and average EER (5 rand. iters) for the DiaRetDB1 baseline method and evaluation protocol. The results include the original and the proposed optimal ground truth.

	Haemorrhage (HA)			Hard exud. (HE)			Microaneurysm (MA)			Soft exud. (SE)			
	Min	Max	Avg	Min	Max	Avg	Min	Max	Avg	Min	Max	Avg	Overall
In [5]	0.233	0.333	0.273	0.200	0.220	0.216	0.476	0.625	0.593	0.250	0.333	0.317	0.349
Our (min)	0.263	0.476	0.322	0.250	0.250	0.250	0.286	0.574	0.338	0.333	0.333	0.333	0.311
Our (max)	0.263	0.476	0.322	0.250	0.250	0.250	0.386	0.574	0.338	0.200	0.268	0.241	**0.288**

does not utilize pixel-based confidence information, and therefore, the algorithm was run separately for all different confidence levels of the original data (S1: 0.25, S2: 0.75 and S3: 1.00). STAPLE outperforms the DiaRetDB1 method, but is inferior to the proposed method for all lesion types.

3.2 Revised DiaRetDB1 Baseline Results

The purpose of this experiment was to study whether the new combination procedure has any effect on the performance of the DiaRetDB1 baseline method. For the two lesion types, Hard exudate (HE) and Soft exudate (SE), the proposed method produced multiple optimal thresholds: HE $\in [0.8, 0.9]$ and SE $\in [0.8, 1.0]$, and thus the DiaRetDB1 baseline method was run multiple times with both the minimum and maximum values. The results are in Table 2.

The minimum and maximum thresholds for the proposed disambiguation rule produce equal results except in the case of soft exudates, for which the maximum in the equally performing interval (1.0) is clearly better. The main difference to the original DiaRetDB1 method occurs with microaneurysms, as expected, since the optimal threshold (0.1) significantly differs from the original (0.75). For haemorrhages, the original result was too optimistic since the optimal confidence yields to worse minimum and average EER. On average, the optimal confidence provided 11–17% better performance. This can be explained by the fact that

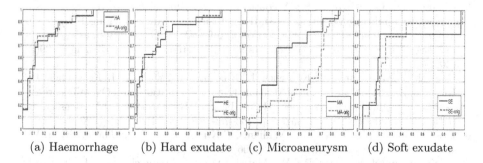

(a) Haemorrhage   (b) Hard exudate   (c) Microaneurysm   (d) Soft exudate

Fig. 2. ROC curves for the DiaRetDB1 baseline method using the original and proposed (max) method to generate training and testing data

the training and testing segments are now consistent with experts' opinion. The findings can be verified by the ROC curves in Fig. 2.

4   Discussion and Conclusion

In this work, the multiple ground truth combination and disambiguation problem was studied in the context of medical images where lesions are delineated by multiple experts (raters). A simple yet effective combining procedure maximizing the mutual agreement of experts' rating was proposed. The procedure corresponds to the clinical practice of "expert/colleague consultation" as it provides the ground truth segments most consistent over all expert opinions. Therefore, the principle of the proposed procedure is well justified and it was exemplified with the DiaRetDB1 database for which our method produced clinically correct and more reliable ground truth. Our work deviates from the state-of-the-art (STAPLE) by being notably simpler, does not require spatial consistency priors and does not produce areas that do not appear in the original expert segments (the upper bound is the complete union). In our experiments, the proposed disambiguation yielded to 11–17% performance improvements compared to the DiaRetDB1 baseline method. For the experts themselves, the mutual agreement, depending on the lesion type, improved 9–40% compared to the original DiaRetDB1 ground truth, and 7–40% compared to the one produced by STAPLE.

Acknowledgements. The authors wish to thank the research collaborators from the University of Eastern Finland and the University of Tampere, and the sponsors of the earlier ImageRet[2] project for their support.

References

1. Kauppi, T., Kalesnykiene, V., Kamarainen, J.K., Lensu, L., Sorri, I., Raninen, A., Voutilainen, R., Uusitalo, H., Kälviäinen, H., Pietilä, J.: The DIARETDB1 diabetic retinopathy database and evaluation protocol. In: BMVC (2007)
2. Warfield, S., Zou, K., Wells, W.: Simultaneous truth and performance level estimation (STAPLE): An algorithm for the validation of image segmentation. IEEE Trans. on Medical Imaging 23(7) (2004)
3. Commowick, O., Warfield, S.: A continuous staple for scalar, vector, and tensor images: An application to dti analysis. IEEE Trans. on Medical Imaging 28(6) (2009)
4. Commowick, O., Warfield, S.: Estimation of inferential uncertainty in assessing expert segmentation performance from staple. IEEE Trans. on Medical Imaging 29(3) (2010)
5. Kauppi, T., Kamarainen, J.-K., Lensu, L., Kalesnykiene, V., Sorri, I., Kälviäinen, H., Uusitalo, H., Pietilä, J.: Fusion of Multiple Expert Annotations and Overall Score Selection for Medical Image Diagnosis. In: Salberg, A.-B., Hardeberg, J.Y., Jenssen, R. (eds.) SCIA 2009. LNCS, vol. 5575, pp. 760–769. Springer, Heidelberg (2009)
6. Everingham, M., Zisserman, A., Williams, C.K.I., Van Gool, L.: The PASCAL Visual Object Classes Challenge (VOC 2006) Results (2006)
7. Kittler, J., Hatef, M., Duin, R.P.W., Matas, J.: On combining classifiers. IEEE Trans. on PAMI 20(3) (1998)

---

[2] http://www2.it.lut.fi/project/imageret/

Cardiac LV and RV Segmentation Using Mutual Context Information

Dwarikanath Mahapatra* and Joachim M. Buhmann

Department of Computer Science, ETH Zurich, Switzerland
dwarikanath.mahapatra@inf.ethz.ch

Abstract. In this paper we propose a graph cut based method to segment the cardiac right ventricle (RV) and left ventricle (LV) by using mutual context information. In addition to the conventional log-likelihood penalty, we also include a 'context penalty' for the RV by learning its geometrical relationship with respect to the LV. Similarly, the RV provides geometrical context information for LV segmentation. The smoothness cost is formulated as a function of the learned context and captures the geometric relationship between the RV and LV. Experimental results on real patient datasets from the STACOM database show the efficacy of our method in accurately segmenting the LV and RV, and its robustness to noise and inaccurate segmentations.

1 Introduction

Cardiovascular diseases are the leading cause of death in the Western world [1]. Magnetic resonance imaging (MRI) has emerged as the preferred diagnostic modality because of its non-invasive nature and gives reliable information on morphology, blood flow, ventricular mass and other parameters. These parameters are obtained by segmenting the left ventricle (LV) and right ventricle (RV) from cardiac MR images [9]. Manual segmentation is tedious and prone to intra- and inter-observer variability. This has necessitated the development of automated/semi-automated segmentation algorithms. An exhaustive review of cardiac segmentation algorithms is given in [9]. While there are many methods for LV segmentation, the RV has not received so much attention [9] because: 1) of its complex crescent shape; and 2) less critical function than LV.

Paragios et al [8] used a signed distance map to incorporate prior shape knowledge in a level set framework for LV segmentation. A multistage active appearance model was used to segment LV and RV in [7], while [3] use a control point representation of the LV prior and deform other images to match the prior. Shape knowledge was combined with dynamic information to account for cardiac shape variability in [13], while orientation histograms were used as shape priors in a graphcut framework for LV segmentation [6].

Auto context was used by Li et al. in [5] to segment the human prostate gland from computed tomography (CT) images, and in [12] to segment brain structures

---

* Corresponding author.

F. Wang et al. (Eds.): MLMI 2012, LNCS 7588, pp. 201–209, 2012.

from MRI. Object interaction priors were used in [2] for inter-vertebral disc segmentation using graph cuts. The geometric relationship between different disc like structures of the vertebrae are modeled using relative distance and orientaion. Based on the segmentation of one disc, other interesting structures are subsequently segmented. Song et al in [10] proposed a surface-region context model for segmenting pulmonary tumors.

We propose a method to segment the RV and LV by learning their mutual context information. For this purpose we make use of geometric relationship between the shapes in the form of relative orientations. The context information is learned from a set of training images in which the RV and LV have been manually segmented. The learned information is encoded on a graphical model of the image as weights between pixel nodes and terminal nodes, as well as the weights between pixel nodes. Graph cuts are used to find the final labels in an iterative fashion. Geometric relationships in the form of orientation angles and distance were used in [2]. However, they try to match distributions of different areas, and hence do not encode costs at levels of pixels or their neighborhoods. Therefore graph cuts cannot be directly used for their formulation. Besides, to optimize for scale parameters the authors introduce sub-modular graphs to optimize over a upper bound which enables use of graph cuts.

This paper makes the following contributions: 1) we encode context information for each pixel as well as between pixels. This allows us to directly use graph cuts without constructing sub-modular graphs as in [2]. Since we do not use distance information we need not optimize over the scale parameters. 2) mutually beneficial context information from the RV and LV is used to segment the individual organs. We describe our method in Section 2, present experimental results in Section 3 and conclude with Section 4.

2 Methods

Method Overview: Our method comprises of the following steps: 1) select seed points on the RV and LV, and use graph cuts to get initial segmentations; 2) fix the RV shape and refine the LV segmentation using contextual information from the RV; 3) fix the new LV shape and refine RV segmentation using contextual information from the LV; 4) repeat steps 2 and 3 till there is no further change in segmentations.

Initial Segmentation of the RV and LV: Small patches on the LV, RV and background were drawn to obtain seed points for intensity distributions. The cost function is formulated as a second order Markov Random Field (MRF) function which is written as

$$E(L) = \sum_{s \in P} D(L_s) + \lambda \sum_{(s,t) \in N} V(L_s, L_t), \tag{1}$$

where P denotes the set of pixels, L_s is the segmentation class of pixel $s \in P$ and N is the set of neighboring pixel pairs. $D(L_s)$, is the data penalty function that measures how well label L_s fits pixel s. V is the smoothness cost that measures the cost of assigning labels L_s and L_t to neighboring pixels s and t. λ is a weight that determines the relative contribution of the two terms. Equation 1 is optimized using graph cuts [4]. The intensity distribution of LV and RV is modeled as a single Gaussian, while the background is modeled as a mixture of two Gaussians. $D(L_s)$ is defined as the negative of the log-likelihood of intensity:

$$D_1(L_s) = -\log Pr(I_s|L_s), \tag{2}$$

where I_s is the intensity at pixel s, Pr is the likelihood, and L_s is the label. V assigns a low penalty at edge points, and favours a piecewise constant segmentation result. It is defined as

$$V_1(L_s, L_t) = \begin{cases} e^{-\frac{(I_s - I_t)^2}{2\sigma^2}} \cdot \frac{1}{\|s-t\|}, & L_s \neq L_t, \\ 0 & L_s = L_t. \end{cases} \tag{3}$$

σ determines the intensity difference up to which a region is considered as piecewise smooth. It is equal to the average intensity difference in the 3×3 neighborhood of s. $\|s - t\|$ is the Euclidean distance between s and t.

Modeling Contextual Relationship between RV and LV: To model the contextual relationship between the RV and LV we use images from 15 patients in which the RV and LV were manually segmented by a radiologist. The STACOM dataset that we use provides only the manual segmentation of the LV. The RV is separately segmented by a radiologist having more than 5 years of clinical experience. We shall denote these shapes as Rv and Lv. Let the set of points on the outer edge of Rv be denoted as $\{Rv_1, \cdots, Rv_i\}$, and those on Lv denoted as $\{Lv_1, \cdots, Lv_j\}$. Edge points are chosen as they give a rich shape descriptor without large computational overhead.

The relative orientation of different organs in the human body does not change and our aim is to exploit this spatial relationship between Lv and Rv. We calculate the normalized histogram (distribution) of orientation angles between each Lv_j and all Rv_i and denote it as $h^o_{Lv,j}$. The superscript o denotes orientation angles. The 32 histogram bins are uniform in log-polar space making the descriptor more sensitive to positions of nearby sample points than points further away. If we consider all the Lv_j over all training images then there are a large number of $h^o_{Lv,j}$. The representative histograms are obtained by principal component analysis (PCA) and we select the first 6 principal histograms which are denoted as $H^o_{Lv,n}$, $n = \{1, \cdots, 6\}$. The 6 largest principal components represent more than 94% energy of the eigen values. Thus we obtain the contextual relationship of the LV wih respect to the RV.

Similarly the contextual relationship of the *RV w.r.t the LV* means the relationship of orientation angles between each point on the RV w.r.t all points on the LV. This relationship is obtained by calculating the distribution of orientation angles between each Rv_i and all Lv_j and denote it as $h^o_{Rv,i}$. Note the difference in notation (i.e., Rv and i). The 6 principal histograms are denoted by $H^o_{Rv,n}$, $n = \{1, \cdots, 6\}$. $H^o_{Rv,n}$ and $H^o_{Lv,n}$ will be different because the relative orientations of one part w.r.t another is different.

Figure 1 (c) shows an example image where the manual segmentations of RV and LV are shown in red. Figure 1 (a) shows the distribution of orientation angles of the RV w.r.t the LV while Fig. 1 (b) shows the distribution of orientation angles of the LV w.r.t the RV. For any one of the figures we observe that the distributions are spread over different angles and has more than one mode.

As mentioned before, contextual information is incorporated to refine the LV segmentation obtained in the initial step. Thus we choose to optimize the cost function over a narrow band around the segmented LV. Figure 1 (c) shows the narrow band (in cyan) around which the pixel labels are updated. For a pixel in the band around the LV let its orientation histogram w.r.t Rv be denoted as h^o. Distance of h^o from each $H^o_{Lv,n}$ is given by the χ^2 metric as

$$d_{Lv}(o, n) = \frac{1}{2} \sum_{k=1}^{K} \frac{\left[h^o(k) - H^o_{Lv,n}(k)\right]^2}{h^o(k) + H^o_{Lv,n}(k)}, \qquad (4)$$

where k denotes the bin index of the histogram and $K = 32$ is the total number of bins. Other measures of histogram distances may also be used. The 'context cost' (D_{cont}) of assigning label 1 (LV) to the pixel (i.e., 'context cost' from RV) is the minimum of $d_{Lv}(o, n)$,

$$D_{cont}(L_s = 1) = \arg_n \min d_{Lv}(o, n). \qquad (5)$$

The principal component among $H^o_{Lv,n}$ giving the minimum cost represents the most similar direction of h^o in the training dataset and hence also the similarity of h^o with Lv. The context cost of assigning label 0 (background) to the pixel is

$$D_{cont}(L_s = 0) = 1 - D_{cont}(L_s = 1). \qquad (6)$$

The pairwise cost is the weight between the two corresponding nodes (pixels) on the graph. If the two pixels should have the same labels then their cost is high such that the link is not severed On the other hand if the two pixels should have different labels then their edge weight should be low. For a neighboring pixel pair s and t we determine their distribution of orientation angles w.r.t the current RV segmentation, which we denote as h^o_s, h^o_t. The difference in histograms is calculated using the χ^2 metric and denoted as $|h^o_s - h^o_t|$. The smoothness cost between s and t due to context is defined as

$$V_{cont}(s, t) = 1 - |h^o_s - h^o_t|. \qquad (7)$$

Similar pixels s and t will have low value of $|h^o_s - h^o_t|$, and the corresponding V_{cont} is high. Dissimilar neighboring pixels s and t will have high value of $|h^o_s - h^o_t|$, and the corresponding V_{cont} is low. Thus the above formulation of V_{cont} serves our desired purpose. A similar reasoning holds during RV segmentation when $|h^o_s - h^o_t|$ are calculated w.r.t the LV. To obtain the updated segmentation we

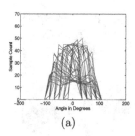 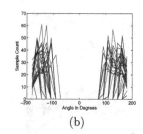 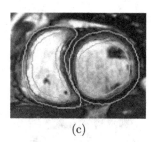

(a)   (b)   (c)

Fig. 1. Illustrations for Context Segmentation. (a) angle distribution for LV w.r.t RV ; (b) angle distribution of RV w.r.t LV. (c) example image with the manual segmentations in red and the corresponding narrow bands in cyan.

incorporate both intensity penalty and contextual penalty in the cost function. Thus the final energy function is

$$E(L) = \sum_{s \in P} [D_1(L_s) + D_{cont}(L_s)] + \lambda \sum_{(s,t) \in N} [V_1(L_s, L_t) + V_{cont}(s,t)], \quad (8)$$

where $\lambda = 0.05$ was set empirically. Equation 8 is used for both RV and LV segmentation although for each stage the individual terms are defined differently. The iterative segmentation is stopped if the Dice Metric (DM) between segmentations of two consecutive iterations is greater than 95%. The optimal segmentations are obtained in $3 - 4$ iterations.

3   Experiments and Results

We test our algorithm on short axis (SA) images from 15 datasets of the STACOM 2011 4D LV Segmentation Challenge run by the Cardiac Atlas Project (CAP). The data were acquired using steady-state free precession (SSFP) MR imaging protocols with thickness ≤ 10 mm, gap ≤ 2 mm, TR $30 - 50$ ms, TE 1.6 ms, flip angle 60°, FOV 360 mm, and 256×256 image matrix. The images consist of an average 12 SA slices and 26 time frames.

We employ a leave-one-out approach where 14 datasets were used for training and one dataset used for testing such that each patient data was part of the training and test data. Automatic segmentations were obtained using three methods: the shape prior based LV segmentation method of [6] (*Met* 1); our method using contextual information in graph cuts (GC_{Cont}) and the method in [2] using object interaction priors (*Met* 2). The automatic segmentations were compared with manual segmentation using Dice Metric (DM) between the *segmented areas* and Hausdorff distance (HD) between their *outer contours*. The intensity of the images was normalized to lie between 0 and 1.

Segmentation Results on Real Patient MRI: Figure 2 shows segmentation results for different algorithms. The advantage of context information is its ability to encode more global knowledge into the segmentation than shape

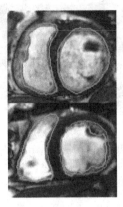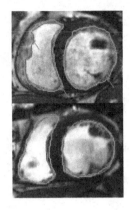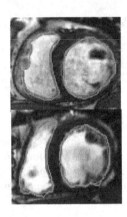

Fig. 2. Segmentation results for different methods. Each row shows results of different patient datasets from the STACOM database. Red contour shows the manual segmentations, and green contours show results for automatic segmentations. Columns $1 - 3$ show segmentation outputs for Met 1, Met 2 and GC_{cont}.

Table 1. Comparative performance of segmentation accuracy using three methods and two metrics (DM and HD). Values indicate the mean and standard deviation.

	Dice Metric (%)			HD (pixels)		
	Met 1	GC_{Cont}	Met 2	Met 1	GC_{Cont}	Met 2
LV Epicardium	79.2±1.1	83.4±1.4	80.5±1.2	3.9±0.9	2.0±0.5	3.1±0.7
LV Endocardium	81.5±1.2	84.9±1.5	82.0±1.3	2.9±0.8	1.5±0.4	2.1±0.5
RV Basal	80.7±1.0	83.2±1.4	81.8±1.1	3.4±0.8	1.5±0.6	2.1±0.7
RV Apex	81.1±0.8	83.7±1.1	81.7±1.0	3.7±0.7	1.4±0.5	2.0±0.5
Mid Ventricular	79.8±0.8	81.3±1.1	80.7±1.0	4.3±0.9	1.8±0.7	2.7±0.8

priors over the same training data. Our method compares favorably with Met 2 and in many cases gives better segmentation accuracy. It also gives comparable results to [11], which gives a summary of results on the same database. Although Met 2 and GC_{cont} are similar in terms of the geometric features used, our method is simpler as we do not need to introduce sub-modular graphs for graph cut optimization. Additionally, we incorporate inter-pixel relationships into the smoothness cost based on training data which contributes to a higher segmentation accuracy. A student $t-$test between results of GC_{Cont} and Met 2 gives $p < 0.03$ indicating statistically different results. Table 1 summarizes the performance of different algorithms.

Performance for noise and initial undersegmentation: Different levels of noise were added to the images and before applying our method. The first row in Fig. 3 shows segmentation results after various iterations of our method for zero mean Gaussian noise with 0.01 variance. Our method was able to extract

Table 2. Performance of various methods for different levels of added noise. σ is variance of added noise which has zero mean.

		$\sigma = 0.01$			$\sigma = 0.08$		
		Met 1	GC_{Cont}	Met 2	Met 1	GC_{Cont}	Met 2
LV	DM	74.8±2.1	79.1±0.9	75.4±1.6	71.5±1.4	76.8±1.3	72.3±1.1
	HD	4.8±1.2	3.1±0.2	4.1±0.9	6.6±1.4	4.4±0.4	5.0±1.0
RV	DM	76.2±1.5	80.5±1.2	77.3±1.7	70.6±2.1	75.1±0.5	71.4±1.0
	HD	5.4±1.4	3.7±0.3	4.3±0.9	6.8±1.3	4.9±0.3	5.1±0.8

Table 3. Performance of various methods for different degrees of undersegmentations. Values indicate mean and standard deviation.

Initial DM		$75 - 79$			$70 - 74$		
		Met 1	GC_{Cont}	Met 2	Met 1	GC_{Cont}	Met 2
LV	Final DM	77.2±2.1	81.9±1.2	78.4±1.3	76.1±2.4	80.3±0.9	77.6±1.7
	HD	3.8±1.2	1.7±0.7	2.6±0.9	5.0±1.4	2.8±0.2	4.0±1.0
RV	Final DM	79.5±2.8	83.9±0.9	80.6±1.4	76.9±2.1	81.5±1.2	77.6±1.7
	HD	4.0±1.3	1.9±0.5	3.1±1.0	5.2±1.7	2.7±0.3	3.9±1.1

Fig. 3. First row shows results for added Gaussian noise of zero mean and variance 0.01. Second rows show results for an initial undersegmentation of $DM = 74\%$. Red contour shows the manual segmentations, and green contours show results for automatic segmentations. Columns $1 - 3$ show segmentation outputs after first, second and third iterations.

the final shape with a fairly high level of accuracy although it is lower than the performance on original images without any added noise. The result for different levels of noise are summarized in Table 2.

In a different set of experiments we deliberately provide a undersegmented mask at the start before applying our method. The second row of Fig. 3 shows the results under such conditions where the first image shows the initial undersegmented contours in green and the subsequent images show the segmentation after each iteration. The performance for different degrees of undersegmentation is summarized in Table 3.

4 Conclusion

We have proposed a novel graph cut framework for cardiac MR image segmentation that incorporates context information from RV and LV for improved segmentation accuracy of each. Context information was modeled in the form of relative orientation of the two organs from a set of training images in which the LV and RV were manually segmented. The learned orientation relationship is used to formulate two penalty and smoothness costs that lead to improved segmentation performance. Experimental results on real patient datasets show the efficacy of our method compared to a previous shape prior based method, and also demonstrate its robustness to noise and initial undersegmentations.

References

1. Allender, S.: European cardiovascular disease statistics. European Heart Network (2008)
2. Ayed, I.B., Punithakumar, K., Garvin, G., Romano, W., Li, S.: Graph Cuts with Invariant Object-Interaction Priors: Application to Intervertebral Disc Segmentation. In: Székely, G., Hahn, H.K. (eds.) IPMI 2011. LNCS, vol. 6801, pp. 221–232. Springer, Heidelberg (2011)
3. Besbes, A., Komodakis, N., Paragios, N.: Graph-based knowledge-driven discrete segmentation of the left ventricle. In: IEEE ISBI, pp. 49–52 (2009)
4. Boykov, Y., Veksler, O.: Fast approximate energy minimization via graph cuts. IEEE Trans. Pattern Anal. Mach. Intell. 23, 1222–1239 (2001)
5. Li, W., Liao, S., Feng, Q., Chen, W., Shen, D.: Learning Image Context for Segmentation of Prostate in CT-Guided Radiotherapy. In: Fichtinger, G., Martel, A., Peters, T. (eds.) MICCAI 2011, Part III. LNCS, vol. 6893, pp. 570–578. Springer, Heidelberg (2011)
6. Mahapatra, D., Sun, Y.: Orientation Histograms as Shape Priors for Left Ventricle Segmentation Using Graph Cuts. In: Fichtinger, G., Martel, A., Peters, T. (eds.) MICCAI 2011, Part III. LNCS, vol. 6893, pp. 420–427. Springer, Heidelberg (2011)
7. Mitchell, S., Lelieveldt, B., van der Geest, R., Bosch, H., Reiver, J., Sonka, M.: Multistage hybrid active appearance models: Segmentation of cardiac mr and ultrasound images. IEEE Trans. Med. Imag. 20(5), 415–423 (2001)
8. Paragios, N.: A variational approach for the segmentation of the left ventricle in cardiac image analysis. Intl. J. Comp. Vis. 50(3), 345–362 (2002)
9. Petitjean, C., Dacher, J.N.: A review of segmentation methods in short axis cardiac mr images. Med. Imag. Anal. 15(2), 169–184 (2011)
10. Song, Q., Chen, M., Bai, J., Sonka, M., Wu, X.: Surface–Region Context in Optimal Multi-object Graph-Based Segmentation: Robust Delineation of Pulmonary Tumors. In: Székely, G., Hahn, H.K. (eds.) IPMI 2011. LNCS, vol. 6801, pp. 61–72. Springer, Heidelberg (2011)

11. Suinesiaputra, A., Cowan, B.R., Finn, J.P., Fonseca, C.G., Kadish, A.H., Lee, D.C., Medrano-Gracia, P., Warfield, S.K., Tao, W., Young, A.A.: Left Ventricular Segmentation Challenge from Cardiac MRI: A Collation Study. In: Camara, O., Konukoglu, E., Pop, M., Rhode, K., Sermesant, M., Young, A. (eds.) STACOM 2011. LNCS, vol. 7085, pp. 88–97. Springer, Heidelberg (2012)
12. Tu, Z., Bai, X.: Auto-context and its application to high-level vision tasks and 3d brain image segmentation. IEEE Trans. Patt. Anal. Mach. Intell. 32(10), 1744–1757 (2010)
13. Zhu, Y., Papademetris, X., Sinusas, A., Duncan, J.: Segmentation of left ventricle from 3d cardiac mr image sequence using a subject specific dynamic model. In: Proc. IEEE CVPR, pp. 1–8 (2008)

Non-parametric Density Modeling and Outlier-Detection in Medical Imaging Datasets

Virgile Fritsch[1,2], Gaël Varoquaux[1-3], Jean-Baptiste Poline[2,1],
and Bertrand Thirion[1,2]

[1] Parietal Team, INRIA Saclay-Île-de-France, Saclay, France
virgile.fritsch@inria.fr
http://parietal.saclay.inria.fr
[2] CEA, DSV, I²BM, Neurospin bât 145, 91191 Gif-Sur-Yvette, France
[3] Inserm, U992, Neurospin bât 145, 91191 Gif-Sur-Yvette, France

Abstract. The statistical analysis of medical images is challenging because of the high dimensionality and low signal-to-noise ratio of the data. Simple parametric statistical models, such as Gaussian distributions, are well-suited to high-dimensional settings. In practice, on medical data reflecting heterogeneous subjects, the Gaussian hypothesis seldom holds. In addition, alternative parametric models of the data tend to break down due to the presence of outliers that are usually removed manually from studies. Here we focus on interactive detection of these outlying observations, to guide the practitioner through the data inclusion process. Our contribution is to use *Local Component Analysis* as a non-parametric density estimator for this purpose. Experiments on real and simulated data show that our procedure separates well deviant observations from the relevant and representative ones. We show that it outperforms state-of-the-art approaches, in particular those involving a Gaussian assumption.

Keywords: Outlier detection, non-parametric density estimation, One-Class SVM, Parzen, Local Component Analysis, neuroimaging, fMRI.

1 Introduction

Group studies based on medical images often attempt to extract representative samples from a given dataset in order to summarize the whole population to one or a few data prototypes. A stronger yet standard assumption is to consider that the data are Gaussian distributed around these prototypes. In the case of neuroimaging, this choice seems convenient because of the high dimensionality of the datasets, but a simple univariate Shapiro-Wilk normality test [9] demonstrates that the Gaussian hypothesis is not correct (see e.g. [10]). Furthermore, a unimodal distribution hypothesis is inconsistent with approaches that emphasize the impact of population stratification such as genome-wise association studies, or diagnosis settings that imply a separation between patients and healthy subjects. More generally, any parametric characterization of the population statistical structure is challenged by the presence of many outliers related to acquisition

F. Wang et al. (Eds.): MLMI 2012, LNCS 7588, pp. 210–217, 2012.
© Springer-Verlag Berlin Heidelberg 2012

or processing issues. Outlier detection and subsequent data cleansing is therefore a first step towards a better understanding of the statistical structure (including between-subjects variability) of medical imaging datasets, which in turn would be of broad interest regarding group analyses. Manifold learning is an alternative solution [2] useful for visualization, but lacking statistical guarantees.

In a recent contribution [1], a regularized version of the standard Mahalanobis distances-based outlier detection method was introduced in this context; it relies on the assumption that inliers are Gaussian distributed. Under mild deviations from this assumption, the approach has been shown to be accurate, making it possible to point out outliers in both high-dimensional and highly polluted neuroimaging datasets. However, although Mahalanobis distances-based approaches can rank the observations accurately (a property that we refer to as *accuracy*), the choice of a threshold on this ranking is strongly related to the actual data distribution.

There has also been interest in non-parametric algorithms such as *One-Class Support Vector Machine (SVM)* [8] for subjects versus patients discrimination [3,5]. One-Class SVM is well suited for medical image models since the algorithm is computationally efficient and does not rely on any prior distribution assumption. However, it defers part of the work to the practitioner, who has to build a training set with already labeled observations, or directly indicate the amount of contamination in the dataset.

The focus of our work is the analysis of the statistical structure of medical imaging datasets through high-dimensional non-parametric density estimation algorithms. We use an algorithm derived from *Parzen windows density estimation* (or *Kernel Density Estimation (KDE)*), that estimate the parameter θ of a given kernel $K(.;.,\theta)$ so that, given a learning set $(x_i)_{i=1,..,n}$, the density probability of an observations $x \in \mathbb{R}^p$ can be written $p(x) = \frac{1}{n} \sum_{i=1}^{n} K(x; x_i, \theta)$. As a new contribution, we subsequently embed this density estimator into a mode-seeking procedure to build a simple representation of the data and thus discard potential outliers. This framework provides an easy and efficient way of checking data homogeneity, a feature often required when performing further data analyzes or clinical studies [5].

In Section 2 and 3, we briefly describe the different tools that we use in this work and our contributions, that adapt these tools to medical imaging settings. In Section 4, we present some experiments on both simulated and real data. We show that the accuracy of density-based outlier detection is greater than the accuracy of state-of-the-art outlier detection methods. We also demonstrate that, starting from the Local Component Analysis density estimator, we can obtain a simple, yet relevant, differentiation between inliers and outliers. Finally, we present the results of our experiments in Section 5 and discuss them in Section 6.

2   State-of-the-Art Methods

Regularized Minimum Covariance Determinant. We consider datasets of n observations $x_1, \ldots, x_n$ in $\mathbb{R}^p$. Based on given mean μ and covariance

Σ parameters, we define the Mahalanobis distance $d^2_{\mu, \Sigma}(x_i)$ of an observation x_i by $d^2_{\mu, \Sigma}(x_i) = (x_i - \mu)^\mathsf{T} \Sigma^{-1}(x_i - \mu)$. The larger this quantity, the more likely x_i is an outlier. We use the *Regularized Minimum Covariance Determinant (RMCD)* [1] as the reference method for outlier detection and also to whiten the data in distance-based approaches (see Section 4).

One-Class SVM. The One-Class SVM *novelty detection* algorithm [8] is a supervised clustering algorithm that relies on a thresholded Parzen windows density estimator to define a frontier between two populations. It can be adapted to the unsupervised problem of outlier detection, but remains a descriptive model that only provides a deviation index for each observation.

Local Component Analysis. Local Component Analysis is another extension of Parzen windows density estimation where the isotropic assumption inherent in most kernels is relaxed to anisotropic covariance parameters. The θ parameter of the kernel hence becomes the local data covariance matrix Σ, which we estimate using a leave-one-out cross-validation scheme as in [7]:

$$\Sigma^* = \arg\min_{\Sigma} \left[-\sum_{i=1}^{n} \log \left(|\Sigma|^{-\frac{1}{2}} (2\pi)^{-\frac{p}{2}} \frac{1}{n-1} \sum_{j \neq i} \exp \left(-\frac{1}{2} d^2_{x_j, \Sigma}(x_i) \right) \right) \right].$$
(1)

3   Theoretical Contributions

Setting the LCA Regularization Term λ. In [7], an internal regularization term is used to ensure LCA computation stability. The proposed default value is set to $\lambda = 10^{-4}$ [7]. In our work, we choose λ so that it models properly the central mode of the data. Since outliers may have a large influence on the observed variance of the dataset along some dimensions, we use a robust heuristic: we select the 50% most concentrated observations according to a Parzen windows density estimation, compute the Ledoit-Wolf [4] coefficient shrinkage α from this subsample, and set $\lambda = \frac{\alpha}{1-\alpha}$.

Building an Interactive Outlier Detection Framework. We propose an efficient procedure to summarize the necessary information about the data structure so that the practitioner can find how many observations to discard: Within the LCA computation, proximity measures of each observation from another are computed as $k_{ij} = \exp\left(-\frac{1}{2}(x_i - x_j)^\mathsf{T} \Sigma^{*-1}(x_i - x_j)\right)$, thus providing a kernel-based representation of the data as a symmetric positive definite matrix $K = (k_{ij})_{i,j \in [1..n]^2}$, that summarizes the whole data set structure. Let $K = UDU^\mathsf{T}$, where U and D are the matrix of the eigenvectors and diagonal matrix of eigenvalues $(\sigma_i, i \in [1..n])$ of K. Let D_δ be the diagonal matrix obtained by shrinking the elements of D by a factor $\delta \geq 0$ like in [11]: $D_\delta(i, i) = 1 - \frac{\delta}{\sigma_i}$ if $\sigma_i > \delta$, $D_\delta(i, i) = 0$ otherwise. D_δ yields a shrunk density estimate at each observation $g_\delta(x_i) = e_i^\mathsf{T} U D_\delta U^\mathsf{T} e$, where e_i is a vector whose entries are 0 except its i-th element which is 1 and e is a vector of ones; note that the normalization constant is omitted as it plays no role in our analysis. We finally define $\Delta(x_i) = \min_\delta\{\delta : g_\delta(x_i) < 0.5\}$, which associates each observation with the minimal shrinkage value δ that –almost– cancels it. Δ can be further used to identify different levels of homogeneity amongst the data. Typically, outliers would correspond to a group of observations that vanish with the smallest values of δ, whereas larger δ also trim off regular observations as in Fig. 2.

We define the *disappearance function*, a ranked version of Δ, as: $\Delta_{\text{rank}}(i) = \Delta(x_i)_{i:n}$, where $\Delta(x_i)_{i:n}$ is the i-th order value of $\Delta(x_i)$. Working with simulated datasets and various values of p, p/n ratios and contamination amount γ, we show that the first knee in the variation of Δ_{sort} provides a reliable estimation of the number of outliers in the dataset, while no such estimation can be made from the LCA's ranked density function $g_{\text{rank}}(i) = g(x_i)_{i:n}$, where $g(x_i) = \frac{1}{Z}e_i^{\mathsf{T}}Ke$ and Z is a normalization factor. As we will show in Section 4, Δ_{rank} better characterizes data structure than g_{rank}.

4 Experiments

In our experiments, we first compare One-Class SVM, Parzen density estimation and LCA outlier detection accuracy on both simulated and real data. Parzen density estimation and One-Class SVM are also applied to whitened data (see Section 2), which we refer to as One-Class SVM_w and Parzen_w. In a second set of experiments, we demonstrate that the subsequent interactive outlier detection framework described in Section 3 provides a usable representation of the data distribution that helps the user to isolate a set of homogeneous samples.

Data Description. We generate a γ-polluted $n \times p$ dataset by drawing $(1-\gamma)n$ observations from a $\mathcal{N}(\mu, \Sigma)$ distribution and γn observations from a $\mathcal{N}(\mu, \alpha\Sigma)$ distribution, $\alpha > 1$. We also consider Student distributed datasets. In both cases, μ can be set to zero without loss of generality. In all our simulations, we generated the outlier observations so that they can be distinguished from the inliers data.

Our real data were functional MRI contrast maps that were acquired with 3T scanners from multiple manufacturers. Each contrast was available for a number of subject n comprised between 1700 and 2000. BOLD time series was recorded using Echo-Planar Imaging, with TR = 2200 ms, TE = 30 ms, flip angle = 75° and spatial resolution 3mm isotropic. Standard pre-processing, including slice timing correction, spike and motion correction, temporal detrending, Gaussian smoothing at 5mm-FWHM, and spatial normalization, were performed on the data using the SPM8 software and its default parameters. Functional contrast maps were obtained by fitting a General Linear Model to this data using SPM8 also. For each available subject, we extract the mean signal of every region of interest defined by an anatomical atlas [6] and concatenate the extracted values so that every subject is represented by a p-dimensional vector in an $n \times p$ matrix.

Outlier Detection Accuracy Measures. With simulated data, for various values of p/n, γ, Σ, and α, we build Receiver-Operating Characteristic (ROC) curves [12] of outlier detection accuracy for each method. ROC curves were averaged over 10 runs for each method and each experiment. We compute Area Under Curve values (AUC) that reflect the general outlier detection accuracy of a method for a realistic range of p/n ratios.

Our real datasets are composed of $n \sim 1900$ (the exact value depends on the contrast) observations, each described by 113 features ($p = 113$). With such a p/n ratio, we can construct a fair approximation of the ground truth with covariance-based outlier detection. Computing AUCs as we did with simulated data, and sub-sampling the original dataset, we assess the ability of the different methods to accurately rank the observations by their *degree of abnormality*.

5   Results

5.1   Quality of Outlier Detection with Density Estimators

Gaussian and Student Distributed Data. On both Gaussian and Student distributed data, the accuracy of outlier detection with LCA dominates the accuracy of the other methods. Generally, all methods perform well with an AUC above 0.9, except when the condition number of the covariance matrix $\kappa(\Sigma)$ is above 100. Table 1 illustrates this phenomenon. In the latter case, one has to whiten the data previously to using One-Class SVM and Parzen. The main advantage of LCA is that such a transformation is part of the algorithm.

Real Dataset. Fig. 1 shows the accuracy of the different methods on a real neuroimaging dataset, using a contrast related to the perception of angry versus neutral faces. All methods perform well with an AUC above 0.8. LCA achieves the highest accuracy yet, which remains above 0.95 for all p/n ratios. Whitening the data prior to outlier detection with One-Class SVM or Parzen density estimation is relevant since it increases the accuracy of the latter methods by roughly 0.1. Similar results were obtained in five other functional contrasts.

Table 1. AUC values of the different outlier detection methods confronted with variance outliers (Gaussian distributed data, $p = 100$, $\gamma = 0.4$, $\kappa(\Sigma) = 1000$, $\alpha = 1.15$)

p/n	0.1	0.5	0.8	1.0
LCA	**0.99** ±0.0017	**0.99** ±0.0054	**0.99** ±0.0080	**0.98** ±0.0078
Parzen	0.98 ±0.0043	0.98 ±0.0103	0.98 ±0.0091	0.96 ±0.0094
Parzen$_w$	**0.99** ±0.0022	0.97 ±0.0055	0.97 ±0.0082	0.97 ±0.0095
One-Class SVM	**0.99** ±0.0037	0.91 ±0.0296	0.77 ±0.0795	0.64 ±0.0593
One-Class SVM$_w$	**0.99** ±0.0022	0.96 ±0.0061	0.97 ±0.0095	0.97 ±0.0104
RMCD	**0.99** ±0.0023	0.95 ±0.0055	0.97 ±0.0083	0.97 ±0.0090

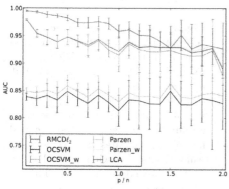

Fig. 1. Outlier detection accuracy of non-parametric density estimation algorithms, represented by their AUC (real data). LCA outperforms both Parzen density estimation and One-Class SVM, even applied on whitened data. RMCD parametric method has the same accuracy than the latter. LCA seems to be sensitive to the p/n ratio as its performance decreases with this ratio.

5.2   Relevance of an Interactive Outlier Detection Procedure

Finding Outliers on Simulated Datasets. We verified with extensive simulations that the first knee of the disappearance function directly provides an estimate of the number of outliers. Fig. 2 illustrates this statement. This result holds for various p, p/n and α values, even though the decision showed to be a bit conservative. This behavior is yet required to guarantee a low false detections rate on heavy tailed distributions such as the Student distribution. Fig. 3 shows that our procedure does not encourage discarding observations when applied to pure Student distributed data.

Investigating the Statistical Structure of Real Data. Fig. 4 gives the spectrum of real neuroimaging datasets as obtained from LCA-learned density transformations. Knees can be easily identified in this curve, indicating that two or more relevant groups of observations are present. This observation rank property could not be inferred from the standard decision function. It is noticeable that many observations (about half of the dataset) seem to be suggested as outliers, while looking at a standard bidimensional PCA plot (not shown for the sake of place) would have suggested a much lower number.

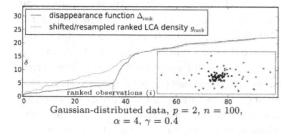

Gaussian-distributed data, $p = 2$, $n = 100$, $\alpha = 4$, $\gamma = 0.4$

Fig. 2. Functions summarizing the data structure from their density. Difference between outliers (red dots) density and inliers (black dots) density only appears in the disappearance function. Choosing $\delta \simeq 5$ yields an outlier detection corresponding to estimating $\hat{\gamma} \simeq 35\%$ for a real value of $\gamma = 40\%$.

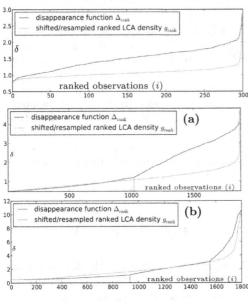

Fig. 3. Data statistical structure investigation in an uncontaminated Student-distributed data. No hard decision seems to be suggested. $p = 100$, $n = 300$, $\gamma = 0$.

Fig. 4. Dataset structure spectrum obtained by density analysis on real neuroimaging datasets. (a) Viewing Angry faces - viewing neutral faces. A slope breakdown is observed at $i \simeq 1000$, suggesting that half the observations should be removed to obtain an heterogeneous set. (b) Rewarding task. The procedure suggests that three observations scales are present in the data. The first one may be composed of outliers. In both cases, g_{rank} does not reveal any structure.

6   Discussion

Statistical modelling of medical images is challenging because of the dimensionality of the data. Most current approaches rely on a Gaussian assumption. Here we use density estimation to rank medical images according to their degree of abnormality in a group study. We demonstrate that outlier detection with Local Component Analysis (LCA) achieves higher accuracy than state-of-the-art methods. This was shown for various p/n settings on both Gaussian and Student distributed data contaminated with up to 40% outliers. Real data experiments showed that LCA accuracy is generally above 0.9, although it seems to slightly decrease in high-dimension. Our choice of the LCA regularization parameter seemed to be optimal in that regard and our experiments demonstrated that LCA should be preferred to other non-parametric methods.

Non-parametric methods do not rely on distributional assumptions, but at the expense of explicit statistical control. We propose a simple way to perform outlier detection in an unsupervised framework that does not require any prior knowledge and guides the user in his final decision about how many observations to discard. Because it uses an internal cross-validation scheme, LCA adapts to the data local structure and comes with a natural kernel-based representation of the data. We apply a trace norm penalization to capture the information carried in the kernel matrix which reveals important features on the structure of the data [11]. As this penalization is the convex relaxation of principal components analysis-based truncation of the kernel matrix, it results in a stable criterion. We used it to characterize the difference between outliers and inliers in a robust procedure. This is meant to provide practitioners a faithful representation of possible inhomogeneities in the population under study. We verified on several simulated and real functional neuroimaging datasets that this heuristic to chose the regularization of LCA does not yield spurious outlier detections. An attractive generalization of the LCA approach for high-dimensional settings is a mixed model, in which some dimensions are simply modeled as a Gaussian, while others are modeled through equation (1) [7].

Conclusion. Local Component Analysis was shown to have a good outlier detection accuracy under more general settings than parametric approaches. The interactive outlier detection framework presented in this contribution is of broad interest in medical imaging where manual data screening is impossible because of the high-dimensionality and sample size of the data, and yet essential due to the poor quality of the datasets used in many clinical studies.

This work was supported by a Digiteo DIM-Lsc grant (HiDiNim project, N°2010-42D). JBP was partly funded by the IMAGEN project, which receives research funding from the E.U. Community's FP6, LSHM-CT-2007-037286. This manuscript reflects only the author's views and the Community is not liable for any use that may be made of the information contained therein.

References

1. Fritsch, V., Varoquaux, G., Thyreau, B., Poline, J.B., Thirion, B.: Detecting outliers in high-dimensional neuroimaging datasets with robust covariance estimators. Medical Image Analysis (in press, 2012)
2. Gerber, S., Tasdizen, T., Joshi, S., Whitaker, R.: On the manifold structure of the space of brain images. Med. Image Comput. Comput. Assist. Interv. 12, 305 (2009)
3. Kalatzis, I., Piliouras, N., Ventouras, E., Papageorgiou, C., Rabavilas, A., Cavouras, D.: Design and implementation of an SVM-based computer classification system for discriminating depressive patients from healthy controls using the P600 component of ERP signals. Comp. Meth. Prog. Bio. 75(1), 11–22 (2004)
4. Ledoit, O., Wolf, M.: A well-conditioned estimator for large-dimensional covariance matrices. Journal of Multivariate Analysis 88(2), 365–411 (2004)
5. Mourao-Miranda, J., Hardoon, D.R., Hahn, T., Marquand, A.F., Williams, S.C., Shawe-Taylor, J., Brammer, M.: Patient classification as an outlier detection problem: An application of the one-class SVM. NeuroImage 58(3), 793–804 (2011)
6. Perrot, M., Rivière, D., Tucholka, A., Mangin, J.F.: Joint bayesian cortical sulci recognition and spatial normalization. Inf. Process Med. Imaging 21, 176–187 (2009)
7. Roux, N.L., Bach, F.: Local component analysis. ArXiv e-prints (2011)
8. Schölkopf, B., Platt, J.C., Shawe-Taylor, J.C., Smola, A.J., Williamson, R.C.: Estimating the support of a high-dimensional distribution. Neural Comput. 13, 1443–1471 (2001)
9. Shapiro, S.S., Wilk, M.B.: An analysis of variance test for normality (complete samples). Biometrika 52(3/4), 591–611 (1965)
10. Thirion, B., Pinel, P., Mériaux, S., Roche, A., Dehaene, S., Poline, J.B.: Analysis of a large fMRI cohort: Statistical and methodological issues for group analyses. NeuroImage 35(1), 105–120 (2007)
11. Wang, J., Saligrama, V., Castañón, D.A.: Structural similarity and distance in learning. ArXiv e-prints (October 2011)
12. Zweig, M., Campbell, G.: Receiver-operating characteristic (ROC) plots: A fundamental evaluation tool in clinical medicine. Clin. Chem. 39(4), 561–577 (1993)

Learning Correspondences in Knee MR Images from the Osteoarthritis Initiative

Ricardo Guerrero*, Claire R. Donoghue, Luis Pizarro, and Daniel Rueckert

Biomedical Image Analysis Group, Imperial College London
{reg09,claire.donoghue08,l.pizarro,d.rueckert}@imperial.ac.uk

Abstract. Registration is a powerful tool that allows mapping images in a common space in order to aid in their analysis. Accurate registration of images of the knee is challenging to achieve using intensity based registration algorithms. Problems arise due to large anatomical inter-subject differences which causes registrations to fail to converge to an accurate solution. In this work we propose learning correspondences in pairs of images to match self-similarity features, that describe images in terms of their local structure rather than their intensity. We use RANSAC as a robust model estimator. We show a substantial improvement in terms of mean error and standard deviation of 2.13mm and 2.47mm over intensity based registration methods, when comparing landmark alignment error.

1 Introduction

In many medical image analysis applications it is important to find mappings to a common space, i.e. non-rigid registration [1], statistical shape models [2], atlas building [3], segmentation [4] and computer aided diagnosis [5]. Many of these methods rely on affine registration as an initialization. In some cases this provides a very good initialization, such as brain images, where the global variations are generally low when compared to other anatomical regions. Unfortunately intensity based affine registrations does not suffice for datasets with large inter-subject anatomical variability, and in occasions it fails completely. Obtaining good initializations in knee MR images can be particularly challenging due to inter-subject variability. This means that intensity-based affine registration may get trapped in a local minimum and hence fail to align the images. For very large population studies manually correcting registration errors is an unfeasible task.

The Osteoarthritis Initiative (OAI) is a multi-center, longitudinal, prospective observational study of knee osteoarthritis, and provides public access to MR images and clinical data. The OIA is a large scale study into this disease with 4796 men and women aged 45-79. A robust and automated registration method that yields accurate and consistent results is essential for such a large scale study.

Several methods have been proposed to address large intra-subject variability registration. Feature based registration methods [6–8], in general, try to find and match features in a pair of images, and use these correspondences to define

---

* This project was partially funded by CONACyT, SEP and the Rabin Enzra trust.

F. Wang et al. (Eds.): MLMI 2012, LNCS 7588, pp. 218–225, 2012.

a transformation from one image's space to the other at these points, while interpolating the intermediate values. However, as stated in [8], the success of point based image registration highly depends on the representative power and accuracy of the feature matching. Graph based methods [9, 10], find geodesic path across a similarity graph between images, and a gradual registration is performed along this path. The main disadvantage of these techniques is a high computational cost. Moreover it is not necessarily straightforward how to treat images that did not form part of the graph building process.

In this work we present an approach to the problem that explores feature matching. We use the recently proposed 3D local self-similarity features [11]. Through saliency measures we compute and match features in a pair of images, that in turn, using a robust parameter estimator define an affine transformation which minimizes the feature alignment error. We show results of using the proposed method on a subset of knee MR images of the OAI cohort, although the method is generalizable to other types of images.

2   Method

To register a pair of images we first use the image structure tensor to filter out image regions that contain no structure and therefore are considered uninformative. Then we calculate 3D local self-similarity features in all the remaining voxels. After this, the feature list is reduced by measuring the energy distribution and level of similarity of the descriptors. The remaining features are fed to a forward-backward matching algorithm that further reduces the list of features by finding and matching stable points in both images. Then the parameters of an affine transformation are learned using random sample and consensus (RANSAC), which again reduces the list of matching points. Fig. 1 shows the pipeline describing the proposed feature analysis and matching methods to drastically reduce the number of potentially stable feature points, which are subsequently fed to a point based registration algorithm.

2.1   Dense 3D Local Self-Similarity Feature Descriptors

For every voxel in an image I a local self-similarity (SS) descriptor can be computed [11]. This can be done by calculating the similarity (using sums-of-squared distances, SSD) between a small spherical patch around the voxel and every other point (another small spherical patch) in a larger surrounding spherical image region. This results in an internal similarity volume map, that is then binned into a log-spherical representation. Each bin is filled with the highest similarity that falls within its supported range. This representation yields three benefits: It compresses the descriptor's length for the voxel, accounts for radially increasing affine deformations, and for small amounts of local non-rigid deformations. The calculated similarities are then normalized to form a *correlation volume* S_q, that is associated with any voxel $q \in \mathbb{R}^3$, and can be written as:

$$S_q(p) = \exp\left(-\frac{SSD_q(p)}{\max(var_{noise}, var_{auto}(q))}\right) \tag{1}$$

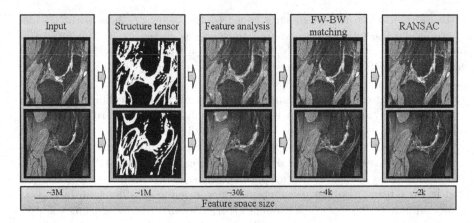

Fig. 1. Proposed feature analysis and matching methods to identify potentially stable feature points (see color figure online)

for all $p \in \mathbb{R}^3$ such that $\|p - q\|^2 < \rho^2$. That is for all points within a distance ρ from pivot point q. The quantities $(var_{noise}, var_{auto})$ are calculated in the same way as in [12]. The correlation volume, which is defined in Cartesian space, is mapped to a spherical coordinate system $S_q(x, y, z) \rightarrow \tilde{S}_q(r', \theta', \phi')$. Thus, the self-similarity descriptor SS_q is given by the maximum correlation value within each bin (r_i, θ_j, ϕ_k): $SS_q(r_i, \theta_j, \phi_i) = \max_{(r', \theta', \phi') \in \mathbb{R}^3} \tilde{S}_q(r', \theta', \phi')$ where

$$
\begin{aligned}
r' \in [r_i, r_{i+1}], & \qquad r_i \in R = \{r_1, ..., r_L\} \\
\theta' \in [\theta_j, \theta_{j+1}], & \qquad \theta_j \in \Theta = \{\theta_1, ..., \theta_M\} \\
\phi' \in [\phi_k, \phi_{k+1}], & \qquad \phi_k \in \Phi = \{\phi_1, ..., \phi_N\}
\end{aligned}
\tag{2}
$$

and R, Θ, Φ denote the sets of discretized radii, elevation and azimuth angles, each with L, M and N values, respectively. This type of descriptor is especially well suited for imaging modalities where there is no intensity consistency across images (i.e. MR images), since they encode the intrinsic surrounding geometry of a point, rather than their intensity distribution. In this way we move away from intensity characterization towards a geometric based description.

2.2 Feature Analysis

Since not all descriptors are informative, we have to remove non-informative ones. Furthermore, we can find in which sections of the image we do not expect to find any informative features at all (i.e. structureless regions). We employ two different techniques to reduce the feature space: a) using the 3D structure tensor of the image we define regions where we would potentially find relevant stable features, hence reducing the feature calculation burden, and b) we measure the energy distribution and level of self-similarity of the calculated features and ignore features that are below a certain threshold to further reduce the number of potential stable feature points. Using a subset of salient features determined by the two mentioned tests, we use a forward-backward feature matching algorithm [14] to determine feature correspondences of stable points.

Image Structure Tensor. The image structure tensor defines the predominant directions of the image gradient around a particular point q [8]. The discrete 3D structure tensor Γ can be written as $\Gamma_w[q] = \sum_r w[r]\Gamma_0[q-r]$ where r defines a set of indices around q, $w[r]$ is a weight on the window such that $\sum w[r] = 1$ and $\Gamma_0[q]$ is the Hessian matrix. Potentially stable features will lie in regions where the structure tensor's eigenvalues are different from zero.

Measures on the Descriptors. There are two tests that are applied directly to the descriptor vector in order to assess if they are considered informative. First, we only consider feature vectors that contain certain level of self-similarity, that is, the similarity between the patch around the voxel for which the descriptor is calculated and the patches in the lager volume being considered, should be above a certain threshold $0 \leq C \leq 1$. Secondly, we also test the energy distribution of the vector. Specifically, we use a sparsity measure to check whether the energy distribution of the descriptor contains peaks or is homogeneous. If the descriptor does not meet both criteria the vector is considered non-informative and is ignored. Where the sparsity metric [13] used is is given by

$$\sigma\left(SS_q\right) = \frac{\sqrt{n} - \left(\sum |SS_{q_i}|\right)\sqrt{\sum SS_{q_i}^2}}{\sqrt{n} - 1} \tag{3}$$

where n is the number of bins of the descriptor SS_{q_i}, and $0 \leq \sigma \leq 1$.

Finding Feature Matches. The forward-backward matching algorithm was originally designed to find distinctive and stable point between two stereoscopic images [14]. Given a set of points $A = \{a_1, a_2, ..., a_n\}$ belonging to an image I_1, a point a_i is considered stable if its best match in a set of points $B = \{b_1, b_2, ..., b_n\}$ belonging to an image I_2, say b_j (forward), also has as best match the original point a_i in image I_1 (backward). Using the Euclidean distance as a measure of similarity between feature vectors we use this algorithm to find the stable points.

2.3   Point Based Affine Registration

Feature correspondences that were established in the previous stages are fed to a point based image registration algorithm that fits an affine transformation model to the set of features by minimizing the root mean square error (RMS) between correspondences. The image is then transformed and interpolated according to this affine transformation. It is worth noting that only the RMS drives the fitting optimization procedure and not the image intensities.

A reasonable assumption to be made is that feature correspondences are noisy, that is, they are contaminated by outliers, where matching features do not correspond to matching structures. Using random sample consensus (RANSAC) we can learn the parameters of an affine transformation model that is robust against outliers. Initially published by [15], it is a non-deterministic algorithm that iteratively estimates parameters of a model in the presence of large amounts of outliers. Rather than using the full set of points to estimate a model, RANSAC uses a minimal random subset to estimate an initial model. This model is then tested on the remainder of the data points and if any other point is well represented by the model (up to an error tolerance) it is added to the subset. This process is repeated on different subsets until the probability that we will find a subset with a higher rank drops below a certain threshold, where the rank is determined by the number of points contained in the subset. The higher the number of points, the higher the rank, the better the model explains the data.

3   Data and Results

Images used to evaluate the proposed method where obtained from the Osteoarthritis Initiative (OAI) public use dataset (groups 1.C.0 and 1.E.0, available at http://www.oai.ucsf.edu). A subset of 75 images where randomly selected and manually annotated by an expert using three orthogonal views by placing four landmark points on the anterior and posterior collateral ligament (ACL and PCL) insertions on the femur and the tibia. The middle voxel of each ligament insertion is selected at the bone interface. The fat-suppressed, sagittal 3D dual-echo in steady state (DESS) sequence with selective water excitation (WE) has in plane resolution of 0.36 x 0.36mm, and slice thickness of 0.7mm [16].

Following the work-flow of Fig. 1 we applied some variations of the method. Using down-sampled images, we filtered out smooth regions of the image using the structure tensor (Sec. 2.2). After this, we calculated 3D local self-similarity features in these regions in a regular grid with 2 x 2 x 1 spacings using a correlation window and a patch size of radius of 5 voxels (empirically found to be adequate for representing the structures at hand). We then reduced the number of features, using sparsity and self-similarity thresholds of 0.25 and 0.9 respectively (Sec. 2.2). For a given pair of images we used the forward-backward matching algorithm to find stable points, using a search window of ± 30 voxels. From this point two different routes were explored: In one we fed the matching features to a point based affine registration algorithm to obtain a transformation model (FBR). In the other we used RANSAC to estimate the parameters of the affine transformation model (FBR$^+$). Using the output from FBR and FBR$^+$ the process was repeated using the transformed image as input for a second iteration (same parameters). At this stage two different search window sizes where tested ± 15 (FBR$_{2a}$) and ± 40 (FBR$_{2b}$ and FBR$^+_{2b+}$). To assess the performance of the proposed method, the alignment error of the previously defined landmarks was compared to an intensity based affine registration (AfR), that minimizes the normalized mutual information using gradient descend optimization.

Tab. 1 shows landmark alignment errors for the proposed methods Our method shows a very substantial improvement in terms of mean error and standard

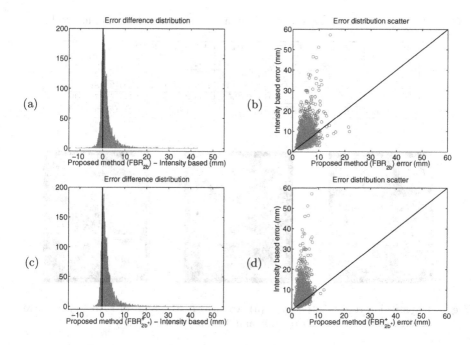

Fig. 2. Landmark alignment error comparison of our method with two different parameter setting and intensity based affine registration

deviation, 2.13mm and 2.47mm respectively, ~36% over intensity based affine registration. Fig. 2 (a-d) shows a landmark alignment error difference histogram and a scatter plot relating intensity based registration and the proposed method, of all the possible pairwise registration (n=5550) for experiments FBR_{2b} and FBR_{2b+}^+ in comparison to AfR. In Fig. 2 (a,c) the landmark alignment error using our proposed method is subtracted from the error achieved by intensity based affine registration. Positive values indicate that our method better aligns the landmarks, and therefore values to the right of the vertical line (at zero) represent an improvement in mm of the value indicated in x-axis over intensity based registration, the distribution is clearly skewed towards the right, which points out the overall improvement. Fig. 2 (b,d) shows scatter plots on the distribution of the landmark alignment error obtained by FBR_{2b}, and FBR_{2b+}^+ vs AfR, values above the diagonal line are an improvement of the proposed method over AfR, values under the line represent cases where our method performed worse and values exactly on the line are cases where no improvement was made. Furthermore, outliers (in regards to the alignment error of the four landmarks) are almost completely removed in the cases of FBR_{2b} and FBR_{2b+}^+, which shows the robustness of the algorithm. Fig. 3 shows a comparison between AfR, FBR_{2b} and FBR_{2b+}^+. In the background is the target image, while the overlaid contours correspond to the source image after registration, a clear improvement is shown.

Table 1. Accuracy of methods. Errors in mm with standard deviation in brackets.

Landmark	AfR	FBR	FBR$^+$	FBR$_{2a}$	FBR$_{2b}$	FBR$^+_{2b+}$
ACL femur	5.62(3.88)	4.43(2.75)	3.15(1.94)	3.52(2.11)	3.66(1.74)	**3.05(1.41)**
ACL tibia	6.17(4.10)	5.70(3.72)	4.50(2.73)	4.75(3.03)	5.03(2.62)	**4.12(2.04)**
PCL femur	6.08(3.97)	5.04(2.97)	**3.68**(2.11)	4.19(2.38)	4.42(2.25)	**3.68(1.79)**
PCL tibia	5.56(3.82)	4.86(3.03)	4.36(2.58)	4.38(2.51)	4.12(2.17)	**4.07(2.00)**
All mean error	5.86(3.53)	5.00(2.58)	3.92(1.77)	4.21(1.93)	4.38(1.41)	**3.73(1.06)**

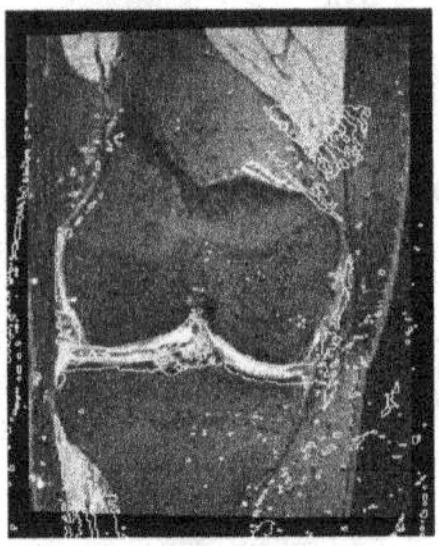

Fig. 3. Registration results after using (a) AfR, (b) FBR$_{2b}$ and (c) FBR$^+_{2b+}$. Average landmark alignment errors of 25.19, 7.08 and 3.15mm, respectively.)

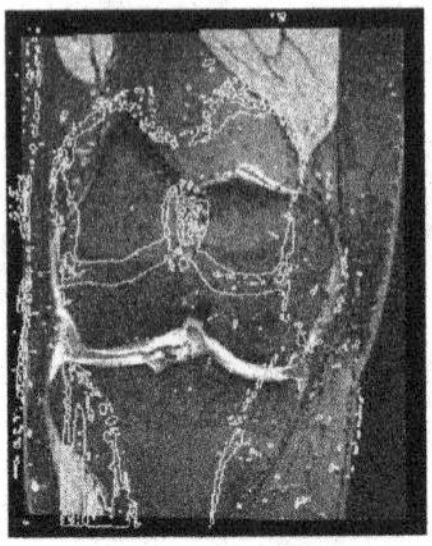

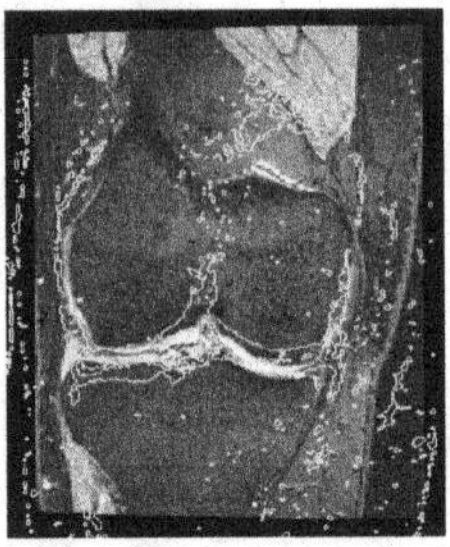

4   Discussion and Future Work

We have proposed a method that uses self-similarity features, rather than raw intensities, to establish feature point matches between a pair of images. This enables us to register images in a more robust and accurate way. We have shown quantitative results about the improvements made over raw intensity based registration, using a subset of images from the Osteoarthritis Initiative, that consists of 75 randomly sampled baseline images. Using every pairwise registration we obtain a landmark alignment accuracy improvement in ~82% of the cases, while virtually eliminating any outliers. It was observed that a two-iteration approach, where the output of the previous step is the input of the next one, helped eliminate outliers. Future experiments would consist of determining the optimal number of iterations in order to achieve more accurate results. We also observed that adding a further intensity based registration only degradates the results, reaffirming that the contribution was due to the use of the 3D local self-similarity features. Another interesting path that we would like to explore, is using RANSAC as a robust estimator of a non-rigid model.

Acknowledgement. The OAI is a public-private partnership comprised of five contracts (N01-AR-2-2258; N01-AR-2-2259; N01- AR-2-2260; N01-AR-2-2261; N01-AR-2-2262) funded by the National Institutes of Health, a branch of the Department of Health and Human Services, and conducted by the OAI Study Investigators. Private funding partners include Merck Research Laboratories; Novartis Pharmaceuticals Corporation, GlaxoSmithKline; and Pfizer, Inc. Private sector funding for the OAI is managed by the Foundation for the National

Institutes of Health. This manuscript uses an OAI public use data set and does not necessarily reflect the opinions or views of the OAI investigators, the NIH, or private funding partners.

References

1. Rueckert, D., Sonoda, L.I., Hayes, C., Hill, D.L.G., Leach, M.O., Hawkes, D.J.: Nonrigid Registration Using Free-Form Deformations: Application to Breast MR Images. IEEE Transactions on Medical Imaging 18(8), 712–721 (1999)
2. Cootes, T.F., Hill, A., Taylor, C.J., Haslam, J.: The Use of Active Shape Models for Locating Structures in Medical Images. In: Barrett, H.H., Gmitro, A.F. (eds.) IPMI 1993. LNCS, vol. 687, pp. 33–47. Springer, Heidelberg (1993)
3. Carballido-Gamio, J., Majumdar, S.: Atlas-based knee cartilage assessment. Magnetic Resonance in Medicine 66(2), 574–583 (2011)
4. Aljabar, P., Heckemann, R.A., Hammers, A., Hajnal, J.V., Rueckert, D.: Multiatlas based segmentation of brain images: Atlas selection and its effect on accuracy. NeuroImage 46(3), 726–738 (2009)
5. Donoghue, C., Rao, A., Bull, A.M.J., Rueckert, D.: Manifold learning for automatically predicting articular cartilage morphology in the knee with data from the osteoarthritis initiative (OAI). In: SPIE Medical Imaging, vol. 7962 (2011)
6. Rohr, K., Stiehl, H.S., Sprengel, R., Buzug, T.M., Weese, J., Kuhn, M.H.: Landmark-based elastic registration using approximating thin-plate splines. IEEE Transactions on Medical Imaging 20(6), 526–534 (2001)
7. Pennec, X., Guttmann, C.R.G., Thirion, J.-P.: Feature-Based Registration of Medical Images: Estimation and Validation of the Pose Accuracy. In: Wells, W.M., Colchester, A.C.F., Delp, S.L. (eds.) MICCAI 1998. LNCS, vol. 1496, pp. 1107–1114. Springer, Heidelberg (1998)
8. Rohr, K.: On 3D differential operators for detecting point landmarks. Image and Vision Computing 15(3), 219–233 (1997)
9. Hamm, J., Ye, D.H., Verma, R., Davatzikos, C.: GRAM: A framework for geodesic registration on anatomical manifolds. Medical Image Analysis 14(5), 633–642 (2010)
10. Jia, H., Wu, G., Wang, Q., Wang, Y., Kim, M., Shen, D.: Directed graph based image registration. Computerized Medical Imaging and Graphics: The Official Journal of the Computerized Medical Imaging Society 36(2), 139–151 (2012)
11. Guerrero, R., Pizarro, L., Wolz, R., Rueckert, D.: Landmark localisation in brain MR images using feature point descriptors based on 3D local self-similarities. In: IEEE International Symposium on Biomedical Imaging, pp. 1535–1538 (2012)
12. Shechtman, E., Irani, M.: Matching Local Self-Similarities across Images and Videos. In: IEEE Conference on Computer Vision and Pattern Recognition (2007)
13. Hoyer, P.O., Dayan, P.: Non-negative matrix factorization with sparseness constraints. Journal of Machine Learning Research 5, 1457–1469 (2004)
14. Fua, P.: A parallel stereo algorithm that produces dense depth maps and preserves image features. Machine Vision and Applications 6(1), 35–49 (1993)
15. Fischler, M.A., Bolles, R.C.: Random Sample Consensus: A Paradigm for Model Fitting with Applications to Image Analysis and Automated Cartography. Communications of the ACM 24(6), 381–395 (1981)
16. Peterfy, C., Schneider, E., Nevitt, M.: The osteoarthritis initiative: report on the design rationale for the magnetic resosnace imaging protocol for the knee. Osteoarthritis and Cartilage 16(12), 1433–1441 (2008)

Gradient Projection Learning for Parametric Nonrigid Registration[*]

Stefan Pszczolkowski[1],[**], Luis Pizarro[1],
Declan P. O'Regan[2], and Daniel Rueckert[1]

[1] Biomedical Image Analysis Group, Imperial College London
{sp2010,l.pizarro,d.rueckert}@imperial.ac.uk
[2] Robert Steiner MRI Unit, Imperial College London
declan.oregan@imperial.ac.uk

Abstract. A potentially large anatomical variability among subjects in a population makes nonrigid image registration techniques prone to inaccuracies and to high computational costs in their optimisation. In this paper, we propose a new learning-based approach to accelerate the convergence rate of any chosen parametric energy-based image registration method. From a set of training images and their corresponding deformations, our method learns offline a projection from the gradient space of the energy functional to the parameter space of the chosen registration method using partial least squares. Combined with a regularisation term, the learnt projection is subsequently used online to approximate the optimisation of the energy functional for unseen images. We employ the B-spline approach as underlying registration method, but other parametric methods can be used as well. We perform experiments on synthetic image data and MR cardiac sequences to show that our approach significantly accelerates the convergence –in number of iterations and total computational cost– of the chosen registration method, while achieving similar results in terms of accuracy.

1 Introduction

Nonrigid image registration is a very important and widely investigated topic in medical image analysis, since it aids to remove the, potentially very large, natural structural variablity present in pairs or groups of medical images. A popular approach for nonrigid registration is to find a deformation field as the solution of an energy minimisation approach. There exist non-parametric methods [1–5] and parametric methods [6–11]. A typical energy functional E is composed of a data term E_D that measures the degree of alignment of a target (fixed) image and a source (moving) image, and a regularisation term E_R that imposes smoothness on the deformation field that aligns the images:

$$E = E_D + \lambda E_R \tag{1}$$

where $\lambda \geq 0$ is a tradeoff parameter between the two terms.

---

[*] This work was partially funded by CONICYT.
[**] We are grateful to Dr. Wenjia Bai for his comments and support.

F. Wang et al. (Eds.): MLMI 2012, LNCS 7588, pp. 226–233, 2012.

Learning-based image registration techniques have captured the interest of many researchers in the last few years. A popular approach is to capture the statistics of deformation by applying PCA over each band of wavelet coefficients [12] or over the control point values of B-splines that provide a parametric representation of the deformation fields [13–16]. In [17], the parameters of the deformation are estimated by a nearest neighbour search over training images generated according to a special criteria. A low dimensional representation of images, with maximally discriminative power is obtained in [18] by combining generative and discriminative objective functions in a constrained optimisation problem. The work in [19] presents a method where features extracted from regions obtained by adaptively partition brain images and the statistics of deformation field are used to robustly place the control points that parameterise the deformations. Also, a partial least squares approach is employed to relate cardiac deformation due to respiration with surface intensity traces in [20]. Finally, in [21], support vector regression is utilised to estimate the principal modes of a brain deformation model given low dimensionality image features.

One of the main issues of registration thechniques is their high computational cost. Recently, a new type of methods for increasing optimisation convergence have been developed, albeit they are not learning-based. This type of scheme is the so-called *preconditioning schemes*, where the image gradient is scaled differently for different areas of the image. The main contributions on this kind of approaches are [22, 23]. The difference is that in [23], the preconditioner is thought to work specificly for sum of squared differences, while the precontitioning scheme by [22] works for any similarity measure.

In this paper, we propose a learning-based parametric registration method that learns a projection from the gradient space of the energy functional to the parameter space of the chosen registration method using partial least squares. This learnt mapping can be seen as an approximation of the energy gradient, which we utilise to accelerate the convergence of the registration.

The rest of the paper is organised as follows. Section 2 introduces the concepts required by our approach, to then describe the learning and registration procedures, and a multi-resolution extesion for the method. Experiments and results on synthetic and medical data are shown on section 3. Finally, we conclude on section 4.

2 Method

2.1 Gradient Projections

Optical flow methods, e.g. [1], estimate a dense (voxel-wise) displacement field $\mathbf{u}$ that aligns the target and source images. This flow $\mathbf{u}$ is obtained as the solution of an energy functional (1). A standard gradient ascent (similarly, descent) scheme updates the solution with a speed-up factor $\eta > 0$,

$$\mathbf{u} \leftarrow \mathbf{u} + \eta \cdot \frac{\partial E}{\partial \mathbf{u}}. \tag{2}$$

where

$$\frac{\partial E}{\partial \mathbf{u}} = \frac{\partial E_D}{\partial \mathbf{u}} + \lambda \frac{\partial E_R}{\partial \mathbf{u}}. \tag{3}$$

The gradients are computed according to the specific choice of the data and regularisation functions. For our later developments, we call the term $\frac{\partial E_D}{\partial \mathbf{u}}$ *similarity gradient image* (SGI).

In parametric registration approaches, such as the B-spline based free-form deformation (FFD) registration algorithm [9], the unknown deformation field is parameterised by $N = n_x \cdot n_y \cdot n_z$ control points. In order optimise the parameters (control point values) Φ_i^ξ, with $i = 1 \dots N$ and $\xi \in \{x, y, z\}$, it is necessary to compute the energy gradient in parametric space rather than voxel space. Thus, the energy gradient is calculated w.r.t. the control point values, by taking the SGI and regularisation terms, and projecting them from voxel space to parameter space

$$\frac{\partial E}{\partial \Phi_i^\xi} = \frac{\partial E_D}{\partial \mathbf{u}} \cdot \frac{\partial \mathbf{u}}{\partial \Phi_i^\xi} + \lambda \frac{\partial E_R}{\partial \mathbf{u}} \cdot \frac{\partial \mathbf{u}}{\partial \Phi_i^\xi}. \tag{4}$$

For the B-spline FFD approach, the projection term $\frac{\partial \mathbf{u}}{\partial \Phi_i^\xi}$ is given by the tensor product of the 1D cubic B-splines

$$\frac{\partial \mathbf{u}}{\partial \Phi_i^\xi} = \sum_{l=0}^{3} \sum_{m=0}^{3} \sum_{n=0}^{3} B_l(u) B_m(v) B_n(w) \tag{5}$$

where u, v, w correspond to relative positions in control point space. Finally, the update step used by the optimisation procedure is

$$\Phi_i^\xi \leftarrow \Phi_i^\xi + \eta \cdot \frac{\partial E}{\partial \Phi_i^\xi}. \tag{6}$$

2.2 Learning the Projection

We introduce an learning-based method (LB-FFD) to project the SGI from the gradient space of the energy functional to parameter space, that yields to faster convergence. In our setting, the projection is not constrained to be computed using the B-Spline tensor product. Instead, it is estimated as follows.

Given M training SGIs based on any similarity metric like normalised mutual information (NMI), sum of squared differences (SSD) or cross correlation (CC), the first step of our method is to extract patches $\mathbf{P}_{i,j} \in \mathbb{R}^{s_x \cdot s_y \cdot s_z \times 1}$ for all control point locations $i = 1 \dots N$ and training SGIs $\left(\frac{\partial E_D}{\partial \mathbf{u}}\right)_j$, $j = 1 \dots M$:

$$\mathbf{P}_{i,j} = \mathbb{P}_i^s \left(\frac{\partial E_D}{\partial \mathbf{u}}\right)_j \tag{7}$$

where $\mathbb{P}_i^s$ is an operator that extracts an intensity patch of size $s = s_x \cdot s_y \cdot s_z$ around the location of the control point i. The motivation of using these patches comes from the fact that the B-spline tensor model has local support, i.e., only the voxels of the SGI within a neighbourhood of a control point have to be considered to perform the corresponding projections.

Since the patches $\mathbf{P}_{i,j}$ are of high dimensionality, a PCA dimensionality reduction step over the training images is performed, yielding low dimensionality patches $\mathbf{p}_{i,j} \in \mathbb{R}^{C \times 1}$

$$\mathbf{p}_{i,j} = \Gamma_i^\top \cdot (\mathbf{P}_{i,j} - \overline{\mathbf{P}_{i,j}}) \tag{8}$$

where $\overline{\mathbf{P}_{i,j}}$ is the mean patch over the training images and $\Gamma_i \in \mathbb{R}^{s_x \cdot s_y \cdot s_z \times C}$ is the basis matrix containing the first C modes of variation of the patches around control point i.

Finally, for each training SGI, a nonrigid FFD registration is performed between the target and source images that define it, yielding the optimal FFD control point values $\Phi_{i,j}^\xi$. After that, we estimate the projection term for each of these control points by fitting a partial least squares regression model on each direction ξ that relates the control point value with the low dimensionality patch centered on it. Thus, the regressed coefficients β_i^ξ satisfy

$$\Phi_{i,j}^\xi \approx \left(\beta_i^\xi\right)_0 + \sum_{k=1}^{C} \left(\beta_i^\xi\right)_k \cdot (\mathbf{p}_{i,j})_k \tag{9}$$

At this point we regard $\Phi_{i,j}^\xi$ as a good approximation of the term $\frac{\partial E}{\partial \Phi_i^\xi}$ in (6), because it approximates a solution to the registration problem. As a consequence, if we use the regressed coefficients and the low dimentional patches to compute this approximation for the optimisation, the speed of convergence should increase.

2.3   Registration of Unseen Images

Once the learning procedure described in the previous section is performed, it is possible to register an unseen image to any of the target images used to produce the training SGIs, like the ones depicted in figures 1(c) and 1(d). For this purpose, we devise an optimisation scheme similar to (6) using our approximation of the energy gradient, and an additional regularisation term to account for possible non-smoothness coming from errors in the regression model

$$\Phi_i^\xi \leftarrow \Phi_i^\xi + \eta \cdot \mathbf{G}_{\text{LB}} \tag{10}$$

$$\mathbf{G}_{\text{LB}} := \left(\left(\beta_i^\xi\right)_0 + \sum_{k=1}^{C} \left(\beta_i^\xi\right)_k \cdot (\mathbf{p}_{i,j}^*)_k\right) + \lambda_2 \frac{\partial E_R}{\partial \mathbf{u}} \cdot \frac{\partial \mathbf{u}}{\partial \Phi_i^\xi} \tag{11}$$

where $\lambda_2 \geq 0$ weights the regularisation term, and the unseen low dimensional patch $\mathbf{p}_i^*$ is computed by projecting the corresponding high dimensionality patch, taken from the SGI between the target and the current transformed source, using the PCA projection rule (8).

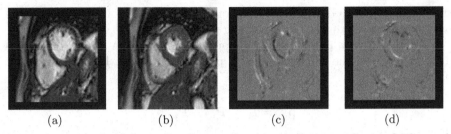

| | | | |
| (a) | (b) | (c) | (d) |

Fig. 1. One example of the cardiac data used and its similarity gradient in both x and y-direction. **a)** Target ROI. **b)** Source. **c)** SGI in x-direction. **d)** SGI in y-direction.

2.4 Multi-resolution Framework

The procedure described in section 2.2 is only valid for a single-resolution registration framework. In order to extend it to be able to perform in a multi-resolution framework with L levels starting from the coarsest level L down to the finest level 1, some considerations have to be made. For level L, the method needs no change, but for all other levels l with $1 \leq l \leq L-1$, the source images used to generate the training SGIs are previously deformed according to the FFD deformation field obtained down to level $l+1$ (while the target remains the same), and the FFD control point values used for regression are the difference between the FFD control point values down to level l and the FFD control point values down to level $l+1$.

3   Results

To test our method we perform two experiments, where we use the SSD between the target and source images as a data term, and the bending energy of the deformation field [24] as a regularisation term.

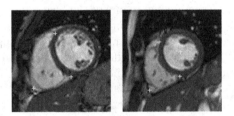

Fig. 2. Examples of the 4 landmarks used by the point-based affine registration

First, we generate 130 synthetic images by randomly scaling a target circle image in both x- and y-direction. 100 of these images are used in the training phase, by computing the SGI and performing FFD registrations between the target and source images that define them. The remaining 30 images are used for testing. The number of principal components retained is set to $C = 5$ and

$\lambda = 0.001$. The value for λ_2 is set to 0.01 due to the unsmooth nature of some of the synthetic deformations.

We compare the mean number of iterations, mean error and total execution time over the 30 testing images of both the FFD approach and our learning-based method, in a single resolution setting. The results are summarised in Table 1.

Table 1. Mean iterations, mean error and total time for the FFD and LB-FFD methods using synthetic data

Algorithm	Iterations	Error (normalised SSD)	Total time (sec)
FFD	29.53	46.32	47.75
LB-FFD	2.70	48.44	3.88

It is possible to see that a reduction in the number of iterations for the learning-based approach is achieved and that, as a consequence, our algorithm performs faster, but mantaining good enough accuracy.

We also evaluate our method on 1.5T Philips Achieva MR cardiac sequences from 10 subjects covering one complete cardiac cicle over 30 frames. Fig. 1 depicts an example of the cardiac data used and its similarity gradient. From the obtained images, we extract one mid-ventricular short-axis slice to produce 2D sequences and then, since the images are on different spatial coordinates for different subjects, a point-based affine registration using 4 landmarks was used to align them, taking the first frame of one of the subjects as a reference. Fig. 2 shows two examples of the landmarks used.

For our experiments on cardiac data, we use $C = 15$ as the number of principal components to retain for our method, since we empirically found that almost no variation in the number of iterations needed to converge is appreciated for $C \in [5, 10, 15, 20, 25, 30]$. The values of λ and λ_2 are both set to 0.001.

We perform a cross-validation procedure where a region of interest from the first frame of each subject is fixed as target image. Then, the second frame of each subject is registered to its corresponding target using both FFD registration with 3 resolution levels and our learning-based method trained using all other frames, also with 3 resolution levels. We repeat this process for the third frame, fourth frame, and so on. Table 2 summarizes the results over the 290 registrations performed for both methods.

Table 2. Mean iterations and total time for the FFD and LB-FFD methods using cardiac data

Algorithm	Iterations Lev. 3	Iterations Lev. 2	Iterations Lev. 1	Total time (sec)
FFD	4.57	7.73	7.93	94.52
LB-FFD	2.02	2.38	2.87	43.08

A clear reduction in the number of iterations can be seen on each resolution level, which in turn makes our algorithm achieve a speedup of over 50%.

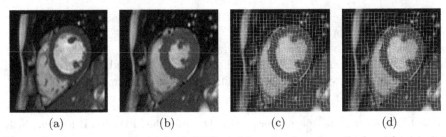

(a)   (b)   (c)   (d)

Fig. 3. Registraton results for both FFD and learning-based methods with superimposed deformation grid. **a)** Target ROI. **b)** Source. **c)** FFD result with linear interpolation. **d)** LB-FFD result with linear interpolation.

Finally, to demonstrate the registration quality of our method, Fig. 3 depicts the registration result between the region of interest on the first frame of a subject and frame number 10, where the end of systole occurs, for both the FFD and learning-based methods, with superimposed deformation grid. It can be seen that our learning-based method performs comparably to the FFD approach.

4 Conclusion

We developed a new general learning-based nonrigid registration approach to accelerate the convergence rate of any chosen parametric energy-based image registration method. A projection from the gradient space of the energy functional to the parameter space is learnt offline and subsequently used online to approximate the optimisation of the energy functional for unseen images. Our preliminary results from experiments on synthetic image data and MR cardiac sequences show that our approach significantly accelerates the convergence, both in number of iterations and total computational cost of the chosen registration method, while achieving similar results in terms of accuracy.

References

1. Horn, B.K.P., Schunck, B.G.: Determining optical flow. Artificial Intelligence 17(1-3), 185–203 (1981)
2. Christensen, G.E., Rabbitt, R.D., Miller, M.I.: Deformable templates using large deformation kinematics. IEEE Transactions on Image Processing 5(10), 1435–1447 (1996)
3. Thirion, J.P.: Image matching as a diffusion process: an analogy with Maxwell's demons. Medical Image Analysis 2(3), 243–260 (1998)
4. Beg, M.F., Miller, M.I., Trouvé, A., Younes, L.: Computing large deformation metric mappings via geodesic flows of diffeomorphisms. International Journal of Computer Vision 61(2), 139–157 (2005)
5. Ashburner, J.: A fast diffeomorphic image registration algorithm. NeuroImage 38(1), 95–113 (2007)
6. Little, J.A., Hill, D.L.G., Hawkes, D.J.: Deformations incorporating rigid structures. In: Computer Vision and Image Understanding, vol. 66, pp. 223–232 (1997)

7. Yoshida, H.: Removal of normal anatomic structures in radiographs using wavelet-based nonlinear variational method for image matching. In: Proceedings of SPIE, vol. 3458, p. 174 (1998)
8. Ashburner, J., Friston, K.J.: Nonlinear spatial normalization using basis functions. Human Brain Mapping 7(4), 254–266 (1999)
9. Rueckert, D., Sonoda, L.I., Hayes, C., Hill, D.L.G., Leach, M.O., Hawkes, D.J.: Nonrigid registration using free-form deformations: application to breast MR images. IEEE Transactions on Medical Imaging 18(8), 712–721 (1999)
10. Wu, Y.T., Kanade, T., Li, C.C., Cohn, J.: Image registration using wavelet-based motion model. International Journal of Computer Vision 38(2), 129–152 (2000)
11. Fornefett, M., Rohr, K., Stiehl, H.S.: Radial basis functions with compact support for elastic registration of medical images. Image and Vision Computing 19(1), 87–96 (2001)
12. Xue, Z., Shen, D., Davatzikos, C.: Statistical representation of high-dimensional deformation fields with application to statistically constrained 3D warping. Medical Image Analysis 10(5), 740–751 (2006)
13. Loeckx, D., Maes, F., Vandermeulen, D., Suetens, P.: Temporal subtraction of thorax CR images using a statistical deformation model. IEEE Transactions on Medical Imaging 22(11), 1490–1504 (2003)
14. Rueckert, D., Frangi, A.F., Schnabel, J.A.: Automatic construction of 3-D statistical deformation models of the brain using nonrigid registration. IEEE Transactions on Medical Imaging 22(8), 1014–1025 (2003)
15. Tang, S., Fan, Y., Wu, G., Kim, M., Shen, D.: RABBIT: rapid alignment of brains by building intermediate templates. NeuroImage 47(4), 1277–1287 (2009)
16. Pszczolkowski, S., Pizarro, L., Guerrero, R., Rueckert, D.: Nonrigid free-form registration using landmark-based statistical deformation models. In: Proceedings of SPIE, vol. 8314, p. 831418 (2012)
17. Tian, Y., Narasimhan, S.G.: A globally optimal data-driven approach for image distortion estimation. In: IEEE Conference on Computer Vision and Pattern Recognition (CVPR), pp. 1277–1284. IEEE (2010)
18. Batmanghelich, N., Taskar, B., Davatzikos, C.: Generative-Discriminative basis learning for medical imaging. IEEE Transactions on Medical Imaging (2011)
19. Wu, G., Qi, F., Shen, D.: Learning Best Features and Deformation Statistics for Hierarchical Registration of MR Brain Images. In: Karssemeijer, N., Lelieveldt, B. (eds.) IPMI 2007. LNCS, vol. 4584, pp. 160–171. Springer, Heidelberg (2007)
20. Ablitt, N.A., Gao, J., Keegan, J., Stegger, L., Firmin, D.N., Yang, G.Z.: Predictive cardiac motion modeling and correction with partial least squares regression. IEEE Transactions on Medical Imaging 23(10), 1315–1324 (2004)
21. Kim, M., Wu, G., Yap, P., Shen, D.: A General Fast Registration framework by learning deformation-appearance correlation. IEEE Transactions on Image Processing (99), 1823–1833 (2011)
22. Zikic, D., Kamen, A., Navab, N.: Natural gradients for deformable registration. In: IEEE Conference on Computer Vision and Pattern Recognition (CVPR), pp. 2847–2854. IEEE (2010)
23. Klein, S., Staring, M., Andersson, P., Pluim, J.P.W.: Preconditioned Stochastic Gradient Descent Optimisation for Monomodal Image Registration. In: Fichtinger, G., Martel, A., Peters, T. (eds.) MICCAI 2011, Part II. LNCS, vol. 6892, pp. 549–556. Springer, Heidelberg (2011)
24. Wahba, G.: Spline models for observational data, vol. 59. Society for Industrial Mathematics (1990)

Learning to Rank from Medical Imaging Data*

Fabian Pedregosa[1,2,4], Elodie Cauvet[3,2], Gaël Varoquaux[1,2],
Christophe Pallier[3,1,2], Bertrand Thirion[1,2], and Alexandre Gramfort[1,2]

[1] Parietal Team, INRIA Saclay-Île-de-France, Saclay, France
fabian.pedregosa@inria.fr
[2] CEA, DSV, I²BM, Neurospin bât 145, 91191 Gif-Sur-Yvette, France
[3] Inserm, U992, Neurospin bât 145, 91191 Gif-Sur-Yvette, France
[4] SIERRA Team, INRIA Paris - Rocquencourt, Paris, France

Abstract. Medical images can be used to predict a clinical score coding
for the severity of a disease, a pain level or the complexity of a cognitive
task. In all these cases, the predicted variable has a natural order. While
a standard classifier discards this information, we would like to take it
into account in order to improve prediction performance. A standard
linear regression does model such information, however the linearity assumption is likely not be satisfied when predicting from pixel intensities
in an image. In this paper we address these modeling challenges with a
supervised learning procedure where the model aims to order or rank images. We use a linear model for its robustness in high dimension and its
possible interpretation. We show on simulations and two fMRI datasets
that this approach is able to predict the correct ordering on pairs of images, yielding higher prediction accuracy than standard regression and
multiclass classification techniques.

Keywords: fMRI, supervised learning, decoding, ranking.

1 Introduction

Statistical machine learning has recently gained interest in the field of medical
image analysis. It is particularly useful for instance to learn imaging biomarkers
for computer aided diagnosis or as a way to obtain additional therapeutic indications. These techniques are particularly relevant in brain imaging [4], where the
complexity of the data renders visual inspection or univariate statistics unreli-
able. A spectacular application of learning from medical images is the prediction
of behavior from functional MRI activations [7]. Such a supervised learning problem can be based on regression [11] or classification tasks [6].

In a classification setting, *e.g.* using support vector machines (SVM) [12], class
labels are treated as an unordered set. However, it is often the case that labels
corresponding to physical quantities can be naturally ordered: clinical scores,
pain levels, the intensity of a stimulus or the complexity of a cognitive task are

* This work was supported by the ViMAGINE ANR- 08-BLAN-0250-02, IRMGroup
ANR-10-BLAN-0126-02 and Construct ANR grants.

F. Wang et al. (Eds.): MLMI 2012, LNCS 7588, pp. 234–241, 2012.

examples of such naturally ordered quantities. Because classification models treat these as a set of classes, the intrinsic order is ignored leading to suboptimal results. On the other hand, in the case of linear regression models such as Lasso [13] or Elastic Net [2], the explained variable is obtained by a linear combination of the variables, the pixel intensities in the present case, which benefits to the interpretability of the model [2, 14]. The limitation of regression models is that they assume linear relationship between the data and the predicted variable. This assumption is a strong limitation in practical cases. For instance, in stroke studies, light disabilities are not well captured by the standard NIHSS score. For this reason most studies use a classification approach, forgoing the quantitative assessment of stroke severity and splitting patients in a small number of different classes. A challenge is therefore to work with a model that is able to learn a non-linear relationship between the data and the target variable.

In this paper, we propose to use a *ranking* strategy to learn from medical imaging data. Ranking is a type of supervised machine learning problem that has been widely used in web search and information retrieval [16, 1] and whose goal is to automatically construct an order from the training data. We first detail how the ranking problem can be solved using binary classifiers applied to pairs of images and then provide empirical evidence on simulated data that our approach outperforms standard regression techniques. Finally, we provide results on two fMRI datasets.

Notations. We write vectors in bold, $a \in \mathbb{R}^n$, matrices with capital bold letters, $A \in \mathbb{R}^{n \times n}$. The dot product between two vectors is denoted $\langle a, b \rangle$. We denote by $\|a\| = \sqrt{\langle a, a \rangle}$ the ℓ_2 norm of a vector.

2 Method: Learning to Rank with a Linear Model

A dataset consists of n images (resp. volumes) containing p pixels (resp. voxels). The matrix formed by all images is denoted $X \in \mathbb{R}^{n \times p}$.

In the supervised learning setting we want to estimate a function f that predicts a target variable from an image, $f : \mathbb{R}^p \to \mathcal{Y}$. For a classification task, $\mathcal{Y} = \{1, 2, 3, ..., k\}$ is a discrete unordered set of labels. The classification error is then given by the number of misclassified images (0-1 loss). On the other hand, for a regression task, $\mathcal{Y}$ is a metric space, typically $\mathbb{R}$, and the loss function can take into account the full metric structure, *e.g.* using the mean squared error.

Here, we consider a problem which shares properties of both cases. As in the classification setting, the class labels form a finite set and as in the regression setting there exists a natural ordering among its elements. One option is to ignore this order and classify each data point into one of the classes. However, this approach ignores valuable structure in the data, which together with the high number of classes and the limited number of images, leads in practice to poor performance. In order to exploit the order of labels, we will use an approach known as *ranking* or *ordinal regression*.

Ranking with binary classifiers. Suppose now that our output space $\mathcal{Y} = \{r_1, r_2, ..., r_k\}$ verifies the ordering $r_1 \leq r_2 \leq .. \leq r_k$ and that $f : \mathbb{R} \to \mathcal{Y}$ is our prediction function. As in [8], we introduce an increasing function $\theta : \mathbb{R} \to \mathbb{R}$ and a linear function $g(\mathbf{x}) = \langle \mathbf{x}, \mathbf{w} \rangle$ which is related to f by

$$f(\mathbf{x}) = r_i \iff g(\mathbf{x}) \in [\theta(r_{i-1}), \theta(r_i)[\tag{1}$$

Given two images $(\mathbf{x}_i, \mathbf{x}_j)$ and their associated labels (y_i, y_j) $(y_i \neq y_j)$ we form a new image $\mathbf{x}_i - \mathbf{x}_j$ with label $\text{sign}(y_i - y_j)$. Because of the linearity of g, predicting the correct ordering of these two images, is equivalent to predicting the sign of $g(\mathbf{x}_i) - g(\mathbf{x}_j) = \langle \mathbf{x}_i - \mathbf{x}_j, \mathbf{w} \rangle$ [8].

The learning problem is now cast into a binary classification task that can be solved using standard supervised classification techniques. If the classifier used in this task is a Support Vector Machine Classifier, the model is also known as *RankSVM*. One of the possible drawbacks of this method is that it requires to consider all possible pairs of images. This scales quadratically with the number of training samples, and the problem soon becomes intractable as the number of samples increases. However, specialized algorithms exist with better asymptotic properties [10]. For our study, we used the Support Vector Machine algorithms proposed by scikit-learn [15].

The main benefit of this approach is that it outputs a linear model even when the function θ is non-linear, and thus ranking approaches are applicable to a wider set of problems than linear regression. Compared to multi-label classification task, where the number of coefficient vectors increase with the number of labels (ranks), the number of coefficients to learn in the pairwise ranking is constant, yielding better-conditioned problems as the number of unique labels increases.

Performance evaluation. Using the linear model previously introduced, we denote the estimated coefficients as $\hat{\mathbf{w}} \in \mathbb{R}^p$. In this case, the prediction function corresponds to the sign of $\langle \mathbf{x}_i - \mathbf{x}_j, \hat{\mathbf{w}} \rangle$. This means that the larger $\langle \mathbf{x}_i, \hat{\mathbf{w}} \rangle$, the more likely the label associated to $\mathbf{x}_i$ is to be high. Because the function θ is non-decreasing, one can project along the vector $\hat{\mathbf{w}}$ to order a sequence of images. The function θ is generally unknown, so this procedure does not directly give the class labels. However, under special circumstances (as is the case in our empirical study), for example when there is a fixed number of samples per class this can be used to recover the target values.

Since our ranking model operates naturally on pairs of images, we will define an evaluation measure as the mean number of label inversions. Formally, let $(\mathbf{x}_i, y_i)_{i=1,...,n}$ denote the validation dataset and $\mathcal{P} = \{(i, j) \text{ s.t. } y_i \neq y_j\}$ the set of pairs with different labels. The prediction accuracy is defined as the percentage of incorrect orderings for pairs of images. When working with such a performance metric, the chance level is at 50% and the error is defined as $\# \{(i, j) \in \mathcal{P} \text{ s.t. } (y_i - y_j)(f(\mathbf{x}_j) - f(\mathbf{x}_i))\rangle < 0\} / \# \mathcal{P}$

Model selection. The Ranking SVM model has one regularization parameter denoted C, which we set by nested cross-validation on a grid of 50 geometrically-spaced values between 10^{-3} and 10^3. We use 5-folds splitting of the data: 60% of the data is used for training, 20% for parameter selection and 20% for validation. To establish significant differences between methods we perform 20 such random data splits.

3 Results

We present results on simulated fMRI data and two fMRI datasets.

3.1 Simulation Study

Data generation The simulated data $\mathbf{X}$ contains $n = 300$ volumes (size $7 \times 7 \times 7$), each one consisting of Gaussian white noise smoothed by a Gaussian kernel with standard deviation of 2 voxels. This mimics the spatial correlation structure observed in real fMRI data. The simulated vector of coefficients $\mathbf{w}$ has a support restricted to four cubic Regions of Interest (ROIs) of size $(2 \times 2 \times 2)$. The values of $\mathbf{w}$ restricted to these ROIs are $\{5, 5, -5, -5\}$.

We define the target value $\mathbf{y} \in \mathbb{R}^n$ as a logistic function of $\mathbf{Xw}$:

$$\mathbf{y} = \frac{1}{1 + \exp\left(-\mathbf{Xw}\right)} + \epsilon \tag{2}$$

where $\epsilon \in \mathbb{R}^n$ is a Gaussian noise with standard deviation $\gamma > 0$ chosen such that the signal-to-noise ratio verifies $\|\epsilon\|/\|\sqrt{\mathbf{Xw}}\| = 10\%$. Finally, we split the 300 generated images into a training set of 240 images and a validation set of other 60 images.

Results. We compare the ranking framework presented previously with standard approaches. Ridge regression was chosen for its widespread use as a regression technique applied to fMRI data. Due to the non-linear relationship between the data and the target values, we also selected a non-linear regression model: support vector regression (SVR) with a Gaussian kernel [5]. Finally, we also considered classification models such as multi-class support vector machines. However, due to the large number of classes and the limited number of training samples, these methods were not competitive against its regression counterpart and were not included in the final comparison.

One issue when comparing different models is the qualitatively different variables they estimate: in the regression case it is a continuous variable whereas in the ranking settings it is a discrete set of class labels. To make both comparable, a score function that is applicable to both models must be used. In this case, we used as performance measure the percentage of incorrect orderings for pairs as defined in the performance evaluation paragraph.

Figure 1-a describes the performance error of the different models mentioned earlier as a function of number of images in the training data. We considered a validation set of 60 images and varied the number of samples in the training set from 40 to 240. With a black dashed line we denote the optimal prediction error, i.e. the performance of an oracle with perfect knowledge of $\mathbf{w}$. This error is

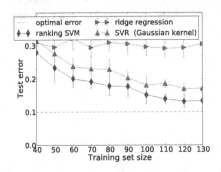 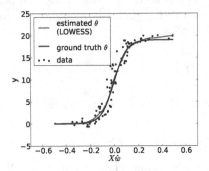

Fig. 1. a) Prediction accuracy as the training size increases. Ranking SVM performs consistently better than the alternative methods, converging faster to the empirical optimal error. b) Estimation of the θ function using non-parametric local regression and ranking SVM. As expected, we recover the logistic function introduced in the data generation section.

non zero due to noise. All of the model parameters were set by cross-validation on the training set. The figure not only shows that Ranking SVM converges to an optimal model (statistical consistency for prediction), but also that it converges faster, *i.e.* has lower sample complexity than alternative approaches, thus it should be able to detect statistical effects with less data. Gaussian kernel SVR performs better than ridge regression and also reaches the optimal error. However, the underlying model of SVR is not linear and is therefore not well-suited for interpretation [2]; moreover, it is less stable to high-dimensional data.

As stated previously, the function θ can be estimated from the data. In Fig. 1-b we use the knowledge of target values from the validation dataset to estimate this function. Specifically, we display class labels as a function of $\mathbf{X}\hat{w}$ and regularize the result using a local regression (LOWESS). Both estimated function and ground truth overlap for most part of the domain.

3.2   Results on Two Functional MRI Datasets

To assess the performance of ranking strategy on real data, we investigate two fMRI datasets. The first dataset, described in [3], consists of 34 healthy volunteers scanned while listening to 16 words sentences with five different levels of complexity. These were 1 word constituent phrases (the simplest), 2 words, 4 words, 8 words and 16 words respectively, corresponding to 5 levels of complexity which was used as class label in our experiments. To clarify, a sentence with 16 words using 2 words constituents is formed by a series of 8 pairs of words. Words in each pair have a common meaning but there is meaning between each pair. A sentence has therefore the highest complexity when all the 16 words form a meaningful sentence.

The second dataset is described in [17] and further studied in [9] is a gambling task where each of the 17 subjects was asked to accept or reject gambles

Table 1. Prediction accuracy of the ranking strategy on two real fMRI datasets: language complexity (lang. comp.) in 3 ROIs and gambles. As a comparison, scores obtained with alternative regression techniques (ridge regression and SVR using a non-linear Gaussian kernel) are presented. As confirmed by a Wilcoxon paired test between errors obtained for each fold using Ranking SVM and ridge regression, Ranking SVM leads to significantly better scores than other approaches on 4 of the 5 experiments.

	RankSVM	Ridge	SVR	P-val
lang. comp (aSTS)	**0.706**	0.661	0.625	2e-3***
lang. comp. (TP)	**0.687**	0.645	0.618	7e-4***
lang. comp. (IFGorb)	**0.619**	0.609	0.539	0.3
lang. comp. (IFG tri)	**0.585**	0.566	0.533	5e-2*
gambling	**0.58**	0.56	0.53	1e-2**

that offered a 50/50 chance of gaining or losing money. The magnitude of the potential gain and loss was independently varied across 16 levels between trials. No outcomes of these gambles were presented during scanning, but after the scan three gambles were selected at random and played for real money. Each gamble has an amount that can be used as class label. In this experiment, we only considered gain levels, yielding 8 different class labels. This dataset is publicly available from http://openfmri.org as the *mixed-gambles task* dataset. The features used in both experiments are SPM β-maps, *a.k.a.* GLM regression coefficients.

Both of these datasets can be investigated with ranking, multi-label classification or regression. We compared the approaches of regression and ranking to test if the added flexibility of the ranking model translates into greater statistical power. Due to the high number of classes and limited number of samples, we found out that multi-label classification did not perform significantly better than chance and thus was not further considered.

To minimize the effects that are non-specific to the task we only consider pairs of images from the same subject.

The first dataset contains four manually labeled regions of interest: Anterior Superior Temporal Sulcus (aSTS), Temporal Pole (TP), Inferior Frontal Gyrus Orbitalis (IFGorb) and Inferior Frontal Gyrus triangularis (IFG tri). We then compare ranking, ridge regression and Gaussian kernel SVR models on each ROI separately. Those results appear in the first three rows of Table 1 and are denoted as language complexity with its corresponding ROI in parenthesis. We observe that the ranking model obtains a significant advantage on 3 of the 4 ROIs. This could be explained by a relatively linear effect in IFGorb or a higher noise level.The last row concerns the second dataset, denoted gambling, where we selected the gain experiment (8 class labels). In this case, since we were not presented manually labeled regions of interest, we performed univariate dimensionality reduction to 500 voxels using ANOVA before fitting the learning models. It can be seen that the prediction accuracy are lower compared to the first dataset. Ranking SVM however still outperforms alternative methods. Locations in the brain of the ROIs for the first dataset, with a color coding for their

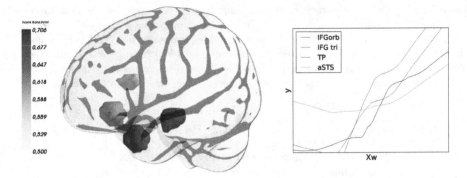

Fig. 2. a) Scores obtained with the Ranking SVM on the 4 different ROIs. The regions with the best predictive power are the temporal pole the anterior superior temporal sulcus. b) The target variable **y** as a function of **Xŵ** for the four regions of interest. We observe that the shape of the curves varies across brain regions.

predictive power are presented in Fig. 2-a. As shown previously in the simulated dataset, Fig. 2-b shows the validation data projected along the coefficients of the linear model and regularized using LOWESS local regression for each one of the four highest ranked regions of interest. Results show that the link function between **Xŵ** and the target variable **y** (denoted θ in the methods section) varies in shape across ROIs, suggesting that the BOLD response is not unique over the brain.

4   Discussion and Conclusion

In this paper, we describe a ranking strategy that addresses a common use case in the statistical analysis of medical images, which is the prediction of an ordered target variable. Our contribution is to formulate the variable quantification problem as a ranking problem. We present a formulation of the ranking problem that transforms the task into a binary classification problem over pairs of images. This approach makes it possible to use efficient linear classifiers while coping with non-linearities in the data. By doing so we retain the interpretability and favorable behavior in high-dimension of linear models.

From a statistical standpoint, mining medical images is challenging due to the high dimensionality of the data, often thousands of variables, while the number of images available for training is small, typically a few hundreds. In this regard, the benefit of our approach is to retain a linear model with few parameters. It is thus better suited to medical images than multi-class classification.

On simulations we have shown that our problem formulation leads to a better prediction accuracy and lower sample complexity than alternative approaches such as regression or classification techniques. We apply this method to two fMRI datasets and discuss practical considerations when dealing with fMRI data. We confirm the superior prediction accuracy compared to standard regression techniques.

References

1. Burges, C.J.C.: From RankNet to LambdaRank to LambdaMART: An overview. Learning 11(MSR-TR-2010-82), 23–581 (2010)
2. Carroll, M.K., Cecchi, G.A., Rish, I., Garg, R., Rao, A.R.: Prediction and interpretation of distributed neural activity with sparse models. NeuroImage 44(1), 112–122 (2009)
3. Cauvet, E.: Traitement des Structures Syntaxiques dans le langage et dans la musique. Ph.D. thesis, Ecole doctorale n158, Cerveau - Cognition - Comportement (2012)
4. Cuingnet, R., Rosso, C., Chupin, M., Lehéricy, S., Dormont, D., Benali, H., Samson, Y., Colliot, O.: Spatial regularization of SVM for the detection of diffusion alterations associated with stroke outcome. Medical Image Analysis (2011)
5. Drucker, H., Burges, C.J.C., Kaufman, L., Smola, A.J., Vapnik, V.: Support vector regression machines. In: NIPS, pp. 155–161 (1996)
6. Haxby, J.V., Gobbini, M.I., Furey, M.L., Ishai, A., Schouten, J.L., Pietrini, P.: Distributed and Overlapping Representations of Faces and Objects in Ventral Temporal Cortex. Science 293(5539), 2425–2430 (2001)
7. Haynes, J.D., Rees, G.: Decoding mental states from brain activity in humans. Nat. Rev. Neurosci. 7, 523 (2006)
8. Herbrich, R., Graepel, T., Obermayer, K.: Large margin rank boundaries for ordinal regression, vol. 88, pp. 115–132. MIT Press, Cambridge (2000)
9. Jimura, K., Poldrack, R.A.: Analyses of regional-average activation and multivoxel pattern information tell complementary stories. Neuropsychologia, 1–9 (2011)
10. Joachims, T.: Training linear SVMs in linear time. In: Proceedings of the 12th ACM SIGKDD International Conference on Knowledge Discovery and Data Mining, KDD 2006, pp. 217–226. ACM, New York (2006)
11. Kay, K.N., Naselaris, T., Prenger, R.J., Gallant, J.L.: Identifying natural images from human brain activity. Nature 452, 352–355 (2008)
12. LaConte, S., Strother, S., Cherkassky, V., Anderson, J., Hu, X.: Support vector machines for temporal classification of block design fMRI data. NeuroImage 26(2), 317–329 (2005)
13. Liu, H., Palatucci, M., Zhang, J.: Blockwise coordinate descent procedures for the multi-task lasso, with applications to neural semantic basis discovery. In: Proceedings of the 26th Annual International Conference on Machine Learning, ICML 2009, pp. 649–656. ACM, New York (2009)
14. Michel, V., Gramfort, A., Varoquaux, G., Eger, E., Thirion, B.: Total variation regularization for fMRI-based prediction of behaviour. IEEE Transactions on Medical Imaging 30(7), 1328–1340 (2011)
15. Pedregosa, F., Varoquaux, G., Gramfort, A., Michel, V., Thirion, B., Grisel, O., Blondel, M., Prettenhofer, P., Weiss, R., Dubourg, V., Vanderplas, J., Passos, A., Cournapeau, D., Brucher, M., Perrot, M., Duchesnay, E.: Scikit-learn: Machine Learning in Python. Journal of Machine Learning Research 12, 2825–2830 (2011)
16. Richardson, M., Prakash, A., Brill, E.: Beyond PageRank: machine learning for static ranking. In: WWW 2006, pp. 707–715. ACM, New York (2006)
17. Tom, S.M., Fox, C.R., Trepel, C., Poldrack, R.A.: The neural basis of loss aversion in decision-making under risk. Science 315(5811), 515–518 (2007)

Integrating Statistical Shape Models into a Graph Cut Framework for Tooth Segmentation

Johannes Keustermans[1], Dirk Vandermeulen[1], and Paul Suetens[2]

[1] KU Leuven, Faculty of Engineering, ESAT - PSI, Leuven, Belgium
[2] IBBT-KU Leuven Future Health department, Leuven, Belgium
johannes.keustermans@esat.kuleuven.be

Abstract. The segmentation of teeth is of great importance for the computer aided planning of dental implants, orthodontic treatment, and orthognathic surgery. However, it is hampered by metallic streak artifacts present in Computed Tomography (CT) images in general, and the lack of contrast between the teeth and bone in Cone-Beam CT (CBCT) images particularly. Therefore, we propose a novel graph cut based algorithm that effectively integrates a statistical shape model based on a probabilistic shape representation. The statistical shape model is obtained from a set of training samples and imposes a Gaussian distribution on the shape space. The presented algorithm minimises an energy function that is formulated according to a maximum a posteriori criterion and consists of three terms: an image likelihood term, a segmentation likelihood term integrating the shape model into the graph cut framework, and a shape model term favoring shapes that are more likely according to the statistical shape model.

1 Introduction

Recently, three-dimensional orthognathic surgery and dental implant planning software systems became available, enabling visualization, quantification, non-invasive diagnosis, treatment planning, and evaluation of treatment outcome in an unprecedented way. The introduction of Cone-Beam Computed Tomography (CBCT) has instigated a breakthrough towards the routine use of these three-dimensional treatment planning software systems, due to the low radiation dose, unique accessibility and low cost. The segmentation of teeth from CBCT images is of particular interest for these software systems as it may significantly broaden or help their applicability, e.g. virtual tooth extraction, dental implant planning, and orthodontic treatment planning and evaluation. Yet, the segmentation of teeth from CBCT images is challenging problem, as it is hampered by various factors. First, the presence of metal streak artifacts in the CBCT images, caused by orthodontic braces or dental fillings. Next, since the teeth are anchored in the jaw bone there is only little contrast between the bone and the teeth, predominantly at the level of the apex. Subsequently, the signal to noise ratio of CBCT images is in general lower compared to CT images. Finally, the shape of teeth shows a significant variability over individuals. In the literature a number of methods for the segmentation of teeth have been proposed [1,2]. To our knowledge, however, none of these methods are capable of coping with the mentioned problems.

F. Wang et al. (Eds.): MLMI 2012, LNCS 7588, pp. 242–250, 2012.

Since a manual segmentation is very time-consuming and subjective, hindered even more by the dimensionality and size of the CBCT images, as well as the number of teeth, there is a strong need for an automated or semi-automated approach. In the last decades the computer vision community has produced a large variety of image segmentation algorithms. Earlier approaches to the segmentation problem are based on heuristic rules. Despite being not robust, these methods are still widely known and used in practice due to their simplicity, predictability, and speed. More recently, optimization methods have become established as being more powerful and mathematically sound. These algorithms minimize an appropriate energy function, leading to an optimal image segmentation in some sense. The Bayesian formulation of the energy function allows to introduce prior shape knowledge into the image segmentation framework. To make the algorithm as generic as possible, a statistical learning approach can be used, in which the prior shape knowledge can be obtained from training data.

This paper presents an algorithm that integrates a statistical shape model into the graph cut framework. The graph cut algorithm defines a graph $\mathcal{G} = \{\mathcal{V}, \mathcal{E}\}$ consisting of a set of nodes $\mathcal{V}$, representing image voxels, and a set of edges $\mathcal{E}$ connecting neighboring nodes. Two extra terminal nodes s (*source*) and t (*sink*) are added, representing the object and background label. All edges $e \in \mathcal{E}$ are assigned some non-negative weight w_e. The goal of the graph cut algorithm is the optimal separation of source and sink by slicing a set of edges that no remaining path exists between the source and the sink. The cost of a cut $\mathcal{C}$ is defined by the sum of the weights of the edges sliced by the cut. This cut can be computed efficiently in low order polynomial time using the max-flow/min-cut algorithm [3].

Integrating statistical shape models into the graph cut framework is not straightforward. Malcolm et al. [4] present an interactive graph cut framework employing statistical shape models based on an implicit shape representation. Freedman et al. [5] integrate a deformable template based on an implicit representation into the interactive graph cut framework. Although not based on graph cuts, Schoenemann et al. [6] present a model-based segmentation algorithm providing global minima. First, however, only a deformable template is used compared to the statistical shape models used in this work. Second, the algorithm is inherently two dimensional, so extending the method to higher dimensions is not straightforward.

Compared to previous work we have chosen to integrate a statistical shape model based on a probabilistic shape representation reflecting the probability of a point to belong to the object boundary, originally presented by Hufnagel et al. [7], into the graph cut framework. As such, we retain advantages of both explicit and implicit shape representations combined with an effective optimization algorithm. The segmentation algorithm presented in this paper is applied to the segmentation of teeth from CBCT images. The organization of this paper is as follows. Section 2 presents the statistical shape model. Section 3 further details the segmentation algorithm itself. Subsequently, section 4 discusses some experiments and results. Finally, section 5 formulates a conclusion and some ideas for future work.

2 Statistical Model Building

This section presents the procedure for constructing the statistical shape models. This procedure was originally presented by Hufnagel et al. [7], and is extended here. A clear distinction is made between the observation parameters and the model parameters. Since the proposed statistical shape model imposes a Gaussian distribution on the shape space, the set of model parameters Θ consists of the mean shape $\bar{M} = \{\bar{\mathbf{m}}_j\}_{j=1}^{N_m}$, the eigenmodes $v_p = \{\mathbf{v}_{pj}\}_{j=1}^{N_m}$, the eigenvalues λ_p and the number of eigenmodes n. The observation parameters $Q = \{Q_k\}_{k=1}^{N}$ are the bandwidth parameters σ_k, the rigid transformations $T_k = \{\mathbf{R}_k, \mathbf{t}_k\}$, and the deformation coefficients $W_k = \{w_{kp}\}_{p=1}^{n}$ with respect to the eigenmodes that fit the statistical shape model to each of the training samples $\mathcal{S}_k = \{\mathbf{s}_{ki}\}_{i=1}^{N_k}$. Unlike Hufnagel et al., the bandwidth parameters are training sample specific, and included with the observation parameters. As such, their values are estimated in an optimal and automated manner. In order to optimize both model and observation parameters a maximum a posteriori criterion is formulated

$$p(Q, \Theta | \mathcal{S}) = p(\Theta) \prod_{k=1}^{N} \frac{p(\mathcal{S}_k | Q_k, \Theta) \, p(Q_k | \Theta)}{p(\mathcal{S}_k)} \; . \tag{1}$$

The term $p(Q_k | \Theta)$ can be further expressed according to the Gaussian shape model and by assuming a constant prior for the rigid transformations. Furthermore, the term $p(\mathcal{S}_k | Q_k, \Theta)$ can be further expressed by imposing the probabilistic object representation based on a kernel density estimator with Gaussian kernels

$$p(\mathcal{S}_k | Q_k, \Theta) = \prod_{i=1}^{N_k} p(\mathbf{s}_{ki} | Q_k, \Theta) = \prod_{i=1}^{N_k} \sum_{j=1}^{N_m+1} p(j) \, p(\mathbf{s}_{ki} | j, Q_k, \Theta) \; , \tag{2}$$

where $p(j)$ are equal membership probabilities, and $p(\boldsymbol{x} | N_m + 1, Q_k, \Theta) = \frac{1}{N_m}$ is a uniform (pseudo) outlier distribution. Unlike Hufnagel et al., an outlier distribution is added to improve the robustness against outliers. The term $p(\boldsymbol{x} | Q_k, \Theta)$ can be further expanded as,

$$p(\boldsymbol{x} | Q_k, \Theta) = \frac{1-\omega}{N_m} \sum_{j=1}^{N_m} \frac{\exp\left(-\frac{\|\mathbf{s}_{ki} - \mathbf{R}_k \mathbf{m}_{kj} - \mathbf{t}_k\|^2}{2\sigma_k^2}\right)}{\left(2\pi\sigma_k^2\right)^{d/2}} + \frac{\omega}{N_m} \; , \tag{3}$$

where $0 \leq \omega \leq 1$ is parameter balancing the relative importance of the (pseudo) outlier distribution. Furthermore, $\mathbf{m}_{kj}$ can be expanded as a linear combination of the principal components and the mean, $\mathbf{m}_{kj} = \bar{\mathbf{m}}_j + \sum_{p=1}^{n} w_{kp} \mathbf{v}_{pj}$.

Assuming $p(\Theta)$ to be uniform and taking the negative logarithm yields the energy function to be minimized. Unlike Hufnagel et al., the energy function is optimized using the EM algorithm [8]. In the E-step an optimal upper bound to the energy function is formulated, by applying Jensen's inequality and introducing specific probability distributions $q_k(i,j)$, representing probabilistic correspondences. The probabilistic correspondences $q_k(i,j)$ are determined as to optimize the upper bound that it touches the energy function using the current model Θ^t and observation parameters Q^t and adding the constraints $\sum_{i=1}^{N_k} q_k(i,j) = 1$ and $\sum_{j=1}^{N_m+1} q_k(i,j) = 1$. As such, the E-step consists of iterating the following equations until convergence

$$\hat{q}_k^{t+\frac{1}{2}}(i,j) = \frac{\hat{q}_k^t(i,j)}{\sum_{j=1}^{N_m} \hat{q}_k^t(i,j) + \frac{\omega(2\pi\sigma_k^2)^{d/2}}{1-\omega}} \quad \text{and} \quad \hat{q}_k^{t+1}(i,j) = \frac{\hat{q}_k^{t+\frac{1}{2}}(i,j)}{\sum_{j=1}^{N_m} \hat{q}_k^{t+\frac{1}{2}}(i,j)},$$

$$(4)$$

where $\hat{q}_k^0(i,j) = \exp\left(-\frac{\|\mathbf{s}_{ki} - \mathbf{m}_{kj}\|^2}{2\sigma_k^2}\right)$. This approach is similar to the softassign approach of Chui et al. [9], and leads to more accurate probabilistic correspondences compared to Hufnagel et al. [7]. In the M-step the obtained upper bound is minimized with respect to the observation parameters Q and the model parameters Θ while keeping, respectively, Θ and Q fixed. This upper bound can be formulated as

$$C_k^M(Q_k, \Theta) \simeq \frac{1}{2\sigma_k^2} \sum_{i=1}^{N_k} \sum_{j=1}^{N_m} q_k(i,j) \| \mathbf{s}_{ki} - \mathbf{R}_k\mathbf{m}_{kj} - \mathbf{t}_k \|^2 +$$

$$\frac{N_{qk}d}{2}\log(\sigma_k^2) + \sum_{p=1}^{n}\left(\log(\lambda_p) + \frac{w_{kp}^2}{2\lambda_p^2}\right), \quad (5)$$

where $N_{qk} = \sum_{i=1}^{N_k} \sum_{j=1}^{N_m} q_k(i,j)$. Closed-form solutions for almost all parameters can be obtained. For the rotation matrix $\mathbf{R}_k$ and translation vector $\mathbf{t}_k$, the expressions are similar to the rigid coherent point drift algorithm [10]. For the bandwidth parameter σ_k the following expression can be derived

$$\sigma_k = \sqrt{\frac{1}{N_{qk}d} \sum_{i=1}^{N_k} \sum_{j=1}^{N_m} q_{ki}(j) \| \mathbf{s}_{ki} - \mathbf{m}_{kj} \|^2}. \quad (6)$$

For the deformation coefficients, as well as all model parameters we refer to Hufnagel et al. [7], since similar expressions are obtained, differing only in the probabilistic correspondences $q_k(i,j)$.

3   Image Segmentation

This section will provide details of the energy function and the optimization thereof. In the following paragraphs we will formulate this energy function and derive expressions for the edge weights in the graph cut framework. The objective of the presented algorithm is the optimal segmentation of teeth from CBCT images according to some criterion. This criterion is formulated through a maximum a posteriori probability formulation of the segmentation $\phi : \Omega \mapsto \{0, 1\}$ and the observation parameters Q given the image $\mathcal{I} : \Omega \mapsto \mathbb{R}$ and the shape model Θ. The segmentation ϕ is evolved such that $p(\phi, Q|\mathcal{I}, \Theta)$ is maximal which, according to the rule of Bayes, can be stated as follows:

$$\arg\max_{\phi, Q} \frac{p(\mathcal{I}|\phi, Q, \Theta)\, p(\phi|Q, \Theta)\, p(Q|\Theta)}{p(\mathcal{I})}. \quad (7)$$

Since the observation parameters Q and the shape model Θ do not add any information when the segmentation ϕ is known, $\mathcal{I}$ is conditionally independent with respect to Q and Θ. Therefore, and since $p\left(\mathcal{I}\right)$ is constant, $p\left(\phi, Q | \mathcal{I}, \Theta\right)$ can be expressed as

$$p\left(\phi, Q | \mathcal{I}, \Theta\right) \propto p\left(\mathcal{I} | \phi\right) p\left(\phi | Q, \Theta\right) p\left(Q | \Theta\right) . \tag{8}$$

Maximization of the probability is converted to energy minimization by taking the negative logarithm of equation 8. The following paragraphs formulate expressions for the different terms of this energy function.

3.1 Image Likelihood Term

The term $p\left(\mathcal{I} | \phi\right)$ of equation 8 is the image likelihood. Since the main contribution of this paper lies in the integration of statistical shape models into the graph cut framework, we restrict ourselves to a simple term. Therefore we exploit the knowledge that object boundaries typically coincide with edges in the image and is based on an edge detector function $g\left(|\nabla I|\right)$.

$$E\left(I, \phi\right) = \int_{\partial \Omega} g\left(|\nabla I|\right) \mathrm{dx} , \tag{9}$$

where $\partial \Omega$ denotes the segmentation boundary. To translate this image likelihood term into edge weights for the *n-links* we can use the geo-cut method of Boykov et al. [11]. It should be noted that the image likelihood supports a variety of different energy terms, such as regional ones. This is application specific and can greatly improve the segmentation outcome.

3.2 Segmentation Likelihood Term

The second term $p\left(\phi | Q, \Theta\right)$ of equation 8 is the segmentation likelihood, and connects the segmentation and the statistical shape model. Due to the probabilistic shape representation reflecting the probability of a point to belong to the object boundary, the shape model nicely integrates in the graph cut framework. As such we can formulate

$$p\left(\phi | Q, \Theta\right) = \prod_{e \in \mathcal{C}_n} p\left(e | Q, \Theta\right) , \tag{10}$$

where $\mathcal{C}_n$ is the subset of *n-links* belonging to the cut corresponding to segmentation ϕ and $p\left(e | Q, \Theta\right)$ is the probability of cutting edge $e \in \mathcal{E}$ given the observation parameters Q and the shape model Θ. This probability is given by the sum of the probabilities for each point along the edge to belong to the object boundary.

$$p\left(e | Q, \Theta\right) = \int_0^1 p\left(u\left(\mathbf{h_e} - \mathbf{t_e}\right) + \mathbf{t_e} | Q, \Theta\right) \mathrm{d}u . \tag{11}$$

where u is the parametrization variable and $\mathbf{t}_e$ and $\mathbf{h}_e$, respectively, are the tail and head node of edge e. This can be further expressed as

$$p\left(e | Q, \Theta\right) = \sum_{j=1}^{N_m} \frac{|\mathbf{a}_e| e^{\left(-\frac{|\mathbf{a}_e \times \mathbf{b}_e^j|^2}{\sigma^2}\right)}}{N_m 2 \pi \sigma^2} \left(\mathrm{erf}\left(\frac{|\mathbf{a}_e|^2 + \mathbf{a}_e \cdot \mathbf{b}_e^j}{\sigma}\right) - \mathrm{erf}\left(\frac{\mathbf{a}_e \cdot \mathbf{b}_e^j}{\sigma}\right)\right) , \tag{12}$$

where $\mathbf{a}_e = \mathbf{h}_e - \mathbf{t}_e$, $\mathbf{b}_e^j = \mathbf{t}_e - \mathbf{m}_j$, $\sigma_e = \sqrt{2}\sigma|\mathbf{a}_e|$, $|\mathbf{x}|$ is the norm of vector $\mathbf{x}$, $\mathbf{x} \cdot \mathbf{y}$ is the dot product and $\mathbf{x} \times \mathbf{y}$ is the cross product between vectors $\mathbf{x}$ and $\mathbf{y}$.

Taking the negative logarithm of equation 10 converts the probability of a cut given the observation and model parameters into the energy of the cut. From this energy function, the weights assigned to the *n-links* e can be defined in a straightforward manner as $w_e = -\log\left(p\left(e|Q, \Theta\right)\right)$. As such, an effective means for the integration of a statistical shape model into the graph cut framework is achieved. However, a bias is introduced favoring shorter object contours, as can be seen from equation (10). This is also reflected in the work of Hufnagel et al. [12], as can be seen from the curvature term in equation 7.

3.3 Shape Model Prior Term

The term $p\left(Q|\Theta\right)$ favors objects that are more probable according to the statistical shape model. Again assuming a constant prior for transformations leads to the following equation

$$\log\left(p\left(Q|\Theta\right)\right) \simeq \sum_{p=1}^{n} \left(\log\left(\lambda_p\right) + \frac{w_p^2}{2\lambda_p^2}\right) , \tag{13}$$

with $Q = \{T, W\}$ and $W = \{w_p\}_{p=1}^n$, being the observation parameters. This term does not influence the edge weights of the graph.

3.4 Optimization

The statistical shape model term in the energy function enforces an iterative optimization procedure. In each iteration, starting from an initial segmentation, alternatively the observation parameters Q and the segmentation ϕ are optimized while keeping, respectively, ϕ and Q fixed. The observation parameters are optimized in a similar manner as explained in section 2. Optimization of the segmentation is performed by the max-flow/min-cut algorithm [3]. Although the graph cut algorithm provides global minima, since an iterative optimization is pursued, depending upon the initialization, only local minima can be proven to be obtained.

The statistical shape model in this framework causes the next segmentation boundary after a complete iteration to be located close to the current segmentation boundary. Therefore, computing the edge weights throughout the entire graph and applying the max-flow/min-cut algorithm to the full graph is not needed. In order to enforce a significant speedup of the algorithm, a narrow-band approach is pursued.

3.5 Initialization

As stated above, the outcome of the optimization is highly dependent upon the initialization. Therefore the initialization procedure is an important aspect of the algorithm. Different approaches can be used in order to provide a fast, yet accurate initial segmentation. Here we used the interactive graph cut segmentation algorithm of Boykov et al. [3]. Hereby, based on the edge-consistency prior explained in paragraph 3.1 and manually indicated seed points an initial segmentation is obtained. These manually indicated seed points are included in the graph cut framework as hard constraints, by setting the weights of the corresponding *t-links* to $+\infty$.

4   Experiments and Results

The segmentation algorithm presented in this paper is applied to the segmentation of teeth from Cone-Beam Computed Tomography (CBCT) images. A training data set of 22 patients is used of which the upper and lower left incisors, canines, premolars and molars are manually segmented. Since a manual segmentation of all left teeth is available, statistical shape models of the right teeth can be obtained as well, by a simple mirroring operation. Training the algorithm on all except one of the training samples and testing on the remaining data sample produces the results shown in figure 1. The leave-one-out validation results for all left teeth are provided in table 1. Here the Dice coefficient is used to measure the overlap between the ground truth (manual) segmentation and the segmentation provided by the algorithm. The results for the lower teeth are slightly worse compared to the upper teeth. The main reason for this is the lower contrast between the bone and teeth in the lower jaw compared to the upper jaw. Comparison to the results reported by Gao et al. [1] reveals a seemingly inferior performance of the algorithm presented in this paper. However, comparison of the results is not straightforward. At first, the algorithm presented in this paper is validated on a different data set. Second, the data set used by Gao et al. [1] does not contain orthodontic braces. Third, no range of results is reported by Gao et al. Fourth, a more advanced image likelihood term will most likely further improve the results, but was not the main scope of this paper.

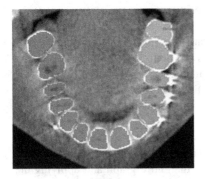

Fig. 1. Segmentation of teeth in a CBCT image. A single slice is shown with a different color for each tooth. The metallic streak artefacts caused by the othodontic braces are visible.

Table 1. Validation results for the algorithm presented in this paper obtained from a leave-one-out approach applied to the training data. For each tooth the Dice coefficient is given as a measure of overlap between the ground truth (manual) segmentation and the segmentation provided by the algorithm.

Tooth	Root number	Dice coefficient
incisor 1 (lower)	1	0.8535 ± 0.0302
incisor 2 (lower)	1	0.8047 ± 0.1057
canine (lower)	1	0.8625 ± 0.1004
premolar (lower)	1	0.8369 ± 0.2164
molar (lower)	2	0.8522 ± 0.0766
incisor 1 (upper)	1	0.8820 ± 0.0332
incisor 2 (upper)	1	0.8734 ± 0.0641
canine (upper)	1	0.8882 ± 0.0431
premolar (upper)	1 or 2	0.8780 ± 0.0331
molar (upper)	2 or 3	0.8517 ± 0.0588

5   Discussion

In this paper a novel graph cut based segmentation algorithm is presented for the segmentation of teeth from CBCT images. Using a probabilistic shape representation a statistical shape model is constructed that integrates into the graph cut framework. The algorithm optimizes an energy function, formulated according to a maximum a posteriori criterion. This energy function consists of three components: an image likelihood, a shape model term, and a segmentation likelihood term efficiently integrating the shape model into the graph cut framework. The energy function is optimized in an iterative manner. In future work we would like to extend this framework. At first, the linear shape model is not perfectly suited to segment objects that arise from a complex underlying distribution. We therefore would like to extend the probabilistic object representation framework to nonlinear shape models. Next, the image likelihood term is very general and can easily be replaced by a variant more tailored to a specific application. Finally, since the segmentation likelihood term introduces a shrinking bias, favoring objects with shorter contours, we would like to circumvent this. However, care must be taken in order to ensure that the derived metric is graph-representable.

References

1. Gao, H., Chae, O.: Individual tooth segmentation from ct images using level set method with shape and intensity prior. Pattern Recognition 43(7), 2406–2417 (2010)
2. Hosntalab, M., Zoroofi, R.A., Tehrani-Fard, A.A., Shirani, G.: Segmentation of teeth in ct volumetric dataset by panoramic projection and variational level set. International Journal on Computer Assisted Radiology and Surgery 3(3-4), 257–265 (2008)
3. Boykov, Y., Funka-Leah, G.: Graph cuts and efficient n-d image segmentation. International Journal of Computer Vision 70(2), 109–131 (2006)
4. Malcolm, J., Rathi, Y., Tannenbaum, A.: Graph cut segmentation with nonlinear shape priors. In: IEEE International Conference on Image Processing, vol. 4, pp. 365–368 (2007)
5. Freedman, D., Zhang, T.: Interactive Graph Cut Based Segmentation with Shape Priors. In: CVPR 2005: Proceedings of the 2005 IEEE Computer Society Conference on Computer Vision and Pattern Recognition (CVPR 2005), vol. 1, pp. 755–762. IEEE Computer Society (2005)
6. Schoenemann, T., Cremers, D.: A combinatorial solution for model-based image segmentation and real-time tracking. IEEE Transactions on Pattern Analysis and Machine Intelligence 32(7), 1153–1164 (2010)
7. Hufnagel, H., Pennec, X., Ehrhardt, J., Handels, H., Ayache, N.: Shape Analysis Using a Point-Based Statistical Shape Model Built on Correspondence Probabilities. In: Ayache, N., Ourselin, S., Maeder, A. (eds.) MICCAI 2007, Part I. LNCS, vol. 4791, pp. 959–967. Springer, Heidelberg (2007)
8. Dempster, A.P., Laird, N.M., Rubin, D.B.: Maximum likelihood from incomplete data via the em algorithm. Journal of the Royal Statistical Society, Series B 39(1), 1–38 (1977)
9. Chui, H., Rangarajan, A.: A new point matching algorithm for non-rigid registration. Computer Vision and Image Understanding 89(2-3), 114–141 (2003)
10. Myronenko, A., Song, X.: Point set registration: Coherent point drift. IEEE Transactions on Pattern Analysis and Machine Intelligence 32(12), 2262–2275 (2010)
11. Boykov, Y., Kolmogorov, V.: Computing geodesics and minimal surfaces via graph cuts. In: Proceedings of International Conference on Computer Vision, vol. I, pp. 26–33 (2003)
12. Hufnagel, H., Erhardt, J., Pennec, X., Schmidt-Richberg, A., Handels, H.: Level set segmentation using a point-based statistical shape model relying on correspondence probabilities. In: Proc. of MICCAI Workshop Probabilistic Model for Medical Image Analysis, PMMIA 2009 (2009)

A Random Forest Based Approach
for One Class Classification in Medical Imaging

Chesner Désir[1], Simon Bernard[2], Caroline Petitjean[1], and Laurent Heutte[1]

[1] Université de Rouen, LITIS EA 4108, BP 12, 76801 Saint-Etienne-du-Rouvray, France
[2] Université de Liège, Department of EECS et GIGA-Research, B-4000 Liège - Belgium

Abstract. In this paper, we address the problem of one-class classification for medical image classification. Indeed, in some situations, pathological samples may be difficult to acquire. In this case, one class classification (OCC) is a natural learning paradigm to be used. It consists in learning from only one class of objects, while two or more classes may be presented in prediction. We propose an original OCC method called One-Class Random Forest (OCRF), that combines ensemble learning principles from traditional Random Forest algorithm with an original outlier generation method. These two key processes complement each other for responding to OCC issues, and are shown to perform well on medical datasets in comparison to few other state-of-the-art OCC methods.

Keywords: One-class classification, decision trees, ensemble methods, random forests, medical image classification.

1 Introduction

Image classification, image retrieval and object detection are usual tasks in medical imaging. When such tasks are performed for medical diagnosis purposes, pathological cases may be difficult to acquire and only healthy samples may be available for learning data of the problem, while both classes of images are likely to be presented to the classifier in the prediction stage. This is the case for example when healthy tissue samples outweigh cancer tissue samples [1,2]. These situations may be dealt with using the one-class classification (OCC) learning paradigm that consists in discriminating a class of interest, the target class, from one or several other classes of objects, the outlier class, with no prior knowledge about the outlier class.

As for traditional supervised learning, OCC literature usually opposes density-based methods to discriminative (or boundary-based, or frontier-based) methods [3]. Density-based methods aim at estimating the probability density function of the target data and are thus straightforwardly applicable to OCC. The most used techniques among these methods are Parzen windowing and Mixtures of Gaussians (MoG) [4]. However, density-based methods are rarely effective for high dimensional data and usually require a large number of training samples to provide a reasonably good estimate of the distribution [4]. Discriminative approaches, based on the construction of a decision frontier between classes to discriminate, have also been introduced for OCC [5]. Their main difficulty is to synthesize the class of outlier data in order to model the decision frontier. This is usually done by either using kernels, as in SVM-based methods [5], or by artificially generating outliers during training as in [6]. In this latter case, artificially

F. Wang et al. (Eds.): MLMI 2012, LNCS 7588, pp. 250–257, 2012.
© Springer-Verlag Berlin Heidelberg 2012

generated outliers are often assumed to be uniformly distributed, so as to cover the whole domain of variation of the feature space. This implies to generate an exponential and thus expensive amount of outliers with respect to the dimension of the feature space, and as a consequence, this way of generating outliers is often inaccurate or unusable.

Now, ensemble methods, as we will show, offer some interesting randomization mechanisms that may be used to reduce both the number of outliers to generate and the size of the feature space in which outliers are generated. Though these methods are known to be powerful for traditional learning tasks [7], they are little used to tackle OCC [3,4]. We investigate in this paper the use of such ensemble methods for medical image one-class classification. Among ensemble methods, we have chosen ensembles of decision trees, such as random forests [8], since they embed the interesting randomization mechanisms evoked above and have proved their efficiency over single classifiers on various standard classification tasks [7,9]. We thus propose a new ensemble approach for OCC, called One-Class Random Forest (OCRF), based on random forest algorithm that is designed to tackle issues relative to the generation of outliers. The remainder of the paper is organized as follows. In Section 2, our method is detailed. Section 3 is devoted to the experimental protocol and results, and Section 4 gives conclusions and future works.

2   One-Class Random Forests

The new discriminative approach we propose for OCC, named One-Class Random Forests (OCRF), is based on a random forest algorithm.

Let us recall that the random forest (RF) principle is one of the most successful ensemble techniques, and has shown to be competitive with SVM and with Adaboost [8]. It uses randomization to produce a diverse pool of individual tree-based classifiers. In the reference RF learning algorithm, two powerful randomization processes are used: bagging and Random Feature Selection (RFS). The first one, bagging, consists in training each individual tree on a bootstrap replica of the training set. Bagging is used to create the expected diversity among the individual classifiers and is particularly effective on unstable learning algorithms, like tree-based classifiers, where small changes in the training set result in large changes in predictions. The second one, RFS, is a randomization principle specifically used in tree induction algorithms. It consists, when growing the tree, in randomly selecting at each node of the tree a subset of features from which the splitting test is chosen. The RFS process contributes to the reduction of the dimensionality and has been shown to significantly improve RF accuracy over bagging alone [10,11].

Our OCRF algorithm includes these two randomization principles (bagging and RFS), combined with an outlier generation process. Now the generation of artificial outliers is difficult to implement since the number of outliers to generate for having reasonably good performance is exponential with respect to the size of the feature space, and may also increase as the number of available training samples increases. This issue may be addressed by subsampling the training set for each component classifier of the ensemble. Random forests offer the two randomization mechanisms for subsampling the training set: selection of the training samples through bagging and selection of the features through RFS. Another popular randomization principle, the Random Subspace

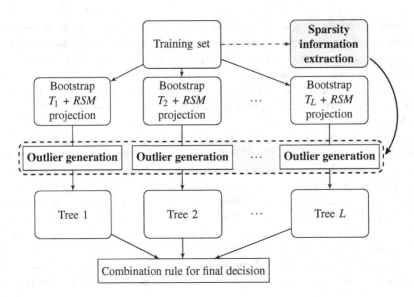

Fig. 1. Overview of the OCRF induction. Additional procedures, in comparison to a traditional RF, are highlighted (in boldface). See also Algorithm 1.

Method (RSM) [12], may also contribute to solve the dimensionality issue for outlier generation. It consists in randomly selecting a subset of features before the training of each individual classifier. These two latter principles, RFS and RSM, are thus used to generate outliers in smaller feature spaces.

Now let us describe our outlier generation process. A first naive approach would be to generate outliers uniformly, before the induction of the RF, which would imply to generate a very large amount of data to cover the whole feature space. But such a process would not allow to take full advantage from ensemble methods. We thus propose to generate outliers in each bootstrap sample before the induction of each individual tree, as shown in Figure 1. It allows to reduce the number of outliers to generate, thanks to RFS and RSM that reduces the dimensionality upstream. Then, regarding the distribution of outliers, our idea is to identify areas where the target data are sparsely located in the original feature space, and to generate a lot of outliers in these areas. Conversely, fewer outliers are generated in areas containing a lot of target samples. The distribution of outliers is designed to be complementary to the distribution of targets.

The OCRF algorithm is thus made of two main steps: (i) extraction of prior information from the target data in the original feature space, in order to generate outliers in adequate areas, and (ii) induction of a random forest with RSM that reduces the dimension of the feature space, and as a consequence the number of outliers to generate for having reasonably good performance (see Figure 1 and Algorithm 1).

In summary, the OCRF method takes advantage of: (i) combining a diverse ensemble of weak and unstable classifiers, which is known to be accurate and to increase the generalization performance over single classifiers, and (ii) subsampling the training dataset, in terms of training samples and features, in order to efficiently generate outliers by controlling their location and their number.

Algorithm 1 Training algorithm for OCRF: generation of outliers in projected bootstrap replicates

---

Require: a training set T, the number of outliers to be generated $N_{outlier}$, the domain of definition for the generation of outliers $\Omega_{outlier}$, the number of trees in the forest L, the number of dimensions for RSM K_{RSM}
Ensure: a one-class random forest classifier

1: (A) *Sparsity information extraction*
2: Compute H_{target} the normalized histogram of the target data
3: Compute $H_{outlier}$ the normalized histogram of the outlier data, so that $H_{outlier}$ is the complementary of H_{target}, i.e. $H_{outlier} = 1 - H_{target}$

4: (B) *Outlier generation and forest induction*
5: **for** $l = 1$ to L **do**
6:     (*i*) Draw a bootstrap sample T_l from the training set
7:     (*ii*) Project this bootstrap sample onto a random subspace of dimension K_{RSM}
8:     (*iii*) Generate $N_{outlier}$ outlier data according to the complementary histogram $H_{outlier}$ in the domain $\Omega_{outlier}$, so that the probability that a generated outlier falls in a bin of the histogram $H_{outlier}$ is proportional to the value associated to that bin
9:     (*iv*) Train a standard decision tree on the augmented dataset composed of the target data and the newly generated outlier data
10: **end for**
11: **return** one-class random forest model

---

3   Experiments

Datasets. In some applications of medical imaging, it is difficult and sometimes even impossible to establish the pathological nature of the images. Let us introduce such an example now. Recently, it has been made possible to visualize pulmonary alveoli in vivo and in real time, thanks to a new endoscopic technique [13], called Fibered Confocal Fluorescence Microscopy (FCFM) or alveoscopy. It allows to acquire images of the alveolar structure, which appears as a network of smooth fiber lines, that may be altered by distal lung pathologies. Images are collected from healthy volunteers and patients with distal lung pathologies, diagnosed with another modality (CT scan). Whereas healthy images are guaranteed to represent healthy condition, pathological images may correspond to either a pathological or a healthy lung segment, even when acquired on an ill patient. The ground truth cannot be based on image expertise because the histopathology of the images has not yet been established, as of today. In this case, pathological images are not reliable enough to train a binary classifier and the solution is to train a one-class classifier on healthy images only.

In order to assess the relevance of the OCRF approach, it has also been tested on two other standard medical datasets taken from the publicly available UCI repository [14]: the *Breast Cancer Wisconsin* (BCW), that includes benign and malignant images of cell nuclei, and the *Pima Indians Diabetes* (PID) dataset, made up of statistics regarding diabetes in Pima Indians women population. Table 1 shows the numbers of samples and the distribution of each dataset[1]. For each of them, the OCRF is trained with the healthy (or negative) cases only, whereas as during the testing phase, samples from both classes are used.

Table 1. Description of alveoscopy dataset and datasets taken from the UCI

Dataset	Attributes	Classes	Negative	Positive	Total
Alveoscopy smoker	28	2	60	33	93
Alveoscopy non-smoker	28	2	31	102	133
BCW	9	2	458	241	699
PID	8	2	268	500	768

Evaluation Criteria. In our experiments, results are presented in terms of global recognition rates, but also in terms of target and outlier recognition rates, in order to allow for an analysis of the "target vs outlier" trade-off. However, these evaluation measures, standard in the machine learning field particularly for binary classification, do not take into account the imbalanced nature of OCC datasets [16]. There is still no consensus for the performance assessment of OCC algorithms. For our experiments, the Matthews correlation coefficient (MCC) or "phi coefficient" is used, as it is particularly well-adapted to imbalanced problems since it takes into account the disparities in the data [16]. The MCC is based on the contingency table from the confusion matrix and is given by:

$$MCC = \frac{TP \times TN - FP \times FN}{\sqrt{(TP+FP)(TP+FN)(TN+FP)(TN+FN)}}$$

where TP, TN, FN and FP respectively stands for true positive, true negative, false negative (or non-detection) and false positive (or false alarm). MCC values range from -1 if correct predictions are inverted to $+1$ for perfect classification.

A standard 10-fold stratified cross-validation has been repeated 5 times for *BCW* and *PID* datasets whereas for alveoscopy image datasets, a 50/50 stratified random subsampling scheme has been repeated 100 times to counterbalance the small number of images and to decrease the bias. The classifier performance are then averaged over the different runs.

State-of-the-Art OCC Methods and Parameterization. The OCRF algorithm is compared to four state-of-the-art OCC algorithms: the one-class SVM (OCSVM) [5] taken from the LibSVM toolbox and three density estimators, Gaussian estimator, Parzen windows and Mixture of Gaussians models taken from the Pattern Recognition Toolbox (PRTools) [17]. Each algorithm is run with the default parameterization of its tool-

---

[1] For *Alveoscopy* images, smoker and non-smoker patients have been considered separately, since smoking causes some specific artifacts to appear in alveoscopy images that slightly change the nature of the recognition problem [13]. *Alveoscopy* images are characterized by the local binary pattern (LBP) operator, a powerful texture descriptor that consists in computing the distribution of binary patterns in the circular neighborhood of each pixel [15].

box[2]. Note that the definition of the threshold on the density estimators output is defined thanks to the parameter $fracrej = 0.05$ of the PRTools toolbox. This parameter corresponds to the fraction of legitimate target cases that will be considered as outliers during training. OCRF is also run with standard values for the parameters:

- the number of trees in the random forest is $L = 200$, a value commonly considered as sufficient in practice to ensure statistical convergence of the algorithm [18];
- the number of attributes for the Random Subspace Method is empirically $K_{RSM} = 10$ or $K = M$ if $M < 10$, where M is the dimension of the feature space;
- the number of attributes for the Random Feature Selection is $K_{RFS} = \sqrt{M}$.

Regarding the generation of outliers during training, one must define their number and the range of their values. We have chosen the generation domain of outliers to be 1.2 times greater than the target domain estimated through the training set, assuming that the outlier domain needs to cover the whole target domain. The number of outliers to generate depends obviously on the number of available target samples N_{target} and is empirically set to $N_{outlier} = 10 \cdot N_{target}$.

Experimental Results. Results are presented in Table 2, in which averaged Matthews coefficient (MCC) values, global accuracy rates, target and outlier recognition rates are reported. Firstly, it may be observed that some algorithms have MCC values equal to 0, i.e. they always predict the outlier class (see Gauss, Parzen, MoG on the *Alveoscopy_NS* dataset and OCSVM on the *PID* dataset). The Gaussian classifier obtains rather good performance on *Alveoscopy_S* and *BCW* datasets indicating that the gaussian model fits well the distribution of the target data for these datasets. However, it fails to obtain an adapted model for the other target datasets. Our method achieves the best results on 3 among 4 datasets. It fails to correctly classify the target class for *Alveoscopy_S* and the outlier class for *PID* dataset. For this latter dataset, we can argue that a less flexible model is able to prevent the acceptance of too many outlier data (at the expense of the target data). This could be achieved by either generating more outlier data or reducing the outlier generation domain.

Further experiments were conducted on the *Alveoscopy_S* dataset to show that the target recognition rate, for example, could be improved by generating less outlier data. Indeed, the same number of outliers as targets was generated ($N_{outlier} = N_{target}$), and a mean MCC value of 0.56, an accuracy rate of 80.4% and a target recognition rate of 86.0% were obtained, compared to 0.42, 63.9% and 48% with $N_{outlier} = 10 \cdot N_{target}$, respectively. The set of target samples used for training seems to be overlapped by too many outlier data. Therefore, the number of outliers and the size of the outlier domain may have an impact on performance for difficult datasets and deserve more attention in future works. These parameters result from a trade-off between target and outlier recognition rates. If their values are high, performance on the target data are likely to decrease; if their values are small, it will impact the performance on outlier data like in the *PID* dataset case. The optimal values of these parameters could be investigated for

---

[2] In particular, for the OCSVM, the cost coefficient is $C = 1$ and the kernel is a radial basis function with a bandwidth $\gamma = \frac{1}{dimension}$. Only the ν coefficient, an upper bound on the fraction of support vectors, is set to a more frequently cited value $\nu = 0.1$, instead of $\nu = 0.5$ in LibSVM.

Table 2. Mean OCC results (± standard deviation) for the *Alveoscopy*, *BCW* and *PID* datasets: MCC, global accuracy rate (Acc), target (T) and outlier (O) recognition rates. Best MCC results are indicated in boldface.

		OCRF	OCSVM	Gauss	Parzen	MoG
Alveo_S	MCC	0.42±0.03	0.50±0.01	**0.76±0.00**	0.31±0.00	0.36±0.04
	Acc	0.63±0.02	0.67±0.01	0.89±0.00	0.50±0.00	0.54±0.04
	T	0.48	0.49	0.90	0.23	0.30
	O	0.93	1.00	0.87	1.00	1.00
Alveo_NS	MCC	**0.71±0.03**	0.51±0.07	0.00±0.00	0.00±0.00	0.00±0.00
	Acc	0.88±0.02	0.82±0.03	0.76±0.00	0.76±0.00	0.76±0.00
	T	0.81	0.27	0.00	0.00	0.00
	O	0.91	1.00	1.00	1.00	1.00
BCW	MCC	**0.92±0.05**	0.85±0.10	0.90±0.06	0.71±0.06	0.87±0.06
	Acc	0.96±0.02	0.92±0.03	0.95±0.03	0.83±0.04	0.93±0.03
	T	0.96	0.87	0.94	0.74	0.90
	O	0.96	1.00	0.97	1.00	0.98
PID	MCC	**0.24±0.12**	0.00±0.00	-0.05±0.13	0.06±0.13	0.02±0.10
	Acc	0.68±0.04	0.34±0.02	0.35±0.03	0.55±0.06	0.39±0.04
	T	0.90	0.00	0.93	0.46	0.88
	O	0.28	1.00	0.30	0.60	0.12

instance during a validation process, where training data are only composed of target data and validation set composed of either target data only or augmented with a few artificially generated outliers.

4   Conclusion and Future Works

In this paper, we have proposed a new OCC method that is especially useful for medical image classification where the pathological nature of the images may not be clearly assessed, as this is the case in alveoscopy images for example. The proposed method, called One-Class Random Forest, is based on the reference random forest algorithm combined with an original outlier generation procedure. The generation of artificial outliers is often used with discriminative learning methods but is difficult to implement since the number of outliers to generate for having reasonably good performance is exponential with respect to the dimension of the feature space, and may also increase as the number of available training samples increases. We have shown that the random principles used in traditional RF can be powerful tools to overcome this issue: by subsampling the training set for each component classifier of the ensemble, through the selection of both the training samples (with bagging) and the features (with Random Feature Selection and Random Subspaces methods), and by then combining all of them, we reduce the minimum number of outliers to generate and increase the generalization accuracy of the ensemble.

To assess the efficiency of our method, experiments have been conducted on alveoscopy images as well as on two other medical datasets from the UCI repository and OCRF has been compared to the four most used OCC algorithms. On these datasets and using the default parameterization of each method, results have shown that OCRF performs equally well or better than these state-of-the-art OCC algorithms. Besides, it has been pointed out that parameterization of OCRF needs to be further investigated for taking full advantage of the potential of the method. This will be the scope of our future works.

References

1. Tarassenko, L., Hayton, P., Cerneaz, N., Brady, M.: Novelty detection for the identification of masses in mammograms. In: Fourth International Conference on Artificial Neural Networks, pp. 442–447 (1995)
2. Mourão-Miranda, J., Hardoon, D., Hahn, T., Marquand, A., Williams, S., Shawe-Taylor, J., Brammer, M.: Patient classification as an outlier detection problem: An application of the one-class support vector machine. NeuroImage (2011)
3. Khan, S.S., Madden, M.G.: A Survey of Recent Trends in One Class Classification. In: Coyle, L., Freyne, J. (eds.) AICS 2009. LNCS, vol. 6206, pp. 188–197. Springer, Heidelberg (2010)
4. Tax, D.M.J., Duin, R.P.W.: Combining One-Class Classifiers. In: Kittler, J., Roli, F. (eds.) MCS 2001. LNCS, vol. 2096, pp. 299–308. Springer, Heidelberg (2001)
5. Scholkopf, B., Platt, J., Shawe-Taylor, J., Smola, A., Williamson, R.: Estimating the support of a high-dimensional distribution. Neural Computation 13(7), 1443–1471 (2001)
6. Hempstalk, K., Frank, E., Witten, I.H.: One-Class Classification by Combining Density and Class Probability Estimation. In: Daelemans, W., Goethals, B., Morik, K. (eds.) ECML PKDD 2008, Part I. LNCS (LNAI), vol. 5211, pp. 505–519. Springer, Heidelberg (2008)
7. Dietterich, T.G.: Ensemble Methods in Machine Learning. In: Kittler, J., Roli, F. (eds.) MCS 2000. LNCS, vol. 1857, pp. 1–15. Springer, Heidelberg (2000)
8. Breiman, L.: Random forests. Machine Learning 45(1), 5–32 (2001)
9. Gray, K.R., Aljabar, P., Heckemann, R.A., Hammers, A., Rueckert, D.: Random Forest-Based Manifold Learning for Classification of Imaging Data in Dementia. In: Suzuki, K., Wang, F., Shen, D., Yan, P. (eds.) MLMI 2011. LNCS, vol. 7009, pp. 159–166. Springer, Heidelberg (2011)
10. Bernard, S., Heutte, L., Adam, S.: Forest-RK: A New Random Forest Induction Method. In: Huang, D.-S., Wunsch II, D.C., Levine, D.S., Jo, K.-H. (eds.) ICIC 2008. LNCS (LNAI), vol. 5227, pp. 430–437. Springer, Heidelberg (2008)
11. Geurts, P., Ernst, D., Wehenkel, L.: Extremely randomized trees. Machine Learning 63(1), 3–42 (2006)
12. Ho, T.: The random subspace method for constructing decision forests. IEEE Transactions on Pattern Analysis and Machine Intelligence 20(8), 832–844 (1998)
13. Thiberville, L., Salaün, M., Lachkar, S., Dominique, S., Moreno-Swirc, S., Vever-Bizet, C., Bourg-Heckly, G.: Human in vivo fluorescence microimaging of the alveolar ducts and sacs during bronchoscopy. Eur. Respir. J. 33(5), 974–985 (2009)
14. Blake, C., Merz, C.: Uci repository of machine learning databases. Department of Information and Computer Science, University of California, Irvine, CA, vol. 55 (1998), http://www.ics.uci.edu/~mlearn/mlrepository.html
15. Ojala, T., Pietikäinen, M., Mäenpää, T.: Gray Scale and Rotation Invariant Texture Classification with Local Binary Patterns. In: Vernon, D. (ed.) ECCV 2000, Part I. LNCS, vol. 1842, pp. 404–420. Springer, Heidelberg (2000)
16. Baldi, P., Brunak, S., Chauvin, Y., Andersen, C., Nielsen, H.: Assessing the accuracy of prediction algorithms for classification: an overview. Bioinformatics 16(5), 412 (2000)
17. Duin, R.: PRTools version 3.0: A Matlab toolbox for pattern recognition. In: Proc. of SPIE (2000)
18. Bernard, S., Heutte, L., Adam, S.: Influence of Hyperparameters on Random Forest Accuracy. In: Benediktsson, J.A., Kittler, J., Roli, F. (eds.) MCS 2009. LNCS, vol. 5519, pp. 171–180. Springer, Heidelberg (2009)

Finding Deformable Shapes by Correspondence-Free Instantiation and Registration of Statistical Shape Models

Weiguo Xie[1,2], Steffen Schumann[1], Jochen Franke[2], Paul Alfred Grützner[2], Lutz-Peter Nolte[1], and Guoyan Zheng[1]

[1] Institute for Surgical Technology and Biomechanics, University of Bern, Switzerland
[2] BG Trauma Center Ludwigshafen at Heidelberg University Hospital, Germany
`guoyan.zheng@ieee.org`

Abstract. This paper addresses the problem of finding a deformable shape by instantiation and registration of a statistical shape model (SSM) to the observation. A correspondence-free approach based on expectation conditional maximization (ECM) framework is proposed, and a robust and efficient implementation is presented. Preliminary experiments conducted on SSM of both femur and pelvis resulted in an average mean reconstruction error of 2.7mm (50 sparse observation points) and of 1.1mm/1.0mm (100 sparse points, with/without noise) for femur, as well as a mean reconstruction error of 4.36mm for pelvis, which demonstrated the efficacy of the proposed approach.

1   Introduction

Finding a deformable shape by matching a parameterized model [1] to the observation data is a frequently encountered problem in image registration, object tracking, image segmentation and image recognition. The iterative closest point (ICP) method [2] including its many variants [3-6] is one of the most well-known algorithms. It works by alternating between correspondence establishment and parameter estimation steps until convergence. Due to its dependence on the strong assumption that every closest point pair should correspond to each other, it may fail when the parameterized model and the observation are not coarsely aligned or when occlusion occurs in either side. This has motivated the introduction of various robust methods using the expectation maximization (EM) algorithms [7-13]. In such algorithms, the parameter estimation boils down to an iterative estimation of probabilistic point-to-point correspondences and of the model parameters in turn. Thus the explicit one-to-one correspondence assumption is not needed any more. We define methods in this category as correspondence-free approaches. The method that we will present in this paper belongs to this category.

The closest work in the literature to our proposed method is the one presented by Horaud et al. [12], where they have developed an expectation conditional maximization (ECM) algorithm for rigid and articulated rigid point registration. In this paper, we apply the ECM algorithm to addressing the parameter estimation problem in instantiation and registration of statistical shape models (SSM). Thus, unlike what has been done by Horaud et al., here we need to estimate not only the

F. Wang et al. (Eds.): MLMI 2012, LNCS 7588, pp. 258–265, 2012.

pose parameters (the registration problem) but also the shape parameters (the instantiation problem).

The paper is organized as follows. The next section will focus on the derivation of an ECM algorithm for correspondence-free registration and instantiation of a SSM to the sparse point data. Section 3 presents results of two experiments conducted on two different SSMs, followed by conclusions and discussion in Section 4.

2   Methods

2.1   SSM Instantiation and Registration with ECM

Given m three-dimensional (3D) observation/reference points $\{Y_j\}_{1 \leq j \leq m}$ and n 3D model/target points $\{X_i\}_{1 \leq i \leq n}$, we define a scaled rigid transformation as $\mu(X_i; \theta) = s(RX_i + \vec{t})$ with the rigid transformation parameters $\theta := \{R, \vec{t}\}$ where R is a 3×3 rotation matrix and $\vec{t}$ is a 3×1 translation vector, and s is the scaling parameter.

For SSM instantiation [14], the to-be-estimated model with n vertices $\{X_i\}$ can be expressed as $[X_1 \ X_2 \ \cdots \ X_n]^t = [\bar{S}_1 \ \bar{S}_2 \ \cdots \ \bar{S}_n]^t + [\vec{V}_1 \ \vec{V}_2 \ \cdots \ \vec{V}_K]\vec{b}$, where $[\bar{S}_1 \ \bar{S}_2 \ \cdots \ \bar{S}_n]^t$ is the mean shape, $[\vec{V}_1 \ \vec{V}_2 \ \cdots \ \vec{V}_K]$ are K eigenvectors corresponding to K largest eigenvalues $[\lambda_1 \ \lambda_2 \ \cdots \ \lambda_K]$ of the covariance matrix of the training population, and $\vec{b} = [b_1 \ b_2 \ \cdots \ b_K]^t$ are the eigenvector weights (the shape parameters). For each target point X_i, we can write $X_i = \bar{S}_i + \emptyset_i \vec{b}$ where $\emptyset_i$ is the i-th row of the matrix $[\vec{V}_1 \ \vec{V}_2 \ \cdots \ \vec{V}_K]$.

Following [12], we denote the prior probability of an observed point Y_j with the assignment to a $\mu(X_i; \theta)$-centered Gaussian cluster as $p_i = P(Z_j = i)$, where Z_j is the assignment variable for the observed point Y_j. We assume that $P(Y_j | Z_j = i)$, i.e. the probability of Y_j given its cluster assignment (the conditional likelihood of Y_j), follows Gaussian distribution with the mean of $\mu(X_i; \theta)$ and the covariance of Σ_i.

E-step: Estimation of Posterior Probabilities. The posterior probability α_{ji} of an assignment $P(Z_j = i)$ conditioned by observations was given as follows:

$$\alpha_{ji} = \frac{|\Sigma_i|^{-\frac{1}{2}} \exp\left(-\frac{1}{2}\|Y_j - \mu(X_i; \theta)\|_{\Sigma_i}^2\right)}{\sum_{i=1}^{n} |\Sigma_i|^{-\frac{1}{2}} \exp\left(-\frac{1}{2}\|Y_j - \mu(X_i; \theta)\|_{\Sigma_i}^2\right) + P_{outlier}} \tag{1}$$

where $P_{outlier}$ corresponds to the outlier probability, which is set according to the suggestion given in [12].

Conditional Expectation (CM)-step: Estimation of SSM Instantiation and Registration Parameters. We propose to minimize energy below in order to instantiate and register the SSM to sparse point data:

$$\varepsilon(\psi) = \frac{1}{2} \sum_{j=1}^{m} \sum_{i=1}^{n} \alpha_{ji} \left(\|Y_j - \mu(X_i; \theta)\|_{\Sigma_i}^2 + \log|\Sigma_i| \right) + \rho \frac{1}{2} \sum_{k=1}^{K} \frac{b_k^2}{\lambda_k} \tag{2}$$

where the first term is the probabilistic matching likelihood energy and the second term is the prior energy term, which is often referred to as Mahalanobis Distance [14-17]; $\psi = \{\theta, s, \Sigma_1, \dots, \Sigma_n, \vec{b}\}$ is the parameter set and ρ is a balancing coefficient. Details about the ECM algorithm for instantiation and registration of a SSM to the sparse point data will be explained below.

2.2   ECM Algorithm for Instantiation and Registration of a SSM

Our ECM algorithm for instantiation and registration of a SSM to sparse point data consists of following three stages.

- Initialization stage: initialize pose, shape, and covariance matrix parameters.
- ECM-based scaled rigid registration stage.
  − E-step 1: estimate the posterior probability α_{jl} **according to Eq. (1).**
  − CM-step 1-1: estimate the current rigid transformation parameters of R and $\vec{t}$.
  − CM-step 1-2: estimate the current scale parameter s.
  − CM-step 1-3: estimate the current covariance matrices $\{\Sigma_i\}$.
  − Convergence check: if converged, go to the next stage. Otherwise, go back to the E-step 1.
- ECM-based SSM instantiation stage.
  − Initialize the SSM with R, $\vec{t}$ and s estimated in the last stage
  − E-step 2: estimate the posterior probability α_{jl} **according to Eq. (1).**
  − CM-step 2-1: estimate the current covariance matrices $\{\Sigma_i\}$.
  − CM-step 2-2: estimate the current shape parameters $\vec{b}$.
  − Convergence check: if converged, algorithm ends. Otherwise, go back to the E-step 2.

The detailed derivation of parameter estimation at each step in our proposed algorithm is described as follows. It is assumed that the cluster of Gaussian mixture model (GMM) is the isotropic covariance model, i.e., $\{\Sigma_i = \sigma_i^2 I_{3\times3}, i = 1, \dots, n\}$, where $I_{3\times3}$ is the identity matrix of size 3.

Estimation of Rigid Parameters. This is done by introducing the virtual observation concept of $W_i (1 \le i \le n)$ and their weights $\beta_i (1 \le i \le n)$ as [12] did:

$$W_i = \frac{1}{\beta_i} \sum_{j=1}^{m} \alpha_{ji} Y_j \tag{3}$$

$$\beta_i = \sum_{j=1}^{m} \alpha_{ji} \tag{4}$$

Then the problem of estimating the rigid parameters can be formulated as:

$$\Theta^* = \text{argmin}_{R,\vec{t}} \frac{1}{2} \sum_{i=1}^{n} \left\| \frac{\sqrt{\beta_i}}{\sigma_i} W_i - \frac{\sqrt{\beta_i}}{\sigma_i} s(RX_i + \vec{t}) \right\|^2 \tag{5}$$

Set the derivative of above equation with respect to $\vec{t}$ equal to zero, we have

$$\bar{t} = s^{-1}(p' - sRp)/a \tag{6}$$

where $a = \frac{1}{n}\sum_{i=1}^{n}\frac{\sqrt{\beta_i}}{\sigma_i}$, $p' = \frac{1}{n}\sum_{i=1}^{n}(\frac{\sqrt{\beta_i}}{\sigma_i})W_i$ and $p = \frac{1}{n}\sum_{i=1}^{n}(\frac{\sqrt{\beta_i}}{\sigma_i})X_i$. Replacing Eq. (6) to Eq. (5), we obtain

$$\Theta^* = \text{argmin}_{R,\bar{t}}\frac{1}{2}\sum_{i=1}^{n}(q_i'^t q_i' - 2q_i'^t sRq_i + s^2 q_i^t q_i) \tag{7}$$

where $q_i' = \frac{\sqrt{\beta_i}}{\sigma_i}(W_i - \frac{p'}{a})$ and $q_i = \frac{\sqrt{\beta_i}}{\sigma_i}(X_i - \frac{p}{a})$.

Minimizing Eq. (7) is equal to maximizing $\sum_{i=1}^{n}(q_i'^t s)Rq_i$ [18]. By computing the singular value decomposition (SVD) of $\sum_{i=1}^{n}q_i(q_i'^t s)$ as $U\Lambda V^t$, we can estimate the rotation matrix via $R = VU^t$. $\bar{t}$ is then estimated according to Eq. (6).

Estimation of the Scale Parameter. When Θ^* is minimized, the scale parameter s can be calculated by setting the partial derivative of (2) with respect to s equal to 0, i.e., $\frac{\partial \varepsilon(\psi)}{\partial s} = 0$, which leads to

$$s = \frac{\sum_{j=1}^{m}\sum_{i=1}^{n}\frac{\alpha_{ji}}{\sigma_i^2}\left[(RX_i+\bar{t})^t Y_j + Y_j^t(RX_i+\bar{t})\right]}{2\sum_{j=1}^{m}\sum_{i=1}^{n}\frac{\alpha_{ji}}{\sigma_i^2}(RX_i+\bar{t})^t(RX_i+\bar{t})} \tag{8}$$

Estimation of Covariance Matrices $\{\Sigma_i\}$. When the rigid transformation and scale parameters are updated, each covariance matrix Σ_i can be estimated with $\frac{\partial \varepsilon(\psi)}{\partial \Sigma_i} = 0$, which in the case of the isotropic covariance model gives us the following equation:

$$\sigma_i^2 = \frac{\sum_{j=1}^{m}\alpha_{ji}(Y_j - s(RX_i+\bar{t}))^t(Y_j - s(RX_i+\bar{t}))}{3\sum_{j=1}^{m}\alpha_{ji}} \tag{9}$$

Estimation of Shape Parameters. Similarly, by setting the partial derivative of $\varepsilon(\psi)$ with respect to each shape parameter b_k $(k = 1, ..., K)$ equal to zero, we have

$$\frac{\partial \varepsilon(\psi)}{\partial b_k} = \frac{-\frac{1}{2}\sum_{j=1}^{m}\sum_{i=1}^{n}\alpha_{ji}\partial\left(\|Y_j - \mu(X_i;\theta)\|_{\Sigma_i}^2\right)}{\partial \bar{b}} \times \frac{\partial \bar{b}}{\partial b_k} - \frac{\partial\left(\rho\frac{1}{2}\sum_{k=1}^{K}\frac{b_k^2}{\lambda_k}\right)}{\partial b_k} = 0 \tag{10}$$

The shape parameter b_k is thus estimated with

$$b_k = \frac{\left\{\sum_{j=1}^{m}\sum_{i=1}^{n}\frac{\alpha_{ji}}{\sigma_i^2}\left[(Y_j - s\bar{t} - sR\bar{s}_i)^t sR\emptyset_{ik}\right] - \sum_{j=1}^{m}\sum_{i=1}^{n}\frac{\alpha_{ji}}{\sigma_i^2}\left[s^2\left(\sum_{\tau=1(\tau\neq k)}^{K}b_\tau\emptyset_{i\tau}^t\right)\emptyset_{ik}\right]\right\}}{\left\{\sum_{j=1}^{m}\sum_{i=1}^{n}\frac{\alpha_{ji}}{\sigma_i^2}\left[s^2\emptyset_{ik}^t\emptyset_{ik}\right] + \frac{\rho}{\lambda_k}\right\}} \tag{11}$$

3   Experiments and Results

We designed and conducted two experiments to validate the proposed approach. For all studies described in both experiments, the parameters were initialized as: $s = 1$,

$\{\sigma_i = 1000.0, i = 1, ... n\}$, $R = I_{3\times3}, \vec{t} = 0_{3\times1}$ and $\vec{b} = 0_{K\times1}$, where $0_{3\times1}$ and $0_{K\times1}$ are zero vectors of size 3 and of size K, respectively.

The first experiment was conducted on a SSM of the proximal femur by performing leave-one-out studies. More specifically, each time we took one of the 18 training models out and used the rest of 17 training models to build the SSM. The left-out object was then transformed by a scaled rigid transformation constructed with randomly generated parameters as follows: its scale parameter was randomly generated from the range of [0.8, 1.2], rotation angle around each axis from the range of [-45°, 45°], and the translation along each axis from the range of [-100mm, 100mm].

This leave-one-out experiment consisted of three studies. For the 1st study, 50 landmarks were randomly picked on the surface model of the left-out object. These landmarks were used to reconstruct the shape of the associated left-out object. For the 2nd study, 100 landmarks were randomly picked on the surface model of the left-out object. Both of studies were noise-free, whereas for the 3rd study 25 landmarks were randomly chosen from the 100 landmarks and random Gaussian noise with the standard deviation of 2mm was added to the coordinates of these 25 landmarks.

The error was calculated between the reconstructed surface model and the ground truth model (i.e. the associated left-out object) using the open-source software called MESH (http://mesh.berlios.de/) [19]. The results of the three studies are presented in Table 1. When 50 landmarks were used as the input, an average mean reconstruction error of 2.7mm was found. This value changed to 1.0mm when 100 landmarks were used as the observation. In the presence of Gaussian noises added to the coordinates of the 25 randomly chosen landmarks, the reconstruction accuracy was slightly worse and an average mean reconstruction error of 1.1mm was observed. Video 1 submitted as the supplemental material of this paper shows one of the aforementioned trials in 2nd study while 100 noise-free landmarks were used as the input.

Table 1. Femur SSM instantiation and registration results

Stu-dies	Average distances between the reconstructed model and the ground truth model of each left-out object (mm)																	
	1	2	3	4	5	6	7	8	9	10	11	12	13	14	15	16	17	18
1st	2.0	2.5	2.2	3.4	4.2	1.8	2.3	3.4	2.6	2.8	1.9	3.2	2.4	3.3	2.3	3.0	3.0	3.7
2nd	0.8	0.6	1.1	1.9	1.1	1.4	0.6	0.7	0.9	0.6	1.7	1.6	0.4	1.3	0.6	0.9	0.9	1.0
3rd	0.9	0.6	1.1	1.9	1.2	1.5	1.2	0.7	0.7	1.0	1.6	1.6	0.4	1.5	0.7	0.9	1.0	1.1

The second experiment was conducted on a SSM of the pelvis constructed from 14 training pelvis models, whose mean model contains 24994 points and eight most significant modes of the deformable variation were used. The observation data for this experiment were prepared as follows: we segmented 10 real clinical CT datasets of the pelvis with software Amira 5.3.0 (Visage Imaging GmbH, Berlin, Germany) to obtain 10 pelvis bony surface models (without sacrum). On each of pelvis surface models, we randomly picked 540 points from regions of bilateral anterior superior iliac spines (ASISs), bilateral anterior inferior iliac spines (AIISs), the pubis, the left and right ischia, and the left and right iliac crest. The reason why we chose such regions is that usually only these regions are clinically available for point digitization with e.g. ultrasound (US) or a traced pointer. Thus the collected 540 points could be utilized to simulate the real clinical data and to validate our proposed method in a simulated clinical scenario.

Through the aforementioned preparation, we acquired 10 test datasets (each of them consists of 540 digitized points). Using these datasets as the sparse observation points, we performed 10 trials to register and instantiate the pelvis SSM. Table 2 lists the reconstruction errors of 10 trials in terms of the root mean square (RMS) distance of the found correspondences between the observation data and the instantiated SSM. A mean reconstruction error of 4.36mm was observed. Fig. 1 and the supplemental Video 2 illustrate one of the 10 trials detailedly.

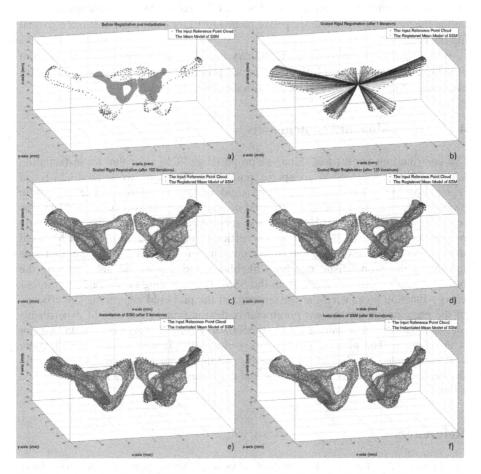

Fig. 1. An example of pelvis SSM registration and instantiation with ECM. a) Input picked points (blue) and the mean model of SSM (green). b) and c) Scaled rigid registration: after 1st iteration and 100th iteration. For each input sparse point, its correspondence on the mean model that has the largest posterior probability is connected with it by the blue dotted line. d) The result of the scaled rigid registration (after 120 iterations). e) Instantiation of SSM: after 3rd iteration. f) The instantiated SSM (after 50 iterations).

Table 2. Pelvis SSM instantiation and registration results

Trial No.	1	2	3	4	5	6	7	8	9	10
RMS Error (mm)	4.25	4.45	2.72	5.27	3.64	5.88	5.44	4.24	4.27	3.45

Here we did consider the RMS error of the found correspondences between the observation data and the instantiated SSM instead of the reconstruction error between the whole surface of the instantiated SSM and the ground truth surface model (the segmented one), because we are more interested in the reconstruction accuracy of certain local anatomy e.g. pubic tubercles and bilateral ASISs which are important to define the intra-operative anterior pelvic plane (APP) for certain applications e.g. total hip arthroplasty (THA).

Both experiments showed the preliminary but comparable results with those from other scholarly work e.g. [4-5], whereas our proposed approach requires no coarse alignment of the parameterized model with the observation data.

4   Discussion and Conclusions

Our contributions are twofold. First, we proposed an ECM algorithm for instantiation and registration of a SSM to sparse point data. Previous work on ECM-based registration [11-12] only addressed the rigid or articulated rigid pose estimation problem whereas our algorithm addressed not only the pose estimation problem (the registration problem) but also the shape reconstruction problem (the instantiation problem). Second, we designed a new efficient energy function for ECM-based registration. This new energy function consists of two terms with the first one measuring the probabilistic matching likelihood and the second one encoding the prior probability that is learned from the SSM. Incorporating the second term in our energy function guaranteed the convergence of the proposed algorithm. The efficacy of the presented approach was preliminarily demonstrated by results of experiments on instantiation and registration of two SSMs to different sparse point data, with or without noise. The planned future work includes the further validation with more (~20) segmented CT datasets of the pelvis and in a simulated surgical scenario with the digitized data acquired from plastic and dry cadaver pelvises by US or the tracked pointer.

References

1. Cootes, T.F., Taylor, C.J.: Statistical Models of Appearance for Computer Vision. Technical report, University of Manchester, UK (2004)
2. Besl, P.J., McKay, N.D.: A Method for Registration of 3-D Shapes. IEEE Transactions on Pattern Analysis and Machine Intelligence 14(2), 239–256 (1992)
3. Chan, C.S.K., Edwards, P.J., Hawkes, D.J.: Integration of Ultrasound-based Registration with Statistical Shape Models for Computer-assisted Orthopaedic Surgery. In: Proc. of SPIE, vol. 5032, pp. 414–424 (2003)

4. Chan, C.S.K., Barratt, D.C., Edwards, P.J., Penney, G.P., Slomczykowski, M., Carter, T.J., Hawkes, D.J.: Cadaver Validation of the Use of Ultrasound for 3D Model Instantiation of Bony Anatomy in Image Guided Orthopaedic Surgery. In: Barillot, C., Haynor, D.R., Hellier, P. (eds.) MICCAI 2004, Part II. LNCS, vol. 3217, pp. 397–404. Springer, Heidelberg (2004)
5. Barratt, D.C., et al.: Instantiation and Registration of Statistical Shape Models of the Femur and Pelvis Using 3D Ultrasound Imaging. Medical Image Analysis 12(3), 358–374 (2008)
6. Foroughi, P., Song, D., Chintalapani, G., Taylor, R.H., Fichtinger, G.: Localization of Pelvic Anatomical Coordinate System Using US/Atlas Registration for Total Hip Replacement. In: Metaxas, D., Axel, L., Fichtinger, G., Székely, G. (eds.) MICCAI 2008, Part II. LNCS, vol. 5242, pp. 871–879. Springer, Heidelberg (2008)
7. Rangarajan, A., Chui, H., Mjolsness, E., Pappu, S., Davachi, L., Goldman-Rakic, P.S., Duncan, J.: A Robust Point Matching Algorithm for Autoradiograph Alignment. Medical Image Analysis 1(4), 379–398 (1997)
8. Chui, H., Win, L., Schultz, R., Duncan, J.S., Rangarajan, A.: A Unified Non-rigid Feature Registration Method for Brain Mapping. Medical Image Analysis 7, 113–130 (2003)
9. Jian, B., Vemuri, B.C.: A Robust Algorithm for Point Set Registration Using Mixture of Gaussians. In: 10th IEEE International Conference on Computer Vision (ICCV 2005), pp. 1246–1251 (2005)
10. Granger, S., Pennec, X.: Multi-scale EM-ICP: A Fast and Robust Approach for Surface Registration. In: Heyden, A., Sparr, G., Nielsen, M., Johansen, P. (eds.) ECCV 2002, Part IV. LNCS, vol. 2353, pp. 418–432. Springer, Heidelberg (2002)
11. Myronenko, A., Song, X.: Point-Set Registration: Coherent Point Drift. IEEE Transactions on Pattern Analysis and Machine Intelligence 32(12), 2262–2275 (2010)
12. Horaud, R., Forbes, F., Yguel, M., Dewaele, G., Zhang, J.: Rigid and Articulated Point Registration with Expectation Conditional Maximization. IEEE Transactions on Pattern Analysis and Machine Intelligence 33(3), 587–602 (2011)
13. Xie, W., Nolte, L.P., Zheng, G.: ECM versus ICP for Point Registration. In: 33rd Annual International Conference of the IEEE Engineering in Medicine and Biology Society (EMBC 2011), Boston, MA, USA, pp. 2131–2135 (2011)
14. Blanz, V., Vetter, T.: A Morphable Model for the Synthesis of 3D Faces. In: 26th Annual Conference on Computer Graphics and Interactive Techniques (SIGGRAPH 1999), pp. 187–194 (1999)
15. Rajamani, K.T., Styner, M., Talib, H., Zheng, G., Nolte, L.-P., Gonzalez Ballester, M.A.: Statistical Deformable Bone Models for Robust 3D Surface Extrapolation from Sparse Data. Medical Image Analysis 11, 99–109 (2007)
16. Zheng, G., et al.: A 2D/3D Correspondence Building Method for Reconstruction of A Patient-specific 3D Bone Surface Model Using Point Distribution Models and Calibrated X-ray Images. Medical Image Analysis 13, 883–899 (2009)
17. Baka, N., et al.: 2D-3D Shape Reconstruction of the Distal Femur from Stereo X-ray Imaging Using Statistical Shape Models. Medical Image Analysis 15, 840–850 (2011)
18. Arun, K.S., Huang, T.S., Blostein, S.D.: Least-Squares Fitting of Two 3-D Point Sets. IEEE Transactions on Pattern Analysis and Machine Intelligence PAMI-9(5), 698–700 (1987)
19. Aspert, N., Santa-Cruz, D., Ebrahimi, T.: MESH: Measuring Error between Surfaces Using the Hausdorff Distance. In: Proc. of IEEE ICME, vol. I, pp. 705–708 (2002)

Computer Aided Skin Lesion Diagnosis with Humans in the Loop

Orod Razeghi, Guoping Qiu, Hywel Williams, and Kim Thomas

VIPLAB, IMA Group, Computer Science,
University of Nottingham, Nottingham, UK
{Psxor1,Guoping.Qiu,Hywel.Williams,Kim.Thomas}@nottingham.ac.uk
http://www.viplab.cs.nott.ac.uk

Abstract. Despite much progress made in recent years, computer is still incapable of reliably and accurately recognising images of most real world problems, including images of skin diseases. In this paper, we have developed an interactive skin lesion recognition system based on a human in the loop visual recognition technology, where computer vision algorithms and models of human responses to a series of simple perceptual questions are combined together to achieve very high recognition rates (over 96%). We have designed the first ever dermatology "Question and Answer" bank consisting of 21 questions and over 100 possible answers that can be effectively used in a human in the loop skin lesion recognition system. We present experimental results to show that for some diseases, computer vision technique can only achieve a recognition rate of 20%, while with human in the loop the performance can be boosted to over 96%. We also show that users do not require any medical knowledge to answer these questions to achieve excellent recognition rates.

Keywords: Dermatological Image Recognition, Human in the Loop.

1 Introduction

The problem of understanding visual content of an image has been studied for many years in the computer vision community. Despite significant progress, reliable and accurate automatic visual recognition is still an evolving research subject and existing state of the art solutions are not yet ready for real world mission critical applications, such as computer aided medical diagnosis.

Researchers have recently advocated and developed the so-called interactive imaging and vision [11] or human in the loop [4] approach to tackle the aforementioned issue of visual object recognition; an intermediate practical solution to develop technologies that make human and computer work in harmony to exploit their respective strengths. An innovative solution that follows this line of thought is that of [4], where the authors introduced a general framework for incorporating a multi-class object recognition algorithm with human answers to a visual version of the "20 Question" game. The solution harnesses computer to reduce human labour in difficult visual object recognition tasks and resorts

F. Wang et al. (Eds.): MLMI 2012, LNCS 7588, pp. 266–274, 2012.

to human interactively answering simple questions to boost the performance of object recognition algorithms. We believe that an adaptation of this approach is particularly suitable for medical applications, such as computer aided skin diagnosis.

We believe that for the very first time we have applied the promising human in the loop visual recognition technique to computer aided diagnosis of medical images. This paper is one of very few papers that attempts to apply computer vision technique to automatic recognition of various skin diseases, and is certainly one that achieves the best results in the literature. We also believe that our promising accurate results can be evaluated from separate point of views: the role of computer vision in reducing human labour, the role of human in the loop in increasing accuracy of computational models, and computer vision and human in the loop combined in solving real world problems.

Our contributions include, demonstrated for the first time that human in the loop visual recognition can significantly boost computer recognition of a range of different skin diseases and achieving near perfect recognition results, designed a dermatology relevant "Question and Answer" bank suitable for human in the loop visual recognition solutions, and also shown that such system can be used by users without any medical knowledge. We believe our encouraging results should open up new possibilities for applying computer technologies, specifically, human in the loop visual recognition solutions, to other areas of medical imaging and computer aided diagnosis.

2   Related Work

In dermatology, there has been long interest in exploiting computer technology. Recent years have seen increased activities in developing machine learning and computer vision techniques for skin lesion diagnosis, especially for diagnosing melanoma cases. The authors in [13] utilises optical spectroscopy and a multi-spectral classification scheme using SVMs to assist dermatologists in their diagnosis of skin lesions. Another solution is a computer image analysis system presented in [1] that differentiates early melanoma from benign pigmented lesions. The analysis system extracts features related to the size, shape, boundary, and colour of each lesion.

An automated melanoma recognition system is introduced in [6]. Initially, a binary mask of lesion is obtained by a number of basic segmentation algorithms alongside a fusion strategy. A set of shape and radiometric features is calculated to determine the malignancy of a lesion. As a different approach, the physics-based model [5] of tissue colouration provides a cross-reference between image colours and the fundamental histological parameters of skin lesions. The model is built by computing the spectral composition of light remitted from the skin. The model is representative of all the normal human skin colours. Abnormal skin colours do not conform to this model and thus can be detected.

Feature extraction in [15], unlike our unique combination of extracted features, is limited to the quantification of degree of symmetry. The symmetry quantification step presents a six dimensional feature vector that can be exploited to classify pigmented skin lesions as benign or malignant. The solution demonstrates that the underlying scheme outperforms methods based on the principal component decomposition that is generally used for this category of applications. A more practical framework is proposed in [12] that assesses a series of 588 flat pigmented skin lesions. The proposed analyser groups 48 parameters into 4 categories that are used to train an artificial neural network. A feature selection procedure confirms that as few as 13 of the variables are adequate to discriminate the two groups of "melanoma" and "other pigmented" skin lesions.

Although the literature demonstrates a number of attempts at fabricating Content Based Image Retrieval (CBIR) Medical Systems for dermatological purposes [3][7], and quite a few attempts at assessing severity of specific skin diseases automatically [14], the lack of a reliable system for unskilled users or an assistant tool for dermatologists, which is capable of distinguishing different skin diseases in real time, is apparent.

3   Human in the Loop Skin Lesion Recognition

Our human in the loop skin recognition system works as follows: A skin lesion image along with a sequence of questions about attributes of the image are presented to the user, as shown in Fig. 1. The image features and the user's answers to the questions are then modelled together to arrive at a recognition decision.

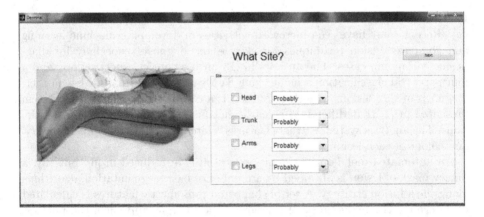

Fig. 1. A skin lesion image is displayed to the user. A question and its possible answers are also displayed. The user selects an answer and provides a confidence vote to quantify the answer. After answering one question, the next question will be displayed and the user repeat the process of answering the questions. The next question is selected from a pre-constructed question bank by looking at the previous user's answers and the image features. After answering a predefined number of questions, the final recognition decision is made by combining image features and user's answers.

Our system adopts the framework of [4] for incorporating any multi-class object recognition algorithm that produces a probabilistic output over different classes of skin diseases, as follows:

$$p(c|x, U) = \frac{p(U|c, x)p(c|x)}{\sum_c p(U|c)p(c|x)} = \frac{p(U|c)p(c|x)}{\sum_c p(U|c)p(c|x)} \tag{1}$$

where c is class of disease, x is skin lesion image, and U is any random sequence of user responses. The assumption that $p(U|c, x) = p(U|c)$ suggests that the types of randomness present in user responses is class-dependent and not image-dependent.

In our implementation of the above framework, we employed 10 image features with specific parametrisation including Coloured Pattern Appearance Model (CPAM) [10], Geometric Blur (GB) [17], Global Image Descriptor (GIST) [8], Pyramid Histogram of Oriented Gradients (PHOG) and its variations [17], Scale-invariant Feature Transform (SIFT) and its variations, Pyramid Histogram of Visual Words (PHOW) and its variations [16], and Self-similarity Feature (SSIM) [17]. We used *OBSCURE* [9], a state of the art, publicly available open source Support Vector Machine (SVM) based classifier for the visual classification, $p(c|x)$.

Assuming that users answer questions independently given a class, user responses $p(U|c)$ captured over time t are modelled by the following:

$$p(U^{t-1}|c) = \prod_i^{t-1} p(u_i|c) \tag{2}$$

Each user response u is a pair containing an arbitrary answer a, and a confidence value r that helps with user's uncertainty in answering questions:

$$p(u|c) = p(a, r|c) = p(a|r, c)p(r|c) \tag{3}$$

Similar to the original work [4], we also used a multinomial distribution with a Dirichlet prior to model user response triplets:

$$Dir(\alpha_r p(a|r) + \alpha_c p(a|c)) \tag{4}$$

where $p(a|r)$ is a global attribute prior, and $p(a|c)$ is estimated by examining certainty labels provided by users. Alpha constants for "guessing", "probably", and "definitely" certainty labels in practice diminish the importance of any user response with certainly label r other than definitely.

Maximum information gain and KL divergence is used to efficiently select the next suitable question. The upcoming question is picked by looking into its set of possible answers and previous user responses. The expected information gain of posing the additional question, where H is entropy, is defined as follows:

$$I(c; u_i|x, U^{t-1}) = E_u[KL(p(c|x, u_i \cup U^{t-1})||p(c|x, U^{t-1}))] \tag{5}$$

$$I(c; u_i|x, U^{t-1}) = \sum_{u_i \in A_i * V} p(u_i|x, U^{t-1})(H(c|x, u_i \cup U^{t-1}) - H(c|x, U^{t-1})) \tag{6}$$

4   Experimental Results

4.1   Datasets

We have collected two datasets from various Internet sources. The first and second datasets contain 90 and 706 dermatological images from 3 and 7 different skin diseases respectively. The lesions were manually segmented using a bounding box that includes pixels of lesion, healthy skin and noise, such as hair. Features were extracted from the entire bounding box, which as a whole is treated as a single instance. Images with their ground truth classification were mainly collected from http://www.dermis.net.

4.2   Dermatology Question and Answer Bank

A set of questions, which both summarise the patient's general conditions as well as her skin lesion characteristics, were designed to help with obtaining user perception of patient in a (fabricated) scenario. We have consulted medical professionals and a dermatological reference [2] to scientifically derive these questions. A simple Graphical User Interface (GUI), as shown in Fig. 1, was also built to capture user responses.

Table 1 lists 8 questions and 36 possible answers used for testing the first dataset and Table 2 lists 13 questions and 67 possible answers used for testing the second dataset. Wherever specific medical terms were used, a guide image with explanations was available for users to avoid confusion.

4.3   Results

Table 3 shows the results for the 1st and 2nd datasets. In the 1st dataset, 15 randomly selected images from each of the 3 diseases were used in training and the rest were used for testing. The experiment was repeated 5 times and the results in the table is the average over 5 rounds of experiments by a group of non-expert users. Here, it is clear that computer vision performs very badly on the Scabies images, achieving only 33% correct recognition rate. With human in the loop, the correct recognition rate boosts to 93% - a very significant improvement.

Table 1. Dermatology First Dataset Questions

Question	Attributes (Possible Answers)
01 Site	Head, Trunk, Arms, Legs
02 Condition	Acute, Chronic
03 Surface	Normal, Scaly, Hyperkeratotic, Warty, Crust, Exudate, Excoriated
04 Lesion	Flat, Raised, Fluid Filled, Surface Broken
04 Colour	Pink, Red, Purple, Mauve, Brown, Black, Blue, White, Yellow, ...
06 Age	Infant, Young, Adult, Old
07 Contagiousness	Contagious, Non-contagious
08 Itchiness	Itchy, Non-itchy

Table 2. Dermatology Second Dataset Questions

Question	Attributes (Possible Answers)
01 Age	Infant, Child, Adult, Elderly
02 History	Personal, Family
03 Site	Face, Scalp, Ears, (Mouth, Tongue, Lips), Trunk, Hands, ...
04 Number	Single, Multiple
05 Distribution	Symmetrical, Asymmetrical, Unilateral, Localised, Generalised
06 Arrangement	Discrete, Coalescing, Disseminated, Annular, Linear, Grouped
07 Erythema	Erythematous, Non-erythematous
08 Duration	Acute, Chronic
09 Type	Flat, Raised Solid, Fluid Filled, Cyst, Comedone, Broken Surface
10 Surface	Normal, Abnormal Keratinisation, Scale, Broken, Crust, Shiny, ...
11 Colour	Due to blood (Red, Pink), Due to pigment (Black, Blue), ...
12 Border	Well defined, Poorly defined, Accentuated edge
13 Shape	Round, Irregular, Rectangular, Serpiginous, Dome shaped, ...

Average correct recognition rate across the diseases is just over 57% for computer vision only solution but it is boosted to over 97% with human in the loop.

In the 2nd dataset, 30 images from each disease were randomly selected for training and the remaining 496 images were used for testing. Here the computer vision technique can only achieve 20% recognition rate for Mycosis Fungoides, but with human in the loop, the recognition rate is boosted to over 96% - again a dramatic improvement. The average across the diseases for the entire dataset is 61% for computer vision only and 96% for introducing human in the loop.

These results clearly demonstrate the effectiveness of human in the loop technique for recognising skin lesions. Compared to computer vision only solutions, adding human in the loop can dramatically improve the correct recognition rates. It is very important to note that the computer algorithm treats the images' classification ground truth as the correct disease diagnosis and the recognition rate should be interpreted as such.

To investigate the respective roles played by the computer vision and human in the loop, Fig. 2 plots the recognition rates of computer vision combined with user answers and without computer vision (solely based on human answers to questions). From these results, we can draw the following observations. Even though the technique can achieve excellent recognition rate without computer vision, computer vision plays an important role in reducing human labour in terms of the number of questions humans have to answer in order to arrive at a correct classification. Given that there are over 1000 skin conditions worldwide, a fully functioning system will need a question bank of hundreds, if not thousands of questions. Therefore, the role computer vision plays in reducing the number of questions needed is important in improving efficiency. Furthermore, some images cannot be classified correctly without computer vision, even after asking all the questions.

More interestingly, it was also found that users do not have to answer all the questions correctly in order to achieve correct recognition. It was observed that although users' questions are asked in different orders and users' answers to the same questions are different, the algorithm still recognises images successfully.

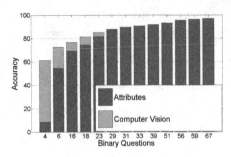

Fig. 2. Attribute results. Computer Vision improves Attributes accuracy. Computer Vision plays an important role in decreasing human labour by reducing the number of questions necessary to ask to achieve high accuracy results (above 80%). Attributes and Computer Vision results almost merge after 29 binary questions. Answering all questions results in very high accuracies.

Table 3. 1st and 2nd Dataset Accuracy Results

Class (1st Dataset)	Visual	Vis+Attr
Discoid Eczema	80%	100%
Infantile Acne	60%	100%
Scabies	33.33%	93%
Average Accuracy	57.78%	97.66%
Class (2nd Dataset)	Visual	Vis+Attr
Allergic Vasculitis	59.52%	100%
Atopic Eczema	48.67%	89.38%
Bullous Pemphigoid	56.09%	100%
Lichen Planus	38.09%	95.23%
Mycosis Fungoides	20.75%	96.22%
S. Cell Carcinoma	67.74%	98.38%
S. S. Melanoma	91.6%	98.6%
Average Accuracy	61.09%	96.16%

Above results were based on using 10 image features together. Although combining multiple features is a popular practice in computer vision and machine learning literature, it is nevertheless interesting to see which visual features will be important in our current application. Table 4 shows the computer vision recognition rates of 10 individual features. It is seen that PHOW-HSV is the most effective feature.

Table 4. Individual Computer Vision Feature's Effectiveness

Feature	CPAM	GB	PHOG-180	PHOW-GREY	SIFT
Accuracy	45.97%	32.86%	27.62%	51.61%	42.54%

Feature	SSIM	GIST	PHOG-360	PHOW-HSV	DENSE-SIFT
Accuracy	34.88%	45.77%	42.34%	57.06%	46.37%

5   Conclusions

It is believed that there are between 1000 to 2000 skin conditions, and about 20% are difficult to diagnose. In the UK typical general practitioners receive minimal dermatology training. Our promising results from non-medical experts illustrate the potential clinical application of our work for health care providers, and also for places where access to health services are scarce.

We believe that we have for the first time applied a human in the loop visual recognition technique to diagnosis of skin diseases from visual images of affected areas. We have shown for some of the conditions, computer vision technique performs very poorly (as low as 20%), while human in the loop technique boosts the recognition rate to over 96%. Our future work is to apply the technique to a larger number of diseases, to refine the "Question and Answer" bank, and to implement the work on a smart mobile phone.

References

1. Pfitzner, J., O'Rourke, M., Knight, N., Green, A., Martin, N.: Computer image analysis in the diagnosis of melanoma. Journal of the American Academy of Dermatology 31, 958–964 (1994)
2. Ashton, R., Leppard, B.: Differential diagnosis in dermatology. Radcliffe (2005)
3. Ballerini, L., Li, X., Fisher, R.B., Aldridge, B., Rees, J.: Content-Based Image Retrieval of Skin Lesions by Evolutionary Feature Synthesis. In: Di Chio, C., Cagnoni, S., Cotta, C., Ebner, M., Ekárt, A., Esparcia-Alcazar, A.I., Goh, C.-K., Merelo, J.J., Neri, F., Preuß, M., Togelius, J., Yannakakis, G.N. (eds.) EvoApplicatons 2010, Part I. LNCS, vol. 6024, pp. 312–319. Springer, Heidelberg (2010)
4. Branson, S., Wah, C., Schroff, F., Babenko, B., Welinder, P., Perona, P., Belongie, S.: Visual Recognition with Humans in the Loop. In: Daniilidis, K., Maragos, P., Paragios, N. (eds.) ECCV 2010, Part IV. LNCS, vol. 6314, pp. 438–451. Springer, Heidelberg (2010)
5. Claridge, E., Cotton, S.D., Hall, P., Moncrieff, M.: From Colour to Tissue Histology: Physics Based Interpretation of Images of Pigmented Skin Lesions. In: Dohi, T., Kikinis, R. (eds.) MICCAI 2002. LNCS, vol. 2488, pp. 730–738. Springer, Heidelberg (2002)
6. Ganster, H., Pinz, P., Rohrer, R., Wildling, E., Binder, M., Kittler, H.: Automated melanoma recognition. IEEE Transactions on Medical Imaging 20, 233–239 (2001)
7. Muller, H., Rosset, A., Vallee, J.-P., Geissbuhler, A.: Integrating content-based visual access methods into a medical case database. In: Proceedings of the Medical Informatics Europe Conference, MIE 2003 (2003)
8. Oliva, A., Torralba, A.: Modeling the shape of the scene: A holistic representation of the spatial envelope. Int. J. Comput. Vision 42, 145–175 (2001)
9. Orabona, F., Luo, J., Caputo, B.: Online-batch strongly convex multi kernel learning. In: Proceedings of the IEEE Conference on Computer Vision and Pattern Recognition (2010)
10. Qiu, G.: Indexing chromatic and achromatic patterns for content-based colour image retrieval. Pattern Recognition 35, 1675–1686 (2002)
11. Qiu, G., Yuen, P.C.: Editorial: Interactive imaging and vision-ideas, algorithms and applications. Pattern Recogn. 43, 431–433 (2010)
12. Rubegni, P., Cevenini, G., Burroni, M., Perotti, R., Dell'Eva, G., Sbano, P., Miracco, C., Luzi, P., Tosi, P., Barbini, P., Andreassi, L.: Automated diagnosis of pigmented skin lesions. International Journal of Cancer 101, 576–580 (2002)
13. Safi, A., Castaneda, V., Lasser, T., Navab, N.: Skin Lesions Classification with Optical Spectroscopy. Springer (2010)
14. Savolainen, L., Kontinen, J., Alatalo, E., Rning, J., Oikarinen, A.: Comparison of actual psoriasis surface area and the psoriasis area and severity index by the human eye and machine vision methods in following the treatment of psoriasis. Acta Dermatovenereologica 78, 466–467 (1998)

15. Schmid-Saugeona, P., Guillodb, J., Thiranaand, J.-P.: Towards a computer-aided diagnosis system for pigmented skin lesions. Computerized Medical Imaging and Graphics 27, 65–78 (2003)
16. Vedaldi, A., Fulkerson, B.: Vlfeat: An open and portable library of computer vision algorithms (2008), http://www.vlfeat.org/
17. Vedaldi, A., Gulshan, V., Varma, M., Zisserman, A.: Multiple kernels for object detection. In: Proceedings of the International Conference on Computer Vision (ICCV) (2009)

Author Index